AMERICAN FOREIGN POLICY 98/99

Fourth Edition

Editor

Glenn P. Hastedt

James Madison University

Glenn Hastedt received his Ph.D. from Indiana University. He is professor of political science at James Madison University, where he teaches courses on U.S. foreign policy, national security policy, and international relations. His special area of interest is on the workings of the intelligence community and the problems of strategic surprise and learning from intelligence failures. In addition to having published articles on these topics, he is the author of *American Foreign Policy: Past, Present, Future,* Second Edition; coauthor of *Dimensions of World Politics;* and editor and contributor to *Controlling Intelligence.* He is currently working on two volumes of readings, *Toward the Twenty-First Century* and *One World; Many Voices.*

Annual Editions
A Library of Information from the Public Press
Dushkin/McGraw-Hill
Sluice Dock, Guilford, Connecticut 06437

Visit us on the Internet—http://www.dushkin.com/

The Annual Editions Series

ANNUAL EDITIONS, including GLOBAL STUDIES, consist of over 70 volumes designed to provide the reader with convenient, low-cost access to a wide range of current, carefully selected articles from some of the most important magazines, newspapers, and journals published today. ANNUAL EDITIONS are updated on an annual basis through a continuous monitoring of over 300 periodical sources. All ANNUAL EDITIONS have a number of features that are designed to make them particularly useful, including topic guides, annotated tables of contents, unit overviews, and indexes. For the teacher using ANNUAL EDITIONS in the classroom, an Instructor's Resource Guide with test questions is available for each volume. GLOBAL STUDIES titles provide comprehensive background information and selected world press articles on the regions and countries of the world.

VOLUMES AVAILABLE

ANNUAL EDITIONS
Abnormal Psychology
Accounting
Adolescent Psychology
Aging
American Foreign Policy
American Government
American History, Pre-Civil War
American History, Post-Civil War
American Public Policy
Anthropology
Archaeology
Astronomy
Biopsychology
Business Ethics
Child Growth and Development
Comparative Politics
Computers in Education
Computers in Society
Criminal Justice
Criminology
Developing World
Deviant Behavior
Drugs, Society, and Behavior
Dying, Death, and Bereavement
Early Childhood Education

Economics
Educating Exceptional Children
Education
Educational Psychology
Environment
Geography
Geology
Global Issues
Health
Human Development
Human Resources
Human Sexuality
International Business
Macroeconomics
Management
Marketing
Marriage and Family
Mass Media
Microeconomics
Multicultural Education
Nutrition
Personal Growth and Behavior
Physical Anthropology
Psychology
Public Administration
Race and Ethnic Relations

Social Problems
Social Psychology
Sociology
State and Local Government
Teaching English as a Second Language
Urban Society
Violence and Terrorism
Western Civilization, Pre-Reformation
Western Civilization, Post-Reformation
Women's Health
World History, Pre-Modern
World History, Modern
World Politics

GLOBAL STUDIES
Africa
China
India and South Asia
Japan and the Pacific Rim
Latin America
Middle East
Russia, the Eurasian Republics, and Central/Eastern Europe
Western Europe

Cataloging in Publication Data
Main entry under title: Annual Editions: American Foreign Policy. 1998/99.
    1. U.S. Foreign Relations—Periodicals. I. Hastedt, Glenn P., comp.
II. Title: American foreign policy.
327.73'05   ISBN 0–697–39127–2   ISSN 1075–5225

© 1998 by Dushkin/McGraw-Hill, Guilford, CT 06437, A Division of The McGraw-Hill Companies.

Copyright law prohibits the reproduction, storage, or transmission in any form by any means of any portion of this publication without the express written permission of Dushkin/McGraw-Hill, and of the copyright holder (if different) of the part of the publication to be reproduced. The Guidelines for Classroom Copying endorsed by Congress explicitly state that unauthorized copying may not be used to create, to replace, or to substitute for anthologies, compilations, or collective works.

Annual Editions® is a Registered Trademark of Dushkin/McGraw-Hill, A Division of The McGraw-Hill Companies.

Fourth Edition

Cover image © 1998 PhotoDisc, Inc.

Printed in the United States of America

Printed on Recycled Paper

Editors/Advisory Board

Members of the Advisory Board are instrumental in the final selection of articles for each edition of ANNUAL EDITIONS. Their review of articles for content, level, currentness, and appropriateness provides critical direction to the editor and staff. We think that you will find their careful consideration well reflected in this volume.

EDITOR

Glenn P. Hastedt
James Madison University

ADVISORY BOARD

Linda S. Adams
Baylor University

Kirsten Bookmiller
Millersville University

Ralph G. Carter
Texas Christian University

Nader Entessar
Spring Hill College

Will Hazelton
Miami University

Donald Mayer
Shippensburg University

Steve Newlin
California State University, Chico

James W. Peterson
Valdosta State University

Helen E. Purkitt
U.S. Naval Academy

Nathaniel Richmond
Utica College

J. Philip Rogers
Central European University

John T. Rourke
University of Connecticut, Storrs

James C. Sperling
University of Akron

Joseph E. Thompson
Villanova University

Kristine Thompson
Concordia College

B. Thomas Trout
University of New Hampshire

Caroline S. Westerhof
University of South Florida

Stephen D. Wrage
U.S. Naval Academy

Staff

Ian A. Nielsen, Publisher

EDITORIAL STAFF

Roberta Monaco, Developmental Editor
Dorothy Fink, Associate Developmental Editor
Addie Raucci, Senior Administrative Editor
Cheryl Greenleaf, Permissions Editor
Deanna Herrschaft, Permissions Assistant
Diane Barker, Proofreader
Lisa Holmes-Doebrick, Program Coordinator

PRODUCTION STAFF

Brenda S. Filley, Production Manager
Charles Vitelli, Designer
Shawn Callahan, Graphics
Lara M. Johnson, Graphics
Laura Levine, Graphics
Mike Campbell, Graphics
Joseph Offredi, Graphics
Juliana Arbo, Typesetting Supervisor
Jane Jaegersen, Typesetter
Marie Lazauskas, Word Processor
Kathleen D'Amico, Word Processor
Larry Killian, Copier Coordinator

To the Reader

In publishing ANNUAL EDITIONS we recognize the enormous role played by the magazines, newspapers, and journals of the *public press* in providing current, first-rate educational information in a broad spectrum of interest areas. Many of these articles are appropriate for students, researchers, and professionals seeking accurate, current material to help bridge the gap between principles and theories and the real world. These articles, however, become more useful for study when those of lasting value are carefully *collected, organized, indexed,* and *reproduced* in a *low-cost format,* which provides easy and permanent access when the material is needed. That is the role played by ANNUAL EDITIONS. Under the direction of each volume's *academic editor,* who is an expert in the subject area, and with the guidance of an *Advisory Board,* each year we seek to provide in each ANNUAL EDITION a current, well-balanced, carefully selected collection of the best of the public press for your study and enjoyment. We think that you will find this volume useful, and we hope that you will take a moment to let us know what you think.

This fourth volume of *Annual Editions: American Foreign Policy* presents an overview of American foreign policy in transition. It is a transition that is proceeding unevenly and at several different levels. At the broadest level, American foreign policy is in a transition from relying upon the grand strategies that shaped definitions of the national interests and mobilized America's resources during the cold war era to developing a new set of fundamental principles and guiding concepts. This transition is evident in the reworking of American relations with other states and in efforts to establish international mechanisms for preserving the peace.

It is uncertain how well prepared the policymakers, American political institutions, or the American public are for this transition. The rush of events in such places as Bosnia, Somalia, the Middle East, Rwanda, Cuba, China, and North Korea has outpaced the ability of the policymakers to develop a coherent strategy. There is also uncertainty in Congress, the bureaucracy, and the American public over how best to respond to events abroad. The contradictory signals sent out by these political forces point to a potentially long and difficult transition to a post–cold war era.

Annual Editions: American Foreign Policy 98/99 examines the many issues and problems involved in making this transition from a cold war–centered American foreign policy to one firmly rooted in the international politics of the 1990s. It is divided into eight units. The first addresses questions of grand strategy. The second unit focuses on selected regional and bilateral relations. In the third unit, our attention shifts inward to the ways in which domestic forces affect the content of American foreign policy. The fourth unit looks at the institutions that make American foreign policy. In the fifth unit, the process by which American foreign policy is made is illustrated by accounts of recent foreign policy decisions. The sixth and seventh units provide an overview of the economic and military issues confronting the United States today. The final unit provides students with a sampling of recent writings by authors whose goal it is to reflect on the past so that American foreign policy in the present and future might be improved.

I would like to thank publisher Ian Nielsen for supporting the concept of an *Annual Editions: American Foreign Policy* and for helping to oversee the process of putting this volume together. Also deserving of thanks are the many people at Dushkin/McGraw-Hill who worked to make the project a success, as well as those faculty on the Advisory Board who provided input on the selection of articles. In the end, the success of *Annual Editions: American Foreign Policy* depends upon the views of the faculty and students who use it. I encourage you to let me know what worked and what did not so that each successive volume will be better than its predecessor. Please complete and return the postage-paid article rating form at the end of this book.

Glenn Hastedt
Editor

Contents

UNIT 1

The United States and the World: Strategic Choices

Four articles review some of the foreign policy choices the United States has today.

To the Reader	iv
Topic Guide	2
Selected World Wide Web Sites	4
Overview	6

1. **Building a Bipartisan Foreign Policy: Diplomacy and Economics,** Madeleine Albright, *Vital Speeches of the Day,* April 15, 1997. — 8
   In one of her first speeches as secretary of state, Madeleine Albright talks about the ways in which *foreign policy affects the everyday lives of Americans.* She singles out ratification of the Chemical Weapons Convention and the Middle East as priorities for Clinton's second term.

2. **Starting Over: Foreign Policy Challenges for the Second Clinton Administration,** Richard N. Haass, *The Brookings Review,* Spring 1997. — 12
   Richard Haass argues that the second Clinton administration began with an uneven inheritance from the first. It is now more experienced in dealing with foreign policy but it still lacks a political consensus on how to deal with the world. Haass examines the *domestic and international challenges* facing the second Clinton administration.

3. **A New Realism,** Ronald Steel, *World Policy Journal,* Summer 1997. — 15
   Focusing on the concept of *national security,* Ronald Steel calls for a reexamination of the concepts we use to think about American foreign policy and international relations. He argues that security is not a condition but a feeling and a process. It is not an absolute or an end in itself.

4. **The Crisis of Liberal Internationalism,** Stanley Hoffmann, *Foreign Policy,* Spring 1995. — 24
   A defender of liberal internationalism as the basis for American foreign policy, Stanley Hoffmann argues that *the neo-Wilsonian vision* is in need of sharpening and refinement. In particular, it is unclear on questions involving *the use of force* and has been overly concerned with *limiting power* rather than dealing with chaos.

UNIT 2

The United States and the World: Regional and Bilateral Relations

Seven selections consider U.S. relations with Russia, Asia, Europe, and the developing world.

Overview — 32

A. RUSSIA

5. **Don't Isolate Us: A Russian View of NATO Expansion,** Alexei K. Pushkov, *The National Interest,* Spring 1997. — 34
   Alexei Pushkov, a former speechwriter for Mikhail Gorbachev, asserts that there is a wide consensus in Russian political circles that NATO expansion is not in the Russian national interest. He argues that Russian concerns need to be considered by the United States, and the outlines of *a counterproposal for a Russian-NATO agreement* are presented.

The concepts in bold italics are developed in the article. For further expansion please refer to the Topic Guide and the Index.

B. ASIA

6. **Reluctant Guardian: The United States in East Asia,** Charles W. Freeman Jr., *Harvard International Review,* Spring 1996. 39

   Charles Freeman argues that beneath what appears to be a surface calm, *the Asia Pacific region* is undergoing profound economic, political, and military changes. This article examines both the American domestic context of a policy response and the *key bilateral issues* that the United States will have to face in the near future.

7. **Chinese Realpolitik,** Thomas J. Christensen, *Foreign Affairs,* September/October 1996. 45

   Much has been made of China's growing power. Less attention has been paid to understanding how Chinese analysts discern their own security environment. Thomas Christensen sheds light on how China views the world and concentrates on two issues: *Chinese foreign policy toward Japan and toward Taiwan.*

C. EUROPE

8. **America and Europe: Is the Break Inevitable?** Werner Weidenfeld, *The Washington Quarterly,* Summer 1997. 53

   Perceptions on both sides of the Atlantic regarding the proper nature of the *American-European relationship* are undergoing radical change. Werner Weidenfeld argues that for a new era of cooperation to emerge, political elites in both the United States and Europe will need to fashion a new sense of transatlantic community.

9. **The Folly of NATO Enlargement,** Ted Galen Carpenter, *The World & I,* July 1997. 60

   NATO enlargement has begun. The controversy over whether or not it is a good idea continues and is likely to become even more heated as other candidates for membership are considered. Ted Carpenter presents the *case against NATO enlargement,* arguing that there are major drawbacks to expanding it.

D. THE DEVELOPING WORLD

10. **Pivotal States and U.S. Strategy,** Robert S. Chase, Emily B. Hill, and Paul Kennedy, *Foreign Affairs,* January/February 1996. 63

    Pivotal states are defined as those "whose fate is uncertain and whose future will profoundly affect their surrounding regions." The great danger they face is not external aggression but that they will become *victims of internal disorder.* The authors identify and discuss the contemporary situation in nine pivotal states.

11. **The U.S. and Islamic Fundamentalists: The Need for Dialogue,** Sami G. Hajjar, *Strategic Review,* Winter 1997. 71

    One of the most controversial issues in American foreign policy is how to deal with *Islamic fundamentalists.* Sami Hajjar reviews the debate over whether Islamic fundamentalism is a secular ideology or a messianic movement. He argues for a policy of dialogue with moderate political forces.

UNIT 3

The Domestic Side of American Foreign Policy

Four selections examine the domestic impact of American foreign policy.

UNIT 4

The Institutional Context of American Foreign Policy

Five articles examine how the courts, state and local governments, Congress, and bureaucracy impact on U.S. foreign policy.

Overview 78

A. THE PUBLIC, PUBLIC OPINION, AND THE MEDIA

12. **The Common Sense,** John Mueller, *The National Interest,* Spring 1997. 80
John Mueller argues that when looked at over time the public's views on American foreign policy are consistent and reasonable. Mueller presents 10 propositions about how American public opinion will influence *foreign policy in the post-cold war era.*

13. **The Shrinking of Foreign News: From Broadcast to Narrowcast,** Garrick Utley, *Foreign Affairs,* March/April 1997. 87
For many Americans television is the primary medium by which they view foreign events. But what is the nature of that coverage? Garrick Utley, former chief foreign correspondent for ABC and NBC, presents an overview of *the decline in foreign coverage* and examines the tension between the demands of journalism and the need for profit.

B. THE ROLE OF AMERICAN VALUES

14. **On American Principles,** George F. Kennan, *Foreign Affairs,* March/April 1995. 94
George Kennan calls a principle "a *general rule of conduct*" that defines the limits within which foreign policy ought to operate. Building on a position argued by President John Quincy Adams when Adams was secretary of state, Kennan says that the best way for a big country such as the United States to help smaller ones is by the *power of example.*

15. **Why America Thinks It Has to Run the World,** Benjamin Schwarz, *The Atlantic Monthly,* June 1996. 99
Benjamin Schwarz asserts that most of the public misunderstands the real *motivations behind American foreign policy.* Much more than simply a response to international crises, American foreign policy has as its fundamental goal the *creation and maintenance of a capitalist world order.*

Overview 106

A. LAW AND THE COURTS

16. **International Judicial Intervention,** David J. Scheffer, *Foreign Policy,* Spring 1996. 108
Atrocities in Bosnia and elsewhere have led to renewed calls for the establishment of international courts to deal with war crimes. This essay discusses U.S. foreign policy as it relates to international law, with special emphasis on the *Dayton Agreement,* and it examines the *relationship between domestic and international law.*

B. STATE AND LOCAL GOVERNMENTS

17. **The Politics of NAFTA: Why Is Texas So Much Hotter for NAFTA than California?** James E. Garcia and Dave McNeely, *State Legislatures,* October/November 1996. 116
Trade with Mexico is big business for many states. At the top of the list are Texas, California, Arizona, Illinois, Michigan, and New York. This article contrasts the positive response of Texas with the negative response of California.

The concepts in bold italics are developed in the article. For further expansion please refer to the Topic Guide and the Index.

C. CONGRESS

18. When Money Talks, Congress Listens, Jennifer Washburn, *The Bulletin of the Atomic Scientists,* July/August 1997. — 120

Frequently, public attention focuses on foreign campaign contributions and the question of whether or not they have distorted American foreign policy. A great deal of money, however, also comes from domestic sources. Jennifer Washburn presents a case study of how *funds from the arms industry* exert an influence in Congress and shape American foreign policy.

D. BUREAUCRACY

19. Racing toward the Future: The Revolution in Military Affairs, Steven Metz, *Current History,* April 1997. — 124

Desert Storm was seen by many in the military as the prologue to a fundamental shift in warfare—a *revolution in military affairs.* The ideas embodied in it now serve as the blueprint for most *long-term thinking in the Defense Department.* Steven Metz questions the long-term value of this change in thinking.

20. Ending the CIA's Cold War Legacy, Melvin A. Goodman, *Foreign Policy,* Spring 1997. — 129

Melvin Goodman argues that the *CIA* must address head-on the legacy of its greatest cold war failure—the failure to see the magnitude of the crisis in the Soviet Union that led to the fall of communism. Goodman traces the process of politicalization that took place within the CIA, and he examines key intelligence estimates during the 1980s.

UNIT 5

The Foreign Policy-Making Process

Four selections review some of the elements that affect the process of American foreign policy.

Overview — 138

21. The Curse of the Merit Class, David Ignatius, *Washington Post,* February 27, 1994. — 140

David Ignatius provides an *intellectual overview of the Clinton administration's foreign policy brain trust.* He poses the question: Why is this administration, which has recruited a large number of able people, having so much trouble making foreign policy? Ignatius suggests that, at least in part, it is because the meritocracy relies upon reason rather than politics to solve problems.

22. How the Warlord Outwitted Clinton's Spooks, Patrick J. Sloyan, *Washington Post,* April 3, 1994. — 143

Patrick Sloyan recounts how some of the key decisions in the Somalian endgame were made by the Clinton administration. He contends that, in trying to deal with the problem in Somalia, *the Clinton administration made many mistakes, as did its predecessors.* Most notably, when confronted with a failed diplomatic initiative, it resorted to the *"quick and dirty solution"* offered by the CIA and the military establishment.

23. **Playing Politics with the Chemical Weapons Convention,** Amy E. Smithson, *Current History,* April 1997. 147
In the spring of 1997, U.S. Senate ratified the **Chemical Weapons Convention.** Amy Smithson reviews the **political maneuvering** between the White House and Congress in the ratification debate that took place in the first years of the Clinton administration. She characterizes Clinton's early efforts as "perfunctory at best."

24. **Inside the White House Situation Room,** Michael Donley, Cornelius O'Leary, and John Montgomery, *Studies in Intelligence,* Number 1, 1997. 152
Established after the Bay of Pigs disaster in 1960, the White House Situation Room provides current intelligence and crisis support to the **National Security Council.** The authors of this report describe the role of the council in the policy-making process in an era of 24-hour-a-day television news. They pay particular attention to its intelligence support role and its relationship with other Washington decision-making centers.

UNIT 6

U.S. International Economic Strategy

Three selections discuss how economics and trade strategies affect American foreign policy choices.

Overview 158

25. **Foreign Aid,** Carol Graham, *The Brookings Review,* Spring 1997. 160
Carol Graham argues that the reluctance of the United States to provide foreign aid is seen by other states as evidence of Washington's unwillingness to pay its global dues. Graham examines **three issues central to the debate over the future of foreign aid**: Would states have performed worse without aid?; How are we allocating aid?; and, Do policies promote growth?

26. **A U.S.–Japan Trade Agenda,** Edward J. Lincoln, *The Brookings Review,* Summer 1997. 162
Edward Lincoln warns against treating **Japan** as "yesterday's problem." He presents a negotiating agenda that includes attention to such bilateral issues as the **World Trade Organization, trade,** monitoring **international agreements,** and Japanese **direct investment** in the United States.

27. **Adjusting to Sanctions,** Jahangir Amuzegar, *Foreign Affairs,* May/June 1997. 165
Economic sanctions have become a favored tool of American foreign policy. Often, however, they have failed to achieve their desired goals. This article presents a case study of how one country, Iran, has adjusted to American economic sanctions. The author examines four policy alternatives that are available to the United States.

The concepts in bold italics are developed in the article. For further expansion please refer to the Topic Guide and the Index.

UNIT 7

U.S. Post–Cold War Military Strategy

Four articles examine U.S. military planning in the context of the post–cold war era.

Overview 170

A. THE USE OF MILITARY POWER

28. **Soldiering On: U.S. Public Opinion on the Use of Force,** Catherine M. Kelleher, *The Brookings Review,* Spring 1994. 172
Unlike the past, recent public opinion polls show that *the American public is increasingly well informed about global issues* and has opinions on most major foreign policy and defense policy questions. Catherine Kelleher reviews recent polling data and finds that Americans favor a case-by-case approach to the use of force. A key factor shaping American public opinion is whether the proposed action is unilateral or multilateral.

29. **Deliberate and Inadvertent War in the Post–Cold War World,** Wallace J. Thies, *Strategic Review,* Spring 1997. 176
Wallace Thies criticizes defense budget cuts, which he claims have eroded military readiness. Thies believes that in the future the greatest threat to regional stability will be *inadvertent war.* He examines this phenomenon and discusses the ways in which the United States might respond to these threats.

B. ARMS CONTROL

30. **Paring Down the Arsenal,** Frank von Hippel, *The Bulletin of the Atomic Scientists,* May/June 1997. 185
In March 1997 Bill Clinton and Boris Yeltsin met in Helsinki and pledged themselves to begin *START III negotiations.* The author of this essay calls for moving rapidly in this direction by pulling missiles off hair-trigger alert and making deep cuts in nuclear stockpiles. A three-stage strategy for bringing this about is presented.

31. **The New Arms Race: Light Weapons and International Security,** Michael T. Klare, *Current History,* April 1997. 192
During the cold war the major nonnuclear arms control problem involved the sale of large and expensive weapons systems. This is no longer the case. Michael Klare argues that *the key weapons affecting the outcome of ethnic and sectarian conflicts* are light weapons such as assault rifles, antitank weapons, and shoulder-fired antiaircraft missiles. He presents a strategy for addressing the sale of these weapons by governments as well as for dealing with black market sales.

UNIT 8

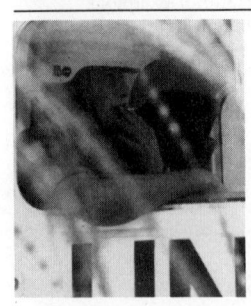

Historical Retrospectives on American Foreign Policy

Three articles examine some of the history of American foreign policy.

Overview 198

32. **Closing the Gate: The Persian Gulf War Revisited,** Michael Sterner, *Current History,* January 1997. 200
The Persian Gulf War is perhaps the most written-about military operation of the post–cold war era. Much has been made over the manner in which the war ended and the failure to remove Saddam Hussein from power. Michael Sterner examines the question of what coalition forces might have done differently at the war's end and what the impact of those actions might have been.

The concepts in bold italics are developed in the article. For further expansion please refer to the Topic Guide and the Index.

33. **Bosnia after Dayton: Year Two,** Susan L. Woodward, *Current History,* March 1997.   208
   The Dayton Accord, which was signed on November 21, 1995, was designed to end the fighting in Bosnia. Susan Woodward notes that while much has been accomplished since then, the tasks set out in the Dayton Accord do not form a coherent strategy. The most likely future facing Bosnia is that of an extremely fragile and relatively unstable country.

34. **Midnight Never Came,** Mike Moore, *The Bulletin of the Atomic Scientists,* November/December 1995.   215
   One of the most recognizable symbols of the *nuclear age* is the **Doomsday Clock** that appeared on the cover of the journal *The Bulletin of the Atomic Scientists.* This article traces the movement of the minute hand on the Doomsday Clock from its first appearance in 1949 through 1991.

Index	225
Article Review Form	228
Article Rating Form	229

Topic Guide

This topic guide suggests how the selections in this book relate to topics of traditional concern to students and professionals involved with the study of the study of American foreign policy. It is useful for locating articles that relate to each other for reading and research. The guide is arranged alphabetically according to topic. Articles may, of course, treat topics that do not appear in the topic guide. In turn, entries in the topic guide do not necessarily constitute a comprehensive listing of all the contents of each selection. **In addition, relevant Web sites, which are annotated on the next two pages, are noted in bold italics under the topic articles.**

TOPIC AREA	TREATED IN	TOPIC AREA	TREATED IN
Arms Control	1. Building a Bipartisan Foreign Policy 23. Playing Politics with the Chemical Weapons Convention 30. Paring Down the Arsenal 31. New Arms Race 34. Midnight Never Came *(29, 30, 31, 33, 34, 35)*	Developing World	10. Pivotal States and U.S. Strategy 29. Deliberate and Inadvertent War 31. New Arms Race *(9, 10, 11, 29, 30, 31)*
Arms Trade	18. When Money Talks, Congress Listens 31. New Arms Race *(24, 30, 31)*	Domestic and Foreign Policy Linkages	1. Building a Bipartisan Foreign Policy 2. Starting Over 15. Why America Thinks It Has to Run the World 17. Politics of NAFTA 18. When Money Talks, Congress Listens *(7, 8, 12)*
Asia	2. Starting Over 6. Reluctant Guardian 7. Chinese Realpolitik 26. U.S.-Japan Agenda *(3, 8, 10, 11, 25, 26, 27, 28)*	Elections	18. When Money Talks, Congress Listens
		Europe	2. Starting Over 8. America and Europe 9. Folly of NATO Enlargement *(8, 12, 18)*
Bosnia	16. International Judicial Intervention 28. Soldiering On 33. Bosnia after Dayton *(1, 2, 3, 11, 12, 18, 31, 32)*	Foreign Aid	10. Pivotal States and U.S. Strategy 15. Why America Thinks It Has to Run the World 25. Foreign Aid *(9, 11, 12, 13, 14, 15, 28)*
Central Intelligence Agency (CIA)	20. Ending the CIA's Cold War Legacy 22. How the Warlord Outwitted Clinton's Spooks *(20, 22, 24)*	Human Rights	4. Crisis of Liberal Internationalism 16. International Judicial Intervention *(31, 32)*
Congress	18. When Money Talks, Congress Listens 23. Playing Politics with the Chemical Weapons Convention *(16, 17, 23)*	International Trade	17. Politics of NAFTA 26. U.S.-Japan Agenda 27. Adjusting to Sanctions *(16, 17, 25, 26, 27, 28)*
Courts and Law	16. International Judicial Intervention *(31)*		

TOPIC AREA	TREATED IN	TOPIC AREA	TREATED IN
Middle East	10. Pivotal States and U.S. Strategy 11. U.S. and Islamic Fundamentalists 27. Adjusting to Sanctions 32. Closing the Gate *(10, 11, 14, 25, 31, 32, 34)*	Presidency	20. Ending the CIA's Cold War Legacy 21. Curse of the Merit Class 24. Inside the White House Situation Room *(8, 12, 21, 22, 24)*
Military Power	4. Crisis of Liberal Internationalism 19. Racing toward the Future 28. Soldiering On 29. Deliberate and Inadvertent War 32. Closing the Gate *(1, 2, 3, 5, 7, 8, 34)*	Public Opinion and the Media	12. Common Sense 13. Shrinking of Foreign News 28. Soldiering On *(13, 14, 15)*
National Interest and American Values	3. New Realism 4. Crisis of Liberal Internationalism 14. On American Principles 15. Why America Thinks It Has to Run the World *(3, 7, 8, 25, 28, 31)*	Russia	2. Starting Over 5. Don't Isolate Us 20. Ending the CIA's Cold War Legacy 34. Midnight Never Came *(7, 11, 20, 21, 30, 35)*
North American Free Trade Association (NAFTA)	17. Politics of NAFTA *(9, 16)*	Somalia	22. How the Warlord Outwitted Clinton's Spooks *(8, 20)*
		State Department and Diplomacy	27. Adjusting to Sanctions 33. Bosnia after Dayton *(19, 31, 32)*
North Atlantic Treaty Organization (NATO)	5. Don't Isolate Us 9. Folly of NATO Enlargement *(12, 18, 19)*	United Nations	4. Crisis of Liberal Internationalism 27. Adjusting to Sanctions *(7, 26)*
Policy Making	20. Ending the CIA's Cold War Legacy 21. Curse of the Merit Class 22. How the Warlord Outwitted Clinton's Spooks 23. Playing Politics with the Chemical Weapons Convention 24. Inside the White House Situation Room *(8, 12, 21, 22, 23, 24)*	Western Hemisphere	17. Politics of NAFTA *(9, 16)*

Selected World Wide Web Sites for *AE: American Foreign Policy*

All of these Web sites are hot-linked through the *Annual Editions* home page: http://www.dushkin.com/annualeditions (just click on a book). In addition, these sites are referenced by number and appear where relevant in the Topic Guide on the previous two pages.

Some Web sites are continually changing their structure and content, so the information listed may not always be available.

General Sources

1. Foreign Affairs—*http://www.foreignaffairs.org/*—This home page of the well-respected, foreign-policy magazine *Foreign Affairs* is a valuable research tool. It allows users to search the magazine's archives and provides indexed access to the field's leading journals, documents, online resources, and so on. Links to dozens of other related Web sites are possible from here.

2. United States Information Agency (USIA)—*http://www.usia.gov/usis.html*—An interesting and wide-ranging home page of the USIA, it provides definition, related documentation, and a discussion of topics of concern to students of foreign policy and foreign affairs. It addresses today's "Hot Topics" as well as ongoing issues that form the foundation of the field. Many Web links are provided.

3. American Diplomacy—*http://www.unc.edu/depts/diplomat/*—*American Diplomacy* is an intriguing online journal of commentary, analysis, and research on U.S. foreign policy and its results around the world. It provides discussion and information on such topics as Life in the Foreign Service and Americanism and Strategy Security.

4. The Federal Web Locator—*http://www.law.vill.edu/Fed-Agency/fedwebloc.html*—Use this handy site as a launching pad for the Web sites of federal U.S. agencies, departments, and organizations. It is well organized and easy to use for informational and research purposes.

The United States and the World: Strategic Choices

5. ISN International Relations and Security Network—*http://www.isn.ethz.ch/*—This site, maintained by the Center for Security Studies and Conflict Research, is a clearinghouse for extensive information on international relations and security policy. The many topics are listed by category (Traditional Dimensions of Security, New Dimensions of Security, and Related Fields) and by major world region.

6. The Heritage Foundation—*http://www.heritage.org/*—This home page offers discussion about and links to many Heritage and other sites having to do with foreign policy and foreign affairs, including News and Commentary, Policy Review, Events, and a Resource Bank.

7. The Henry L. Stimson Center—*http://www.stimson.org*—Stimson, a nonprofit and (self-described) nonpartisan organization, focuses on issues where policy, technology, and politics intersect. Use this site to find assessments of U.S. foreign policy in the post-cold war world and to research many other topics.

8. Clinton Foreign Policy Failure Page—*http://www.geocities.com/CapitolHill/8514/*—For a change of pace from the sites of government organizations and think tanks, check out this personal home page copyrighted by Eddie Roberts, an individual who is very critical of President Bill Clinton's foreign policy. It provides space for you to respond to his opinions.

The United States and the World: Regional and Bilateral Relations

9. Inter-American Dialogue (IAD)—*http://www.iadialog.org/*—This is the Web site for IAD, a premier U.S. center for policy analysis, communication, and exchange in Western Hemisphere affairs. The organization has helped to shape the agenda of issues and choices in hemispheric relations.

10. World Wide Web Virtual Library: International Affairs Resources—*http://info.pitt.edu/~ian/ianres.html*—Surf this site and its extensive links to learn about specific countries and regions; to research various think tanks and international organizations; and to study such vital topics as international law, development, the international economy, human rights, and peacekeeping.

11. The University of Texas at Austin Russian and East European Network Information Center—*http://reenic.utexas.edu/reenic.html*—This site has exhaustive information—from women's issues to foreign relations—regarding more than two dozen countries in Central/Eastern Europe and Eurasia. Also check out University of Texas/Austin's site on Broader Asia (http://asnic.utexas.edu/asnic/index.html) for more insight into bilateral/regional relations.

12. United States Information Service—*http://hps.usis.fi/current/nato17.htm*—This site contains statements on NATO enlargement by President Bill Clinton. It provides links to other views and information associated with that topic as well as other issues of interest to students of American foreign policy.

The Domestic Side of American Foreign Policy

13. Social Influence—*http://www.public.asu.edu/~kelton/*—The Social Influence Web site focuses on the nature of persuasion, compliance, and propaganda, with many practical examples and applications. Students of such topics as the roles of public opinion and media influence in foreign policy making may find these discussions of interest.

14. Carnegie Endowment for International Peace—*http://www.ceip.org/*—One of the most important goals of this organization is to stimulate discussion and learning among both experts and the public at large on a wide range of international issues. The site provides links to the well-respected magazine *Foreign Policy*, to the Moscow Center, and to descriptions of various programs.

15. RAND—*http://www.rand.org/*—RAND is a nonprofit institution that works to improve public policy through research and analysis. Links offered on this home page provide for keyword searches of certain topics and descriptions of RAND activities and major research areas (such as international relations and strategic defense policy).

The Institutional Context of American Foreign Policy

16. NAFTA Border Home Page—*http://www.iep.doc.gov/border/nafta.htm*—This site offers extensive information on the North American Free Trade Agreement, including the full text of NAFTA documents and access to the National Trade Data Bank file. It provides Web links to a variety of NAFTA-related statistics and sources in Canada, Mexico, and the United States.

17. The North American Institute (NAMI)—*http://www.santafe.edu/~naminet/index.html*—This is the home page of NAMI, a tri-national public-affairs organization concerned with the emerging "regional space" of Canada, the United States, and Mexico and the development of a North American community. It provides links for study of trade, the environment, institutional developments, and other topics.

18. The NATO Integrated Data Service (NIDS)—*http://www.nato.int/structur/nids/nids.htm*—NIDS was created to bring information on security-related matters to within easy reach of the widest possible audience. Check out this Web site to review North Atlantic Treaty Organization documentation of all kinds, to read *NATO Review* magazine, and to explore key issues in the field of European security and transatlantic cooperation.

19. United States Department of State—*http://www.state.gov/*—The home page of the State Department is a must for any student of foreign affairs. Explore this site and its links to find out what exactly the Department does, what services it provides, what it says about U.S. interests around the world, and much more information.

20. Central Intelligence Agency (CIA)—*http://www.odci.gov/cia/ciahome.html*—The CIA has historically been a major player in American foreign policy. Use this official home page to learn about many facets of the agency and to get connections to other sites and resources.

The Foreign Policy-Making Process

21. Belfer Center for Science and International Affairs (BCSIA)—*http://ksgwww.harvard.edu/csia/*—BCSIA is the hub of the John F. Kennedy School of Government's research, teaching, and training in international affairs related to security, environment, and technology. This site provides insight into the development of leadership in policy making.

22. Welcome to the White House—*http://www.whitehouse.gov/WH/Welcome.html*—This official Web site provides extensive background information for students interested in studying the policy-making process. It includes a tour of the White House, a search of federal documents and speeches, and "virtual" access to the Briefing Room.

23. InterAction—*http://www.interaction.org/advocacy.html*—InterAction encourages grassroots action and engages government bodies and policymakers on various advocacy issues. The organization's Advocacy Committee provides this site to inform people on its initiatives to expand international humanitarian relief, refugee, and development assistance programs.

24. DiploNet—*http://www.clark.net/pub/diplonet/DiploNet.html*—DiploNet is a network uniquely concerned with the needs of diplomats in the post-cold war era. It provides avenues of research into negotiation and diplomacy. It also addresses conflict management and resolution, peace making, and multilateral diplomacy.

U.S. International Economic Strategy

25. United States Trade Representative—*http://www.ustr.gov/*—This home page explains the important mission of the U.S. Trade Representative and provides background information, access to international trade agreements, and links to other sites.

26. International Monetary Fund (IMF)—*http://www.imf.org/*—This Web site is essential reading for anyone wishing to learn more about this important body's effects on foreign policy and the global economy. It provides information about the IMF, directs readers to various publications and current issues, and suggests links to other organizations.

27. World Bank—*http://www.worldbank.org/*—News (i.e., press releases, summaries of new projects, speeches); publications; and coverage of numerous topics regarding development, countries, and regions are provided at this Web site. It also contains links to other important global financial organizations.

28. United States Agency for International Development—*http://www.info.usaid.gov/*—This Web site covers such broad and overlapping issues as Democracy, Population and Health, Economic Growth, Development, and Regions and Countries.

U.S. Post–Cold War Military Strategy

29. Federation of American Scientists (FAS)—*http://www.fas.org/*—FAS, a nonprofit policy organization, maintains this site to provide coverage of and links to such topics as Global Security, Peace and Security, and Governance in the post-cold war world. It notes a variety of resources of value to students of foreign policy.

30. United States Arms Control and Disarmament Agency (ACDA)—*http://www.acda.gov/*—This official home page of the ACDA provides links to extensive information on the topic of arms control and disarmament. Researchers can examine texts of various speeches, treaties, and historical documents on the subject.

31. The Commission on Global Governance—*http://www.cgg.ch/*—This site provides access to *The Report of the Commission on Global Governance*, produced by an international group of leaders who want to find ways in which the global community can better manage its affairs. It pays particular attention to reform of the United Nations.

32. Human Rights Web—*http://www.hrweb.org/*—The history of the human-rights movement, text on seminal figures, landmark legal and political documents, and ideas on how individuals can get involved in helping to protect human rights around the world can be found on this valuable site.

Historical Retrospectives on American Foreign Policy

33. United States Institute of Peace (USIP)—*http://www.usip.org/*—The USIP, which was created by Congress to promote peaceful resolution of international conflicts, seeks to educate people and disseminate information on how to achieve peace. Click on Highlights, Publications, Grants, Fellowships, Events, Education and Training, Research Areas, Library and Links, and About the Institute.

34. DefenseLINK—*http://www.defenselink.mil/*—Learn about the Department of Defense at this site. News, publications, and other related sites of interest, among other things, are noted. The information systems BosniaLINK and GulfLINK can also be found here.

35. The Bulletin of the Atomic Scientists—*http://www.bullatomsci.org/*—This site allows you to read more about the Doomsday Clock and other issues as well as topics related to nuclear weaponry, arms control, and disarmament.

We highly recommend that you review our Web site for expanded information and our other product lines. We are continually updating and adding links to our Web site in order to offer you the most usable and useful information that will support and expand the value of your book. You can reach us at: *(http://www.dushkin.com/)*

The United States and the World: Strategic Choices

For much of the cold war there was little debate about the proper direction of American foreign policy. A consensus had formed around the policy of containment. It was a policy that identified communism and the Soviet Union as the primary threat to American national interests and prescribed a strategy of constant vigilance, global competition, and unparalleled military strength. That world is no longer with us. We have entered a period that has yet to develop its own identity. It is a world that offers more choices to American foreign policy but also sends contradictory signals as to which of those choices will best protect American national interests in the last years of the twentieth century.

In speaking about the foreign policy challenges of the post–cold war era, R. James Woolsey, President Bill Clinton's first director of the Central Intelligence Agency, suggested that rather than having to contend with a single menacing dragon, the United States now faced a jungle filled with many poisonous snakes. Instead of containing the dragon, the test for any U.S. foreign policy would be how well it handled these snakes.

Not all strategists are convinced that this characterization of the post–cold war international system is correct. For neoidealists, the 1990s represent a moment to be seized. It is a time in which the conflict and confrontation of the cold war can be replaced by strategies designed to foster cooperation among states and lift the human condition. For neoisolationists, the 1990s provide the United States with the long-awaited opportunity to walk away from the distracting and corrupting influence of international affairs. Now, they say, is the time to focus on domestic concerns and embrace traditional American values. Finally, some realists maintain that dragons are still very much with us and that instead of worrying about snakes the United States ought to focus its energy on containing the dragons.

Metaphors alone cannot guide foreign policy. They only provide a point of departure for thinking about problems. What is also needed is the articulation of a strategic perspective in which goals, threats, opportunities, and tactics are linked together by an overall vision and sense of purpose. It was only in September 1993 that the Clinton administration sought to put forward such a grand strategy.

The administration argued that the United States must remain actively engaged in world politics, not out of altruism but because of "real American interests that will suffer if we are seduced by the isolationist myth." It asserted that the successor doctrine to containment should be that of enlargement, which involves (1) strengthening the community of major market democracies, (2) fostering and consolidating new democracies and market economies, (3) countering aggression by "backlash" states hostile to democracy and markets, as well as supporting their liberalization, and (4) working to help democracy and market economics take root in regions of greatest humanitarian concern.

In carrying out this doctrine, administration spokespersons asserted that the United States must be patient, pragmatic, view democracy broadly, and respect diversity.

UNIT 1

Diplomacy was identified as America's first choice as a means for solving problems, but because there will always be times when words and sanctions are not enough, modern military forces were called a continuing necessity. Finally, it was asserted that the choice between unilateralism and multilateralism was a false dichotomy and that elements of each could coexist within the broader strategic framework of American foreign policy.

The articulation of a Clinton Doctrine did little to silence the administration's foreign policy critics. Today, doubts are still expressed by strategists over the wisdom and feasibility of a strategy of enlargement. The readings in this section are designed to introduce the scope of this debate and the range of strategic options now before the United States.

The first two readings provide overviews of the foreign policy challenges facing the Clinton administration in its second term. "Building a Bipartisan Foreign Policy: Diplomacy and Economics," is an address presented by President Clinton's secretary of state, Madeleine Albright, shortly after she assumed this position. Warning against the dangers of isolationism, she reviews Clinton's foreign policy agenda for its second term. Albright argues that foreign policy matters deeply affect the lives of Americans in ways that they do not fully recognize. In her address, she pays particular attention to the need for Senate approval of the Chemical Weapons Convention. The second reading, "Starting Over: Foreign Policy Challenges for the Second Clinton Administration," presents an outsider's view of what is in store for Clinton in his second term. Richard Haass argues that the administration starts with a mixed inheritance of positives and negatives from the first term. He sees two sets of challenges facing it. Overseas the challenges will come from relations with other powers and a series of flash point crises to which the administration will be forced to respond. At home the challenges will come from the low level of public support for international involvement.

The next two readings provide critiques of Clinton's foreign policy as well as overviews of the major lines of argument in the current debate over the proper direction of American foreign policy. Ronald Steel, in "A New Realism," uses the concept of national security as a point of departure for examining the threats and challenges facing the United States. He argues the term was introduced to help make sense of a particular set of circumstances in world politics and is in need of rethinking. For Steel, national security is an attitude more than a policy. In "The Crisis of Liberal Internationalism," Stanley Hoffmann provides a sympathetic critique of President Clinton's foreign policy agenda. He notes that to this point liberalism has not been able to direct American foreign policy in a coherent fashion, with the result that many Americans are deeply ambivalent over how to proceed. Still, Hoffmann believes that, unlike realism, liberalism provides a comprehensive and hopeful vision of world politics?

Looking Ahead: Challenge Questions

How much has the nature of world politics really changed with the passing of the cold war? What trends in world politics are most significant to the United States for the rest of this century?

Stanley Hoffmann speaks of a crisis in liberal internationalism. Is there a crisis in conservative internationalism? If so, what are the major points of debate among conservatives?

Weigh the relative merits of an internationalist foreign policy versus a neoisolationist one.

How do the principles guiding President Clinton's foreign policy differ from those found in earlier presidential foreign policy doctrines?

How much freedom does the United States have in choosing a foreign policy?

What countries are "poisonous snakes" and which are (or could become) "dragons"?

Is Madeleine Albright correct that foreign policy touches the lives of all Americans, or does she overstate the point?

If "national security" is an attitude, what should our attitude be to the challenges facing the United States? Is there a need to rethink our basic ideas about security? How do we move from "attitudes" to "policy" in the arena of world politics?

Article 1

Building A Bipartisan Foreign Policy

DIPLOMACY AND ECONOMICS

Address by MADELEINE ALBRIGHT, *United States Secretary of State*
Delivered to Rice Memorial Center, Rice University, Houston, Texas, February 7, 1997

Mr. Secretary, President Gillis, Ambassador Djerejian, thank you for the introduction and for the Texas hospitality. This is my first official trip as Secretary of State; and I can't imagine a better destination or more distinguished company.

My original thought was to come here next Thursday, on February 13, but one of my advance people who went to Rice told me that you close the University on the 13th of every month, due to your celebration of the ancient academic rite of streaking. And, as the first female Secretary of State, I wasn't sure I was quite ready for that!

In a world where many claim to have all the answers, this Institute and this University understand the importance of asking the right questions.

And, in your search for wisdom, you have certainly found the right guide.

James Baker's memoirs were entitled "The Politics of Diplomacy" and, as his record gives evidence, he was a master of both. He has earned our nation's gratitude, and I am delighted to be a witness to the exciting new work he has initiated here. And I am also glad to learn that former Secretaries of State can get day jobs.

This afternoon, I want to talk with you about some exciting new work of my own. I have just completed my second full week as Secretary of State. Already, I have a reputation for speaking in sound bites. This is not a reputation I have sought. When I speak, I always think I'm sounding like Henry Kissinger; unfortunately, what the audience seems to hear sounds more like David Letterman.

My goal, and it is causing some culture shock back in D.C., is to clear away the fog from Foggy Bottom, a place where the elevator inspection certificates, and I am not making this up, do not refer to elevators, but to "vertical transportation units."

As Secretary, I will do my best to talk about foreign policy, not in abstract terms, but in human terms, and in bipartisan terms; I consider this vital because in our democracy, we cannot pursue policies abroad that are not understood and supported here at home.

When I was nominated by the President, I said that I would have an obligation to explain to you, the "who, what, when, where" and especially the "whys" of the policies we conduct around the world in your name.

Today, I intend to begin that job.

Last Tuesday, in his State of the Union Address, President Clinton said that, "To prepare America for the 21st century, we must master the forces of change in the world and keep American leadership strong and sure for an uncharted time."

Fortunately, thanks to the President's own leadership, and that of his predecessor President George Bush, Houston's most distinguished adopted son, I begin work with the wind at my back.

Our nation is respected and at peace. Our alliances are vigorous. Our economy is strong. And from the distant corners of Asia, to the emerging democracies of Central Europe and Africa, to the community of liberty that exists within our own hemisphere, American institutions and ideals are a model for those who have, or who aspire to, freedom.

All this is no accident, and its continuation is by no means

1. Building a Bipartisan Foreign Policy

inevitable. Democratic progress must be sustained as it was built, by American leadership. And our leadership must be sustained if our interests are to be protected around the world.

That is why our armed forces must remain the best-led, best-trained, best-equipped and most respected in the world. And as President Clinton has pledged, they will.

It is also why we need first-class diplomacy. Force, and the credible possibility of its use, are essential to defend our vital interests and to keep America safe. But force alone can be a blunt instrument, and there are many problems it cannot solve.

To be effective, force and diplomacy must complement and reinforce each other. For there will be many occasions, in many places, where we will rely on diplomacy to protect our interests, and we will expect our diplomats to defend those interests with skill, knowledge and spine.

Unfortunately, in the words of Senator Richard Lugar of Indiana, our international operations today are "underfunded and under-staffed." We are the world's richest and most powerful nation, but we are also the number one debtor to the UN and the international financial institutions. We are dead last among the industrialized nations in the percentage of our wealth that we use to promote democracy and growth in the developing world.

And diplomatically, we are steadily and unilaterally disarming ourselves.

Over the past four years, the Department of State has cut more than 2,000 employees, closed more than 30 overseas posts and slashed foreign assistance by almost one-third.

This trend is not acceptable. Many of you are students. Someday, one of you may occupy the office I hold and that Secretary Baker held. I hope you do. And I assure you that I will do everything I can in my time to see that you have the necessary diplomatic tools in your time to protect our nation and do your job.

Yesterday, the President submitted his budget request to Congress for the coming fiscal year. That budget, which totals some 1.8 trillion dollars, includes about $20 billion for the entire range of international affairs programs. This would pay for everything from our share of reconstruction in Bosnia, to enforcing sanctions against Saddam Hussein, to waging war around the world against drug kingpins and organized crime.

Approval of this budget matters, not only to me, or to those who consider themselves foreign policy experts, but to each and every one of us.

For example, if you live in Houston, more than likely your job, or that of a member of your family, is linked to the health of the global economy, whether through investments, or trade, or competition from workers abroad, or from newly-arrived workers here. This region's robust agricultural and energy sectors are particularly affected by overseas prices, policies and politics.

Your family, like most in America, probably has good reason to look ahead with hope. But you are also anxious. For you see crime fueled by drugs that pour across nearby borders. You see advanced technology creating not only new wonders, but new and more deadly arms. On your television screen, you see the consequences of letter bombs and poisonous serums and sudden explosions, and ask yourself when and where terrorists may strike next.

Whether you are a student, or parent, or teacher, or worker, you are concerned about the future our young people will face. Will the global marketplace continue to expand and generate new opportunities and new jobs? Will our global environment survive the assault of increasing population and pollution? Will the plague of AIDS and other epidemic disease be brought under control? And will the world continue to move away from the threat of nuclear Armaggedon, or will that specter once again loom large, perhaps in some altered and even more dangerous form?

If you are like most Americans, you do not think of the United States as just another country. You want America to be strong and respected. And you want that strength and respect to continue through the final years of this century and into the next.

Considering all this, one thing should be clear. The success or failure of American foreign policy is not only relevant to our lives; it will be a determining factor in the quality of our lives. It will make the difference between a future characterized by peace, rising prosperity and law, and a more uncertain future, in which our economy and security are always at risk, our peace of mind is always under assault, and American leadership is increasingly in doubt.

We are talking here about one percent of the federal budget; but that one percent may determine fifty percent of the history that is written about our era; and it will affect the lives of 100 percent of the American people.

Let me be more specific.

First, foreign policy creates jobs. The Clinton Administration has negotiated more than 200 trade agreements since 1993. Those agreements have helped exports to soar and boosted employment by more than 1.6 million.

For example, earlier today I met with Mexican Foreign Minister, Gurria. Our growing trade with Mexico is a genuine success story. Last year alone, $125 billion dollars in exports were traded. And with NAFTA now in place, we estimate that this coming year some 2.2 million American workers will produce goods for export to our NAFTA partners.

By passing NAFTA, concluding the Uruguay Round, and forging commitments to free trade in Latin America and Asia, we have helped create a growing global economy with America as its dynamic hub.

This matters a lot down here. Houston is one of America's great ports. Texas is our second leading exporting state. Commerce makes you grow. And there are more direct benefits. For years, Texas grains have been among the leading commodities sold through the Food for Peace Program.

America's economic expansion is no accident. It derives primarily from the genius of our scientists, the enterprise of our businesspeople and the productivity of our factories and farms. But it has been helped along by American diplomats who work to ensure that American business and labor receive fair treatment overseas.

For example, if an American businessman or woman bribes a foreign official in return for a contract, that American is fined or goes to jail. If a European bribes that same foreign official, chances are he will get a tax deduction. We are working hard to create higher standards that apply to all. And we have opened the doors of embassies around the world to U.S. entrepreneurs seeking our help in creating a level playing field for American firms and more opportunities for Americans back home.

Have no doubt, these efforts will continue. For as long as I am Secretary of State, America's diplomatic influence will be harnessed to the task of helping America's economy to grow.

We will also use diplomacy to keep America safe.

1 ❖ STRATEGIC CHOICES

The Cold War may be over, but the threat to our security posed be weapons of mass destruction has only been reduced, not ended.

In recent years, with U.S. leadership, much has been accomplished. Russian warheads no longer target our homes. The last missile silos in Ukraine are being planted over with sunflowers, and nuclear weapons have also been removed from Belarus and Kazakstan. North Korea's nuclear weapons program has been frozen. The Nuclear Nonproliferation Treaty has been extended. A comprehensive ban on nuclear tests has been approved.

And we are continuing the job begun under President Bush of ensuring that Iraq's capacity to produce weapons of mass destruction is thoroughly and verifiably dismantled.

The President's budget empowers us to build on these steps. It provides the resources we need to seek further reductions in nuclear stockpiles, to help assure the safe handling of nuclear materials, to back international inspections of other countries' nuclear programs, and to implement the agreements we have reached.

The President's budget also reflects America's role as the indispensable nation in promoting international security and peace.

Our largest single program is in support of the peace process in the Middle East. Even here, the price tag does not compare to the cost to us and to our friends, if that strategic region should once again erupt in war. The oil crisis caused by fighting there in 1973 threw our economy into a tailspin, caused inflation to soar and resulted in gas lines that stretched for miles.

Today, as a result of courageous leaders in the region, and persistent American diplomacy, the peace process launched by Secretary Baker has been sustained. Israel has signed landmark agreements with Jordan and the Palestinian authorities. And as the recent pact on Hebron illustrates, the movement towards peace continues despite episodes of violence, outbreaks of terrorism and a tragic assassination.

As Secretary of State, I will ensure that America continues to stand with the peacemakers and against the bomb throwers in this strategic region. That is in America's interests; it is consistent with the commitments we have made; it reflects the kind of people we are; and it is right.

Because the United States has unique capabilities and unmatched power, it is natural that others turn to us in time of emergency. We have an unlimited number of opportunities to act. But we do not have unlimited resources, nor unlimited responsibilities. We are not a charity or a fire department. If we are to protect our own interests and maintain our credibility, we have to weigh our commitments carefully, and be selective and disciplined in what we agree to do.

Recognizing this, we have good reason to strengthen other instruments for responding to emergencies and conflicts, and for addressing the conditions that give rise to those conflicts.

These other instruments include the United Nations, regional organizations and international financial institutions. Together, these entities remove from our shoulders, the lion's share of the costs of keeping the peace, maintaining sanctions against rogue states, creating new markets, protecting the environment, caring for refugees and addressing other problems around the globe.

Unfortunately, in recent years, we have fallen behind in our payments to these institutions. We owe about $1 billion to the UN and other organizations and almost another $1 billion to the Multilateral Banks.

In his budget, the President requests enough money to repay many of these obligations. The reason is that these debts hurt America. They erode the capacity of these organizations to carry out programs that serve our interests. They undermine the proposals we have made for reform. And, to those around the world who are hostile to our leadership, they are an open invitation to run America down.

The United States can, and should, lead the way in strengthening and reforming international organizations so that they better serve the world community, and American interests. But if we are to succeed, we must also pay our bills. As in poker, if we want a seat at the table, we have to put chips in the pot.

Before closing, I would like to highlight one of the President's top early priorities, which has little to do with money, but much to do with America's standing in the world.

The President has asked the Senate to give its approval to a Convention intended to ban chemical weapons from the face of the Earth. That agreement, known as the Chemical Weapons Convention, or CWC, will enter into force on April 29. Our goal is to ratify the agreement before then so that America will be an original party.

Chemical weapons are inhumane. They kill horribly, massively, indiscriminately and are no more controllable than the wind. That is why the United States decided years ago to eliminate our stockpile of these weapons and to purge from our military doctrine any possibility of their use. Countries that join the CWC will undertake a legal obligation to pursue a similar policy.

The Convention makes it less likely that our armed forces will ever again encounter chemical weapons on the battlefield; less likely that rogue regimes will have access to the materials needed to build chemical arms; and less likely that such arms will fall into the hands of terrorists or others hostile to our interests.

The result will be a safer America and a safer world.

Unfortunately, not everyone sees it that way. Senate approval of the Convention is by no means assured. Opponents of the CWC argue that it does not provide full protection, because we do not expect early ratification by the rogue states. We regret that, but the CWC remains very much in our interests.

The CWC establishes the standard that it is wrong to build or possess chemical weapons. That standard will put added pressure on rogue regimes. It will send a message that if a country wants to be part of the international system, and to participate fully in its benefits, it must ratify and comply with the CWC.

What it comes down to is this question. Who should set the rules for the international community? Law-abiding nations? Or the rogues? Are we barred from establishing any rule that the outlaw nations do not first accept? Or does it serve our interests to draw the clearest possible distinction in law between those who observe international standards and those who do not?

Unfortunately, as General Norman Schwarzkopf recently observed, if the foes of the CWC have their way, the United States would draw a line in the sand, put our friends and allies on one side, and then cross over to the other, joining hands with Libya and Iraq.

If the opponents have their way, we would forgo the right to help draft the rules by which the Convention is enforced and the destruction of chemical weapons assured.

We would lose the right to have Americans help administer and conduct inspections within the CWC.

We would risk the loss of hundreds of millions of dollars in export sales because the American chemical industry would become subject to trade restrictions imposed upon non-members of the CWC.

Finally, we would lose credibility in negotiating arms reduction agreements generally, because our ability to deliver in the Senate what we have proposed at the bargaining table would be undermined, for reasons that friends and allies around the world would find very difficult to understand.

Make no mistake, the Chemical Weapons Convention is in the best interests of the United States. In fact, the CWC has "made in America" written all over it. It was endorsed by President Reagan, and negotiated under President Bush, very ably negotiated I might add, thanks to his Secretary of State.

Now, and until success is achieved, the President, our new Secretary of Defense, Bill Cohen, and I will be working with every member of the Senate to ensure the timely and favorable consideration of this important Convention.

In closing, let me say that I well understand, as I undertake my new job, that there is no certain formula for ensuring public support for American engagement overseas.

Certainly, frankness helps. Consultations with Congress are essential, and we are working with Congressional leaders of both parties to an unprecedented degree. But we Americans are brutally fair. As President Kennedy observed after the Bay of Pigs, success has a thousand fathers, while defeat is an orphan. Ultimately, we will be judged not by our rhetoric or our rationales, but by our results.

The reality is that Americans have always been ambivalent about activism abroad.

At the end of World War I, an American Army officer, stuck in Europe while the diplomats haggled at Versailles, wrote to his future wife about his yearning to go home:

"None of us care if the Russian government is red or not, (or) whether the king of Lollipops slaughters his subjects."

Thirty years later, that same man, Harry Truman, would lead America in the final stages of another great war.

In the aftermath of that conflict, it was not enough to say that what we were against had failed. Leaders such as Truman, Marshall and Vandenberg were determined to build a lasting peace. And together with our allies, they forged a set of institutions that would defend freedom, rebuild economies, uphold law and preserve peace.

Today, the greatest danger to America is not some foreign enemy; it is the possibility that we will ignore the example of that generation; that we will succumb to the temptation of isolation; neglect the military and diplomatic resources that keep us strong; and forget the fundamental lesson of this century, which is that problems abroad, if left unattended, will all too often come home to America.

A decade or two from now, we will be known as the neo-isolationists who allowed totalitarianism and fascism to rise again or as the generation that solidified the global triumph of democratic principles.

We will be known as the neo-protectionists whose lack of vision produced financial chaos or as the generation that laid the groundwork for rising prosperity around the world.

We will be known as the world-class ditherers who stood by while the seeds of renewed global conflict were sown or as the generation that took strong measures to deter aggression, control nuclear arms and keep the peace.

There is no certain roadmap to success, either for individuals or for generations.

Ultimately, it is a matter of judgment, a question of choice.

In making that choice, let us remember that there is not a page of American history of which we are proud, that was authored by a chronic complainer or prophet of despair. We are doers.

We have a responsibility in our time, as others have had in theirs, not to be prisoners of history, but to shape history.

A responsibility to use and defend our own freedom, and to help others who share our aspirations for liberty, peace and the quiet miracle of a normal life.

To that end, I pledge my own best efforts, and solicit yours. Thank you very much.

STARTING OVER

Foreign Policy Challenges for the Second Clinton Administration

RICHARD N. HAASS

The second Clinton administration begins with an uneven inheritance in the area of foreign policy. On the positive side, the president and those around him have four years of experience working with the issues, one another, and foreign leaders. There is as well the momentum that stems from significant accomplishments, most notably in promoting liberal trade; stabilizing or at least defusing situations in Haiti, Bosnia, the Middle East, and North Korea; and managing a severe financial problem in Mexico, one that could have led to a global economic crisis.

The Clinton administration also has the continued luxury of conducting foreign policy in the absence of a major adversary. This is not to say there are no hostile forces—there are, including several so-called rogue states and terrorist and criminal organizations, as well as other governments that can be expected to resist the United States on particular issues. But there is no successor to the Soviet Union, no global competitor of the United States.

At the same time, Mr. Clinton begins his second term with handicaps. It is some seven years after the end of the Cold War, and still there is no intellectual or political consensus on how to view the world or structure America's relationship with it. That we call it the "post–Cold War world" testifies to our confusion, as does the absence of any doctrine or idea to replace containment and guide the country's foreign policy.

Nor did any clear policy consensus emerge from the president's first term. There was not so much a Clinton foreign policy as foreign policies. At various times, Mr. Clinton and his advisers emphasized promoting democ-

racy and human rights, boosting U.S. exports, alleviating humanitarian hardship, or maintaining the balance of power in critical regions such as the Persian Gulf or Northeast Asia. Similarly, the first Clinton administration began by espousing an ambitious concept of what multilateralism could accomplish and ended with a number of actions that were nothing so much as unilateralism in practice.

The 1996 election did little to clarify matters. The presidential campaign as well as the congressional competitions largely ignored events beyond the country's borders. The relative neglect of international affairs means that the winning candidates are not locked into positions that helped them win over voters but would pose an obstacle to intelligent governing. Yet it also means that the Clinton administration cannot lay claim to any mandate in this area. Nor did the campaign prepare the American people for any sacrifice. To the contrary, it only reinforced the impression that the world is a relatively safe place and that international concerns can continue to take a back seat to domestic matters.

This mixed inheritance makes it inevitable that the second Clinton administration will face two sets of challenges. The first will be overseas and will involve relations with the other leading powers of the day and a series of both major and minor flashpoints or crises. The second set of foreign policy challenges will come here at home, where support for international involvement falls short of what is required. How President Clinton deals with both sets of challenges will determine his legacy in the foreign policy realm and, quite possibly, overall.

Richard N. Haass is director of the Brookings Foreign Policy Studies program. He is the author of The Reluctant Sheriff: The United States after the Cold War *(Council on Foreign Relations, forthcoming).*

BEYOND AMERICA'S BORDERS

The most significant foreign policy challenge facing the incoming administration involves relations between the

United States and the other great powers of the era: China, Russia, Japan, and Germany and Western Europe. These countries possess the lion's share of the world's economic and military might. Their ability to agree on the norms or standards that should shape international life will give this period of history its character. Similarly their cooperation is essential if we are to see the emergence and strengthening of the institutions that will help structure or regulate post–Cold War international relations.

Achieving such consensus will be far from easy. Indeed, during Mr. Clinton's first term, U.S. relations with each of these powers deteriorated. To point this out is not to blame the president and his foreign policy team, although it is fair to say that American inconsistency, unilateralism, and above all a lack of regular high-level attention by policymakers did contribute to this development. Improved relations will require a more disciplined agenda on our part and then sustained effort to address U.S. priorities with the leaders of these states.

We will need to continue talking with Russia about its relationship with an enlarged NATO—Moscow deserves a voice, not a veto—and the United States should be willing to adjust arms control arrangements inherited from the Cold War to meet changed circumstances and legitimate Russian concerns. With Germany and Europe there needs to be a greater effort to find common approaches to out-of-area problems, along with less recourse to unilateralism on our part when we disagree, as is the case in policy toward both Iran and Cuba.

No relationship may prove as fateful as that between the United States and China. Indeed, managing China's emergence as a great power could well prove to be the defining foreign policy effort of this era. We would be wise to place our priorities on China's external behavior, the area where the stakes are the largest, the impact the most immediate, and our leverage greatest, and not allow U.S. policy to be determined by hunger for China's market or frustration over human rights. With Japan as well the United States needs a broader relationship, one in which trade concerns do not overwhelm all else but in which we can consult profitably about events in Korea and involving China.

The second principal overseas challenge will involve the Persian Gulf and Northeast Asia. These are the two theaters where the United States has vital national interests, where those interests face clear threats, and where local states are dependent on Washington for help. It may be worth noting that Korea was the site of the first major conflict of the Cold War, and the Gulf the first major conflict of the post–Cold War world. We will require clear communication—both of what we expect and of what we are prepared to do if those expectations are either met or not—as well as the capabilities to back up our words if we are to avoid crises with an increasingly weak North Korea in one region and an increasingly robust Iran and Iraq in another.

The third challenge is not a single one so much as a category. It includes many problems that dominated foreign policymaking during the first term, most notably Bosnia, Haiti, the Middle East, and Mexico. In addition, terrorism, uncertainty over the fate of Hong Kong, growing tensions between Greece and Turkey—these and other problems are sure to intrude. The challenge will be to address them without losing sight of more important if not always more urgent concerns, something best accomplished by early and regular involvement with the full range of foreign policy tools. The worst approach is almost always to wait until a crisis erupts, at which point we are often left with few choices other than those provided by the military.

FOREIGN POLICY BEGINS AT HOME

The world of the next four years is unlikely to be as stable as that of the previous four, which were remarkably calm by any measure. As a result, foreign policy in the second term is likely to be more difficult and demanding. As much as the president and many of those around him may want to focus on domestic matters, they are unlikely to be able to do so.

The president will have to spend a good deal of political capital working with Congress to provide the funds—nearly $300 billion—needed for the United States to continue its leadership role.

The president has already chosen his principal foreign policy lieutenants. Now several relationships must be sorted out, including the degree of presidential involvement, the power of cabinet secretaries relative to one another and to the national security adviser, and the role of the National Economic Council and the weighting of international economic concerns. No one system is right for all presidents, but history strongly suggests the need for regular presidential involvement, a strong national security adviser who can broker differences between the cabinet heads and provide independent counsel as required, and a strong NEC that ensures that trade considerations are factored in but not allowed to dominate national security decisionmaking.

The process of making foreign policy will be complicated by the continuation of divided government. There is no solution to this challenge, just as there is no substitute for constant and regular consultations between the executive and legislative branches.

The president will have to spend a good deal of political capital working with Congress to provide the funds—nearly $300 billion—needed for the United States to continue its leadership role. On spending for defense and intelligence, there seems to be a floor of about $265 billion. Indeed, here the biggest question is less how much is spent overall than what the money is spent on in particular. Balancing among requirements stemming from the need to hedge against great power conflict, planning for the two dominant regional contingencies, and undertaking the many lesser actual and potential deployments is the overarching challenge. What this suggests is the need for capabilities that are not only large but varied and flexible, able to contend with a wide range of challenges in a variety of locales.

No such floor exists under funding for foreign aid and diplomacy. Although economies from consolidating oversight agencies are still possible, and despite the fact that some programs may not yet have been sufficiently revised to meet the changing demands of the post–Cold War world, it is nevertheless true that years of budget cuts have left us resource poor. The result is a loss of leverage and tools that could help us address a host of problems before they reach a point where there is little we can usefully do or where military intervention is the only option.

But as important as dollars are, the most important resource affecting the course of American foreign and defense policy may be time—in particular, the time of the president and his most senior aides. It is often too late once the problem or crisis materializes. We need regular, active involvement as a matter of course—and regular high-level consultations with the other major powers as a matter of schedule.

In the end, all the dollars and all the tools in the world count for little if the American people and their representatives are not prepared to support their use. Only the president has the power to persuade the public that casualties are worth suffering on behalf of certain interests or causes. We need less emphasis on exit strategies and more on the benefits of acting and staying the course. This means that the bully pulpit of the presidency must be used consistently to make the case for foreign policy.

FROM CONTAINMENT TO REGULATION

The lack of an intellectual construct for American foreign policy is not cost-free. Doctrines provide useful guidance for sizing and shaping defense spending, for determining whether and how to intervene with military force or other tools, for deciding where promoting democracy can dominate policy and where it must take a back seat. Without such a structure, policymakers become reactive, all too easily swayed by the latest televised image.

What should this construct be? I would argue for a doctrine of "regulation" to shape the behavior and, in some cases, capabilities of governments and other actors so that they are less likely or able to act aggressively beyond their borders or toward their own citizens and more likely to conduct trade and other economic relations according to agreed norms and procedures.

The focus on inter-state concerns should be dominant rather than exclusive. Considerations of "justice"—democracy, human rights, human welfare—would, though, ordinarily be of a lower priority. So, too, would promoting exports. The reasoning is simple. Order is the more basic concern. One can have order without justice but not the other way around. Similarly, one cannot have trade without stability.

Some of this can be best achieved by creating or expanding multilateral institutions, be they regional (such as NAFTA) or global (such as the World Trade Organization). In other instances, less formal coalitions of the willing and able, organized by the United States, will be the best available mechanism for accomplishing U.S. objectives. In all instances, what is certain is that our ability to realize our goals will be a direct consequence of our willingness and ability to lead, something that in turn will reflect our willingness to devote resources—our wealth, lives, and time—to the tasks before us.

A New Realism
Ronald Steel

Ronald Steel is professor of international relations at the University of Southern California and the author of Temptations of a Superpower.

The most troublesome concepts are the ones we take for granted. This is not only because they are familiar but because they are imbedded in our way of thinking. They roll off our tongues without our ever stopping to think what they really mean. We come to take them as established truths, like Biblical injunctions.

One of these concepts lies at the very heart of our thinking about the outside world: the concept of "national security." It is central to the apparatus of government and enjoys the highest priority over our resources and our lives. Yet like many other familiar terms, it is not a neutral description of an external reality. It is a social construct. It came into being at a specific time and in response to a specific set of circumstances. Those circumstances governed the way we defined the term then and continue to define it now.

It was 50 years ago this summer that President Harry S Truman signed the National Security Act. The very terminology reflected a new American approach to the world and eventually itself became the justification for that approach. The legislation provided for a limited unification of the armed forces, preserving the army and navy, and establishing the air force, as separate departments. In response to enormous pressure from the navy and its supporters—including James Forrestal, then navy secretary and later the first secretary of defense, and also Carl Vinson and other influential legislators—the navy retained its air arm (which it saw as the engine of its future growth) and successfully blocked the full merger of the services and the creation of a general staff.

In addition to partial unification of the armed forces, the act also established the National Security Council to coordinate foreign policy operations, the National Security Resources Board, and the Central Intelligence Agency. The act reflected the arguments favored by the navy and the air force, which sought the lion's share of future budgets, and of the influential Eberstadt Report, which heralded the nation's "new international commitments" and declared that these "have greatly enlarged the sphere of our international obligations, reflecting present concepts of our national security in terms of world security."

The phrasing is significant: "national security in terms of world security." No definition is given, of course, as to what "world security" might mean. It is presumably self-evident. Herein then lies an indication of how, and how early, the new concept of "national security" embraced and then went far beyond the traditional notion of "defense." Indeed, it would have been appropriate to have had, instead of a modestly titled "Defense Department" (which replaced the plain vanilla War Department), a "National Security Department."

Although the familiar phrase can be traced far back, it did not enter the common vocabulary until after the Second World War. It was first popularized by Walter Lippmann in his influential 1943 book, *U.S. Foreign Policy: Shield of the Republic.* There, he wrote that America's long insulation from European quarrels was not due to any inherent virtue on America's part but was a consequence of its protection by two great oceans and a benevolent British navy. This fortuitous combination of circumstances had, he argued, "diverted our attention from the idea of national security."

The phrase, and with it the entire concept, quickly caught on. It captured the feeling of power and exuberance that followed from the victory over Germany and Japan. It repudiated the discredited refuge of isolationism, and it suggested a far broader involvement of the United States in world affairs. In arguing for policies based on what he called a hard calculation of "national interest," Lippmann also added a caveat. A workable foreign policy, he maintained, "consists in bringing into balance, with a comfortable surplus of power in reserve, the nation's commitments and the nation's power." This later came to be honored as much in the breach as in the observance.

What Lippmann inherently recognized—and what later became abundantly clear—was how broadly the new concept of "national security" could be construed. Unlike the term "defense," which connotes repelling an invasive force, it suggests not just resistance to aggression but an outward reach to anticipate and neutralize dangers that might still be only potential. It draws a security perimeter that is determined, in practice, only by the reach of national power. A regional power will have a regional security perimeter; a global power will be satisfied with nothing less than a global one. The perimeter expands in relation to the amount of power available. And the definition of security expands with it.

For this reason security gets unhinged from its geographical moorings. It becomes a function of power and an aspect of psychology. It becomes internalized. It is not a specific reality, and it does not exist entirely in space. It is a function of definition and can be defined broadly or narrowly. Small and weak states define it narrowly, large and powerful ones define it broadly. Security, then, is a reflection of a nation's (or at least of a nation's elite's) sense of its power. It is an operating mechanism, and at the same time an abstraction.

The Paradox of Insecurity
It is striking how quickly the American sense of security, confirmed by the wartime victories and the development of the ultimate weapon, the atomic bomb, developed into a sense of insecurity. The postwar quarrels with the Soviet Union, intensified by a communist ideology that was, in its aspirations (or pretensions), global in sweep—as was, in its own way, the American counter-ideology of democratic capitalism—gave way to a pervasive sense of insecurity.

Virtually no place seemed to be really secure. Where there were not Soviet legions there were communist believers, or sympathizers, enemies without and enemies within. Everything came to seem crucial and everything was up for grabs. This new sense of global security (and as its inseparable companion, global insecurity) was enshrined in the Truman Doctrine of 1947.

Fifty years ago this March, President Truman went before Congress to ask for a relatively modest amount of money to assist the anticommunist governments of Greece and Turkey. But the request was wrapped in packaging that turned out to be far more important than the contents. The packaging was what came to be known as the Truman Doctrine. To legislators who had little inkling of what these modest words would soon justify, Truman declared that Americans must commit themselves to aiding what he described as "free peoples who are resisting attempted subjugation by armed minorities or by outside pressures."

What few asked at the time was how he defined "free peoples," or whether "armed minorities" was not another way of saying "civil war," or what he meant by "outside pressures." Just what kind of situations was he suggesting that the United States get into? "Totalitarian regimes imposed upon free peoples, by direct or indirect aggression," Truman continued, "undermine the foundations of international peace and hence the security of the United States."

Again, there was a little problem of vagueness. Which free peoples, and how free must they be to qualify? What was "indirect aggression," and how did the United States propose to counter it? Furthermore, what was "international peace"? Taken at face value, it meant a beatific state of affairs that had probably never existed. Most troublesome of all was the key word "hence"—as in "hence the security of the United States" was threatened by the absence of international peace.

Drawing the Line
What Truman was saying was that threats to free (that is, anticommunist) governments anywhere were a security threat to the United States. While presumably one was not supposed to take this literally, what his speech was intended to do was to lay out a new definition of international engagement, one global in scope and without clear political or geographical definition. It was inevitable that at some point the desire of policymakers to push the definition of national security to its outer limits would collide head-on with the anxieties of a public unpersuaded of its necessity. The excesses of globalism, and the disaster that was Vietnam, were foretold in the exuberant language of the Truman Doctrine.

If the first problem with the concept of "national security" is its vagueness, the second is its expansiveness. In its effort to simplify the issue and to win public support for a global level of engagement, the Truman Doctrine often failed to distinguish between the vital and the desirable, the critical and the peripheral. It suggested that everything was vital and security a seamless web. But then some things turned out not to be so vital after all, like South Vietnam. Where does one draw the line? If South Vietnam was not really vital, then how about South Korea, or NATO? If security is to some degree arbitrary, then are interests arbitrary as well?

An example of expansiveness carried to its ultimate extreme as a security doctrine can be found in a declaration by the Clinton administration's former national security adviser, Anthony Lake, that the enemies of the United States, now that the Cold War is over, include no less than "extreme nationalists and tribalists, terrorists, organized criminals, coup plotters, rogue states, and all those who would return newly free societies to the intolerant ways of the past." Aside from the welcome news that intolerant ways are now largely confined to the past, one wonders whether there is anyone left, by this definition, who is not an enemy of the United States.

An Attitude, Not a Policy
The major reason for the intellectual confusion evidenced by such statements lies in the unmooring of the concept of "national security" from the more explicit and narrow concept of defense. Defense is a policy, national security is an attitude; defense is precise, national security is diffuse; defense is a condition, national security is a feeling.

The doctrine of national security emphasizes the nation-state. It came to prominence at a time when states were viewed not only as the dominant but as virtually the only actors. Nothing, however, has deflated the role of the state more than the end of the Cold War. There are two reasons for this. First, the state enjoys, by definition, a monopoly on military power. The Cold War, for all its ideological overlay, was primarily a contest between powerful, militarized states. But as the end of the war has decreased the relevance of military power, so, too, has it reduced the importance of the state.

A second reason for the decline of the state is the growing importance of trade, production, and wealth as determinants of power and influence. The central arena in which advanced industrial societies compete has shifted dramatically from the instruments of war to the instruments of wealth. In this new competition a former military superpower has become a supplicant, and former puny protectorates such as Taiwan, Singapore, and South Korea, not to mention Japan, have become powerful players. In the past, the great trading states—France, Germany, Britain, Japan, Spain, and even Venice—were, for the most part, major military players as well. Today, the economic giants are, for the most part, content to remain militarily weak.

The Security Dilemma
The governing theoretical model for international relations during the Cold War—the "paradigm" in political science talk—was that of realism, or power politics. The state was deemed to be the paramount actor, its sovereignty an absolute, and its protection the ultimate purpose of its military and diplomatic forces. States, being considered independent actors, could be threatened only by other states. Since states exist in a Hobbesian world of international anarchy, they must protect themselves from envious rivals. They must accrue military power (or put themselves under the tutelage of a powerful protector). That this may provoke anxieties among other states and make *them* feel threatened is the self-fulfilling prophecy of the security dilemma. Under these rules, security is defined as the prevention of war with other states, or victory in any conflict that occurs.

This is all very well, if the nation-state is the dominant reality of public life and if it has the ability to command undiluted loyalty. But in some areas of the world, the state has collapsed (as in central Africa), or is an instrument of drug lords and local oligarchies (as in parts of Latin America), or is run by a single family or clan (as in much of the Middle East and the Third World). In these cases, it commands not loyalty, but fear, and rules by intimidation. And instead of providing security for its citizens, it actually threatens it.

In such a case, what allegiance is owed the state? The question is not an abstract one. In recent years, we have seen the disintegration of established states, such as Yugoslavia and the Soviet Union, and the hollowing-out of others that exist only at the convenience of outside forces that sustain their ruling regimes, as in the former African colonies of France. Even in parts of the industrialized world, the state is sometimes incapable of providing security for some of its citizens. One has only to look to the slums of major U.S. cities for confirmation of this sorry fact—or even to affluent areas, with their guarded gates and private police forces.

The problem is not simply that the state is often unable to provide security, which is, after all, the major justification for its existence. It has also become increasingly secondary, even superfluous, to the economic life of peoples everywhere. The export and import of capital, the shifting of hundreds of billions of dollars around the world each day, the decisions over investment and employment, wages, and production—all these are made primarily by private forces under little or no state control. Within the economic realm, we are approaching the condition described by Karl Marx (albeit under different circumstances) where the state seems to be withering away.

No longer can any single state make decisions impervious to market forces and market commands: not unless it wants to commit economic suicide. States, like Gulliver, are confined by an ever-widening web of agreements, regulations, and prohibitions that lay outside their control. The American government, for example, has learned that it cannot enforce against its own European allies and Canada its self-declared embargo against Cuba—not even when it declares the matter to be one vital to its "national security"—which it has recently done. If "national security" now means that store clerks from Toronto and homemakers from Cologne must not be allowed to sun themselves on Cuban beaches, then Karl Marx has once again been proved right in observing that events reappear in history the first time as tragedy and the second time as farce.

What is taking place on every level—in the economy, in communications, in the environment, in public health—is the decline of the state as an autonomous actor. It will continue to exist for a long time, but shorn of its former pretense and majesty: a victim of forces it cannot control. Increasingly, the greatest threats to the well-being of citizens come not from other states, not from independent actors, but from *conditions*: resource scarcity, population growth, rampant urbanization, mass migration, environmental degradation, individual and group terrorism, economic exploitation.

Traffic Cops
How does the so-called realist paradigm—which declares states to be the dominant force of international life and their unhindered pursuit of their self-defined "interests" to be the duty of their citizens—help us to deal with this reality? What indeed are we to make of the concept of "statecraft" when the state itself is only one of the actors, or forces, that influences our lives? And beyond that, what happens to the concept of the majestic state when its role is reduced to that of a facilitator of private transactions?

Consider the international trade organizations that have become so important in the past few years: the North American Free Trade Agreement (NAFTA) and the World Trade Organization (WTO). These entities are really little more than giant trade groups whose purpose is to increase the flow of commerce. They do this by eliminating government regulations and ignoring international frontiers. Their purpose is to make national governments irrelevant. What is novel about them, and a telling mark of their power, is that they have enlisted governments to do this work for them. Governments are being reduced to the role of traffic cops, ensuring that everyone follows the regulations that are, of course, written by and for the most powerful corporations.

In some places, this process has gone so far that the state can hardly be said to exist at all. By this I do not mean such narco-states as Colombia, Mexico, Burma, and Pakistan, where drug lords rule independent fiefdoms. Rather, I have in mind Russia, where the new giant corporate entities (themselves former state enterprises stolen from the people by their former managers and the new mafia entrepreneurs) control the government and refuse to pay taxes to a state that they consider, quite understandably, the servant of their ambition. In effect, the role of such a state is to keep the population in line, to deflect criticism of commercial operations by invoking appeals to patriotism, such as the war in Chechnya, and to keep out competitors.

Russia may be an extreme example, but it is not a unique one. The phenomenon can be seen, to one degree or another, throughout the industrialized world. What this means is that national security, as traditionally conceived, has lost its meaning. There is military security, which is designed to protect the nation-state against other nation-states. This will obviously remain important, just as police forces remain important within cities. But there is another realm for which it is largely irrelevant: the realm of interests that is impervious to borders. Here the tools are far more subtle and complex, and the nation with the biggest military force may well not be best equipped to preserve these interests.

Cultural Identities
In this sense, national interest is an important interest but not the only one. Other interests claim the loyalty of individuals; people do not define themselves only as citizens. In recent years, we have had reason to become aware of cultural sources of identity. Modern Islam furnishes a dramatic, but not unique, example of identities that transcend, and even seek to eradicate, frontiers. We have been told that the conflicts of the post–Cold War world will be of a different nature than those of the past: that the clash of states will give way to the clash of civilizations. Although we need not adopt the apocalyptic conclusions of that analysis, it is clear that states are not always the ultimate objects of loyalty, that societies can be riven from within by individuals whose deeply held social values make their own state itself the enemy. We may think of Algiers, but we need look no farther than Oklahoma City for demonstration of this.

Societies today are being torn apart. There is a deadly struggle between traditionalists and modernists, between those who have embraced technological and social change and those who fear and resist it. The fault lines of future, and even present, wars lie not only between civilizations or between religions, but within them. In this struggle the state, when it is not actually considered to be the enemy, is, at best, irrelevant.

Whether or not war is, as Joseph Schumpeter has written, the health of the state, it is the way by which the state demands its citizens' loyalties and affirms its own primacy. It justifies this by the claim that it is the ultimate, and most reliable, guarantor of its citizens' welfare. Yet there has been an increasing tendency to question the central premise of *raison d'état*.

The U.S. Senate came very close to rejecting President Bush's call for war against Iraq for its invasion of Kuwait. The expeditionary force in Somalia (like the one earlier in Lebanon) had to be pulled out when it encountered casualties, and the intervention in Bosnia was delayed for several years until it became clear that American troops would not likely be drawn into the fighting. Even today it is unlikely that the president would be able to keep U.S. forces there if the intercommunal war resumed.

Only in the case of Haiti was there support for military intervention, and that was because there was a clear national interest at stake: keeping unwanted refugees out of the United States. The American people will apparently not presently support direct participation in other people's civil wars: not even where considerations of "national security" are claimed.

If wars are harder to justify, it may also be that, at least for the foreseeable future, great wars are less likely to occur. There have been no wars between major powers for more than 50 years. If the United States and the Soviet Union, for a variety of good reasons, did not choose to fight each other, what major states can we now imagine doing so—and for what stakes? What possible victory is worth the cost? And what society, democratic or not, would be willing to pay it?

While I would not go so far as to argue that nuclear proliferation is a good thing because it tempers hotheads who might otherwise go to war, the fact is that the possession of nuclear weapons has probably saved Israel and dissuaded India and Pakistan from open war. They are also likely to restrain China in its pursuit of great power status, and also other states that contest its right to do so.

There are other reasons why war among major states may be less likely in the future. One is that industrial societies, under the pressures of economic competition and innovation, are perforce becoming more democratic. Democratic states, while not necessarily peace-prone, are harder to arouse to war against other democratic states than are authoritarian ones. A further, and to my mind more compelling, reason is that the great trading states—those with the capacity to fight major wars—have become far more interdependent than in the past. This is one beneficial result of the global economy. With these economic links come a whole chain of other dependencies, all of which make war more self-defeating than in the past.

Where Are the Threats?
If the danger of a major war has diminished, at least so far as the great powers are concerned, what kind of traditional security threats does the United States face? By "traditional" I mean threats from another state. The fact of the matter is that—insofar as we can envisage the future—there is no one out there capable of causing the United States serious harm.

Russia is a deeply wounded state that was always weaker than Americans believed and that will take decades to recover even a semblance of its former power. For a long time, it will remain the sick man on the fringes of Europe: a problem but not a threat.

Japan is a mercantilist, pacifist society, single-mindedly obsessed with enriching itself, and determined not to make the same mistake that it did in the 1930s. It has no higher ambition than to be America's number one creditor, number one supplier, number one investor, and number one protectorate.

And what of Europe, the potential superpower: more populous, richer, more experienced in the evil ways of the world than the United States? Will it one day be a serious rival? Not likely. Europe—if by that term we mean a political entity equipped and willing to make independent foreign policy decisions involving issues of war and peace—does not exist. Nor, despite the hopes and pretensions of Brussels bureaucrats, is it likely to come into being.

In fact, the movement is quite the other way—away from visions of a European superstate capable of challenging, or even being an equal partner with, the United States. Even the effort to create a common currency—let alone a common defense and foreign policy—has proven to be so costly and contentious that it is problematic whether it will happen at all. The Eurocrats were overly ambitious and their American well-wishers overly optimistic.

This leaves China. Traditionally, Americans have had a paternalistic attitude toward China, an exploited nation that they felt would, with proper guidance, follow U.S. leadership to the promised land of capitalism and Christianity. The Chinese rudely betrayed Americans' hopes, and the smiling Little Brother became his doppelganger, the Yellow Peril. Now America does not know how to think about China: as a limitless market or an unending problem.

With its immense population and burgeoning economy, China is, to be sure, a potential great power. But it also has immense problems of governance, national unity, and political legitimacy. The world has come to enjoy low-cost Chinese exports; but it can do without them. China, however, if it is to prosper, needs strong economic and political ties with the rest of the world. The government has tied its legitimacy to its ability to provide a rising standard of living for the Chinese people. It cannot do that through a path of aggression. For the United States this means that China must be engaged, not confronted. To treat it as a national security threat will contribute to making it one.

If the danger of major war has decreased, what do we mean when we speak of security threats? How will we recognize them when they do not entail the survival of the nation, or even its well-being? Just as the so-called "other side" has disappeared with the end of the Cold War, so has the old meaning of the word "threat." What once seemed clear is now vague, ambiguous, diffuse, and unpredictable both in its source and its impact.

Policymakers draw up a long list of potential security threats. That is one of the things they are paid to do. These range from the emergence of another evil empire at one extreme, to "coup plotters and tribalists" at another. But if we get serious, it is striking how few threats from another state the United States today faces.

America Invulnerable
For all practical purposes, the country is invulnerable. It cannot be invaded. It has no enemy interested in destroying it that has the capacity to do so. It is not dependent on foreign trade, even though parts of the economy benefit from it. It feeds itself. It enjoys allies but has no compelling need for them—and in fact never relied on them for defense during the Cold War. The United States spread its net of protection, and of foreign bases, very wide, but not in self-defense. Because of its economic and military strength, its physical resources, its loyal population, and its privileged geographical position, the United States can afford to ignore a good deal of the turbulence in much of the rest of the world.

There are other reasons why America should involve itself with other nations, but defense, or national security, is not a compelling one. That is why it may seem odd that the class of specialists we call "national security managers" has set out for itself a task of global management. This can be seen in a number of policy pronouncements, strategy scenarios, and Pentagon wish lists but perhaps nowhere more dramatically than in a 1992 Defense Department document that argued that the United States must "discourage the advanced industrial nations from challenging our leadership or even aspiring to a larger regional or global role."

When word of this ambition got around, the document was quickly toned down. But it was an accurate reflection of an attitude that is common in Washington policymaking circles today. It comes out of the quick fix of the Gulf War, but even more from the way the Cold War ended—with not only the retreat of the Soviet Union, but its collapse and disintegration. Because this left only one great power, it gave birth, not surprisingly, to the notion of a unipolar world led by the United States and dedicated to the promulgation of American values. Woodrow Wilson would be resurrected in the body of General Patton.

This ambition is sold to the American public in the name of "security" (since the public has little enthusiasm for running the world), and justified to other nations by claiming that it is good for them. It obviates the need for them to develop powerful armed forces of their own, since America pledges to defend their true interests. It is not surprising that this curious notion has been greeted with less than universal acceptance and even outright skepticism.

Those most compliant are the Europeans and Japanese, who quite rightly see this as a way of avoiding the full cost of their own defense. This does not, of course, prevent them from challenging the United States on economic issues, which are the kinds that concern them most deeply. They are content to let us defend them so long as it does not get in the way of more important things. Thus, too, the expansion of NATO, which they agree to because Washington wants it, and because it spares the west Europeans the costly alternative of admitting the east Europeans into their privileged economic club.

The Costs of Leadership
This leadership strategy is an expensive one. NATO expansion alone is scheduled to cost some $100 billion for the upgrading of east European armed forces. No wonder military contractors like it. Even without it, the United States continues to spend militarily at Cold War levels. Currently, it costs about $100 billion a year to "reassure" the Europeans (though against what is unspecified), and another $45 billion or so to "protect" the Japanese and Koreans.

Today, more than 50 percent of all discretionary federal spending is still devoted to national security, even in the absence of an enemy. While other nations invest for production, the United States borrows for consumption—and in the process becomes further indebted to the trade rivals whose interests it seeks to protect.

There is much the United States can and should do in the world, particularly in the economic and humanitarian realms. But it cannot undertake this task while it tries to maintain a pretense of global primacy that rests on a diminishing leverage in the military and diplomatic realms. It is time to balance America's foreign policy as well as its budget: to bring resources, in Lippmann's useful phrase, into line with commitments, and to take a serious look at other demands on those resources. The American people want the nation to be strong and to stick by its ideals. But they are not interested in grandiose plans of global management.

Americans are not by nature or by inclination imperialists. America is a strong and resilient society that is burdened with serious social needs that require urgent attention. Some of these problems not only prevent the United States from competing more effectively in the international arena, but also threaten the well-being and safety—that is, the security—of Americans. A national security policy that does not take that into account is inadequate, unrealistic, and unworthy. It also is doomed to fail.

A Sense of the Feasible
America's primary foreign policy interests are critical but few. They are to protect the American homeland from destruction and to preserve its institutions and form of government. Beyond this, it has a secondary interest in the expansion of the market economic core that contributes to U.S. prosperity, in access to natural resources, in the protection of the common environment, and in peaceful processes of change in areas to which it is intimately linked culturally and politically. Finally, at a tertiary level, it seeks to promote democracy not because this contributes to U.S. security in any tangible sense, but because it reflects American values.

This is a big list for a country with only 4 percent of the world's population and a steadily declining proportion of its wealth and production. If America is not to exhaust itself in pursuit of grandiose ambitions it must reestablish a sense of the feasible. This is the kind of realism of which the United States is most in need.

Specifically, it should abandon the pretense of global military control, turn over regional security tasks to the major powers of those regions, end its high-cost and high-risk dependency on Persian Gulf oil, focus on global competitiveness as the prime objective of its military posture, transform its role from that of global enforcer to that of conciliator and balancer, and address far more seriously the other kind of national security: the threats to the well-being of people that lies beyond the competition among states.

Security is, after all, not a condition, but a feeling and a process. It is also an abstraction. We may feel secure and not be so, or be secure and not feel so. We are all vulnerable in ways we cannot imagine and cannot fully protect ourselves against. That is our human condition. So therefore let us not seek absolutes but instead measure. And let us put security in its proper place, which is as a means to a greater end but not an end in itself. In a real sense it is true, in the mournful words of Macbeth, that the unbridled pursuit of "security is mortals' chiefest enemy."

Note

This essay is based on presentations given at Dickinson College, the U.S. Army War College, and the George Washington University during the spring of 1997.

The Crisis of Liberal Internationalism

Stanley Hoffmann

Stanley Hoffmann is Douglas Dillon Professor of the Civilization of France and chairman of the Center for European Studies at Harvard University.

Communism is dead, but is the other great postwar ideology, liberal internationalism, also dying? A recent book by political scientist Tony Smith as well as several speeches by National Security Adviser Anthony Lake have reminded Americans that "liberal democratic internationalism, or Wilsonianism, has been the most important and distinctive contribution of the United States to the international history of the twentieth century," as Smith states it. Lake, presenting the Clinton administration's foreign policy as a pragmatic Wilsonianism, has explained that it aims at expanding democracy and free trade, at defending democracy from its foes, at quarantining repressive and pariah states, and at protecting and promoting human rights.

After two years, however, pragmatism is more visible than Wilsonianism. In a speech at Harvard, Lake stated that the promotion of democracy and the defense of human rights would entail the use of force only if, among other qualifications, there were clearly defined American interests. He also suggested that the spread of liberalism was not *ipso facto* an American interest: an inadvertent but remarkable concession to traditional realism. As in the Carter years, the different elements of the liberal agenda are again in competition with one another—human rights versus the expansion of free trade, as one example. Whether the liberal agenda should be carried out by multilateral means or, in case of need, by the United States alone, has again become a source of confusion and grief, as in Bosnia. Meanwhile, the nation's enthusiasm for bearing the human and financial costs of carrying out a policy of liberal internationalism has waned. Whereas containment had provided a reasonably clear rationale for policy and a lever for mobilizing public support, neo-Wilsonianism seems a guideline made of rubber and has left the American public deeply ambivalent.

This is not new. As Tony Smith establishes in *America's Mission*, the golden ages of liberal democratic internationalism were the periods that followed the two world wars, and, to some extent, the 1980s, when the Cold War was being "won" by the West and the "third wave" of democratization occurred. This is not a coincidence; it suggests that in order to understand the current difficulties of liberalism on the world stage there is a need to go far beyond the all too familiar and depressing litany of what is wrong with Bill Clinton's foreign policy. An examination of the plight of liberal internationalism must shift to the flaws and limitations of liberalism itself.

Liberalism, in its various philosophical guises, was and is a ram against authoritarian regimes. It tries to free individuals from tyranny by providing them with the right to consent to their political institutions and to the policies pursued in the framework of these institutions, as well as with a set of freedoms protected from governmental intrusions and curtailments. Whether it was Immanuel Kant's liberalism based on the concept of moral autonomy, Jeremy Bentham's utilitarian liberalism based on pleasure-pain analysis, or the late-twentieth century variety—"the liberalism of fear"—suggested by Judith Shklar at a time when nineteenth-century ideas of progress seemed hollow and incredible in light of the totalitarian horrors, the essence of liberalism remains the protection of individual freedom, the reduction of state power, and the conviction that power is legitimate only if it is based on consent and respects basic freedoms.

The international dimension of liberalism was never an afterthought: Kant, Bentham, and John Stuart Mill, not to mention Woodrow Wilson, were cosmopolitans in contrast to Jean Jacques Rousseau, whose ideal was of small, self-sufficient, and inward-looking democratic communities. But the international dimension of liberalism was little more than the projection of domestic liberalism on a world scale. Liberalism was and is, in large part, an expression of revulsion against illegitimate violence: that of tyrants at home and of aggressors abroad. It held and still holds the belief that the elimination of wars of aggression will result from the spread of liberal democratic regimes and, as in Kant's scheme for Perpetual Peace, from the agreements such regimes sign to ban war and reduce armaments. The vision of a legitimate world order is thus the order that liberal

4. Crisis of Liberal Internationalism

states living in harmony would finally establish. What would make the inevitable competition of states harmless would be the external effect of two fundamental liberal "revolutions." The first is the triumph of constitutional, representative governments based on consent and rational discussion—governments that would be far less prone to resort to war than authoritarian regimes. The second is the emancipation of individuals at home, and the resulting formation of a world public opinion and a transnational economic society of free commerce and industry linking people across borders (and creating strong state interests in cooperation and peace). Thus, the constraints put on government at home would expand into constraints on state power abroad.

Whereas containment had provided a reasonably clear rationale for policy and a lever for mobilizing public support, neo-Wilsonianism seems a guideline made of rubber and has left the American public deeply ambivalent.

Contrary to realist charges, liberalism was thus anything but naive about state power, whose reduction and domestication were deemed essential for the preservation of both peace abroad and liberty at home. Nevertheless, the international side of the liberal coin was far less polished than the domestic one. In particular, two questions remained unanswered. One was, How would the vision of harmony among liberal states with reduced power be realized? That is, should one put one's faith in the irresistible propagation of liberal polities (and if so, would international relations in a world divided into liberal and illiberal states not continue to be the kind of "state of war" Thucydides, Niccolò Machiavelli, Thomas Hobbes, and Rousseau had described)? Or should liberal states intervene actively for the propagation of liberalism, or for its defense abroad whenever it risked being crushed? The domestic program of liberalism counted on either reform or revolution: the former, whenever possible, through the combined effects of enlightenment and the new capitalism; the latter when reform was blocked (though the French Revolution taught a grim lesson about the deviations—*dérapage*—in which a revolutionary course might get caught). The international side of liberalism offered a vision but not really a program, and the issue of intervention for liberalism turned out to be deeply divisive. Kant's scheme was resolutely noninterventionist—among liberal states. Mill saw a fundamental difference between interventions for self-government (which he rejected) and interventions for self-determination (which he endorsed). The gamut ranged from what we today would call isolationism on the one side to moral crusades on the other.

The other great unanswered question for traditional liberalism was suggested by Mill's distinction. Liberalism, a seventeenth- and eighteenth-century philosophy, discussed the relations of state and society in terms of mutual obligations between the individuals and the rulers—a rational relationship (often symbolized by the idea of the social contract). But as the people, or a sizable portion of the people, began to play a role in the management of their affairs, a new issue arose: that of loyalty, of the emotional bonds of allegiance that tie the society to the state. This was the issue of nationalism: a new collective consciousness that could evolve from mere feeling to a passion and an ideology capable of being grafted onto every other conceivable political creed. The French Revolution and its wars, the Napoleonic hurricane, and the revolts of 1848 obliged all ideologies to cope with the nationalist phenomenon. Liberalism embraced the principle of national self-determination because it saw in it the external dimension of the principle of consent. A regime was legitimate if it was based on consent. A state was legitimate (and viable) if it reflected the desire of the individuals to form a nation, free of any oppression or intrusion by other nations. Jules Michelet, Giuseppe Mazzini, and Mill became the intellectual champions of liberal nationalism, with Mill being the most explicit and convincing in explaining why multinational states would have great trouble being liberal, given the demand of each national component for self-rule. Thus, self-determination was seen as the necessary corollary of liberal self-government, and it was this conviction that reshaped the vision of final international harmony into a vision of nation-states with liberal regimes: Wilson's dream.

But liberalism's embrace of national self-determination raised more questions than it answered. There was, once more, the dilemma of intervention for the emancipation of oppressed nationalities. In addition, there were formidable new question marks. Nationalities do not come in neat packages. One could conceive abstractly of a world of distinct liberal states, but a world of separate nation-states would leave vast areas of confusion: minorities in existing nation-states, plus the vexing problem of what is the "self" that is entitled to self-determination (what, in other words, distinguishes a group that deserves to become a nation-state from one that does not). There were also questions of whether self-determination was necessarily synonymous with sovereignty, and whether a world of independent sovereign nation-states would find harmony as easily as the world of states envisaged by seventeenth- and eighteenth-century liberals—precisely because of the conflicts that were likely to result from the problems of minorities and of who can claim to form a nation.

Second, the national cause might be separate from the liberal one: There could be authoritarian versions of nationalism, definitions of the nation in terms of "blood and earth," not consent—conceptions that make of the individual a pure product of his national community, and not the master of his civic fate. Non-liberal nationalisms thus could give new strength and relevance to authoritarian doctrines and might derail the philosophy of historical progress that predicted the gradual triumph of liberal government over tyranny. The replacement, on the illiberal Right, of divine right (or the power of tradition) with the needs and demands of the nation was to give a formidable new lease on life to ideas previously associated with obsolescent aristocracies, a reactionary Church, or frivolous courts.

Third, liberalism's embrace of nationalism introduced into liberalism a philosophical incongruity. The appeal of liberalism had been an appeal to reason—the reason embodied in John Locke's Natural Law, Kant's idea of a Good Will rooted in human reason, and the rationalism of utilitarian calculations of pleasure and pain. Nationalism has much more to do with will than with reason; its connections are with Rousseau's General Will, which is exclusively that of the separate community, and with Jacobinism. If the legitimacy of power is derived not merely from rational consent to a system of checks and balances and to a careful separation between a public sphere and a domain of individual liberty, but also from the existence of a common national will, are there not serious risks that such a will, however democratic, could overrun the restraints on power and remove the barrier that protects individuals? Nationalism, in other words, reopened the inherent tension between liberalism and democracy that had broken out in the French Revolution, and thus threatened both the liberal program at home and the cosmopolitan vision abroad—by creating new sources of intense conflict between states with different conceptions of the nation and overlapping nationalities, and by weakening the two transnational pillars of the liberal international order: a transnational economy and world public opinion.

LIBERAL INTERNATIONALISM AND REALPOLITIK

With such blind spots and contradictions, how could liberal internationalism nevertheless have been as successful as it has been at times, particularly in the period that followed the Second World War? A part of the answer is undoubtedly provided by American hegemony in the vast areas in which the United States was able and willing to exert its influence after the calamitous insulation of the interwar period. It is already paradoxical enough that the progress of liberal vision, in the creation of a transnational economy as well as in the development of cooperation among liberal states, should depend so much on the preponderance of power in one state, and on its willingness to provide others with a variety of public goods. After all, the kind of liberal internationalism achieved through hegemony raises questions both about what happens "after hegemony," and about the fairness of the order thus established. But one has to go deeper and examine both why the "hegemon" acted as decisively as it did and why others were willing to accept some of the costs.

The reason is another paradox. Liberal internationalism, a vision of harmony that remained rather vague about how to reach nirvana, has been best at performing what might be called negative tasks. In the economic realm, this was, of course, exactly what the doctrines of laissez-faire demanded. Liberalism has—under the impulse of a hegemon for which self-interest and liberal conviction converged—succeeded in removing a vast number of barriers to trade and communication, and thus in establishing that transnational economic society that liberalism itself called for. The same result was achieved within the European Community, where many of the powers given up by the states have gone not to the new central institutions, but to the market. And there, progress resulted not from the hegemony of one power, but from a consensus among liberal regimes. In the political realm, however, liberalism, in order to reach its conception of peace, had to give priority to battle. Liberal internationalism has both fueled and supported the revolt against colonialism and imperialism, thus carrying forward Wilson's call that "no nation should seek to extend its polity over any other nation or people." Liberal internationalism has spoken up against violations of human rights, especially in the last 20 years. Above all, it waged a protracted cold war against Soviet totalitarianism in order to "contain" it, in the expectation, formulated in 1946–47 by George Kennan, that the Soviet system would eventually succumb to its internal flaws.

Thus the prelude to liberal harmony had to be a skillful exercise in limited war—limited both because of the liberal aversion to war and because of nuclear weapons. But it was the force of the totalitarian challenge that resolved the ambivalence of liberalism toward international activism and neutralized, for a long while, its noninterventionist potential. Even many of the "positive" missions accomplished by liberal internationalism after 1945—the democratization of Germany and Japan, the establishment of the European Community, the integration of the world capitalist economy—were undertaken or advanced as essential parts of the battle against the Soviet totalitarian threat. It was a remarkable fusion of realpolitik and liberal internationalism. But that fusion was not without strains. Some were over priorities: Was the containment of Soviet influence or of communism's expansion so overriding a goal that it left little space for the nurturing of liberal democracy in, say, Greece in 1967–74, in the Shah's Iran, or in Central American and Caribbean countries? Was the Soviet version of communism so dangerous that it became necessary to court and accommodate Moscow's communist rivals—especially in China—and to close one's eyes to the crimes committed by them against human rights? What should one do when anti-imperialism struck at interests America's main allies deemed essential (Suez), or when there was a dramatic confluence of communism and anti-imperialism (Vietnam)?

There was also a problem of means: Did not the battle against communism entail a risk of using distinctly "illiberal" methods, particularly in the realm of subversion or in so-called revolutionary wars like Vietnam? And there was one issue whose importance was barely realized in the momentous sweep of decolonization: The support the United States and liberals in Europe provided to the revolts against colonialism put the demand for self-determination (that is, against alien

4. Crisis of Liberal Internationalism

rule) ahead of any concern for self-government (that is, liberal democracy). These revolts resulted in the establishment of states within the borders arbitrarily drawn by the imperial powers, and amounted to a grant of self-determination not to nations, but often to heterogeneous collections of peoples living within these borders.

A last question mark hung over the institutions of cooperation a liberal world requires. The United Nations became a double victim of the Cold War. Its Security Council was often paralyzed by the Soviet veto and by the division of the world into rival camps; moreover, the huge financial needs that the advanced liberal powers had to meet in the realm of security—the demands of the "military-industrial complex"—left only relatively meager resources for the development of the poorer states. The concern for equity in this respect was, indeed, more characteristic of social democrats than of liberals, who were ambivalent about providing aid to governments that might either waste it or use it to increase their power, or both. The U.N. was also handicapped by its composition: a congeries not of liberal democracies, but of regimes of every type—a fact that severely limited its ability to protect human rights. Liberal internationalism thus had to rely on partial, rather than global, institutions of cooperation, on military alliances such as NATO, or on the hegemon.

In the late 1980s, Mikhail Gorbachev began to try to reform the Soviet Union and moved its foreign policy in the direction of liberal internationalism: arms control, peaceful settlement of conflicts, retreat from the empire acquired abroad, hymns to interdependence, and so forth. It looked as if the Golden Age had arrived, and a "new world order" based on the principles of liberal internationalism was going to emerge from the sound and fury of the Cold War. Ridiculed for saying it, George Bush had in mind something that was not new: His "new world order" was the order underlying the U.N. Charter of 1945—an order resting on the principle of collective security against aggression and on the cooperation of the major powers, which, with the exception of China, were now all liberal or on the road to liberal democracy. The Persian Gulf war was the one and only triumph of that dream. Once again, "realist" concerns (oil and the security of the Gulf states) and the liberal vision converged, with the United States as the linchpin of the construction and the U.N. as the provider of legitimacy. But ever since, the liberal vision has been in serious trouble.

LIBERALISM'S MODERN PREDICAMENT

Basically, the plight of the liberal vision results from the fallacy of believing that all good things can come together. They rarely do, and many that were expected to be good have turned out rotten. More specifically, the liberal vision was focused on one particular enemy: the Moloch of power, wherever found, either arbitrary and excessive at home or imperial and militaristic abroad. Insofar as abuse of power is a hardy perennial, liberalism remains an indispensable source of inspiration and value. But there is another enemy in

ILLUSTRATION BY DAVE RIDLEY

today's world: not the violence that results from the clash of mighty powers or from the imposition of the power of the strong on the weak, but the violence that results from chaos from below. The world today is threatened by the disintegration of power—by anomie, which denotes the absence of norms but can also refer to the collision of norms.

The Wilsonian edifice, its Rooseveltian version of 1945, the Bush coat of fresh paint of 1990, all were undertaken to deal with a world of interstate conflicts. All three assumed that the nature of the regime is a key determinant of state behavior: that liberal nation-states do not fight each other. It is difficult to provide decisive evidence for such a hypothesis, however, and neo-realists believe that the anarchic "structure" of international relations imposes the same kind of behavior on all states. But even if that hypothesis is true, wars among states are only one of the perils of the post-Cold War international system. What is now at stake is the very nature of the state. The "Westphalian" system that has inspired all theories of international relations presupposed well-determined states, clashing or cooperating. Both realism and liberalism shared that assumption; Marxism rejected it, but only because of its belief that the "logic" of state behavior was merely an expression of the logic, and contradictions, of capitalism that states were, so to speak, puppets manipulated by the global economic system. Liberalism—or the U.N. Charter—finds it difficult to cope with a variety of phenomena: the disintegration of the Soviet Union and Yugoslavia; ethnic conflicts in the successor states; civil wars among rival ethnic, religious, or political factions in countries long ravaged by the Cold War (such as Cambodia or Afghanistan) or in much of Africa; the failure of many post-colonial states, especially in Africa but also in parts of Asia, to become nation-states; and the attempts by Islamic or Hindu fundamentalists to replace a secular with a religious and thus highly exclusionary definition of the state. To arrive at a world of liberal polities, there must be a clear idea of the state. If the world consists of disintegrating states, then the cooperative processes and institutions that are supposed to fuel harmony under the banner of liberal internationalism are easily overwhelmed by millions of refugees who flee massacres and disasters and seek asylum in liberal states, or call for protection whenever they cannot escape.

Liberal internationalism thus faces a predicament. First, it needs a set of clear principles to set goals. Yet, in two crucial respects all it finds is a cacophony of principles governing two issues that are anything but new: what to do about violations of human rights by tyrannical regimes—in places such as Haiti, Burma, or China—and how to react to the imposition of alien rule on reluctant peoples—such as the Kurds of Iraq (or Turkey), the Tibetans of China, the East Timorese of Indonesia. On both issues the old split about whether or not to intervene is as deep as ever. On balance, however, the noninterventionist impulse is strengthened by the disappearance of the Soviet threat and rationalized with the argument that the propagation of political liberalism will ultimately result from the spread of global economic liberalism. Thus, paradoxically, the principle of state sovereignty (which is not particularly liberal, since many states are not based on consent) is often given precedence over the liberal norms of self-government and of national self-determination. The old argument for nonintervention was that intervention even for liberal causes would multiply violent conflicts, whereas liberalism's aim was to dampen them. A new argument is that in a world where chaos is now a major peril, intervention even for good liberal causes may only create more chaos.

It is precisely in the realm of chaos I described above—the realm of disintegrating state—that the clash of norms is the most evident and paralyzing: Sovereignty (as a principle of order and, still, a barrier against aggressive or imperial designs), self-government or democracy, national self-determination (with all its ambiguities and flaws), and human rights (which are not devoid of ambiguities of their own, as debates over the priority of political over economic and social rights, and over the rights of individuals vs. the rights of peoples and groups indicate) are four norms in conflict and a source of complete liberal disarray. Human rights—the major strand of non-utilitarian liberalism—often cannot be protected without infringing upon another state's sovereignty, or without circumscribing the potential for a "tyranny of the majority" entailed by national self-determination and by Jacobin versions of democracy. The trouble-making potential of self-determination, both for interstate order and for human rights, is not so obvious that many liberals want to curb it or even get rid of it, yet the demand for it simply cannot be ignored, and denying its legitimacy would rarely be a recipe for order or democracy. Inconsistency is the result of this confusion: the international "community" has recognized Croatia, Bosnia, and Eritrea, but not Biafra, Chechnya, or the right of the Kurds and Tibetans to states of their own.

In a search for a thread that would allow them to set priorities and a strategy, liberal statesmen receive little help from liberal philosophers. In his recent lectures, titled "The Law of Peoples," John Rawls fails to discuss the meaning of "peoples." Cosmopolitan liberals such as Martha Nussbaum, who stress the moral arbitrariness of borders (between states or between nations), step outside the limits of traditional liberalism (which saw the universal values of its creed realized in and through a world of states, not a world state). They also go far beyond what the moral traffic will bear. Communitarian liberals such as Michael Walzer are torn between the cosmopolitan and interventionist implications of their liberalism—when "domestic brutality, civil war, political tyranny, ethnic or religious persecution" become intolerable—and the noninterventionist and relativist implications of their communitarianism. What is needed, and still missing, is a complex and sophisticated rethinking of liberal internationalism; its Ariadne's thread would be human rights (including the right to participate in one's government, and the right to be part of, but not a slave to, a national community). It would curtail sovereignty—so that the powers entailed by it could be shared at home and pooled abroad—and it would limit self-determination so that minorities everywhere could have a genuine choice between assimilation and protection of their distinctiveness, and so that the desire for self-rule need not take the form of full state sovereignty in every instance.

INTERVENTION AND THE USE OF FORCE

Liberal internationalism is also in disarray over methods for defending or promoting its vision. Among liberals today, two sets of alternatives intersect. On the one hand, there is an argument over intervention. Some remain sufficiently suspicious of outside interventions (whether unilateral or collective) to prefer not stepping beyond humanitarian operations whose aim is to protect the victims of natural or manmade disasters. Others fear that the politics of band-aids will only allow the do-gooders to feel good, and leave unaltered the deeper causes of the disasters: murderous gangs and armies, as in Liberia, Somalia, and Rwanda; ethnic absolutists, like Serbs or Bosnian Serbs; tyrants such as Saddam Hussein, and so on. The logic of that viewpoint leads, of course, to far deeper foreign involvements, indeed to protectorates or trusteeships (Cambodia being one current example).

The other great division is over the use of force. Traditionally, liberalism has tried to limit legitimate force to self-defense and collective defense against aggression. But the scope of state chaos, as well as the murderousness of some contemporary tyrannies, has led many liberals to endorse in principle the idea of an outside resort to force whenever domestic chaos threatens the peace and security of other states (for instance through the mass flight of refugees) or whenever domestic chaos or tyrannical government results in massive violations of human rights, such as ethnic cleansing and genocide. Other liberals are doubly dubious about the resort to force because of a traditional tendency to look at it as an instrument of last resort only, and because of a conviction that many of these uses of force could only lead to quagmires and entrapments. Both sides often agree on the dispatching of U.N. peacekeepers, but when it comes to having these troops actually use force (except in self-defense), or to having "peace-builders" with missions far more extensive than peacekeepers, disagreement reappears. The Bosnia fiasco has been the result of all these cleavages. Bosnia has been the victim of the imbalanced compromise between those who gave priority to the restoration of peace, however unfair the solution may be, and those who gave priority to the suppression of what they saw as a double assault on liberal values: Serb aggression and ethnic cleansing.

A final predicament concerns not norms or methods, but agents. Who should be the secular arm of liberal action? Great powers (global or regional) claiming to act as enforcers of community norms inspire suspicion, even if, as in the case of India's intervention in Bangladesh, the ratio of self-interest to common good was clearly tilted toward the latter. There is a second problem with hegemonic enforcers: What happens when they choose not to act, failing to realize that the spread of chaos or the triumph of tyranny are antithetical to their interests as great powers? What has happened in the Clinton years, and may happen even more in the second, "Republican" half of the Clinton era, is ominous. Deprived of the relatively clear and widely shared goals that had pushed America to the fore of what was propagandistically called the free world, Washington has been left with Anthony Lake's laundry list of worthy goals, but appears incapable of turning them into a coherent strategy. The administration, sensing the reluctance of its public and Congress to have America play the role of world policeman, and marked by memories of Vietnam, suggested that if vital interests were not at stake, force would be used only multilaterally. But the story has been one of a double retreat: from military intervention (except in Haiti, where force was coupled with a very limited or ambivalent mandate) and from multilateralism—except when the latter made inaction or minimal action "legitimate," as in Bosnia. Unilateralism has become a way to appease anti-internationalists (a loose collection of realists and of American nationalists) and to justify doing very little.

The alternative to great powers as enforcers would be international organizations, but the lesson of recent years is that the United Nations tends to act effectively only when great powers provide the necessary leadership. When the powers are divided or predominantly reluctant, operations become fiascoes, as has been the case in Somalia and Bosnia, or too little and too late, as in Rwanda (largely because of American pressure to keep the intervention small in size and scope). The United Nations—like traditional liberalism—was designed for a world of interstate conflicts: Many of the tasks it has had thrust on it since 1991 therefore exceed its capacities. As an institution it suffers from the contradiction between a liberal vision that makes harmony depend on the right kind of state (liberal-national) on the one hand, and an international system that requires a heavy dose of international regimes and organizations aimed at overcoming the drawbacks of state sovereignty on the other. The fact that the U.N. has been provided neither with the enforcement institutions Chapter VII of the U.N. Charter had foreseen for collective security nor with a permanent force capable of preventive action or of peace-build-

4. Crisis of Liberal Internationalism

ing in domestic crises has resulted both in calamitous conflicts of loyalty for the contingents that states placed at the U.N.'s disposal and in massive inefficiencies. It would be unfair to accuse liberals of having neglected international agencies, but the literature on regimes has focused much more on norms and institutions at the crossroads of interstate economic cooperation and the transnational world economy than on norms and institutions that deal with what I have called the domain of chaos. Liberals have also paid a lot of attention to agencies for the international protection of human rights. But the gap between liberal theory and practice on human rights is wide indeed. It is explained by the existence of so many states with skeletons in their closets and no desire to do more than pass resolutions on subjects as thorny as minority rights, political freedoms, the rights of migrants and refugees, and international criminal justice.

THE RISE OF TRANSNATIONAL SOCIETY

So far, we have analyzed the plight of liberalism in the world of states. What about the other side of its vision for the planet: transnational society, constraining the capacity of states for evil? Insofar as world public opinion is concerned, Wilson's hopes have not been realized for many reasons. First, when one looks only at the public opinion of open and liberal societies, as expressed in their media, one finds a reflection of the diversity of ideological and religious positions, as over population issues. One also finds the diversity of national perspectives, such as the frequent American reluctance to look at economic and social rights as genuine claims. Second, this is still a world half free and half not. A large number of authoritarian regimes still control the formation and expression of public opinion. They succeed, especially in discussions of human rights issues, in hiding their abuses behind arguments for relativism and the defense of local customs and norms. A variety of economic issues has also put up road blocks on the way to Wilson's vision. In dealing with the problems of distributive justice associated with the allocation of wealth and resources among and within states, and with the intra- and intergenerational choices in environmental policies, liberalism has traditionally been rather silent. When it has raised its voice, it has been torn between its pure laissez-faire types who favor efficiency over equity, defend the status quo, and maintain their faith in the "trickle down" effects of growth on the one hand, and on the other more socially troubled or New Dealish types who are eager to find safety nets for the poor, to orient free enterprise toward "sustainable human development," and to entrust international agencies with some redistributive functions and resources. As a result, on issues of singular importance for the vast majority of humankind, "world public opinion" has not been a cohesive force orienting governments. It has been divided—often along the lines of the rich vs. the poor, with significant elements in each camp crossing over and adopting the arguments of the other. And it has fluctuated over time. This is not to deny the importance of nongovernmental organizations in many areas and their capacity to graduate from "world public opinion" to "transnational actors." But one must face the limits as well.

Liberalism has succeeded in removing a vast number of barriers to trade and communication, and thus in establishing that transnational economic society that liberalism itself called for.

The formation of a global transnational economy constitutes a triumph of the liberal vision that first appeared in the eighteenth century (when philosophers saw private interests cutting across borders as potential tamers of clashing state passions), but it also provides evidence of the fact that fulfillment of the vision has mounting costs and unexpected consequences. Liberalism has always been a somewhat delicate coalition of two different perspectives on human nature. One of them emphasizes selfishness, defines interests in material terms, and celebrates the (general) benefits from individual greed. The other touts the moral aptitudes of human beings, focuses on rights and duties, and emphasizes both moral self-fulfillment and civic virtues. Many liberal philosophers—particularly the utilitarians—have tried to make the two strands converge. Much of the admiration Alexis de Tocqueville had for America came from his belief that here they had indeed been merged. Many of his doubts about liberal democracy's future came from his fears about the possible victory of greed and individual self-interest. It should not be surprising that in the drive to create a global economy through the dismantling of state barriers, concerns for human rights, democracy, or self-determination have often been submerged or twisted according to the highly debatable assumption that free economies must "ultimately" lead to free polities as well. The assumption may turn out to be correct, but it is fair to say that the jury is still out.

The new transnational economy has not merely, and beneficially, constrained the power of states. It has not only deprived them of much of their capacity to build command economies that ignore the signals given by markets and produce colossal inefficiencies. It has, alas, also deprived them of some of their ability to perform necessary tasks, to carry out basic functions liberalism never intended to remove from them. The free flow of drugs and the free circulation of crime have accompanied the formation of a global world economy. Governments find it difficult to restore against such "bad goods" the controls they have removed to facilitate the flow of the good ones. Moreover, the ability of governments to define their own monetary policies and to orient investments, employment, and growth has been seriously curtailed by the very size and weight of the transnational economy. The case of the European Monetary System and of its two huge crises in the summers of 1992 and 1993, when private capital movements played havoc with the exchange rates set up by the European Community and overwhelmed the efforts of central banks, is an extreme but important example of what is happening. The liberals of past centuries had thought primarily in terms of trade. We are now moving toward an integrated world market of trade, production, and distribution. The new world economy is made of national and multinational corporations operating across borders, and of millions of individual bond holders, shareholders, and holders of savings accounts in search of maximal and quick profits across borders. That has two effects, also unforeseen by liberal internationalism, and both contribute to the prevalence of chaos. One is the creation of a huge zone of irresponsibility: The global economy is literally out of control, not subject to the rules of accountability and principles of legitimacy that apply to relations between individuals and the state. States hesitate to impose their own rules unilaterally, out of fear of inefficiency and self-damage. Thus liberalism, successful in reducing the state's power, has created a formidable anonymous new power. It affects both states and individuals, but is treated as if it were merely an extension of the individual's sphere of protected freedoms. What is desperately needed is a theory that acknowledges the public aspects and effects of such private activities across borders and establishes a kind of common government for those activities—just as within civil societies liberalism aimed at setting up legitimate central institutions in order to rule out the flaws of a "state of nature."

The other effect has been a frequent domestic backlash against the constraints imposed by interdependence in general, a reaction to the sense that the fate of individuals even in liberal polities is no longer under their control or that of their representatives. It is hard to target the force that is most responsible for this loss—the transnational economy—and too late to do more than delay or restrain a bit the removal of barriers to the free circulation of capital, goods, and services that allows this economy to grow in all directions. Thus, the reaction often strikes instead at efforts at interstate cooperation (such as the European Union) and takes various forms of xenophobia, as in attacks on migrant workers and restrictions on asylum. Those are defeats for liberal values. The phenomena one can observe in Europe are now becoming visible in the United States as well.

Because of the difficulties experienced by liberal internationalism in the new post–Cold War world and the inconsistencies in U.N. and U.S. actions, one can now legitimately fear a discrediting of international organizations comparable to the one that submerged the League of Nations in the 1930s, even though the causes, this time, are the problems of chaos rather than the challenges mounted by a few major powers. As for the United States, one can also fear a new edition of its behavior in the 1920s, when it remained a mighty actor in the transnational world economy of that period but returned to a severely restricted role in the realm of interstate politics. The main triumphs of the Clinton administration have been in the vigorous offensive to pry open foreign markets, through the North American Free Trade Agreement, the General Agreement on Tariffs and Trade, and the Asia-Pacific Economic Cooperation forum. This is an area where liberal internationalists and American realists can find common ground, since for the United States today, as for Great Britain in the nineteenth century, the case for free trade and the expansion of national economic power and interests appear to coincide. However, the main Clinton objective has not been free trade per se, but a return to growth, hence to fuller employment at home. The president is more interested in the liberal vision at home than the liberal vision abroad. Or rather, the latter serves the former. Meanwhile, the realists, repeating the mantra of "interests defined as power," fail to account for the fact that with the same amount of power on the whole as a few years ago, and at a time when it is the only superpower, the United States is in the midst of a crisis over defining its interests abroad. It tends, in a world without signposts, to give a far more limited interpretation of them—one that reveals a wide gap between unchanged liberal aspirations and actual policies.

Liberal internationalism has never been very good at specifying what liberal state interests were, beyond physical security and survival, and whether setting up an international system of liberal states was a vital interest, and not merely a legitimate aspiration, of liberal states. It has not been good at confronting the illiberal aspects of nationalism and the destructive potential of national self-determination. It has not paid enough attention to the contradiction between a cosmopolitan but uncontrolled world economy and a world of sovereign albeit cooperating states. Nor has it heeded the need for strong common institutions capable both of coping with whatever states cannot accomplish by themselves and of regulating what may soon be seen as a transnational Frankenstein monster.

Marxism is discredited. Realism promises only the perpetuation of the same old game and is no better equipped to face the politics of chaos than is liberalism. Liberalism remains the only comprehensive and hopeful vision of world affairs, but it needs to be thoroughly reconstructed—and that task has not proceeded very far, either in its domestic or its international dimensions.

The United States and the World: Regional and Bilateral Relations

Russia (Article 5)
Asia (Articles 6 and 7)
Europe (Articles 8 and 9)
The Developing World (Articles 10 and 11)

Having a clear strategic vision of world politics is only one requirement for a successful foreign policy. Another is the ability to translate that vision into coherent bilateral and regional foreign policies. Problems almost inevitably arise in moving from the general to the specific. What looks clear-cut and simple from the perspective of grand strategy begins to take on various shades of gray as policymakers grapple with the domestic and international realities of formulating a foreign policy toward specific countries and situations.

Part of the difficulty lies with the fact that foreign policy problems do not arrive on the agenda in an orderly fashion. Two examples from the Clinton administration illustrate the point. First, President Bill Clinton entered office hoping to focus on domestic issues, only to find U.S. troops in Somalia on a humanitarian mission that was becoming embroiled in political controversy; a refugee influx from Haiti looming on the horizon; and an escalating conflict in Bosnia. Not only did these foreign policy problems detract from the administration's ability to focus on domestic issues, but its many about-faces in trying to solve these problems became a major political liability at home and abroad. Second, in April 1995, President Clinton traveled to South Korea, Japan, and Russia. Major foreign policy announcements and agreements were trumpeted at each stop with great fanfare. Totally unscripted, however, was Israel's attack on Southern Lebanon and the tragic shelling of a UN refugee camp. As a result, in the midst of the trip, Secretary of State Warren Christopher was dispatched from Moscow, where he was to attend an arms-control summit, to the Middle East, in hopes of bringing about a cease-fire.

No single formula exists for constructing a successful policy for dealing with other states and organizations. Goals that are mutually reinforcing in one context may prove to be contradictory in another. The costs of attaining a particular goal may vary greatly from setting to setting. Problems thought to be similar may, upon closer examination, turn out to be driven by a very different set of underlying forces. Still, it is possible to identify three questions that should be asked in formulating a foreign policy. First, what are the primary problems that the United States needs to be aware of in constructing its foreign policy toward a given country or region? Second, what does the United States want from this relationship? That is, what priorities should guide the formulation of that policy? Third, what type of "architecture" should be set up to deal with these problems and realize these goals? Should the United States act unilaterally, with selected allies, or by joining a regional organization?

Each succeeding question is more difficult to answer. Problems are easily catalogued. The challenge is to distinguish between real and imagined ones. Prioritizing goals is more difficult, because it forces us to examine critically what we want to achieve with our foreign policy and what price we are willing to pay. Constructing an architecture is even more difficult because of the range of choices available and the inherent uncertainty that the chosen structure will work as planned.

The readings in this section direct our attention to some of the most pressing bilateral and regional problem areas in American foreign policy today. Which of these regions is most important to the American national interests is a hotly debated topic. For some it remains Russia and Europe. Others anticipate the arrival of the "Pacific Century" and direct their attention to Japan and China. Still others argue that increased attention must be given to the often-ignored conditions in the Developing World.

In the first readings in this unit, Alexei Pushkov, director of foreign affairs at the Russian Public Television, argues that a wide consensus exists within Russia against NATO expansion. Pushkov, in "Don't Isolate Us: A Russian View of NATO Expansion," calls for America's taking Russian objections into account in the formulation of its foreign policy.

UNIT 2

The next readings examine U.S. relations with Asia. Charles Freeman Jr., in "Reluctant Guardian: The United States in East Asia," presents an overview of U.S. relations with the major states in the region. He also examines domestic factors in the United States that impinge on the formation of a coherent policy. The next essay, "Chinese Realpolitik" by Thomas Christensen, provides an overview of Chinese thinking about international relations. Particular attention is paid to Chinese foreign policy thinking about Japan and Taiwan.

The third unit subsection examines U.S.–European relations. One of the key issues that must be resolved is the future of NATO. In "The Folly of NATO Enlargement," Ted Galen Carpenter argues against further expansion of NATO. It is an argument he made at the very time that NATO leaders were agreeing to admit three new members: Poland, Hungary, and the Czech Republic. His essay provides a point of departure for evaluating this decision as well as the prospects for continued expansion. Werner Weidenfeld, in "America and Europe: Is the Break Inevitable?" observes that although U.S.–European relations today are generally seen in a positive light, changes are taking place on both sides of the Atlantic that suggest this may not be the case in the future. In order to prevent a future break in U.S.–European relations, Weidenfeld calls for creating a new transatlantic community.

The final set of readings in this unit examine the complex issues that face the United States in its dealings with the developing world. In the first essay, the authors call for a more selective U.S. foreign policy toward developing states. They argue for giving priority to the "pivotal states." These are states that are struggling with internal problems but whose size and stature cause them to cast a shadow over the surrounding region. The next essay focuses on the Middle East. In "The U.S. and Islamic Fundamentalism: The Need for Dialogue," Sami Hajjar argues that the basic principles that underlie the antidialogue position in Washington are faulty and that a dialogue with moderate Islamic forces is possible and necessary.

Looking Ahead: Challenge Questions

Construct a list of the top five regional or bilateral problems facing the United States. Justify your selections. How does this list compare to one that you might have composed 5 or 10 years ago?

Who should the United States pay more attention to in Asia—China or Japan? Why?

What developing countries should be on a list of "pivotal states"? How does your list compare to the one discussed in the article "Pivotal States and U.S. Strategy"?

Evaluate the arguments presented against NATO expansion and present a case and timetable for continued NATO expansion.

To what extent do the United States and Russia have shared interests?

What is the most underappreciated regional or bilateral foreign policy problem facing the United States? How should the United States go about addressing it?

Is it possible and desirable for the United States to engage in a political dialogue with "extremist" political forces in the Middle East or elsewhere? What should the ground rules be for such discussions and what should the United States hope to achieve by entering into such talks?

Don't Isolate Us

A Russian View of NATO Expansion

Alexei K. Pushkov

RUSSIA'S arguments against NATO expansion are well known. Moscow warns that NATO enlargement would create new dividing lines in Europe. If NATO military structures were to approach Russian borders and its troops were to appear on the territories of new member-states, Russia would be forced to adjust to these challenges to its security. New tensions caused by enlargement would spoil the post-Cold War political climate in Europe, destroy mutual trust, revive old fears, and throw the relationship between Russia and the West back into the past.

Until recently there was a tendency in the West—mostly in the United States—to downplay the significance of these arguments. Many American observers assumed that Boris Yeltsin and his government voiced opposition to NATO expansion mainly for domestic political reasons and in reaction to pre-election pressures from Communists and nationalists in the Russian Duma. The logic was that if Yeltsin won the summer 1996 presidential elections he would be sufficiently relieved of these pressures and become more receptive to the logic of Western assurances.

Alexei K. Pushkov is director of foreign affairs at the Russian Public Television and a member of the board of the Russian Council on Foreign and Defense Policies. Previously he was a speechwriter for General Secretary Mikhail Gorbachev.

This assumption was wrong. There was and is a wide consensus within the Russian political establishment that NATO expansion contradicts basic Russian national interests. The few dissenting voices in the Russian media and academic circles are marginal. Even Anatoly Chubais, a well-known adept of liberal economic reforms and currently Yeltsin's chief of staff, noted at his February 2 press conference in Davos that opposition to NATO expansion was the only point on which he agreed with Communist leader Gennady Zyuganov and nationalist firebrand Vladimir Zhirinovsky.

Will Compensation Work?

WHEN IT BECAME apparent that Russia was serious about opposing the expansion of the alliance, Washington offered to open official consultations that would lead, as President Clinton foreshadowed in his October 1996 speech in Detroit, to a formal agreement—a charter—between Russia and NATO. In December, Russian Foreign Minister Yevgeny Primakov accepted the offer, but stressed that such promises would not change Russia's opposition to the planned expansion. Nor would Moscow sign an agreement or charter unless it was a binding one, containing clear guarantees and obligations.

As a result, the U.S. and Russian positions on this issue are still far apart. It is clear that NATO will formally offer membership to several former Warsaw Pact countries at the alliance summit in Madrid on July 7-8. And the

Clinton administration opposes a binding agreement with Russia—a treaty rather than a charter—that would alleviate fully Moscow's concerns. Recent events have confirmed the impasse. Speaking on February 11 before the U.S. House of Representatives International Relations Committee, Secretary of State Madeleine Albright recognized that the United States "must address Russia's legitimate concerns", but said there was little the United States could do to end Russian opposition to an enlarged alliance—themes repeated and broadened during her subsequent visits to Rome, Paris, London, and Moscow.[1] Meanwhile, the Kremlin voiced concern over the possibility of the Baltic states joining NATO, and characterized Secretary-General Javier Solana's visit to four southern former Soviet Republics as being directed against Russia's "special ties" with them.

In this context, the Yeltsin-Clinton summit scheduled for March 20-21 in Helsinki will be of critical importance, though chances for a real solution to the problem do not seem good. A five-power summit to discuss Europe's future security system, proposed recently by French President Jacques Chirac with German backing, could offer another opportunity to establish the broad lines of an agreement between NATO and Russia; but whether it will take place—or succeed—remains to be seen.

A current popular assumption in Washington holds that Russia will finally agree to NATO enlargement and accept a non-binding charter in exchange for compensations in other areas. This was Richard Holbrooke's position in his debate with Michael Mandelbaum at the Council on Foreign Relations in December: Yeltsin and his associates knew that enlargement was going to happen and were deploying a managed reticence in order to get the best bargain possible. These compensations are said to include a favorable revision of the Conventional Forces in Europe Treaty (CFE), the possibility of increased bilateral economic assistance, and a permanent G-7 seat for Moscow, as advocated by France and Germany.

What counts most for Moscow, however, is the nature of the special relationship with NATO itself. While other gestures would alleviate the growing tension between Russia and the West, the compensatory approach misses the point. The new Russia, which parted decisively from the USSR's domestic and foreign policy heritage, strongly believes that it has every right to comprehensive inclusion in modern Europe—economically, politically, and with regard to its security dimensions as well. What Russia seeks is an arrangement that would assure its full participation in European affairs, rather than its isolation from, or marginalization in, Europe. This is the crux of the matter.

Speaking recently on Russia-NATO relations, Deputy Secretary of State Strobe Talbott asserted that the key to a breakthrough is to "really show the Russians that this is not a NATO trick, a grab for a few countries, but really a sincere effort to secure political stability and promote prosperity in Europe for a long time."[2] In Moscow, however, this key must amount to more than verbal assurances—it must mean Russian inclusion in the European security system now under construction. If Russia is to be included in this system, which is in everyone's best interest, the Russia-NATO equation must be defined specifically and not left to the rhetorical vagaries of a non-binding charter.

Preventing New Military Tensions

UNTIL RECENTLY Moscow has shown restraint in formulating what specifically it would like to obtain from NATO, and has directed its efforts instead to the larger issue of opposing enlargement as such. The absence of a clear platform concerning direct relations with an enlarged NATO has been the

---

[1] "Long Delay Over NATO Is Opposed by Albright", *International Herald Tribune*, February 12, 1997.
[2] Joe Fitchett, "Moscow Faces Host of Offers in NATO Talks", *International Herald Tribune*, February 6, 1997; see also Strobe Talbott, "Russia Has Nothing to Fear", *New York Times*, February 18, 1997.

source of a number of contradictory declarations by Russian officials. In this context, on January 6 President Yeltsin convened a top-level meeting on Russia's policy toward NATO, and appointed Mr. Primakov as chief coordinator over the elaboration of this policy. Subsequently, despite vows of confidentiality made between Primakov and Solana when they met in Moscow on January 20, the nature of Russian aspirations has become apparent thanks to the public comments of senior Russian officials.

First, Moscow has suggested that NATO rule out the deployment of nuclear weapons on the territories of the new East European member-states. The Kremlin took careful notice of the "THREE NOs" policy announced by Warren Christopher on December 10—that NATO countries have "no intention, no plan, and no reason" to deploy such weapons on new members' territory. Yet the reluctance of the United States to obligate itself formally on this score creates uneasiness in Moscow. "The American declaration does not remove the issue of nuclear weapons. There should be a formal obligation not to deploy such weapons, and not to engage in preparations for their deployment", says one top Russian diplomat.

The Americans argue that under no condition could NATO possibly offer such a commitment. But in refusing to do so what they overlook is that a binding agreement between NATO and Russia would be relevant only in times of peace. If serious military tension were to develop between the two sides, which is highly unlikely, any standing agreement would become irrelevant. In this case nuclear-capable aircraft and tactical missiles could be quickly transferred to NATO's eastern flank. An agreement on nuclear weapons in Eastern Europe is important not for military reasons, for Russia does not consider NATO a military threat, but because of its political and psychological impact. Nuclear arsenals confronting each other in Europe is a thing of the past. Even the remote possibility of a NATO nuclear missile deployment closer to Russian borders, or in Poland, which has a common border with Russia, would subvert the newly established, fragile sense of mutual trust in Europe. An official refusal to place such weapons in Eastern Europe should not be seen as a concession to Moscow, but as a precondition of any working relationship between Russia and the Atlantic Alliance. It must be codified and confirmed in a Russia-NATO agreement and removed once and for all from the European agenda.

Russia is also opposed to the stationing of NATO troops on the territories of future member-states, and to the spread of NATO military infrastructures to these territories. As in the case of nuclear weapons, Moscow is assured that a forward deployment of NATO troops will not occur. But once again, verbal assurances alone do not suffice. On the eve of the reunification of Germany, Helmut Kohl promised Mikhail Gorbachev that NATO's military infrastructures would not move eastward into the territory of East Germany, a fact since confirmed by the former U.S. Ambassador to Moscow Jack Matlock. Later, as the Warsaw Pact fell apart and new treaties were signed between the Soviet Union and East European states, Moscow was privately assured by their leaders that these states would not seek membership in NATO. All of these promises lay broken three years later.

Clearly, in considering its own security, Russia cannot rely on benign intentions and high-sounding promises alone. Governments change, as do interests. Only a binding agreement—one that addresses the issue of conventional forces, best achieved through a revised CFE Treaty, and that fixes new, reduced ceilings of men and conventional weaponry in Eastern Europe—can remove Russia's concerns as to the military aspects of NATO expansion.

A Real Voice For Russia

DIFFERENCES OVER the military aspects of NATO enlargement, however, are not the only ones to be resolved. A Russia-NATO agreement should introduce a mechanism of political cooperation between NATO and Russia. Moscow cannot be satisfied by the present "16+1" formula, or the standing NATO offer of regularized political consultations. The workings of the contact group on Bosnia and the process by which the Dayton Accord was reached taught Russian diplomats that in the loose framework of "consultations" Moscow risks being relegated to outsider status, to be included only occasionally as a sign of courtesy but otherwise having no real role or standing in any significant decision making process.

In order to feel itself an integral part of the evolving European security system, Russia must have a real voice in that process. In early February, on his trip to the United States, Prime Minister Victor Chernomyrdin suggested creating a mechanism, possibly a NATO "Council of 17", which would include Russia and give it an equal say on all issues directly concerning its own security. This is problematic for Brussels, which is clearly unwilling to give Moscow any veto powers, but it would demonstrate that the expansion of the alliance is not directed against Russia, and it could radically improve the relationship between the two sides.

A Russia-NATO agreement should also establish a joint crisis-management mechanism that would facilitate Russia's participation in the decision making process, as well as in the planning and conduct of out-of-area peacekeeping operations. On the American side the experience of Russia-NATO cooperation over Bosnia in this regard is often cited as a promising precedent for future cooperation. The Bosnian experience, however, is not an ideal precedent from the Russian perspective. It is often forgotten that the whole operation was planned in Washington and Brussels, with no Russian participation. It can hardly be a model for future crisis management operations, especially those involving the territories of the former Soviet Union.

Finally, there is the extremely serious and delicate problem raised by the prospect of enlarging NATO to include states that have a protracted border with Russia, namely the Baltics and Ukraine.[3] Moscow has warned Western leaders that the acceptance of those states into NATO, some of which display an open animosity toward Russia, would spark a serious crisis in relations between Russia and the West. Such a move is clearly unacceptable for Moscow, as it would bring NATO military structures to the northern Russian coastline and result in the strategic encirclement of the Kaliningrad region.

A realistic alternative to NATO membership for the Baltic states would be their acceptance into the European Union. It would confirm their European identity and would give them political guarantees of the security they are seeking. As for their eventual membership in NATO, this might well become less of a problem in the future should Russia and NATO reach a comprehensive, binding agreement along the lines sketched above. If NATO accepts Russia as a real partner, it would lead to profound changes in the alliance and in its military doctrine, as well as in Russia's attitude toward the alliance. If Russia were to approach a status close to that of a NATO member-state, the acceptance of the Baltics would not provoke the kind of response in Moscow that it now does.

The Need for a Binding Agreement

A NON-BINDING CHARTER or declaration of intent that lacks the elements outlined above will accomplish little, and the reason is clear: Anything less will lack the power to put an end to old, mostly bad, habits on both sides.

First, the militaries on both sides would still derive their strategic and operative planning from old assumptions and old doctrines. On the NATO side, moreover, the predisposition to see Russia as a potential enemy would likely be strengthened as new members with strong and fresh anti-Russian feelings join the alliance. The Russian military, meanwhile,

---

[3] See my essay "Russia and NATO: On the Watershed", *Mediterranean Quarterly* (Spring 1996), pp. 26-8.

would have to plan not on the basis of intentions but on the enhanced military, intelligence, and logistical capabilities of the other side. Worse, Russia's present conventional military disadvantage would incline it to rely more heavily on nuclear weapons in planning its defenses—just as NATO did in similar circumstances starting in the late 1950s.

Second, a charter void of contractual obligations would be impossible to sell to the Russian Federal Assembly and political establishment. That means, in turn, that the State Duma, facing the prospect of a foreign military alliance approaching Russian borders, would not ratify the START-II treaty, and any prospect for a START-III agreement would be nil. Nor would the Chemical Weapons Convention or the Open Skies agreement win Duma support. And ongoing negotiations to revise the 1972 Anti-Ballistic Missile Treaty to mutual satisfaction would stall as well.

These demurrals and setbacks could generate a reciprocal reaction in the U.S. Congress that could lead to the collapse of the whole system of bilateral arms control and reduction agreements reached during the last ten years. As long as Russia's economy remains weak, no extensive new arms race will resume, but by conserving their huge nuclear arsenals Russia and the United States would enter into a gray zone of heightened strategic insecurity. The deterioration of Russia's nuclear command and control systems, of which Russian Defense Minster Igor Rodionov recently warned, would create still additional dangers.

Still other problems might come from an asymmetrical interpretation of a non-binding charter in Russia and in the West. If NATO countries were to consider such a charter a serious declaration while most Russians were to regard it as a meaningless piece of paper, a serious disruption of mutual trust could result. The West might accuse Moscow of violating the spirit of the charter; Moscow would respond by accusing the West of anti-Russian motives in the process of expansion and of holding out the prospect for another round of enlargement ever closer to Russia. Under such circumstances, clearly, there would be no way to escape a revived animosity—even a new Cold War.

Why Take Russia Into Account?

IT IS TRUE that Russia cannot stop NATO expansion or deny the East Europeans their right to join the alliance. That being the case, some ask, why strain so hard in the first place to take Russia into account, let alone to allow Moscow a veto over NATO enlargement? The answer is that the implications of enlargement—if it is not accompanied by a compromise with Russia—are very serious ones.

In addition to the disruption of the present security arrangements between Russia and the United States, the political fallout could include a deterioration of the larger bilateral relationship; a Russian policy toward China, Iran, and Iraq that would disregard American interests and concerns; a more frequent invocation by Russia of its veto in the UN Security Council; a more assertive Russia in the former space of the Soviet Union. In short it could mean a Russia that, while not directly challenging the U.S. role in Europe, might become a "loose cannon" of world politics.

A progressive rapprochement with the West is by far the most reasonable and natural path for future Russian diplomacy. Yet this depends not only on Russia's own will, but also on the will of its Western partners. If Russia finds that the door to the West is closed, if it finds itself cut off from Europe, it will have to look for alternatives. Such a development is in neither the Russian, American, or European interest, but this is where the present NATO policy toward Russia, unless seriously reconsidered, will inescapably lead.

EAST ASIAN SECURITY

Reluctant Guardian
The United States in East Asia

By Charles W. Freeman, Jr.

Charles W. Freeman, Jr. is Chairman of Projects International Associates and is former Assistant Secretary of Defense for International Security Affairs.

SINCE THE END OF THE COLD WAR, only the Asia Pacific region has seemed at peace and relatively free of change. The collapse of multiethnic states and empires has rocked Europe, Eurasia, and Africa. Anarchy and ethnic or religious strife have broken out in the former Yugoslavia, Afghanistan, Tajikistan, the trans-Caucasus, Liberia, Zaire, Somalia, and Rwanda. The Middle East has seen a brutal Iraqi attempt to annex Kuwait and the end of civic consensus in Algeria. Major changes have taken place in the relationships between Israelis, Palestinians, and other Arabs, and civil society has gradually reemerged in Lebanon. Confrontation with military regimes in Panama and Haiti and a border war between Peru and Ecuador has marked the advent of a new era in Latin America. Many of these situations have occasioned US military intervention or serious consideration of it—either in the name of the United States itself or under the banner of the United Nations.

At the same time, there have been major adjustments in US military spending and personnel levels. As a percentage of GNP, US military spending is now at the level of the mid- to late 1930s. The size of the US armed forces has shrunk to numbers last seen in 1939. Outside the Asia Pacific region, the United States has radically adjusted the pattern of its military deployments. The United States has built up its forces in the Persian Gulf, and the Atlantic Alliance, which France has now rejoined, is expanding eastward through the Partnership for Peace. The United States had withdrawn two-thirds of its forces from Europe by the time it joined the operation in the Balkans, the first military operation in NATO history.

In contrast, with US forces out of the Philippines, the United States seeks no further adjustments in the pattern of Asia Pacific alliances it developed during the Cold War. On the contrary, Washington affirms that the United States will keep the same number of soldiers, sailors, marines, and airmen—about 100,000—in the Asia Pacific region that it has stationed there for the past decade or more. Few in Asia are confident that such a US presence will in fact be sustained. Southeast Asians and South Koreans hope that it will be. Increasingly, however, Chinese, and even some Japanese, question whether it should be. They are joined in their skepticism by some US citizens who espouse America-first policies. Others in the United States doubt the relevance of military alliances. Despite the mounting evidence from other regions, these Americans continue to expect the coming decades to be dominated by economic, rather than political or military contention. We must all hope they are right.

Beneath the surface calm, however, the Asia Pacific region is undergoing changes no less profound than those that are transforming other regions. These changes go well beyond the well-publicized economic miracle in the People's Republic of China (PRC) and adjacent areas that is making the region the center of gravity for global trade and investment. They include political and military trends that challenge both the existing strategic balance in the region and the US role in it. A February 1995 paper from the Pentagon's directorate for International Security Affairs defined the role preferred by the United States for its forces in the East Asia. The "United States Security Strategy for the East Asia Pacific Region" envisages maintenance of the existing US alliance structure and military presence "as a foundation of regional stability and a means of promoting American influence on key Asian issues." It posits continued cooperation with Asian allies and friends "to deter potential threats, counter regional aggression, ensure regional peace, monitor attempts at proliferation of weapons of mass destruction, and help protect sea lines of communication both within the region and from the region to the Indian Ocean and the Persian Gulf." In short, the United States sees its alliances and cooperative engagement with non-allies as enabling it to underwrite the Asia Pacific balance and the peaceful evolution of the status quo while facilitating the nonviolent resolution of disputes within the region.

For this strategy to work, a number of conditions must prevail. First, the US public must be prepared to support an indefinite military presence in the Western Pacific similar to the present commitment. Second, Japan must be prepared to support a continued, substantial US ground, air, and naval presence in Japan and to sustain the division of labor by which Japan's Self-Defense Forces defend their home islands while US forces manage the strategic defense of Japan and its more distant interests. Third, the United States must have a non-hostile relationship with China that includes dialogue and elements of military cooperation.

Also, Southeast Asian nations must continue to conduct military exercises with and afford access to US forces based in Japan and the United States, and the US-Australia alliance must remain close and strong. Major changes in subregions like the Korean peninsula and the Taiwan Strait, which have the potential to overthrow the existing military balance, must take place by peaceful means rather than war. Finally, East Asians must perceive the United States as a wise, reliable, and sympathetic partner in the management of the region's security problems.

Many of these conditions are now being challenged, and the outcome is far from clear. The most significant challenges emanate from domestic factors in the United States, the uncertain evolution of US-Japan relations, and the deteriorating US relationship with China. The United States cannot hope to manage either Korean or Southeast Asian security issues, such as disputes in the South China Sea, if the American people do not support active US military diplomacy in the region, if US-Japan security ties weaken, or if Sino-American suspicion blossoms into hostility.

The Home Front

Public support for a continued US military role in the Western Pacific cannot be taken for granted. Strong leadership will be needed to sustain it. The collapse of the Soviet Union ended any apparent threat to the survival and independence of the United States. Now that these supreme national interests are no longer at stake, the mood in the United States has turned selfish and inward-looking. This is reflected in the collapse of budgets for the traditional instruments of American statecraft—a global diplomatic and consular presence, direct and indirect economic aid to nations of strategic or commercial significance, cultural exchange and other forms of public diplomacy, contributions to international organizations, and subsidized transfers of weapons to allies to raise the threshold at which they must call for US intervention.

US embassies around the world are closing. The US Agency for International Development (AID) and the foreign assistance programs it administers are being drastically downsized and may even be abolished outright. The US Information Agency and its programs face a similar threat. US contributions to the World Bank and other international financial institutions are being cut or eliminated. The United States is now notoriously in arrears in its contributions to the United Nations Organization, and has begun to withdraw from several of the UN's subordinate agencies. US military assistance to allies and friends ended some years ago for all but Israel and its Camp David peace process partner, Egypt. The US public seems

> *Were Korea to be reunified or North Korea to renounce its nuclear weapons and missile programs, the United States would still wish to maintain forces in Japan.*

increasingly to define the appropriate international role for the United States solely in terms of trade and investment. Americans expect the United States to continue as the world's preeminent political and military power, but no longer seem prepared to pay the bills or sacrifice the lives that this role has traditionally entailed. Even popular issues, like non-proliferation and the environment, can no longer find much support for funding in Congress. More and more of what the United States attempts to do internationally must be done with other peoples' money.

This trend toward US withdrawal from a leading position in world affairs has yet to have much effect on the US presence in the Asia Pacific region, though AID missions are being closed and the diplomatic presence drawn down there as elsewhere. So far, with the exception of an unsuccessful challenge to the home porting of US Navy ships in Japan by West Coast shipyard interests, no real debate about the US military presence in the region has emerged. Nevertheless, with the exception of the long-standing US commitment to the defense of South Korea, the justification for continued US military presence in the Western Pacific is poorly understood and thinly supported by Americans. It remains to be seen whether that presence could withstand serious questioning. A compelling case can be made for continuing US military engagement in the region, but no US leader has yet been stimulated to make it.

The US-Japan Alliance

The cornerstone of the US presence in the Western Pacific, as well as of US power and reach in Asia and adjacent areas, is the US-Japan Alliance. Without Japanese bases and financial support, the United States would be

6. Reluctant Guardian

Safeguarding peace and stability in Asia requires US leadership and cooperation.

hard pressed to project power in the region, let alone beyond it into the Indian Ocean and Arabian Peninsula theater. Japan's alliance with the United States has precluded any Japanese requirement to develop substantial military forces, power projection capability, or a nuclear deterrent of its own. By furnishing these capabilities to Japan, the United States has made the reemergence of Japan as a potential military rival in Asia unthinkable. It has prevented the possible outbreak of military rivalry and arms races between Japan and China and managed the emotionally charged Japan-Korea security relationship to the benefit of both sides. By maintaining bases in Japan, the United States has gained a relatively secure forward position from which to guarantee peace in Korea and the Taiwan Strait, project an ongoing presence in Southeast Asia, and secure sea lines of communication to the Indian Ocean. The United States has shared the financial burden of doing all this with Japanese taxpayers. The US-Japan alliance has been, and remains, the basis for the status of the United States as the dominant military power in the Western Pacific.

Smaller US forces, a more constrained defense budget, and reduced basing overseas have increased the importance of Japan to the United States. For the Japanese, however, the elimination—at least for the next decade or two—of Russia as an active strategic rival at once raised questions about the value of the US-Japan alliance and the US military presence that it authorizes. With the Soviet Union gone, many Japanese asked what enemy they now needed the United States to help them deter. Neither Americans nor Japanese wished to posit China as such an enemy. (No one in the region believes that containment is a necessary or appropriate response to growing Chinese power or wishes to foster hostility and confrontation between Japan, China, and the United States.) Before Japan's debate could gather steam, however, North Korea's nuclear and missile threat emerged to provide an apparent answer to the question of who might threaten Japan. The threat of attack or intimidation from North Korea has now been adopted officially by Japan as the organizing principle for its defense. Since North Korea, unlike the Soviet Union, cannot invade Japan, Tokyo is reducing the size of the Japanese land forces to reflect the diminished risk of ground combat in the home islands.

The new Japanese focus on the North Korean threat set aside the debate in Japan. North Korea alone, however, does not provide a long-term basis for US-Japan defense cooperation. Under some circumstances, North Korea might pose a direct threat to Japan. In the event of conflict on the Korean peninsula, Pyongyang would wish to deter active Japanese cooperation with Seoul and Washington. It would also wish to deny the United States a secure rear area in Japan from which US forces could act against North Korean forces and targets. Presumably, that is a major motivation for Pyongyang's nuclear and missile programs. By no measure, however, is North Korea as compelling a threat to Japan as the former Soviet Union was. Were Korea to be reunified or North Korea to renounce its nuclear weapons and missile programs, the United States would still wish to maintain forces in Japan. Washington would see this as serving common US and Japanese regional and global interests. Would Tokyo? The rationale for US-Japan security ties needs broadening, redefinition, and renewal. That is why the Pentagon, through former Assistant Secretary Joseph Nye, sought a security dialogue with Tokyo. Nye's sudden departure from office, however, raised doubts in Tokyo about how vigorously his successors will pursue this dialogue.

Meanwhile, the Japanese people's sense of diminished external threat has made them less willing than they once were to tolerate the inevitable frictions that arise from foreign bases and forces on their territory. The end of Liberal Democratic Party dominance in Japanese politics has weakened Tokyo vis-à-vis Japanese local authorities. The trend toward less centralized Japanese politics is likely to accelerate as a new election law, replacing proportional representation with geographic constituencies, takes hold. As local issues assume greater salience in Japanese politics, it will be harder for Tokyo to constrain local resentment and objections to the US military presence and for Washington to finesse complaints from local Japanese communities. The Okinawa child rape case has served to warn Tokyo and Washington of this problem. The incident has galvanized a long overdue dialogue about how to redeploy US forces to minimize friction between them and their Japanese hosts. This process, timely and necessary as it is, is likely to be protracted and contentious. Repeated eruptions in troubled US-Japan trade and investment relations will not ease its management.

US Presence in Korea

US forces in South Korea have been and continue to be an essential deterrent to efforts by the failing North Korean regime to solve its problems by conquering the South. The danger of such an attack is now cresting, as Pyongyang's military capabilities reach their apogee amidst economic bankruptcy and political uncertainty. North Korea cannot sustain its extraordinary burden of war preparations much longer. As its capabilities recede, attention will naturally turn to how to arrange a soft landing for the North Korean regime. Having seen the strain reunification placed on Germany, Koreans hope for a gradual rather than sudden disappearance of the border between North and South.

As long as US forces must deter North Korean attack, they are strategically immobilized. Their departure from the Korean peninsula would risk North Korean adventurism. Such adventurism could also be stimulated by an outbreak of major conflict elsewhere that could delay reinforcement of US forces in Korea. Should the threat from the North disappear, however, Washington and Seoul would have to consider whether to withdraw US forces from Korea.

Some in Seoul argue strongly that US forces should remain even after reunification. They see a continuing US presence as enabling Korea to play a pivotal role in Northeast Asia between China and Japan. They also see utility in a continuing US force presence in Japan to serve as a bridge between the Korean and Japanese military. Many Japanese wish US forces to remain in both countries for the same reason. Others see a continuing US presence in Korea as facilitating a US drawdown in Japan. After reunification, US forces would be available for regional or global missions outside the Korean peninsula. Popular attitudes in Korea are, however, increasingly hostile to the US military presence. Koreans might well prove responsive to a Chinese campaign arguing for US withdrawal, if the Chinese came to see a continuing US presence in Asia as threatening or adverse to China's interests.

The US-Chinese Relationship

Cooperative interaction between the United States and China is essential to any US role as balancer and facilitator in Asia Pacific security matters. How Beijing pursues adjustment of its multiple differences with other Asian capitals—territorial disputes with Japan, the Philippines, Vietnam, Brunei, Malaysia, and India; seabed disputes with both Koreas and with Indonesia; and an undefined relationship with the democratically elected Chinese authorities in Taipei—will determine whether Asia remains at peace or drifts toward confrontation. Without an active dialogue with China, the United States cannot play a moderating role in these disputes. Nor can peace, stability, or proliferation issues in Korea and South Asia be easily managed. Asia Pacific transnational issues, such as drug trafficking and illegal migration, also are intractable without Beijing's help. Regional considerations alone furnish ample reason for the United States and China to cooperate. The Sino-US relationship is, however, increasingly troubled.

The collapse of a common enemy, the Soviet Union, at the end of the 1980s destroyed the strategic rationale for US-China relations. As the Washington-Moscow-Beijing strategic triangle vanished into history, so did the mutual tolerance of ideological differences and the patient problem-solving approach that the United States and China had made guiding principles of their relations. The catalytic event was the uprising in Tiananmen Square and the sharp US reaction to its brutal suppression. Since June 4, 1989, the Sino-US relationship has been dominated by US criticism of Chinese human rights practices and Chinese defiance of US efforts to coerce internal change in China through ostracism and economic pressure.

Mutual understanding between the United States and China on matters normally as remote from politics as, for example, the environment, has atrophied along with strategic dialogue. For US politicians, China is no longer "politically correct." For Chinese politicians, the United States is now a bully to be resisted. This atmosphere is not conducive to problem-solving, and differences between Washington and Beijing on issues as varied as territorial disputes, the rules for global trade, technology transfer, investment, and non-proliferation, and the regional balances in South Asia and the Persian Gulf have widened and deepened.

The most dangerous differences between the United States and China are those that have arisen over Taiwan. These differences have their roots in the domestic changes taking place in Taiwan. On the one hand, Taiwan's emergence as a prosperous, modernized, democratic Chinese society has attracted the admiration of many Chinese across the Strait as well as most Americans. Many on the mainland hope that Taiwan's evolution, in which economic liberalization preceded political liberalization, will be repeated in the rest of China. They see the gradual reunification of the two sides of the Taiwan Strait as central to the realization of this hope. On the other hand, Taiwan's politics have come to center on the island's identity crisis. The dream of reunification has steadily lost ground to the vision of a distinct Taiwanese national identity, expressed through Taiwan's achievement of status separate from China or outright independence.

For decades, Taipei sought US support in insisting at the United Nations and elsewhere that there was only one China and only one legitimate Chinese government, that Taiwan was part of China, and that the capital of China was Taipei, not Beijing. Now that Beijing is almost universally acknowledged as the capital of China, Taipei is seeking to enlist the United States in support of the contrary thesis that, whatever China may be, it consists of "two equal political entities" that should be recognized as such by the international community and should enjoy separate seats in the United Nations. Taipei's efforts to separate itself from the "One China" principle through "pragmatic diplomacy" have already generated serious friction between Beijing and Washington. Taiwanese separatist impulses now risk military action by Beijing against Taiwan itself.

On one level, the US position is clear. In 1979, the United States switched its diplomatic recognition from Taipei to Beijing as the sole legal government of China. It acknowledged the Chinese position that Taiwan is part of China. Within this context, the United States traded the form of its relations with Taipei for their substance, undertaking to maintain only "economic, cultural and other unofficial relations with the people of Taiwan." On this "One China" basis, Washington's relations with Beijing were normalized while unofficial US ties with Taiwan flourished.

The end of the US military presence in Taiwan and of the US defense treaty with Taipei permitted Beijing to set aside threats to "liberate" Taiwan in favor of "a fundamental policy of striving for peaceful reunification." Continuing US arms sales to Taiwan, authorized by domestic US legislation (the "Taiwan Relations Act"), underscored the abiding American interest in a "peaceful settlement" of the Taiwan issue by the two sides and assured that Taiwan could maintain a formidable military deterrent against attack from the mainland and gave Taiwan's people the sense of security they needed to risk rapprochement with Chinese across the Strait. Taipei's and Beijing's common view that there was only one China removed any sense of urgency about reunification. This consensus was the basis for a tacit modus vivendi in the Taiwan Strait, which produced a remarkable relaxation of tensions and facilitated surprisingly rapid expansion of relationships and dialogue between the two sides. These developments, in turn, made possible the end of martial law in Taiwan and the island's transformation into a democratic society.

It is this tacit modus vivendi that has now broken down. Taipei's drive for international recognition as the capital of a state distinct from the rest of China found dramatic expression in the spring of 1995. Taiwan's president, Lee Teng-hui, made a private but highly political visit to the United States while Taiwanese premier Lien Chan was received officially in central Europe. On their return to Taipei, they offered the United Nations US$1 billion for a separate seat for Taiwan in the General Assembly. Beijing saw these actions as a frontal assault by Taipei on the "One China" principle that had undergirded the understanding in the Taiwan Strait. It saw the series of policy decisions in Washington that culminated in Lee Teng-hui's visit as signaling an American intention to abandon a "One China" policy. China believed the United States was complicitous in Taiwanese separatism.

The Chinese leadership concluded that the United States was attempting to divide China by permanently slicing off Taiwan, detaching Tibet, and subverting Chinese control of post-1997 Hong Kong; attempting to weaken China politically by supporting dissidents and fostering opposition to Communist Party rule; and attempting to retard China's modernization by restricting technology transfer and excluding China from the World Trade Organization. The subsequent US normalization of relations with Vietnam only strengthened perceptions in Beijing that Americans were moving to "contain" China in order to generate a Soviet-style collapse.

Beijing's first priority was to obtain renewed assurances that the United States would remain faithful to a "One China" policy. It withdrew its ambassador from Washington, withheld agreement for a new US ambassador, canceled high level defense and military exchanges, and broke off dialogue on issues of special concern to the United States until it obtained such assurances. Now that the United States has reaffirmed its commitment to the "One China" policy, Beijing has turned its attention to Taipei.

The PRC has not abandoned its policy of a negotiated settlement with Taipei. Rather than waiting patiently for negotiations to evolve from the past few years' informal "Ku-Wang talks," however, Beijing now seeks to compel Taipei either to desist from further efforts at achieving an identity separate from China or to agree to "reunification" on the very loose terms Beijing has proposed. According to Chinese officials, under reunification Taiwan would retain its armed forces and continue to buy arms abroad. No mainland officials would be stationed on Taiwan, which would maintain its own distinct political system and administration. Taiwanese officials would, however, be invited to participate in governing the mainland. Recently, Beijing has unofficially suggested that it might be prepared to negotiate a change in the PRC's name, flag, and anthem; that arrangements could be negotiated for Taiwan to take a seat at the United Nations; and that a division of diplomatic labor could be worked out by which

Taipei's embassies could represent China in some foreign capitals.

Beijing has given military backing to its drive to replace the shattered tacit modus vivendi in the Taiwan Strait with an explicit one. For the first time in decades, it is mounting military operations against Taiwan. (Initially, these were called exercises, directed by the headquarters of a "military region." They are now called "operations" in a "war zone.") If Taipei shows no convincing sign of willingness to turn from "separatism" and open negotiations with Beijing, the People's Liberation Army vows that it is prepared for further escalation, including low intensity conflict and possibly direct missilestrikes on targets in Taiwan or other military actions to shake Taipei's recent complacency.

In addition to the breakdown of peace and stability in the Taiwan Strait, such an outcome would also discredit long-standing US efforts to deter conflict over Taiwan. At some point, the United States would have to choose between combat support of Taiwan against the PRC and neutrality in the conflict. It is no exaggeration to say that the consequences of either choice to strategic stability in the Asia Pacific region would be dire, even catastrophic.

Given the strategic importance of Taiwan to Japan, a US decision to stand aside from conflict in the Taiwan Strait would be seen by Japanese as a default on the US responsibility to manage Japan's strategic defense. The Japanese reaction would be all the stronger because of the emotional links between Japanese and many Taiwanese. (Taiwanese are the only former subjects of the Japanese emperor who remain close to their ex-colonial masters.) No longer confident that the United States could be depended upon to do the job, Japan would have to reassume responsibility for its own strategic defense.

If the United States decided to intervene in support of Taiwan, it would have to use Japanese bases to do so. Tokyo would then have to decide between its policy of good relations with Beijing on the one hand, and its alliance with Washington and interests in Taiwan on the other. It would almost certainly opt for Washington and Taipei. No future Japanese government, however, would ever again be willing to be put in a position where foreigners made such fundamental choices for Japan. The result would be a slow resumption by Japan of responsibility for its own defense.

The strategic consequences of conflict in the Taiwan Strait therefore include not just the poisoning of US-China relations for decades and a setback for China's modernization, but also fundamental realignment of the Asian strategic balance. Japanese rearmament, in the context of hostility between Japan and China, would polarize the Asia Pacific region and marginalize the role of the United States. Japan might even, in time, turn to Russia, India, and Southeast Asia as partners in a strategy of containing the rising power of China.

These effects of the outbreak of war in the Taiwan Strait would unfold regardless of whether the United States intervened, and regardless of whether Beijing succeeded in regaining Taiwan for China. Beijing's arguments that the Taiwan issue is legally a matter of Chinese internal affairs may be right, but these arguments miss the most important point. Politically and strategically, Taiwan is anything but a local affair. How this issue unfolds in the coming months will decide whether harmony or confrontation prevail in the Asia Pacific region. It may also determine whether the United States can retain the highly influential role it has come to take for granted in East Asia.

It is clearly in the interest of the United States to avoid an outbreak of conflict in Taiwan. The United States does not want to have to make a choice between intervention and non-intervention in the Taiwan Strait—between war and peace with China. It is therefore in the interest of the United States that Beijing and Taipei to negotiate a renewed modus vivendi. The United States should vigorously promote such negotiations as the only viable alternative to confrontation and conflict. Doing so would not be easy. Neither Taipei nor Beijing wants war, but neither wants to compromise. Each side needs to be brought to face unpalatable realities and needs to reach difficult accommodations with the other.

Taipei must recognize that it cannot determine its status in defiance of Beijing's views. Taiwan's past, present, and future are linked to the Chinese mainland. Whoever rules Taiwan, and whatever the island calls itself, Taipei must have a working relationship with Beijing. The quality of that relationship—not whether Taiwan sits in international councils—will determine the level of security and prosperity Taiwan and its people will enjoy. Taipei can win a battle with Beijing, but it cannot win a war. At the same time, Beijing must confront the reality that confrontation and combat with Taiwan are likely to create a fundamentally adverse and hostile international environment for China. China's modernization, its links to the outside world, and its relationships with other great powers in the Asia Pacific region and beyond would be the victims of such an environment.

Conclusion

The vision of the United States as the manager of an evolving cooperative security system in the Asia Pacific region is appealing. Without greater efforts by Washington, however, this vision is unlikely to become reality. Leadership is like muscle tissue. Unless it is exercised, it atrophies. Many in Asia see the last minute decision by President Clinton, in the face of domestic political distractions, not to attend the Asia Pacific Economic Cooperation meeting in Osaka as emblematic of a lack of US interest and commitment to participate actively in the affairs of the region. Others fear that the drift in US-Japan security relations, which efforts by both sides had begun to reverse, may now resume. Asians are especially disturbed by the erratic course of US relations with China.

US aspirations to help Asians resolve disputes by measures short of war now face a major test in the Taiwan Strait. So far, however, the United States has seemed reluctant to recognize that there is a problem, let alone to bring US diplomacy to bear on the PRC and Taiwan. A US default on this urgent challenge will not augur well for the prolongation of the "American century" in the Asia Pacific region.

Chinese Realpolitik

Thomas J. Christensen

THOMAS J. CHRISTENSEN is assistant professor of government at Cornell University and author of *Useful Adversaries: Grand Strategy, Domestic Mobilization, and Sino-American Conflict, 1947–58* from Princeton University Press. Research for this article was funded by the Asia Security Project at Harvard University's Olin Institute for Strategic Studies.

READING BEIJING'S WORLD-VIEW

SCHOLARS AND policy analysts seem almost obsessed with China's continuing rise toward the status of a great power. Debates rage about whether there is a "China threat" to East Asia or the United States, how to measure China's present military and economic power, and which trends best project China's growth into the next century. Less attention has been given to how Chinese government analysts view their own security environment. Because they influence the thinking of government decision-makers and are privy to their thoughts, an analysis of their views on security is valuable. By providing a better understanding of both China's baseline realpolitik view of international politics and two significant divergences from that baseline—Beijing's attitudes toward Japan and Taiwan—such a study can help contribute to a more prudent American East Asia strategy.[1]

China may well be the high church of realpolitik in the post–Cold War world. Its analysts certainly think more like traditional balance-of-power theorists than do most contemporary Western leaders and policy analysts.[2] For example, although China has not actively opposed multilateral humanitarian efforts, the rationales for international missions in Bosnia, Somalia, and Haiti are alien to the thinking of most Chinese analysts. They are also much less likely than their Western counterparts to emphasize political, cultural, or ideological differences with foreign countries. The United States considers the "enlargement of areas of democracy" a core element of its grand strategy, but China has made almost no effort, with the possible exception of its relations with North Korea, to export its ideas about "market socialism."

China is not interested in pressing either allies or rivals to comply with global norms of human rights. On occasion, it will return fire when a country criticizes its human rights record, but this seems purely tactical. It is hard to believe that Chinese elites are truly concerned with the plight of Native Americans, African-Americans in south central Los Angeles, or Turkish guest workers in Berlin. Chinese analysts raise these topics only when defending China from attack on human rights grounds.

China's elites are suspicious of many multilateral organizations, including those devoted to economic, environmental, nonproliferation, and regional security issues. In most cases, China joins such organizations to avoid losing face and influence. But Beijing does not allow these organizations to prevent it from pursuing its own economic and security interests. Chinese analysts often view international organizations and their universal norms as fronts for other powers. Particularly in times of tension with the United States, such as mid-1995 when the United States allowed Taiwanese President Lee Teng-hui to visit, they view complaints about China's violations of international norms or laws as part of an integrated Western strategy, led by Washington, to prevent China from becoming a great power. Many analysts, particularly those in the military, believe that criticisms by foreign governments and nongovernmental organizations are plots to keep Beijing off balance and encourage domestic forces bent on the overthrow of the Chinese Communist Party or the breakup of the country.

China has not been cavalier in its attitudes toward multilateral organizations; it has been con-

---

[1] For this essay, I conducted dozens of interviews with military and civilian government analysts during three separate month-long trips to Beijing. These government think tank analysts are not decision-makers, but they advise and brief decision-makers in all relevant government organizations: the People's Liberation Army, the Foreign Ministry, the State Council, and the Chinese intelligence agencies. The research trips were hosted by the China Institute of Contemporary International Relations.

[2] I argue that, in general, Chinese security analysts think about their nation's security like Western scholars of realpolitik (e.g., E. H. Carr, Hans Morgenthau, and Henry Kissinger). One recent work argues that realpolitik thinking in China may have its roots in the dynastic era. See Alastair Iain Johnston, *Cultural Realism: Strategic Culture and Grand Strategy in Chinese History*, Princeton: Princeton University Press, 1995.

2 ❖ REGIONAL AND BILATERAL RELATIONS: Asia

Never let down your guard: A 1993 billboard promotes China's unsuccessful campaign to host the Summer Olympics in 2000.

cerned and vigilant for reasons consistent with a hard-nosed view of international politics. For example, in 1994 Chinese analysts seemed wary of the Association of Southeast Asian Nations (ASEAN) and its new security forum, the ASEAN Regional Forum (ARF). Civilian and military experts were concerned that after Vietnam's acceptance into ASEAN, the organization might become an expanded, tacitly anti-Chinese alliance with links to the United States. They have argued against trying to create a formal security regime in East Asia to parallel the Organization for Security and Cooperation in Europe. Their fear seems to have been that in a more formal ARF, China might play Gulliver to Southeast Asia's Lilliputians, with the United States supplying the rope and stakes. If ARF were to adopt specific norms of transparency and rules on force deployment, it might enable the region to monitor and limit the growth of China's ability to project power.

China worries that a military buildup by Japan may be on the horizon.

China has participated fully in ARF activities since 1994, and its attitudes toward the organization have clearly softened on a range of issues. But Beijing still seems reluctant to use the multilateral forum to settle sovereignty disputes in the South China Sea, where islets, subject to overlapping territorial claims by the People's Republic of China, Taiwan, Malaysia, Vietnam, the Philippines, and Brunei are sprinkled across a vast stretch of seabed believed to contain rich oil and mineral deposits. Since China is the most powerful claimant, its wariness about the potential formation of a local anti-Chinese coalition is fully in accord with traditional balance-of-power politics.

WATCHING JAPAN

CHINESE ATTITUDES toward Japan mix elements of realpolitik with less antiseptic emotions rooted in China's bitter history of occupation by Japanese imperialists. Chinese security analysts, particularly military officers, anticipate and fear Japan's renaissance as a world-class military power in the early 21st century. These predictions are consistent with balance-of-power theories but not with the analysis of many Japan experts throughout the West, who believe that cultural pacifism after World War II, domestic political constraints, and economic interests will steer Japan away from such ambitions. Chinese analysts do not always dismiss these arguments out of hand, but many believe those obstacles will merely delay Japan's long-term military buildup. The two related and most important delaying factors, in the minds of these analysts, are the U.S.-Japan relationship, particularly the security alliance, and the political and economic stability of Japan. They believe that the United States, by reassuring Japan and providing its security on the cheap, fosters a political climate in which the Japanese public remains opposed to buildup and the more hawkish elements of the Japanese elite are kept at bay. If, however, the U.S.-Japan security alliance either comes under strain or undergoes a transformation in which Japan assumes a much more prominent military role, then, Chinese analysts believe, the ever-present hawks could more easily foment militarization.

Realpolitik would predict that the one-sided U.S.-Japan alliance will collapse after the demise of the common Soviet enemy. But Beijing's dread of various scenarios for change goes beyond the abstract logic of balance-of-power politics. According to that logic, China should be at least as concerned about coercion or attack by the world's only superpower, the United States, as about the remilitarization of Japan. As Secretary of Defense William Perry recently reminded China, America has by far the strongest military in the western Pacific. If one considers only military power, one might expect China to welcome the ejection of American forces from Japan and the rise of a new regional power that, in collaboration with China, might counter

American regional hegemony. One might argue that Japan's geographic proximity alone would make a new regional power more of a threat to China than the more distant United States. But having lost hundreds of thousands of soldiers fighting the American military in the Korean War, China is unlikely to consider the United States a removed power. In any case, a conclusion about which nation poses a greater threat to China—a distant superpower or a local great power—cannot be reached by Chinese analysts or Western scholars weighing the international balance of power alone. It must be based largely on historical legacies and national perceptions.

If U.S.-Japan relations fray, China will want to quickly brace its arms.

The real reason that Chinese military and civilian analysts are so afraid of a breakdown or a fundamental change in the U.S-Japan alliance is a historically rooted and visceral distrust of Japan. Although they harbor suspicion toward the United States, they view Japan with even less trust and, in many cases, with a loathing rarely found in attitudes toward America. This is more a legacy of Japanese atrocities in the 1930s than a byproduct of contemporary Japanese power.[3] Like many other countries in the region, China seems grateful that America restrains Japanese militarization by guaranteeing Japanese security and replacing what would otherwise be Japanese aircraft carriers and marines with American ones. Although Chinese analysts are rarely so direct as to say that American forces should stay in Japan indefinitely, they are quick to say that they hope the United States will not leave anytime soon.

Through 1993 China's civilian and military analysts had similar takes on Japanese remilitarization. Japan's reemergence as a great power after World War II had been interpreted as the goal of a three-part grand strategy long pursued by the Liberal Democratic Party (LDP) leadership: first, become an economic superpower; next, a political superpower, by using increased economic aid and coercion and securing a Security Council seat; and finally, a significant military power that would vie for regional power and project force around the world. Many Chinese analysts were pessimistic about the ability of the U.S.-Japan security arrangement or domestic pacifism in Japan to prevent the timely completion of this long-term design.

In 1994 and 1995 this consensus seemed to break down in ways that may influence China's defense policy and international posture. Many analysts were influenced by Clinton administration pronouncements in 1994 and by the February 1995 Department of Defense East Asia strategy report, which underscored the importance for American post–Cold War strategy of the U.S.-Japan security alliance and the maintenance of at least 100,000 U.S. troops in the region. Some who had been skeptical about America's commitment to the region were reassured that the Soviet collapse and U.S. domestic politics were not going to render the remaining superpower isolationist and self-absorbed. Many Chinese analysts still agreed on the threat posed by the long-term goals of some Japanese elites, but the more liberal and moderate analysts in Beijing believed that, despite the domestic political shakeups in Japan, the desire for economic and social stability could dissuade Japan from launching any significant military initiatives, such as massive increases in defense spending or abrogation of the current Japanese ban on forces designed to project power more than 1,000 nautical miles from the home islands (e.g., aircraft carriers or aerial refueling planes). Also, these analysts seemed willing to believe that the U.S. military might be indefinitely engaged in the region, particularly in Japan.

Conservative Chinese analysts, many of whom are in the military, remained more skeptical about the durability of the American brake on Japan's military modernization. In 1993 and 1994, several of these analysts argued that the lack of a common enemy meant that Japan and the United States not only lost an incentive to cooperate in the western Pacific but gained an incentive to compete for economic and military influence in the region. They argued that the bilateral alliance would be poisoned by several factors: the effect of trade disputes and nationalist issues on domestic politics in both nations, the natural laws of international politics, and the zero-sum nature of Japanese and American rivalry in East Asia.

Since early 1995, Chinese security elites have found a new source of pessimism in the Clinton administration statements about "upgrading" or "strengthening" the U.S.-Japan defense relationship. If it were to occur, a U.S. withdrawal from Japan would still worry Chinese analysts most. However, America's presence in East Asia is only reassuring because it replaces—not strengthens—Japanese military forces. American efforts to improve Japanese defense technologies, introduce

---

[3] For the classic study of China's attitudes toward Japan, see Allen S. Whiting, *China Eyes Japan*, Berkeley: University of California Press, 1989.

new weapons systems, and, most recently, encourage an expansion of Japanese roles in joint operations are perceived to undercut that role. The February 1995 Department of Defense East Asia strategy report received mixed responses from Beijing analysts. They seemed relieved that the United States set a formal floor for the size of its regional forces. However, they seemed worried by the suggestion that Japan and the United States might develop new weapons systems, including theater missile defense systems (TMD), that might counter China's deterrent capabilities against both Japan and Taiwan.

In the past, Chinese experts have worried about seemingly innocuous changes in Japan's defense policy, such as sending peacekeepers to Cambodia and minesweepers to the Persian Gulf. So the seemingly mild changes in policy that President Clinton and Prime Minister Ryutaro Hashimoto announced in the April 1996 U.S.-Japan communiqué—e.g., increased Japanese logistic support for American missions in the region and consideration of future cooperation on theater missile defense systems—triggered strong negative responses from Beijing. Chinese analysts argue that unless the U.S.-Japan alliance were to turn sharply against Beijing and seek to contain China, little upgrading would be needed. Moreover, they believe that new roles for the Japanese military would only encourage independence from the United States and the development of Japan's force projection capabilities. One Chinese military analyst warned against American efforts to strengthen Japan's defense capabilities by citing a traditional Chinese expression, *yang hu yi huan*, which means, "When one raises a tiger, one courts calamity."

Whether or not they believe American abandonment or encouragement might spark Japanese militarization, few Chinese military or civilian analysts seem to believe that Chinese behavior could have much effect on the timing or intensity of a Japanese military buildup. Chinese analysts seem incredulous that Japan, given its history of aggression toward China dating back to the 1890s, could sincerely view China as a threat and alter its defense policy accordingly. If the current U.S.-Japan security relationship seems to be in trouble, there is likely to be a widening consensus among Chinese analysts that China should quickly build up its military power and settle various sovereignty disputes in the East and South China seas, by force, if necessary. Otherwise, China would have much less leverage against a Japanese navy and air force the is larger and could project power effectively into those areas. Chinese analysts realize that if Japan decided to strengthen its military capabilities its technological and economic base would allow it to do so quickly. They point to Tokyo's ongoing investment in defense-related technologies and to its defense budget, which is small as a percentage of GNP but second only to America's in absolute size. Although outside observers might believe that China would be creating a self-fulfilling prophecy by anticipating an eventual Japanese buildup and threatening Japanese interests in the near term, most Chinese analysts do not believe China's behavior will affect Japanese policy. Consequently, Beijing is unlikely to factor Japanese fears of China into its policy equation.

Chinese analysts vary widely in their degree of pessimism about the likely pace and intensity of Japanese militarization, but there is a basic consensus that Japanese power would be more threatening than American power and that the status quo in the U.S.-Japan security arrangement—without upgrades—is desirable. This view is not immutable, however, and when the United States appears to be threatening core Chinese security interests, particularly the one-China policy barring Taiwanese independence, the U.S.-Japan alliance is perceived in a different light. In the summer of 1995, after Taiwanese President Lee Teng-hui's visit to Cornell University, Chinese analysts began to view the United States and Japan as collaborators in an attempt to break Taiwan away from the mainland. Suddenly American forces were not guarantors of Japanese restraint but instruments of tacit Japanese designs on China. The deployment of two U.S. aircraft carrier battle groups to Taiwan during Chinese missile exercises in March (including the *Independence*, based in Yokosuka, Japan) almost certainly affected Beijing's negative reaction to President Clinton's April trip to Japan and the resulting U.S.-Japan communiqué.

WORRYING ABOUT TAIWAN

ANOTHER AREA where realpolitik alone cannot account for Beijing's security attitudes is China's violent opposition to Taiwan's legal independence. China will almost certainly use force against Taiwan or Taiwanese interests (for example, shipping and offshore islands) if Taipei actively seeks independence. China will act even if it means damaging its profitable trade and investment relations with Taiwan, and it will do so regardless of the level of the U.S. military commitment to Taiwan's security. Since realpolitik would suggest attention to political realities, not legalities, it is puzzling why the change from de facto independence, which Taiwan has had since 1949, to legal independence would drive China to risk damage to its economy and war with the world's only superpower. But there is convincing evidence that China is prepared to do just that.

In China's century of humiliation, which began with a loss to the British in the Opium War and ended with the surrender of Japan in World War II, no event was more demeaning than the 1895 defeat at the hands of Japan, after which Taiwan was ceded to Tokyo. For the traditional Chinese state, it was degrading enough to be vanquished by "barbarians" from far-off lands like Britain and France. But given China's historical superiority to its tributary neighbors, succumbing to a local power was a much greater blow. Although Taiwan had little material value for China at the time, it became a symbol of this national tragedy. For Chinese, the return of Taiwan to China after World War II, as promised by the United States and Britain in the 1943 Cairo Declaration, was also a symbol of China's considerable contribution to the death of Japanese imperialism. Rectifying the century of humiliation is a core nationalist goal for any modern Chinese regime, and that means preventing the loss of Taiwan.

Preventing Taiwan's independence would be important to any Chinese regime, but it is a critical nationalist issue for the Chinese Communist Party government. The party has, by way of market reforms, all but obliterated the second of the two adjectives in its name. Almost no influential figure in Chinese government or society believes in communism anymore, and that has created a vacuum that nationalism, always a strong element in the party's legitimacy, is filling. As many analysts have noted, nationalism is the sole ideological glue that holds the People's Republic together and keeps the CCP government in power. Since the Chinese Communist Party is no longer communist, it must be even more Chinese.

China's military wants to regain the pride it lost at Tiananmen.

As continuing economic reforms and exposure of the Chinese people to Western ideas and international news cut ever more deeply into CCP legitimacy, there are few issues left that do not trigger debate and exacerbate tensions between the state and society. Yet in all sectors of politically aware Chinese society a consensus remains on the legitimacy of using force, if necessary, to prevent Taiwan's independence. On that issue one is almost as likely to hear a hawkish reaction from scholars who protested in Tiananmen Square in 1989 as from a military officer who fired on them.

Chinese leaders will go to extraordinary lengths to prevent Taiwan's independence in part because they fear a national breakup. Chinese analysts believe that national integrity would be threatened by an uncontested declaration of Taiwanese independence, especially because of the decades of propaganda about Taiwan's unbreakable links to the motherland. They subscribe to a domestic domino theory in which the loss of one piece of sovereign territory will encourage separatists elsewhere and hurt morale among the Chinese forces who must defend national unity. Their most notable concerns are with traditionally non-Han regions such as Tibet, Xinjiang, and Inner Mongolia.

Not surprisingly, People's Liberation Army officers are even more hawkish than civilian analysts on sovereignty issues, particularly Taiwan. To justify increasing military budgets after the collapse of the Soviet Union, which was regarded as China's main military threat, the army needs a mission, and defending sovereignty is not a hard sell. On political grounds, tensions with Taiwan make the military even more important in the succession struggles that will follow the death of Deng Xiaoping. Although few China experts in the West expect a military coup, almost all believe that the military will play kingmaker. Gaining early military support and avoiding opposition from the military should prove critical to any leader hoping to succeed Deng.

PLA leaders, particularly the influential officers living in and around Beijing, also desperately want to regain their social standing after the Tiananmen massacre. Almost all PLA officers believe that the pro-democracy protests should have been suppressed forcibly, but several expressed embarrassment over the level of force used and the damage to the military's image. Chinese military officers, like professional soldiers around the world, take pride in their work. The chance to show that their main mission is defending national integrity, not shooting unarmed civilians, will not be forfeited lightly.

One may get the impression that civilian leaders will grapple with Taiwan as a central issue if there is a succession struggle following Deng's death. Although attempts to endear themselves to the military and hard-liners may make economically oriented technocrats more macho and nationalistic, the jockeying is more likely to manifest itself in their attitudes toward the defense budget, the Spratly Islands disputes, or Western criticism of Chinese human rights violations than in their opposition to Taiwan's independence. Strong differences of opinion apparently have formed between more moderate and more hawkish Chinese over the wisdom of using military exercises to deter Taiwan from pursuing independence. Many elites apparently had strong reservations about the last and most provocative round of exercises in March, before the Taiwanese elections. But these differences would likely disappear if Taiwan appeared to be on the brink of declaring independence. In that case a broad consensus, including dovish liberal technocrats as well as hawkish conservatives, would likely form around a hard-line policy.

Democracy is served by having Taiwan remain nominally part of China.

Succession struggles are not meaningless, however. The political process may make China more sensitive about what constitutes a significant move toward independence by President Lee Teng-hui's government. Taiwan's self-styled "pragmatic diplomacy" has been presented publicly as a bid to increase the island's diplomatic space and recognition without abandoning the one-China principle that Taipei has so strongly adhered to since 1949. But Beijing believes that Lee is tacitly pursuing independence. Chinese analysts say that Lee has not said so in public for purely pragmatic reasons, the most important of which is the threat of violent retaliation from the mainland. When nerves are raw in Beijing and succession politics are under way, Taipei must be very careful not to take actions that might seem mild in Taipei and elsewhere but might be interpreted in Beijing as significant advances toward independence.

IMPLICATIONS FOR U.S. POLICY

BY KEEPING American forces in Japan, the United States can simultaneously reassure Japan and its major potential rival, China, and thereby stabilize the region. Washington should do more than stay engaged; it should reassure Japan and other regional powers publicly and often that it intends to do so indefinitely. Any suggestion that the United States might withdraw its forces from Japan may set off an arms race, escalating tensions, and self-fulfilling prophecies about Japanese militarization, all of which will destabilize the region. Chinese security analysts watch closely what the United States says about its relationship with Japan, and the division between Chinese conservatives and moderates is most visible in predictions about the hardiness of the current U.S.-Japan defense arrangement. Anything that underscores America's long-term commitment to protect Japan with American forces will have a positive impact on China and helps the moderate analysts sell their message of stability and optimism to CCP leaders. Anything that suggests either fragility or fundamental reform in the U.S.-Japan security relationship has a negative impact on China and helps conservative, hard-line analysts sell their portrayal of a threat from Japan and prescriptions for a tougher Chinese security posture. For example, any linkage of the U.S.-Japan security arrangement with reduction of America's trade deficit with Japan would be irresponsible because it would quickly be interpreted in Beijing as an omen of discord in the U.S.-Japan alliance. Encouraging Japan to take on more military roles also may not be a good short-term strategy. For example, the United States should weigh carefully the political cost of U.S.-Japan TMDs against their military benefits. The political implications should be taken at least as seriously as the political costs of ballistic missile defenses and scrapping the Antiballistic Missile Treaty for America's Russia policy. Since China, like Russia, is in a transition period, U.S.-Japan TMD should be considered using a similar type of cost-benefit analysis.

The United States should make a clear distinction between its general goal of spreading democracy and its policy on Taiwanese sovereignty. Taiwanese democracy and Taiwanese independence are logically and morally separate issues. The United States should support the former and distance itself from the latter. Indeed, if the United States wants to spread democracy, it should encourage Taiwan to remain nominally part of China. When Taiwan claims to be both Chinese and democratic, it puts the lie to Beijing officials' claim that Chinese culture and Western-style democracy do not mix. In the "enlargement" strategy of the United States, China is a prize 55 times larger than Taiwan. American idealists should not be myopic and settle for current Taiwanese independence at the expense of future Chinese democracy.

Until tensions settle down, both in relations between Taipei and the mainland and in the succession politics of Beijing, Washington should discourage President Lee from aggressively pursuing his pragmatic diplomacy agenda. For example, Washington should not only refuse to support Taiwan's bid for entry into the United Nations, it should discourage Taipei from vigorously pursuing that goal in the near term. The United States should provide a guarantee of support for Taiwanese security, including direct American intervention if necessary, but this guarantee should be conditional: Taiwan's democracy will be assisted only if it does not provoke an attack by moving toward formal independence.

Taiwan should not provoke an attack just to transform a de facto reality into a legal one.

Even generally hawkish military and civilian analysts in Beijing have firmly stated that the current Chinese government would never attack Taiwan out of the blue, so it would be fair to deduce that a reversal in this policy would carry grave implications. A China that would launch an unprovoked, military reunification campaign that violates its own economic and political interests would have to be a radically more aggressive China. The United States would have to contain such a China vigorously or expect to face it in battle soon. For either of those tasks, Taiwan is a better platform than most.

If, however, Taiwan takes provocative diplomatic steps toward a more independent legal status, the United States should let Taiwan know unequivocally that it will also stand alone in security matters. Taiwan and the United States stand to lose too much in a fight against the mainland, particularly for the mere purpose of transforming a de facto reality—Taiwan's independence—into a legal one. If Taiwan declared independence and was then attacked by the mainland, one could not draw conclusions about Beijing's expansionist designs any more than one could draw conclusions about American expansionism from the northern states' reaction to the South's secession. If Taiwanese independence provokes the attack, Taiwan could hardly be portrayed as China's Sudetenland, and American aloofness could not be compared to Chamberlain's appeasement at Munich.

Some American security analysts believe that Taiwan is a logical place for Washington to draw the first unconditional containment line around any potential Chinese aggression. Taiwan is, as MacArthur said long ago, an unsinkable aircraft carrier, and it has a strong military and economy with which the United States could join forces. But if the United States were to draw a line in the Taiwan Strait now and offer unconditional assurances to Taiwan, this would encourage Taiwanese independence and spark hypernationalism in China, creating just the kind of expansionist, hard-line regime in Beijing that America and everyone else in the region fear.

On military grounds alone, Washington should recognize that, while Taiwan may be an unsinkable aircraft carrier, it is also an immovable one. Although China probably could not invade Taiwan successfully even if America stood on the sidelines, the United States can do little to defend Taiwan from attacks that, though a far cry from invasion, would devastate its economy. China can use force effectively against Taiwan without the slightest pretense of a D-Day–style invasion. The mere announcement that shipping around Taiwan was no longer safe from assault would cripple Taiwan's trade-dependent economy. If a few missiles landed in Taipei, the stock market there would likely crash. The drop in Taipei stocks from the first P.R.C. missile exercises last July to the last round of exercises preceding this year's March 23 elections testifies to the danger of even limited threats, let alone force.

In March the Clinton administration may have finally found a balance in its policy toward the dispute over Taiwan. Although the current leadership in Beijing was almost certainly not preparing to attack Taiwan even if America stood idly by, Washington's deployment of two carrier battle groups to the area sent a long-term signal to any hypernationalists in Beijing who might vie for power after Deng's death: the cost of an unprovoked attack on Taiwan will likely be high. At the same time, the United States avoided the politically provocative and militarily imprudent option of placing carrier battle groups in the Taiwan Strait itself.

Although it received far less news coverage than the deployment of the carriers, an equally important message was apparently sent to Taiwan through back channels and carefully worded public statements by high-level administration officials: Washington supports Taiwan's security conditionally, and it expects Taipei to avoid provoking the mainland. While the United States cannot and should not dictate policy to the democratically elected government of Taiwan, it should stress the dangers and costs of certain options so that Taiwanese officials do not base their strategic policies on misperceptions and false hopes of unconditional U.S. support.

The United States should not limit its regional role to helping Taiwan defend against unprovoked attack. Instead, it should continue to commit itself to the peaceful settlement of the sovereignty disputes in the South China Sea. The United States need not and should not take sides there, but it should guarantee peaceful resolutions. By doing so, the United States is not "containing" China, it is protecting international sea-lanes in the region.

This policy is more prudent than a containment policy and an unconditional commitment to Taiwan's security. Beijing's claim to the Spratly Islands does not carry the same emotional baggage as its claim to Taiwan. By adopting a neutral stance on the sovereignty disputes, the United States would reduce the risk of appearing imperialistic and fueling Chinese hypernationalism. Most important, the United States would be taking actions with the express purpose of protecting Japan's sea-lanes. A large percentage of Japan's trade and the majority of its oil imports from the Middle East pass through those international waters, and keeping them open and safe is a vital security interest for Japan. If the United States explained to China and all other regional actors that the alternative to U.S. Navy patrols would be Japanese navy patrols, the message probably would not fall on deaf ears.

America has huge stakes in the political transitions of China and other East Asian nations. By remaining engaged in the region and rejecting short-sighted strategies such as a Cold War–style containment policy toward China, the United States will improve the odds that China's next generation of leaders will be moderate at home and abroad. As the differences between Deng Xiaoping and Mao Zedong make clear, leadership matters, especially in nondemocratic countries. Chinese elites' current realpolitik tendencies are infinitely preferable to the messianic versions of Chinese nationalism that might come to the fore if the United States, Japan, or other powers treat Beijing as an enemy. By engaging China and encouraging its participation in multilateral forums and confidence-building regimes, over the long term the United States may help soften China's skepticism about these institutions, which could help stabilize East Asia.

America and Europe: Is the Break Inevitable?

Werner Weidenfeld

APART FROM A few contentious trade issues, a cursory look at U.S.–European relations today reveals a general picture of harmony. In particular, an almost perfect symbiosis has prevailed in U.S.–German relations ever since the United States lent unparalleled support for German reunification. President Bill Clinton spoke of a "unique partnership" during his visit to Berlin in 1994. The often wearisome discussions during the 1980s on the deployment of medium- and short-range missiles, the heated dispute between the United States and Europe on the Soviet gas pipeline deal, and the anti-American demonstrations of the 1970s and '80s in front of U.S. embassies and consulates in Europe, so hurtful to the United States, are now forgotten.

Yet, despite U.S.—European congeniality, the way each side views its partner and the expectations placed on cooperation are currently undergoing radical change. Europe's significance in U.S. politics has diminished drastically since the end of the Soviet threat. Western Europe is no longer considered to be threatened militarily from the outside. As a result, less and less attention is being paid to internal developments on the old continent. The United States used to be keen to promote a positive image of itself to the European public to preserve the cohesion of the Western defense community. This required Americans to devote a great deal of effort to assessing the mood in Europe. Today, interest in Europe has been reduced to certain spheres: as an ally in resolving international crises and perhaps as a trading partner—that is, as a market for U.S. goods.

The America Houses in Munich and Hamburg are now under threat of closure. The U.S. cultural institutes in Hanover and Stuttgart were closed in 1995. U.S. exchange programs with Europe are being cut drastically at all levels, a prime example being the renowned Fulbright scholarships. U.S. consulates are closing their doors. In the last few years, 200,000 U.S. troops left European bases, and now the official U.S. political and cultural presence in Europe is noticeably diminishing, too.

Washington points to financial difficulties, claiming that, because of the desire to balance the U.S. budget, public funds are no longer available in abundance and that, in any case, relations with Europe today are far more relaxed than they were during the Cold War. Reducing the U.S. commitment to Europe was thus something less than dramatic.

The results of the 1996 U.S. elections gave further momentum to this change in Americans' view of Europe. It is of secondary importance to Europeans which party the U.S. president belongs to or whether Republicans or Democrats have the majority in Congress. What does matter is that the emergence of a new generation of politicians further accelerated the dramatic decrease in knowledge about Europe. Fourteen senators with proven experience in issues related to the Atlantic Alliance—among them, Sam Nunn, Bill Bradley, and Claiborne Pell—did not stand for reelection last year and were replaced by younger and less-experienced colleagues. Although the younger generation of politicians generally has a large measure of goodwill toward Europe, it seems reluctant to follow European affairs closely. In 1995, not one member of Congress visited Bonn. In 1996, only five visited Germany. Europe is in danger of disappearing from the radar screen of U.S. politics.

In Europe as well, a radical change is taking place in self-perception and in expectations of the United States as a partner. The forthcoming deepening and enlargement of the European Union (EU) is increasingly the all-pervasive domestic and foreign policy issue. Reshaping Europe following the end of the Cold War requires that all European countries undertake painful reform, in particular the reform of their social welfare systems and the abolition of government subsidies.

At the same time as Europe is becoming more introspective, however, the call is getting louder from the outside, especially from the United States, for the Union to assume global politi-

---

Werner Weidenfeld is the coordinator for German–American Cooperation in the Foreign Ministry of the Federal Republic of Germany and member of the Executive Board of the Bertelsmann Foundation.

cal responsibility. Demands on Europeans to carry an ever larger share of the joint international burden are mounting as the United States's own resources are increasingly needed to master domestic challenges.

Flagging interest coupled with heightened expectations about Europe's capability to act decisively and cohesively in the field of foreign policy will inevitably lead in the medium term—5–10 years—to a dangerous alienation within the transatlantic relationship. The already perceptible weakening of U.S.–European networks are thus only harbingers of a much more radical development: The United States and Europe are at risk of experiencing a political and cultural continental drift. Even a complete break is possible.

The transatlantic community as it was during the days of the East–West conflict no longer exists. Certainly, the alliance remains, but without the mentality of a defense organization designed to protect against a major attack. Certainly, the political links are still in place, but without the challenge of an antagonistic system of values. The partnership still exists but it lacks a definition of what specific contribution it has to make in responding to issues arising in international politics. The old loyalties will not be enough to provide the necessary political and analytical parameters for the next phase in U.S.–European cooperation. Sooner or later, Europe and the United States will find themselves redefining their interests.

It would be desirable if this were a process that resulted in positive gains for both sides. But it is entirely possible that the opposite will happen—in terms of foreign policy, a drifting apart of the partners under the influence of the centrifugal forces of international crisis; in terms of economic policy, an escalation of transatlantic trade rivalries; and in social and cultural terms, a refocusing of interests away from the transatlantic partner.

This negative scenario would mean more than just a difficult restructuring of foreign policy priorities for Europe and the United States. In fact, it would shake the very foundations of the European and U.S. self-image. Historically speaking, each partner has always formed part of the other's identity. The commitment of the United States to the reconstruction of Europe after World War II is a central element in their collective consciousness. For the United States too, the contribution made by Europeans toward the development of politics and society has become a basic element of the U.S. psyche—beyond demographical and ethnic shifts. Thus, for both sides, the loss of their transatlantic partner would do more than just inflict damage in foreign policy terms—it would lead to a cultural split with disastrous consequences. So, if the redefinition of the transatlantic relationship is to succeed, is has to offer both partners not only a common agenda in practical terms, but also a redefinition of their own identity that incorporates the partner on the other side of the Atlantic.

For a new era of transatlantic cooperation to emerge, the political elites of Europe and the United States will have to display the sort of vision shown by the founders of the postwar order. A reorientation of the relationship is inevitable, but it remains to be seen whether it will be possible to develop further this valuable transatlantic friendship and enable it to operate effectively under new conditions.

The United States in a New Era

The end of the Cold War allowed both Europe and the United States to turn to internal problems that had been neglected or concealed for decades. In Europe, the fall of the Iron Curtain made dramatically clear the wretched state of the economies of the formerly socialist half of the continent, with all the consequences that the economic demise of Eastern Europe poses for the nations of Western Europe. In the United States, the full attention of politicians and the public turned for the first time in decades to the country's domestic economic and social difficulties. Paradoxically, the election of President Clinton in 1992 and the Republican landslide victory at the 1994 congressional elections sent the same message: U.S. society is less interested in the "new world order" proclaimed by former president George Bush than in solving domestic problems that have grown dramatically.

The United States is now engaged in a debate unprecedented in its sheer breadth—a dialogue that, albeit superficially, contrasts strangely with the carefully celebrated restoration of U.S. self-confidence vis-à-vis the outside world, a restoration that had taken place only a few years earlier under presidents Ronald Reagan and George Bush. At the center of the debate lies concern about the serious structural problems of the U.S. economy that, in the view of many Americans, will be an increasing burden on current and future generations. For instance, the total federal debt has grown from $3 trillion in 1991 to a current figure of more than $5 trillion. Each year, approximately $300 billion—or approximately 20 percent of the federal budget—goes toward paying interest on this debt.

The problem of the budget deficit is made worse by the extremely low level of savings in the United States. On average only 5 percent of disposable income is saved, whereas the figures for Germany and Japan are 12 percent and 15 percent respectively. Thus, the deficit in the United States has to be financed from foreign sources to a much greater degree than in Europe. This has led to a situation whereby, in the space of a few years, the United States has moved from being the world's biggest creditor country to being the biggest debtor country. Internationally, it is some $650 billion in the red. At the same time, the effects of economic globalization are now making their full impact felt on the United States. Cheap suppliers from East Asia have surpassed many U.S. producers in their own market: Color televisions, for example, are no longer manufactured in the United States. This and similar developments are reflected in the already chronic U.S. trade deficit, which has reached record levels the last two years. The United States's technological lead, which in the eyes of Americans is the crucial factor underlying the country's leading role in the world, has disappeared completely in many areas and has been noticeably reduced in others. Growth in productivity and investment are currently not high enough in the United States to turn the situation around in the short term—that is, in 2–3 years. Americans have, quite simply, been consuming too much for too many decades and neglecting the modernization of the country's infrastructure and production sites in the process.

The concrete results of this for most Americans are stagnant or sinking real wages. For example, the income of employees without a college degree has dropped by 18 percent during the last 15 years. Although greater wage flexibility means that the United States does not have the European problem of mass unemployment, the fact is that, in the United States, a job does not guarantee a secure income: More than 3 million Americans living below the poverty line have full-time jobs. The phenomenon of the "working poor" has become a stock-in-trade of the U.S. social debate.

Furthermore, the increasingly visible shortcomings in social integration are closely connected to the state of the economy. An ever greater number of Americans is missing out on the American dream. Today, nearly 15 percent of the population—37 million U.S. citizens—is officially classified as poor. Likewise, about 37 million Americans have no health insurance whatsoever. The increasingly evident shortcomings in the education system pose a particularly severe problem, in that they contribute to the growing marginalization of large sections of the population. At its best, the U.S. education system leads the world. But a concentration on excellence at the top end has led to an increasing neglect of education and training for the masses.

In view of these facts it is not surprising that many Americans demanded a fundamental change in policy and saw the dissolution of the Cold War system as an opportunity to question aspects of domestic and foreign policy that until then had been taken for granted. President Clinton tried to react to the new mood with a fundamental reform of health and social policy during his first years in office. The attempt failed because the majority of Americans viewed the expansion of "big government," rather than the administration's lack of action, as the root cause of economic decay. The main target of all reform attempts during the last two years—both those of the Republican majority in Congress and those of the Clinton administration—has therefore been the federal deficit, which both sides hope to master through an endless succession of budget cuts in the areas of domestic, social, and foreign policy.

The new approach is far more radical than all previous attempts to consolidate the budget. The current focus of U.S. politics almost solely on the national agenda could be seen as a relapse into provincialism. Against the background of the ambitious domestic agenda, for example, voters generally find a [number] of Congress's overseas contacts highly suspect because they distract attention from what are perceived as the real tasks at hand.

Yet, the effects of budget cuts on the actual content of U.S. foreign policy have been even more dramatic than this shifting of priorities. Since 1994, influential elements—the leadership in Congress in particular—have devoted themselves to a far-reaching reinterpretation of U.S. foreign policy, using domestic challenges as a guideline for foreign policy initiatives. As with home affairs, they view U.S. foreign policy as being unnecessarily constrained by excessive bureaucracy and inefficiency and generally take the view that it has drifted too far from the ideas and interests of the American public. Thus, various members of Congress have called for the abolition of institutions such as the United States Information Agency that have long been part of the U.S. foreign policy "establishment." Furthermore, they demand budget cuts for development aid, personnel and the number of U.S. diplomatic missions abroad, and exchange programs such as Fulbright scholarships.

The proponents of this new U.S. foreign policy strategy vehemently reject the suggestion, already made by some Europeans, that budget cuts constitute a prelude to a new period of U.S. isolationism. On the contrary, they say, they are concerned about reasserting the United States's claim to lead the world and wish to rid the foreign policy establishment of unnecessary ballast in the form of both government bureaucracy and multilateral commitments. The proponents of the strategy can thus be best described as "unilateralists." Their criticism that the United States has failed to assert its claim to world leadership in recent years may well be justified. Yet, it would be a mistake to conclude that the continued need for U.S. involvement and leadership in the world can be served by a reduction in the country's foreign policy resources.

U.S. policies to reduce "big government" in domestic affairs cannot automatically be applied to the field of U.S. foreign policy. It is precisely because the United States must concentrate increasingly on its own economic and social problems that it must also renew its foreign policy efforts: to ensure that the burden of U.S. international involvement, which is as necessary as ever, can be shared more efficiently with its allies and partners.

Europe in Transition

Like the United States, Europe is undergoing far-reaching changes in its self-perception and experiencing internal upheavals of an unpredictable nature. Processes of integration are occurring concurrently with processes of disintegration, and both are affecting the European Union. Supranational political interweaving is running parallel to new splits along social and ethnic lines. The old borders between Catholic and Orthodox Europe, between the Ottoman and Habsburg empires, have reemerged. It is less clear than ever before where Europe begins and ends. The acceleration in the process of developing the EU is being met with a growing degree of skepticism at the national level. The importance of national and regional concerns is increasing.

At the same time, the internationalization of economics and politics is intensifying, and creating several problems. But the development of appropriate decision-making structures at the European level continues to lag and cannot yet offer an adequate response to pressures that are already too great for individual nation-states. Europe is trapped: On the one hand, the magnet of integration is attracting more and more politicians and states—specifically, Eastern European ones—keen to accede to the EU; on the other, the structures that would enable the Union to take political action at the supranational level are not being developed quickly enough. The continent is in danger of becoming a victim of its own success.

In a transitional era like the present one, the foreign policy of many states has reverted to a familiar pattern in the European context—the maintenance of a "balance of power." Behind the multilateralist rhetoric of the Conference on Security and Cooperation in Europe (CSCE), behind the wrangling about the heritage of the Soviet Union and the question of the timetable for accepting new members into the EU, there lie national calculations as to the best way to counterbalance the potential power wielded by neighboring states.

In Western Europe, integration has become an instrument for such an approach. The shift in the internal balance caused by German unification has prompted France to offer to deepen the European Union. Britain has countered the prospect of greater integration with the prospect of widening, in the expectation that this will lead to a looser type of integration.

Yet, under present conditions, this process should not be seen as a return to the European tradition of grand diplomacy by nation-states. One of the peculiarities of the present-day policy of maintaining a balance of power is that it combines classic diplomacy with modern levels of integration. Even within the European Union, it is possible to pursue a policy of national interest. European politicians now face the task of giving form to this complex, transitional constellation. National ambitions need to be brought into harmony with the challenges resulting from the situation.

This simultaneity of contrasting developments is what makes Europe such a special case. And it is from this complex Europe that the United States will demand a clear definition of interests. It will expect Europe to have at its disposal the instruments necessary to pursue clearly defined policies. Thus, any realignment of the transatlantic partnership is going to require that Europeans do some very basic homework.

No action based on maintaining equilibrium can be considered an adequate solution or an appropriate way of solving far-reaching challenges. In particular, balance of power policies do not do justice to U.S. expectations concerning a more mature partnership. Rather, current political problems demand that European politicians devise strategic policies to meet four specific goals: to change the institutions responsible for integration, including their capacity to act; to develop the EU further along the path toward a true political, economic, and monetary union; to stabilize and integrate Central and Eastern Europe; and to preserve peace and security on the continent. The European Union's Intergovernmental Conference (IGC) for 1996–97 will determine the way forward; it is intended to give the process of integration new impetus and pave the way for amendments to the Treaty on the European Union. The whole idea of taking integration further will thus be subjected to careful consideration.

At first glance it appears paradoxical: Of all the times to start raising the issue of the continent's leading role, the United States has to do so in a period of deep-seated insecurity in Europe about the Union's future shape. Yet, given its increasing problems at home and its lonely position as the sole global superpower following the collapse of the Soviet Union, the United States is understandably applying increasing pressure on Europeans to play a greater role in solving global problems. It is thus in the U.S. interest that Europe learn, as soon as possible, to speak with one voice politically, militarily, and economically—or at least to channel the chorus of voices more effectively. The United States, as Europe's main partner, has the important role of constantly reminding the Europeans not to get tied up in seemingly trivial internal quarrels relating to European integration and not to lose sight of wider global challenges.

Europe has to bear responsibility worldwide simply because of its economic might; together with the United States, Europe is one of the main sources of hope in the developing world in terms of support for democracy and economic liberalization. In the future, the United States will increasingly remind Europe of its duty to take on political responsibilities commensurate with its position as a world economic power.

Today, Europe has the full potential to take on this new role of equal partner to the United States. One condition for the full exploitation of this potential is that Europe be politically aware of the new international challenges that have emerged in the wake of the end of the Cold War. If it fails to react to these challenges, or if it reacts inadequately, it risks permanent erosion of the transatlantic community: The United States, in searching for partners prepared to share its burdens, will increasingly begin looking outside Europe if it does not believe the Union is up to the task.

The Rise and Fall of the Transatlantic Community

Internal social and political changes taking place on both sides of the Atlantic will have several consequences on the transatlantic relationship. Both parties find themselves in a relatively serious identity crisis and lack a firm sense of direction. It is becoming increasingly difficult for Europe and the United States to calculate one another's actions—especially given the shifting political importance of economy, security, and culture. Under circumstances such as these, conflicts could be triggered very easily.

Crises beyond the domain of the North Atlantic Treaty Organization (NATO), trade conflicts both within and outside the Western community, and global challenges such as environmental pollution or nuclear terrorism have moved to the fore as topics demanding high-level political decision-making, yet the transatlantic partners have no commonly accepted guidelines for dealing with them. Differences on individual issues that have always existed are now becoming clearly visible and are being allowed to develop unchecked.

Yet, for the foreseeable future, no alternative exists to the transatlantic relations that have developed over the last 50 years. Europe and the United States have created a network of relations unprecedented throughout the world; they have succeeded in building more common understanding concerning democracy, pluralism, human rights, and the market economy than has ever before existed. Moreover, this common understanding is accepted by, and serves as a model for, more and more nations all over the world. This fact is increasingly ignored or forgotten because the West lacks a common orientation and a new agenda to take into account altered external conditions.

To establish transatlantic consensus, the West continues to use the old structures left over from the era of East–West conflict. But these structures cannot meet new challenges. New guiding principles for common action are needed to change the old backdrops and to form a consensus on how to tackle the tasks of the future. The ability of the Western partners to develop a new outline for a common direction in transatlantic relations will ultimately decide their fate.

If the West does not step up to this challenge, U.S.–European relations seem headed for a cultural split, one whose effects would radically question the structure of 50 years of transatlantic links. This split in the culture of political and social contact would not come about in the form of abrupt cuts or spectacular arguments. Rather, it would lead decisionmakers on both sides of the Atlantic in the medium term to drift apart in terms of their attitudes and subjective political and social designs.

Signs of a possible start of this process have already become manifest in the creeping erosion of bilateral links. Thus, the parliamentary contacts between Europe and the United States have recently been thinning visibly. According to U.S. insiders in the policy planning staff of the U.S. executive, the transatlantic relationship is also moving to the fringe of the operative radar screen. If this trend continues and extends to other fields, in the medium term the ability to conduct transatlantic policy will disappear.

As this erosion is below the surface, the whole extent of the current split would become visible only when the damage could no longer be repaired by using the reliable pattern of direct contacts and pulling the relevant strings. Strings can be pulled only when they exist—that is, when political and social contacts are constantly cultivated and a high level of agreement exists concerning the expectations each party has toward the other. As the attitudes of leading opinion makers in Europe and the United States drift apart, the basis for short-term successful crisis management will also vanish.

This process would not only lead to a far-reaching drift of political and social orientations, but also, in the worst case, to a direct political division between Europe and the United States—in other words, to a complete abandonment of the concept of the fundamental community of interests. The danger of such a split can be surmounted only if a future-oriented concept for deepening the transatlantic relationship can be developed that takes both partners' topical interests into consideration. Without a renewal of the U.S.–European community along such strategic lines, the very existence and success of the transatlantic relationship will be in jeopardy.

Creating a New Transatlantic Community

Players on both sides of the Atlantic have felt the increasingly painful unraveling of the network of transatlantic relations, the lack of a common new direction, and the ensuing dangers of substantial erosion of the U.S.–European partnership. Thus, politicians are, with increasing intensity, creating new models for the future prospects of U.S.–European cohesion. Leading European and U.S. politicians, in particular the German minister for foreign affairs, Klaus Kinkel, and his previous U.S. counterpart, former secretary of state Warren Christopher, declared their support for new treaty arrangements between Europe and the United States, as well as for the drawing-up of a binding transatlantic agenda or the establishment of new forums for cooperation at all conceivable levels.

All these approaches have one thing in common: namely, the worry about the creeping erosion of the transatlantic partnership following the disappearance of a common foe. To reshape cooperation to bring it in line with the times—a move that is absolutely imperative—the partners must develop a structure that is binding for all involved.

The task of finding a new direction can certainly be compared to that facing the transatlantic partners after World War II, one that demanded a radical paradigmatic shift on both sides of the Atlantic. The founders of the postwar order were aware that this change of direction and the quality of the U.S.–European ties they hoped to achieve would not be possible if relations within the Western community were governed only by loose arrangements. The degree of organization within the Western community had to be improved and this improvement found expression in the form of NATO, complemented by its economic counterpart, the Marshall Plan.

Today's new challenges, too, call upon the U.S.–European partnership to take a great step forward in terms of commitment. The first step must be the renaissance of the transatlantic community uniting the United States and the European Union. This task involves defining a clear vision of a continued transatlantic success story, in the face of different external conditions, that is obvious to both domestic and external observers and that will give all partners involved a highly exigent, common goal toward which to work. Furthermore, the new community has to create an organizational framework that enables the diverse and far-reaching common traits of the transatlantic partners to be developed into a coordinated and well-defined strategy for political action.

New Structures for Political Cooperation

Unlike during the period of East–West confrontation, when all partners could rely on a common security policy, no all-encompassing *raison d'être* exists today as a basis for reestablishing the transatlantic community. The creation of new binding structures must therefore revolve around issues in which the partners have an obvious interest in joint action as a matter of paramount importance.

If one considers the focus of European or U.S. political action, the need for binding structures is evident particularly in the coordination of strategy in response to global challenges and/or international crises. Today, Europe and the United States remain the only reliable makers or guarantors of stability in the world. The variety of burning issues in international politics calls for action by the transatlantic partners almost daily, often in regions where the existing institutions of the Atlantic Alliance have no jurisdiction. Thus far, no permanent mechanism exists to coordinate European and U.S. policy to deal with these issues. Moreover, both the United States and members of the European Union have fallen prone to navel-gazing because of problems and challenges at home. Yet, now that the traditional security partnership has been somewhat watered down, there is an increasing danger that the fallout from these conflicts may affect the transatlantic community, too.

Therefore, it is vital to establish a binding structure for transatlantic political consultation and cooperation that would give the transatlantic partners a reliable mandate to coordinate all issues relevant to the transatlantic agenda. The structure of this consultation and cooperation could be similar to that of the European Political Cooperation (EPC) forum, introduced in 1970 as the first permanent forum for coordinating the common policy of the members of the European Economic Community, as the EU was then known. It is now time for the transatlantic partners to institute a similar mechanism, to set up some form of Euro-American Political Cooperation (EAPC), which could deal with all the issues that the international community directs at the transatlantic partners but for which no organizational form has yet been found.

Creating a Transatlantic Common Market

Nowhere is the level of existing transatlantic interdependency more visible than in economic relations. This policy area constitutes one of the central vehicles of previous—and future—progress in transatlantic integration. Great care must therefore be taken to shape the political framework for this tightly woven network of relations so it can become the catalyst driving integration forward rather than—as has often been the case—the brakes holding it back. The high degree of transatlantic economic interdependency somehow seems to evade the collective consciousness of the European and U.S. populations. What they never fail to notice, however, are the recurring clashes over trivial matters such as bananas, feta cheese, or spaghetti, although the respective trade volumes in these goods account for a mere fraction of their governments' economic interests.

Similarly unheeded by the public at large, countless negotiating teams of European and U.S. officials in various different forums endeavor to thrash out progress concerning individual aspects of transatlantic trade, such as liberalizing public procurement, standardizing product norms, and dismantling export subsidies.

If one measures the results of this dialogue on regulatory policy against both the extent and the dynamic potential of real economic trade between Europe and the United States, however, a serious policy deficit emerges. Transatlantic settlement mechanisms lag far behind the supranational vitality of trade between Europe and the United States and seriously hamper the further development of trade relations.

Removing existing barriers to trade can succeed only if Europe and the United States manage to make their removal part of a strategic vision and manage to win over their populations by means of proactive arguments. Europe and the United States must categorically declare their faith in a revival of their trade relations; the founding of a Transatlantic Common Market, anchored in an agreement between the European Union and the United States, would be an optimal way of achieving this aim. This agreement should provide for specific objectives aimed at dismantling existing tariffs that hamper trade and, furthermore, it should formulate the timetable for a standardized U.S.–European economic area. In other words, it should dismantle any barriers to trade caused by regulatory policy.

Founding a Transatlantic Learning Community

The internal challenges facing the members of the transatlantic partnership increasingly require consultation between Europe and the United States, too. Concerning problems such as international crime, drug trafficking, and immigration, a need for joint action is clear. But other issues, such as reform of social security systems, appear merely to have a national character. Yet, strategies aimed at solving domestic problems can draw on models from other countries within the transatlantic community.

By way of example, President Clinton's health care reforms were clearly inspired by European models. By the same token, U.S. limits on automobile emission levels were crucial for European policymakers in this field. Countless other examples illustrate how the transatlantic partners can learn from each other's experiences. This has created the ideal conditions for founding a transatlantic learning community that would give some structure to the contacts and cross-referencing that have, until now, been somewhat ad hoc.

For the strategic planning of such a learning community, one must realize that the future of international relations will no longer be governed by the *raison d'être* of the security partnership—that is, by a so-called superior motive. In the future, such exchanges will have to serve a specific aim or make a practical contribution to the future lives of citizens on both sides of the Atlantic. It is the job of politicians to tap this potential appropriately, to create the optimum space for it to unfold as creatively as possible, and in so doing, to increase the acceptance of transatlantic relations among both Americans and Europeans.

Using the Opportunities of a New Beginning

The tenacity of the institutions of the postwar order has, until now, stalled the tendency for Europe and the United States to drift further apart. For example, no one seriously calls into question the existence of NATO, although the reason for its inception—the threat from Eastern Europe—has been reduced considerably. The after-effects of Western cohesion during the

East–West confrontation will be available to the transatlantic partners as spiritual armor for some time yet. The imminent celebrations commemorating the fiftieth anniversary of the Marshall Plan, the Berlin airlift, and the founding of NATO will certainly contribute to this.

Furthermore, the potential for differences of opinion between the Western partners has decreased considerably since the end of the Cold War. Constant points of friction over the appropriate reaction to the Soviet threat have disappeared. Compared to the controversies of the 1980s, the present state of transatlantic relations exudes considerable harmony. Yet, the current risk is that of increasing transatlantic indifference on a scale to match the disputes of old. Potential sources of friction concerning security policy coordination have ceased to exist, dealing with one's partners seems less and less necessary, and, given the more promising topics of everyday politics, cooperation is now frequently seen as a tiresome obligation.

Any analysis of transatlantic circumstances and options brings us to this central dilemma. On the one hand, as indicated above, no two other regions in the world enjoy such close ties, characterized by friendship and shared common values as well as by political and economic efficiency, as do Europe and the United States. On the other hand, the historical development of this alliance over the last 50 years makes it clear that, without a revitalization of these ties that is both forward-looking and geared toward the changing geopolitical situation, the two partners will inevitably grow apart.

The closeness of the transatlantic community in recent decades has been possible only because the security partnership founded in the postwar era provided the necessary framework. In the future, this framework will no longer be available. Thus far, only the initiated have been able to discern the first tiny cracks in the superstructure, demonstrated by the sharp decline in the number of visits to Europe by members of Congress and the cutbacks in U.S. funding for transatlantic cultural exchanges.

On both sides of the Atlantic, the everyday routine of politics is creating ever-greater distance between what were once the closest of partners. If this tendency is not halted, this slight indifference will eventually develop into more sharply defined differences of perception concerning international politics and strategies. This will become visible as a serious problem for Europe and the United States only when this perceptual difference turns into conflict, most likely when the partners face a concrete international challenge, such as peacekeeping in a crisis region of the world. The expectation that tried-and-tested methods of long-standing transatlantic cooperation will be able to solve this conflict of ideas may be deceptive.

Successful U.S.–European conflict management rests on the permanent agreement between policymakers and their public on a common direction. If this agreement is lacking on the minor issues, or if politicians begin to prefer solving domestic problems at the cost of dealing with their foreign partners (for example, in trade policy), then, when a serious issue arises, neither the politicians nor the general public will see the value of maintaining a transatlantic consensus. The ultimate consequences of such a split could be a permanent break in the transatlantic culture of close political and social interaction.

Eventually, all parties involved will have to ask how transatlantic relations can be placed on a new footing for the future. The longer it takes to answer this question, the more difficult a new beginning will be. For now, however, the opportunity to refound the transatlantic community is still ripe. The latest discussions on a Transatlantic Treaty, a Charter, or a "New Agenda" have made major political, industrial, and social policymakers aware of the need for a new initiative. The generation of committed supporters of the transatlantic partnership from the days of the East–West conflict are still involved in policymaking and opinion-shaping. Both Europe and the United States must therefore make decisive use of these conditions for a new beginning.

No one should make the mistake of thinking that such a new foundation will be easy to build. It will require a lot of effort on both sides and, more specifically, new and unconventional strategies. At the moment, because of the dominance of domestic issues, it is more difficult to gauge how much foreign policy strain Europe and the United States can take. Founding the transatlantic community anew would require both partners to open up unreservedly toward each other in areas such as trade, economic relations, and the transfer of experiences in social affairs.

In the coming decades, these new forms of cooperation will give both sides entirely new chances for development. In the short term, however, they could lead to painful adjustments, especially for the guardians of certain individual interests desirous of protection, such as agriculture or textiles. Transatlantic renewal requires Europeans and Americans to change their attitudes to a degree, not unlike reestablishing relations after World War II. Citizens on both sides of the Atlantic have to be won over if this new beginning is to succeed.

It is only by opening up the transatlantic community to the challenges of the future that we can ensure its continued existence and success. Merely preserving the status quo based on a transfigured romantic view of the past would be the surest way to guarantee the erosion of this partnership. Europe and the United States must seize this historic opportunity to found the transatlantic community anew before the emerging tendency to ignore solidarity means it slips through our fingers for good.

The Folly of NATO Enlargement

by Ted Galen Carpenter

When NATO leaders meet in Madrid this July, they intend to invite several central European nations to join the alliance. Poland, the Czech Republic, and Hungary are almost certain to receive invitations, and Romania and Slovenia are possible candidates.

Advocates of NATO enlargement insist that the step will foster cooperation and promote stability throughout Europe. But an enlarged NATO is a dreadful, potentially catastrophic idea. Instead of healing the wounds of the Cold War, it threatens to create a new division of Europe and dangerous security obligations for the United States.

There are four major drawbacks to NATO enlargement. One of the most troublesome is its effect on Russia. The enlargement issue undermines pro-Western democrats in that country and plays into the hands of communists and ultranationalists. Clinton administration officials and other supporters of NATO expansion profess to be baffled by the hostile reaction of Russians across the political spectrum. But even democratically inclined Russians find it difficult to countenance a powerful, U.S.-led military alliance perched on their country's western frontier. The few political figures who fail to oppose enlargement are excoriated by their opponents as stooges of foreign powers.

Given the fragility of Russian democracy, that development is exceedingly worrisome. Just as the foolish "war guilt" clause in the Versailles Treaty after World War I undermined domestic support for Germany's democratic Weimar Republic and eventually helped bring the Nazis to power, NATO enlargement could produce a similar tragedy in Russia.

The expansion of NATO also threatens to poison Russia's relations with the West even if a democratic regime retains control. We should not be lulled into complacency by the likelihood that Boris Yeltsin will sign a charter outlining a "special relationship" between Russia and NATO.

Given their country's weakened condition, Russian leaders understand that they cannot block the first round of enlargement. Therefore, they have adopted Foreign Minister Yevgeny Primakov's strategy to "limit the damage to Russia's interests." Moscow's underlying objective is to raise the political costs of the initial round of enlargement so high that there will never be a subsequent round. Further expansion might bring the alliance into Russia's "near abroad," including the Baltic region. Russians of diverse political persuasions would regard that as an intolerable provocation.

Yeltsin will likely be seething with resentment even as he signs the face-saving charter containing a few sops offered by NATO. The danger is that when Russia recovers economically and militarily, Russians will remember that the West exploited their country's temporary weakness to establish hegemony in central and eastern Europe, and they will seek revenge.

Even now, Moscow can take several disagreeable actions. Hopes for a START III nuclear-arms agreement to further reduce the Russian and U.S. arsenals are likely to be an early casualty of NATO enlargement. There are indications that the Russian Duma might even reject the START II agreement.

Moscow also has an incentive to seek closer strategic relationships with Iran, China, and other powers outside Europe. There are already ominous signs of a Moscow-Beijing axis. Russian and Chinese leaders speak of a "strategic partnership" between the two countries, and China is now Russia's largest arms customer.

As NATO expands eastward, Russia can also create its own political-military bloc among those nations that are not included on the roster of new NATO members. The agreement between Russia and Belarus, which seems so contrary to Russia's political and economic interests, suggests an intention to construct such a bloc. From Moscow's perspective, Belarus is a security buffer between an expanded NATO and Russia—and a potential forward staging area for Russia's forces.

A second problem with NATO enlargement is that the alliance could become entangled in parochial disputes among the central and east European states. Article 5 of the North Atlantic Treaty obligates the United States and its allies to help a fellow member repel aggression from any source. That is a matter of concern, since there are several potential flash points along the alliance's prospective security frontier. Hungary has ethnic problems with three neighboring states: Serbia, Slovakia, and Romania. Although it has signed accords with the latter two countries, there is little evidence that the underlying grievances have been resolved.

Even more worrisome is that part of NATO's eastern frontier would be the border between Poland and Belarus. The political situation in the latter country is ominous. Ruled by the autocratic and eccentric Alexander Lukashenko and possessing one of the weakest economies in Europe, Belarus is a political volcano waiting to erupt. There is considerable danger in having the United States obligated to protect Poland if trouble breaks out along the Polish-Belarussan border—especially since Belarus is a political and military client of Russia.

Enlargement Invites Danger

▲ Russians find it difficult to countenance a powerful U.S.-led military alliance perched on their country's western frontier.

▲ Russian and Chinese leaders speak of a strategic partnership between the two countries, and China is now Russia's largest arms customer.

▲ For the American taxpayer, an enlarged NATO would mean an outlay of $25 billion to $35 billion over the next 10 years.

COST PROJECTIONS

A third major problem is that enlargement is likely to be expensive. A 1996 study by the Congressional Budget Office concluded that the costs could run as high as $124 billion by 2012. Subsequent RAND Corporation and Pentagon studies have produced far lower figures, but those calculations are based on the assumption that Europe's security environment will remain quiescent for the next 15 years. They further assume that an enlarged NATO can meet its obligations merely by upgrading central European defenses and by creating a small (five ground divisions and five air wings; a mere 80,000 troops and 45 aircraft) rapid-reaction force. The RAND analysis estimates the probable costs of enlargement at between $30 billion and $52 billion over 10 to 15 years. The Pentagon's figures are even lower—$27 billion to $35 billion.

Basing cost projections on a rosy scenario is dubious methodology. There is no guarantee that Europe's strategic environment will remain placid for 15 years. One need only recall how different that environment looked 15 years ago to appreciate how rapidly radical transformations can occur.

The comment of a senior U.S. official following the release of the Pentagon report reveals much about the underlying motives of those advocating NATO enlargement. "There was a strong political imperative to low-ball the figures," admitted the official. "Everybody realized the main priority was to keep costs down to reassure Congress, as well as the Russians."

If the overall cost projections in the RAND and Pentagon studies are excessively sanguine, the assumption that the European countries will pay the overwhelming majority of those costs is even worse. Poland, Hungary, and the Czech Republic face daunting financial problems that make it difficult to spend additional billions of dollars on bringing their military forces up to NATO standards. Moreover, there is a dearth of domestic support for undertaking expensive military burdens, even if the costs were theoretically affordable.

Prospects for generous funding by the current European members of NATO are no better. The west European countries have slashed their military spending, in some cases at a rate even greater than that of the United States, since the end of the Cold War. There is no evidence that such trends will be reversed to fund NATO's enlargement.

Indeed, the populaces in several west European countries seem preoccupied with thwarting efforts to trim their bloated welfare states. French President Jacques Chirac's attempt to make modest cuts in such programs provoked mass demonstrations, eventually impelling Chirac to seek the resignation of the cabinet minister responsible for the austerity plan. Similarly, German Chancellor Helmut Kohl has encountered ferocious opposition to his efforts to scale back domestic welfare programs.

Given such political realities, it is naive to assume that there will be meaningful public support for increased military outlays to bring the central European states into NATO. Given the financial crunch afflicting west European governments, the conclusion of Walther Stuetzle, a former senior defense planner for the German government, seems prophetic. "So who will pick up the tab? I think that it will have to be the United States."

American taxpayers could be on the hook for an additional $25 billion to $35 billion over the next 10 to 12 years—even if one accepts the extraordinarily low RAND and Pentagon projections. The burden could be as much as $115 billion if the more realistic (in fact, conservative) CBO numbers are correct.

Those who believe that NATO enlargement can be done "on the cheap" ignore the fact that the new members are expecting reliable security guarantees, not just the status symbol of alliance membership.

That is the fourth problem with enlargement: The United States will be assuming extremely dangerous obligations if it is serious about providing such protection. Extending security commitments to nations in Russia's geopolitical "backyard" virtually invites a challenge. The United States would then face the choice of failing to honor treaty obligations or risking war with a nuclear-armed great power.

It is important to understand the extent of America's risk exposure. The United States is not merely pledging to contribute troops to a NATO rapid-reaction force in the event of trouble; it is promising to do whatever is necessary to defend its new allies. That includes shielding those countries with the U.S. strategic nuclear arsenal.

Indeed, it would be difficult to mount an effective conventional defense of the easternmost members of an expanded NATO against a capable adversary. That is especially true if NATO goes beyond the first round and brings in the Baltic states. Most military experts believe that there is no way to defend the Baltic republics by conventional means. The only alternative is a U.S. nuclear guarantee.

Such grave risks should never be incurred except to defend America's vital security interests. Proponents of enlargement must show why the nations of central and eastern Europe are so indispensable to America's security and well-being that U.S. leaders are justified in putting the lives of American troops and the existence of American cities at risk.

Advocates of enlargement sometimes act as though a bigger NATO is merely an institutional mechanism whereby everyone can gather in the center of Europe for a group hug. It is not. It is an unnecessary, expensive, and provocative initiative with perilous implications.

Ted Galen Carpenter is vice president for defense and foreign policy studies at the Cato Institute and the author of several books, including **Beyond NATO: Staying Out of Europe's Wars** *(1994).*

Pivotal States and U.S. Strategy

Robert S. Chase, Emily B. Hill, and Paul Kennedy

Robert S. Chase is a Ph.D. candidate in economics at Yale University. Emily B. Hill is a Ph.D. candidate in history at Yale University. Paul Kennedy is Professor of History at Yale University.

THE NEW DOMINOES

HALF A DECADE after the collapse of the Soviet Union, American policymakers and intellectuals are still seeking new principles on which to base national strategy. The current debate over the future of the international order—including predictions of the "end of history," a "clash of civilizations," a "coming anarchy," or a "borderless world"—has failed to generate agreement on what shape U.S. policy should take. However, a single overarching framework may be inappropriate for understanding today's disorderly and decentralized world. America's security no longer hangs on the success or failure of containing communism. The challenges are more diffuse and numerous. As a priority, the United States must manage its delicate relationships with Europe, Japan, Russia, and China, the other major players in world affairs. However, America's national interest also requires stability in important parts of the developing world. Despite congressional pressure to reduce or eliminate overseas assistance, it is vital that America focus its efforts on a small number of countries whose fate is uncertain and whose future will profoundly affect their surrounding regions. These are the pivotal states.

The idea of a pivotal state—a hot spot that could not only determine the fate of its region but also affect international stability—has a distinguished pedigree reaching back to the British geographer Sir Halford Mackinder in the 1900s and earlier. The classic example of a pivotal state throughout the nineteenth century was Turkey, the epicenter of the so-called Eastern Question; because of Turkey's strategic position, the disintegration of the Ottoman Empire posed a perennial problem for British and Russian policymakers.

Twentieth-century American policymakers employed their own version of a pivotal states theory. Statesmen from Eisenhower and Acheson to Nixon and Kissinger continually referred to a country succumbing to communism as a potential "rotten apple in a barrel" or a "falling domino." Although the domino theory was never sufficiently discriminative—it worsened America's strategic overextension—its core was about supporting pivotal states to prevent their fall to communism and the consequent fall of neighboring states.

Because the U.S. obsession with faltering dominoes led to questionable policies from Vietnam to El Salvador, the theory now has a bad reputation. But the idea itself—that of identifying specific countries as more important than others, for both regional stability and American interests—is sensible. The United States should adopt a discriminative policy toward the developing world, concentrating its energies on pivotal states rather than spreading its attention and resources over the globe.

Indeed, the domino theory may now fit U.S. strategic

needs better than it did during the Cold War. The new dominoes, or pivotal states, no longer need assistance against an external threat from a hostile political system; rather, the danger is that they will fall prey to internal disorder. A decade ago, when the main threat to American interests in the developing world was the possibility that nations would align with the Soviets, the United States faced a clear-cut enemy. This enemy captured the American imagination in a way that impending disorder does not. Yet chaos and instability may prove a greater and more insidious threat to American interests than communism ever was. With its migratory outflows, increasing conflict due to the breakdown of political structures, and disruptions in trade patterns, chaos undoubtedly affects bordering states. Reacting with interventionist measures only after a crisis in one state threatens an important region is simply too late. Further, Congress and the American public would likely not accept such actions, grave though the consequences might be to U.S. interests. Preventive assistance to pivotal states to reduce the chance of collapse would better serve American interests.

A strategy of rigorously discriminate assistance to the developing world would benefit American foreign policy in a number of ways. First, as the world's richest nation, with vast overseas holdings and the most to lose from global instability, the United States needs a conservative strategy. Like the British Empire in the nineteenth and early twentieth centuries, the interests of the United States lie in the status quo. Such a strategy places the highest importance on relations with the other great powers: decisions about the expansion of NATO or preserving amicable relations with Russia, China, Japan, and the major European powers must remain primary. The United States must also safeguard several special allies, such as Saudi Arabia, Kuwait, South Korea, and Israel, for strategic and domestic political reasons.

The United States has the most to lose; thus, its interests lie in the status quo.

Second, a pivotal states policy would help U.S. policymakers deal with what Sir Michael Howard, in another context, nicely described as "the heavy and ominous breathing of a parsimonious and pacific electorate." American policymakers, themselves less and less willing to contemplate foreign obligations, are acutely aware that the public is extremely cautious about and even hostile toward overseas engagements. While the American public may not reject all such commitments, it does resist intervention in areas that appear peripheral to U.S. interests. A majority also believes, without knowing the relatively small percentages involved, that foreign aid is a major drain on the federal budget and often wasted through fraud, duplication, and high operating costs. Few U.S. politicians are willing to risk unpopularity by contesting such opinions, and many Republican critics have played to this mood by attacking government policies that imply commitments abroad. Statesmen responsible for outlining U.S. foreign policy might have a better chance of persuading a majority of Congress and the American public that a policy of selective engagement is both necessary and feasible.

Finally, a pivotal states strategy might help bridge the conceptual and political divide in the national debate between "old" and "new" security issues. The mainstream in policy circles still considers new security issues peripheral; conversely, those who focus on migration, overpopulation, or environmental degradation resist the realist emphasis on power and military and political security.

In truth, neither the old nor the new approach will suffice. The traditional realist stress on military and political security is simply inadequate—it does not pay sufficient attention to the new threats to American national interests. The threats to the pivotal states are not communism or aggression but rather overpopulation, migration, environmental degradation, ethnic conflict, and economic instability, all phenomena that traditional security forces find hard to address. The "dirty" industrialization of the developing world, unchecked population growth and attendant migratory pressures, the rise of powerful drug cartels, the flow of illegal arms, the eruption of ethnic conflict, the flourishing of terrorist groups, the spread of deadly new viruses, and turbulence in emerging markets—a laundry list of newer problems—must also concern Americans, if only because their spillover effects can hurt U.S. interests.

Yet the new interpretation of security, with its emphasis on holistic and global issues, is also inadequate. Those who point to such new threats to international stability often place secondary importance (if that) on U.S. interests; indeed, they are usually opposed to invoking the national interest to further their cause. For example, those who criticized the Clinton administration in the summer of 1994 for not becoming more engaged in the Rwandan crisis paid little attention to the relative insignificance of Rwanda's stability for American interests. The universal approach common to many advocates of global environmental protection or human rights, commendable in principle, does not discriminate between human rights abuses in Haiti, where proximity and internal instability made intervention possible and even necessary, and similar abuses in Somalia, where the United States had few concrete interests.

Furthermore, the new security approach cannot make a compelling case to the American public for an internationalist foreign policy. The public does not sense the

10. Pivotal States and U.S. Strategy

danger in environmental and demographic pressures that erode stability over an extended period, even if current policies, or lack thereof, make this erosion inexorable and at some point irreversible. Finally, the global nature of the new security threats makes it tempting to downplay national governments as a means to achieving solutions.

A pivotal states strategy, in contrast, would encourage integration of new security issues into a traditional, state-centered framework and lend greater clarity to the making of foreign policy. This integration may make some long-term consequences of the new security threats more tangible and manageable. And it would confirm the importance of working chiefly through state governments to ensure stability while addressing the new security issues that make these states pivotal.

HOW TO IDENTIFY A PIVOT

ACCORDING TO which criteria should the pivotal states be selected? A large population and an important geographical location are two requirements. Economic potential is also critical, as recognized by the U.S. Commerce Department's recent identification of the "big emerging markets" that offer the most promise to American business. Physical size is a necessary but not sufficient condition: Zaire comprises an extensive tract, but its fate is not vital to the United States.

What really defines a pivotal states is its capacity to affect regional and international stability. A pivotal state is so important regionally that its collapse would spell transboundary mayhem: migration, communal violence, pollution, disease, and so on. A pivotal state's steady economic progress and stability, on the other hand, would bolster its region's economic vitality and political soundness and benefit American trade and investment.

For the present, the following should be considered pivotal states: Mexico and Brazil; Algeria, Egypt, and South Africa; Turkey; India and Pakistan; and Indonesia. These states' prospects vary widely. India's potential for success, for example, is considerably greater than Algeria's; Egypt's potential for chaos is greater than Brazil's. But all face a precarious future, and their success or failure will powerfully influence the future of the surrounding areas and affect American interests. This theory of pivotal states must not become a mantra, as the domino theory did, and the list of states could change. But the concept itself can provide a necessary and useful framework for devising American strategy toward the developing world.

A WORLD TURNING ON PIVOTS

TO UNDERSTAND this idea in concrete terms, consider the Mexican crisis a year ago. Mexico's modernization has created strains between the central and local governments and difficulties with the unions and the poorest groups in the countryside, and it has damaged the environment. Like the other pivotal states, Mexico is delicately balanced between progress and turmoil.

Given the publicity and political debate surrounding the Clinton administration's rescue plan for Mexico, most Americans probably understood that their southern neighbor is special, even if they were disturbed by the means employed to rescue it. A collapse of the peso and the consequent ruin of the Mexican economy would have weakened the U.S. dollar, hurt exports, and caused convulsions throughout Latin America's Southern Cone Common Market and other emerging markets. Dramatically illustrating the potency of new security threats to the United States, economic devastation in Mexico would have increased the northward flow of illegal immigrants and further strained the United States' overstretched educational and social services. Violent social chaos in Mexico could spill over into this country. As many bankers remarked during the peso crisis, Mexico's troubles demonstrated the impossibility of separating "there" from "here."

Because of Mexico's proximity and its increasing links with the United States, American policymakers clearly needed to give it special attention. As evidenced by the North American Free Trade Agreement, they have. But other select states also require close American attention.

EGYPT

EGYPT'S LOCATION has historically made its stability and political alignment critical to both regional development and relationships between the great powers. In recent decades, its proximity to important oil regions and its involvement in the Arab-Israeli peace process, which is important for the prosperity of many industrialized countries, has enhanced its contribution to stability in the Middle East and North Africa. Furthermore, the government of President Muhammad Hosni Mubarak has provided a bulwark against perhaps the most significant long-term threat in the region—radical Islamic fundamentalism.

The collapse of the current Egyptian regime might damage American interests more than the Iranian revolution did. The Arab-Israeli peace process, the key plank of U.S. foreign policy in this region for the past 20 years, would suffer serious, perhaps irreparable, harm. An unstable Egypt would undermine the American diplomatic plan of isolating fundamentalist "rogue" states in the region and encourage extremist opposition to governments everywhere from Algeria to Turkey. The fall of the Mubarak government could well lead Saudi Arabia to reevaluate its pro-Western stance. Under such conditions, any replay of Operation Desert Storm or similar military intervention in the Middle East on behalf of friendly countries such as Kuwait or Jordan would be extremely difficult, if not impossible. Finally, the effect on oil and financial markets worldwide could be enormous.

Egypt's future is not only vital, but very uncertain. While some signs point to increasing prosperity and stability—birth rates have declined, the United States recently forgave $7 billion of debt, and Egypt's international reserves reached $16 billion in 1995—the preponderance of evidence paints a dimmer picture. Jealously guarding its power base and wary that further privatization would produce large numbers of resentful former state employees, the government fears losing control over the economy. Growth rates lurch fitfully upward, and although reform has improved most basic economic indicators, it has also widened the gap between rich and poor. Roughly one-third of the population now lives in poverty, up from 20–25 percent in 1990.

A harsh crackdown on fundamentalism has reduced the most serious short-term threat to the Mubarak regime, but a long-term solution may prove more elusive. The government's brutal attack on the fundamentalist movement may ultimately fuel Islam's cause by alienating the professional middle class; such a policy has already greatly strengthened the more moderate Muslim Brotherhood and radicalized the extremist fringe.

Environmental and population problems are growing. Despite the gradually decreasing birthrate, the population is increasing by about one million every nine months, straining the country's natural resources, and is forecast to reach about 94 million by 2025.

Recognizing Egypt's significance and fragility, successive U.S. administrations have made special provisions to maintain its stability. In 1995 Egypt received $2.4 billion from the U.S. government, making it the second-largest recipient of American assistance, after Israel. That allocation is primarily the result of the Camp David accords and confirms Egypt's continuing importance in U.S. Middle East policy. Current attempts by American isolationists to cut these funds should be strongly resisted. On the other hand, the U.S. government and Congress should seriously consider redirecting American aid. F-16 fighters can do little to help Egypt handle its internal difficulties, but assistance to improve infrastructure, education, and the social fabric would ease the country's troubles.

INDONESIA

WHILE EGYPT'S prospects for stability are tenuous, Indonesia's future appears brighter. By exercising considerable control over the population and the economy for the last several decades, Indonesia's authoritarian regime has engineered dramatic economic growth, now expected to be about 7 percent annually for the rest of the decade. Poverty rates have dropped drastically, and a solid middle class has emerged. At first glance, Indonesia's development has been a startling success. However, the government now confronts strains generated by its own efforts.

Along with incomes, education levels, and health status, Indonesia's population is increasing dramatically. With the fourth-largest population in the world and an extra three million people added each year, the country is projected to reach 260 million inhabitants by 2025. The main island of Java, one of the most densely populated places on earth, can scarcely accommodate the new bodies. In response, the government is forcing many citizens to migrate to other islands. This resettlement program is the focal point for a host of other tensions concerning human rights and the treatment of minorities. The government's brutal handling of the separatist movement in East Timor continues to hinder its efforts to gain international respect. President Suharto's regime has made a point of cooperating with Chinese entrepreneurs to boost economic expansion, but ethnic differences remain entrenched. Finally, the government's favoring of specific businesses has produced deep-rooted corruption.

Because of the government's tight control, it can maintain stability even while pursuing these questionable approaches to handling its people. However, as a more sophisticated middle class emerges, Indonesians are less willing to accept the existing concentration of economic and political power. These opposing forces, one for continued central control and one for more dispersed political power, will clash when Suharto leaves office, probably after the 1998 elections.

If Indonesia falls into chaos, it is hard to see its region prospering.

A reasonable scenario for Indonesia would be the election of a government that shares power more broadly, with greater respect for human rights and press freedoms. The new regime would maintain Indonesia's openness to foreign trade and investment, and it would end favoritism toward certain companies. Better educated, better paid, and urbanized for a generation, Indonesians would have fewer children per family. Indonesia would continue its leadership role in the Association of Southeast Asian Nations (ASEAN) and the Asia-Pacific Economic Cooperation forum (APEC), helping foster regional growth and stability.

The possibility remains, however, that the transfer of power in Jakarta could trigger political and economic instability, as it did in 1965 at the end of President Sukarno's rule. A new regime might find it more difficult to overawe the people while privately profiting from the economy. Elements of the electorate could lash out in frustration. Riots would then jeopardize Indonesia's growth and regional leadership, and by that stage the United States could do nothing more than attempt to rescue its citizens from the chaos.

Instability in Indonesia would affect peace and prosperity across Southeast Asia. Its archipelago stretches across key shipping lanes, its oil and other businesses attract Japanese and U.S. investment, and its stable economic condictions and open trade policies set an example for ASEAN, APEC, and the region as a whole. If Indonesia, as Southeast Asia's fulcrum, falls into chaos, it is hard to envisage the region prospering. It is equally hard to imagine general distress if Indonesia booms economically and maintains political stability.

Despite the difficulty, the United States must have a strategy for encouraging Indonesia's stability. Part of this will involve close cooperation with Japan, which is by far the largest donor to Indonesian development. A more sensitive aspect of the strategy will be encouraging the regime to respect human rights and ethnic differences. The strategy also calls for calibrated pressure on Indonesia to decrease its widespread corruption, which in any case is required to achieve the country's full integration into the international business world.

BRAZIL

BRAZIL BORDERS every country in South America except Ecuador and Chile, and its physical size, complex society, and huge population of 155 million people are more than enough to qualify it as a pivotal state.

Brazil's economy appears to be recovering from its 1980s crisis, although the indicators for the future are inconsistent. President Fernando Henrique Cardoso's proposals for economic reform, which include deregulation and increased openness to foreign investment in key industries, have advanced in Brazil's congress. Many basic social and economic indexes point to a generally improving quality of life, including the highest industrial growth since the 1970s (6.4 percent in 1994), declining birth and death rates, increasing life expectancy, and an expanding urban infrastructure. In the longer term, however, Brazil must address extreme economic inequality, poor educational standards, and extensive malnutrition. These realities, together with a burgeoning current account deficit and post-peso crisis skittishness, help diminish investor confidence.

Were Brazil to founder, the consequences from both an environmental and an economic point of view would be grave. The Amazon basin contains the largest tropical rain forest in the world, boasting unequaled biodiversity. Apart from aesthetic regrets about its destruction, the practical consequences are serious. The array of plants and trees in the Amazon is an important source of natural pharmaceuticals; deforestation may also spread diseases as the natural hosts of viruses and bacteria are displaced to other regions.

A social and political collapse would directly affect significant U.S. economic interests and American investors. Brazil's fate is inextricably linked to that of the entire South American region, a region that before its debt and inflation crises in the 1970s bought large amounts of U.S. goods and is now potentially the fastest-growing market for American business over the decades to come. In sum, were Brazil to succeed in stabilizing over the long term, reducing the massive gap between its rich and poor, further opening its markets, and privatizing often inefficient state-run industries, it could be a powerful engine for the regional economy and a stimulus to U.S. prosperity. Were it to fail, Americans would feel the consequences.

SOUTH AFRICA

APARTHEID'S END makes South Africa's transition particularly dramatic. So far, President Nelson Mandela's reconciliation government has set an inspiring example of respect for ethnic differences, good governance, and prudent nurturing of the country's economic potential. In contrast to other conflicts, in which different groups have treated each other with so much acrimony that they could not negotiate, the administration has successfully overcome some of its political divisions: it includes both former apartheid president Frederik Willem de Klerk and Zulu Chief Mangosuthu Buthelezi. Moreover, South Africa is blessed with a strong infrastructure, a sound currency, and vast natural resources. These assets make its economy larger and more vital than any other on the continent, accounting for a colossal 75 percent of the southern African region's economic output. No longer an international pariah, it is working to develop robust trade and financial links around the region and the globe. A hub for these connections, South Africa could stimulate growth throughout the southern cone of Africa.

There are indications, however, that South Africa could succumb to political instability, ethnic strife, and economic stagnation. Power-sharing at the cabinet level belies deep ethnic divisions. Any one of several fissures could collapse this collaboration, plunging the country into civil war. Afrikaner militias may grow increasingly intransigent, traditional tribal leaders could raise arms against their diminished influence, and when Mandela no longer leads the African National Congress, the party may abandon its commitment to ethnic reconciliation.

As Mandela's government struggles to improve black living standards and soothe ethnic tensions, the legacy of apartheid creates a peculiar dilemma. It will be hard to meet understandable black expectations of equity in wages, education, and health, given the country's budget deficits and unstable tax base. As racial inequalities persist, blacks are likely to grow impatient. Yet if whites feel they are paying a disproportionate share for improved services for blacks, they might flee the country, taking with them the prospects for increased foreign direct investment.

South Africa can show other ethnically tortured nations the way to democracy.

While the primary threats to South Africa's stability are internal, its effectiveness in containing them will have repercussions beyond its borders. Even before apartheid ended, South Africa had enormous influence over the region's political and economic development, from supporting insurgencies throughout the "front-line states" to providing mining jobs for migrant workers from those same countries. If South Africa achieves the economic and political potential within its grasp, it will be a wellspring of regional political stability and economic growth. If it prospers, it can demonstrate to other ethnically tortured regions a path to stability through democratization, reconciliation, and steadily increasing living standards. Alternatively, if it fails to handle its many challenges, it will suck its neighbors into a whirlpool of self-defeating conflict.

Although controlling the sea-lanes around the Cape of Good Hope would be important, especially if widespread trouble were to erupt in the Middle East, American strategic interests are not otherwise endangered in southern Africa. Yet because South Africa is the United States' largest trading partner in Africa and possesses vast economic potential, its fate would affect American trading and financial interests that have invested there. It would also destabilize key commodity prices, especially in the gold, diamond, and ore markets. More generally, instability in South Africa, as in Brazil and Indonesia, would cast a large shadow over confidence in emerging markets.

American policy toward South Africa should reflect its importance as a pivotal state. While recognizing South Africa's desire to solve its problems without external interference, the United States should promote South Africa's economic and political stability. Of $10.5 billion in American economic aid given in 1995, a mere one percent ($135 million) was for South Africa. A strategy that acknowledges this nation's importance to American interests would surely be less parsimonious.

ALGERIA AND TURKEY

ALGERIA'S geographical position makes its political future of great concern to American allies in Europe, especially France and Spain. A civil war and the replacement of the present regime by extremists would affect the security of the Mediterranean sea-lanes, international oil and gas markets, and, as in the case of Egypt, the struggle between moderate and radical elements in the Islamic world. All the familiar pressures of rapid population growth and drift to the coastal cities, environmental damage, increasing dependence on food imports, and extremely high youth unemployment are evident. Levels of violence remain high as Algerian government forces struggle to crush the Islamist guerrilla movement.

While a moderate Islamist government might prove less disturbing than the West fears, a bloody civil war or the accession of a radical, anti-Western regime would be very serious. Spain, Italy, and France depend heavily on Algerian oil and gas and would sorely miss their investments, and the resulting turbulence in the energy markets would certainly affect American consumers. The flood of middle-class, secular Algerians attempting to escape the bloodshed and enter France or other parts of southern Europe would further test immigration policies of the European Union (EU). The effects on Algeria's neighbors, Morocco and Tunisia, would be even more severe and encourage radical Islamic elements everywhere. Could Egypt survive if Algeria, Morocco, Tunisia, and Muammar al-Qaddafi's Libya collaborated to achieve fundamentalist goals? Rumors of an Algerian atomic bomb are probably premature, but the collapse of the existing regime would undoubtedly reduce security in the entire western Mediterranean. All the more reason for the United States to buttress the efforts of the International Monetary Fund and for the Europeans to improve Algeria's well-being and encourage a political settlement.

Although Turkey is not as politically or economically fragile as Algeria, its strategic importance may be even greater. At a multifold crossroads between East and West, North and South, Christendom and Islam, Turkey has the potential to influence countries thousands of miles from the Bosporus. The southeast keystone of NATO during the Cold War and an early (if repeatedly postponed) applicant to enlarged EU membership, Turkey enjoys solid economic growth and middle-class prosperity. However, it also shows many of the difficulties that worry other pivotal states: population and environmental pressures, severe ethnic minority challenges, and the revival of radical Islamic fundamentalism, all of which test the country's young democratic institutions and assumptions. There are also a slew of external problems, ranging from bitter rivalries with Greece over Cyprus, various nearby islands' territorial boundaries, and Macedonia, to the developing quarrel with Syria and Iraq over control of the Euphrates water supply, to delicate relationships with the Muslim-dominated states of Central Asia. A prosperous, democratic, tolerant Turkey is a beacon for the entire region; a Turkey engulfed by civil wars and racial and religious hatreds, or nursing ambitions to interfere abroad, would hurt American interests in innumerable ways and concern everyone from pro-NATO strategists to friends of Israel.

INDIA AND PAKISTAN

CONSIDERED separately; the challenges facing the two great states of South Asia are daunting enough. Each confronts a population surge that is forecast to take Pakistan's total (123 million in 1990) to 276 million by 2025, and India's (853 million in 1990) to a staggering 1.45 billion, thus equaling China's projected population. While such growth taxes rural environments by causing the farming of marginal lands, deforestation, and depletion of water resources, the urban population explosion is even more worrisome. With 46 percent of Pakistan's and 35 percent of India's population under 15 years old, according to 1990 census figures, tens of millions of young people enter the job market each year; the inadequate opportunities for them further strain the social fabric. All this forms an ominous backdrop to rising tensions, as militant Hindus and Muslims, together a full fifth of the population, challenge India's democratic traditions, and Islamic forces stoke nationalist passions across Pakistan.

The shared borders and deep-rooted rivalry of India and Pakistan place these pivotal states in a more precarious position than, for example, Brazil or South Africa. With three wars between them since each gained independence, each continues to arm against the other and quarrel fiercely over Kashmir, Pakistan's potential nuclear capabilities and missile programs, and other issues. This jostling fuels their mutual ethnic-cum-religious fears and could produce another bloody conflict that neither government could control. What effect a full-scale war would have on the Pakistan-China entente is hard to predict, but the impact of such a contest would likely spread from Kashmir into Afghanistan and farther afield, and Pakistan could find support in the Muslim world. For many reasons, and perhaps especially the nuclear weapons stakes, the United States has a vital interest in encouraging South Asia's internal stability and external peace.

Could this short list of important states in the developing and emerging-markets regions of the globe include others? Possibly. This selection of pivotal states is not carved in stone, and new candidates could emerge over the next decades. Having an exact list is less important than initiating a debate over why, from the standpoint of U.S. national interests, some states in the developing world are more important than others.

BETTER WISE THAN WIDE

THE UNITED STATES needs a policy toward the developing world that does not spread American energies, attention, and resources too thinly across the globe, but rejects isolationist calls to write it off. This is a realistic policy, both strategically and politically. Strategically, it would permit the United States, as the country that can make the greatest contribution to world security, to focus on supporting pivotal states. Politically, given the jaundiced view of Americans and their representatives toward overseas engagements, a strategy of discrimination is the strongest argument against an even greater withdrawal from the developing world than is now threatened.

As the above case studies suggest, each pivotal state grapples with an intricate set of interrelated problems. In such an environment, the United States has few clearcut ways to help pivotal states succeed. Therefore, it must develop a subtle, comprehensive strategy, encompassing all aspects of American interaction with each one. Those strategies should include appropriate focusing of U.S. Agency for International Development assistance, promoting trade and investment, strengthening relationships with the country's leaders, bolstering country-specific intelligence capabilities and foreign service expertise, and coordinating the actions of government agencies that can influence foreign policy. In short, the United States must use all the resources at its disposal to buttress the stability of key states around the globe, working to prevent calamity rather than react to it. Apart from avoiding a great-power war, nothing in foreign policy could be more important.

This focus on the pivotal states inevitably means that developing states not deemed pivotal would receive diminished attention, energy, and resources. This will seem unfair to many, since each of the pivotal states examined above enjoys a higher per capita GDP than extremely poor nations like Mali and Ethiopia. Ideally, U.S. assistance to the entire developing world would significantly increase, but that will not happen soon. A pragmatic refocusing of American aid is better than nothing at all being given to the developing world, which may happen if the isolationist mood intensifies.

Such a refocusing could improve the American public's confidence that its money can be used effectively abroad. Relative to what other states give for development, the American contribution is declining. By continuing to spread those resources across a broad swath of developing countries, the United States might further diminish the impact of its assistance in many countries. In contrast, concentrating on a few pivotal states would increase American influence in them and improve the chances of convincing the public to spend resources overseas.

Current patterns of assistance to developing and emerging countries do not reflect American global security interests and in many cases seem glaringly inconsistent with U.S. strategic priorities. While conceding that by far the largest amounts of American aid will go to Israel and Egypt, is it not curious that India, like South

Africa, receives less than one percent of total U.S. assistance? Pakistan receives virtually nothing. Algeria receives nothing. Brazil is given one-fifth of the aid awarded to Bolivia. Turkey gets less than Ethiopia (although, like Egypt, Ankara is given a large amount of military assistance that is hard to explain in the post-Cold War environment). Surely this requires serious examination?

A pragmatic refocusing of aid is better than no aid at all.

In changing these patterns, diplomatic and political objections will be inevitable. Questions will arise about countries not on the list, particularly when one of them faces a crisis. Some will plead that exceptions be made for states that have been encouraged to undertake internal political changes, like Haiti, El Salvador, and the Philippines. Foreign service professionals will caution against making this strategy part of the declared policy of the United States, for that could indicate likely American reactions in a crisis. The more critics raise theme problems, the more controversial this idea will become.

However, the pivotal states strategy merits such a debate, and it is high time for such a policy discussion to begin. As Mackinder pointed out, democracies find it difficult to think strategically in times of peace. All the above-mentioned problems and reservations, far from weakening the case for helping pivotal states, point to the importance of identifying how better to order U.S. policies in different parts of the world. A debate over pivotal states would also provide a way of checking the extent to which American agencies already carry out a discriminative strategy and the degree to which they recognize that the traditional types of external threats are not the only sources of danger to countries important to U.S. interests.

Would this formula solve all of America's foreign policy challenges? By no means. Priority should always be given to managing relations with the other great powers. In view of the international convulsions of the past 10 years, who would be rash enough to predict American relations with Russia, Japan, and China a decade or more hence and the dire implications if they go badly? Yet even if those countries remain our primary concern, the developing world still needs a place in U.S. global strategy. By identifying pivotal states to Congress and the public and providing the greatest possible support to those countries, this strategy has a greater chance of coherence and predictability than vague and indiscriminate assurances of good will to all developing countries, large and small. America's concern about traditional security threats would then be joined by a heightened awareness of the newer, nonmilitary dangers to important countries in the developing world and the serious repercussions of their collapse. Whichever administration steers the United States into the next century, American priorities would be ordered, and its foreign policy toward the developing world would have a focus—that of supporting those pivotal states whose future affects the fate of much of the planet.

THE U.S. AND ISLAMIC FUNDAMENTALISTS: THE NEED FOR DIALOGUE

SAMI G. HAJJAR

Sami G. Hajjar is a Professor in the Department of National Security and Strategy and Director of the Middle East Studies Program at the U.S. Army War College, Carlisle Barracks, PA. He is a former foreign service officer with the U.S. Information Agency with assignments in Saudi Arabia and the United Arab Emirates. For over twenty years he was also a professor of political science at the University of Wyoming. A graduate of the American University of Beirut, Lebanon, he received his Ph.D. from the University of Missouri-Columbia.

IN BRIEF

Some influential scholars argue that the U.S. should not engage in dialogue with Islamic fundamentalist opposition groups because all are extremists. But the basic assumptions about Islamic fundamentalists that underlie the anti-dialogue position are faulty. There are fundamentalists who advance positions that are at least compatible with the precepts of Western liberalism. Engaging such moderates is justified in light of U.S. national interests.

Terrorist bombings in Israel during the early months of 1996 by Hamas suicide bombers have seriously threatened the peace process. These attacks have focused attention not only on the immediate question of security in the region but also on the broader issue of how to deal with Islamic fundamentalists. American scholars have been divided on the latter issue, but those urging a tough stance against fundamentalists by the United States and other Western governments have gained credibility as terrorist activities escalate.[1] A leading representative of this viewpoint is Middle East scholar Daniel Pipes, who has concluded that all Muslim fundamentalists are dangerous and has urged the United States Government to adopt a policy of preventing fundamentalist opposition groups from seizing power in Islamic countries.[2]

Pipes is strongly opposed to the Clinton Administration's discussions with Palestinian, Egyptian and Algerian fundamentalist movements. Such a policy, he claims, is based on "terribly misguided ideas about fundamentalists in opposition." According to Pipes, the seizure of power by these groups would lead to disastrous consequences, including a threat to the survival of Israel, political unrest in the Gulf, high energy costs, an accelerated arms race, more international terrorism, and unending wars. Additionally, he argues, the massive refugee outflow to Europe could enhance the appeal of fascism.[3]

Pipes' view is mistaken. The official U.S. policy toward Islamic fundamentalist opposition groups is justified, and is the right strategy for dealing with fundamentalism's post-Cold War growth in popularity. Pipes' basic assumptions about fundamentalists are faulty; consequently, the thrusts of his conclusions and policy recommendations are unjustified.

Fundamentalism: Secular Ideology or Messianic Movement?

Pipes' starting postulate is that fundamentalist Islam is a radical utopian movement closer in spirit to communism and fascism than to traditional religions. He goes on to characterize Islamic fundamentalism as totalitarian, extremist, revolutionary, anti-democratic, anti-Semitic, and anti-Western, rejecting the very possibility of coexistence with Western civilization. In short, Pipes regards fundamentalist Islam as a "movement standing in direct competition to Western civilization and challenging it for global supremacy."[4]

Pipes further suggests that fundamentalist Islam has replaced the traditional totalitarian systems of the Twentieth Century—communism and fascism—as the source of world conflict in its opposition to the West and the liberal democratic tradition. Now that the right and left totalitarian ideologies have been defeated, Pipes is ready to embrace Samuel Huntington's paradigm of the "Clash of Civilizations," but with a crucial refinement. The fault line is not the West and traditional Islam, as Huntington thought, but the West and fundamentalist Islam.

But the affinity between fundamentalist Islam and the totalitarian ideologies of communism and fascism is superficial. Communism and fascism are secular ideologies, and despite their heterogeneity they share important characteristics. Foremost, both operate exclusively on the political level of existence. The institution of the state (dictatorship of the proletariat in communist theory) is regarded as the vehicle by and through which the individual and the group can attain the ultimate values of social life—liberty and justice. The state thus becomes the only source of legislation, the giver and supreme arbiter of morality. Under these systems, the spheres of personal and social domains become increasingly blurred. The belief in the power and righteousness of the state (or party) becomes an article of faith and the basis for the popular support that these systems generate.[5]

By contrast, fundamentalist Islam, like Messianic Christian movements that from time to time erupted in Europe from the Middle Ages up to the Eighteenth Century, is concerned with both the temporal (political) and spiritual (transcendental) planes.

What Talmon wrote about Christian revolutionaries of centuries past applies perfectly to post-Cold War fundamentalist Islam: "[they] fought for the individual's freedom to interpret God's order; their sovereign was not man, but God. They aimed at personal salvation and an egalitarian society based on the law of Nature because they had it from God that there lies salvation, and believed that obedience to God is the condition of human freedom."[6]

For Muslims, as for Christians and Jews, this life is but a journey whose completion lies in the Hereafter. And because the Islamic doctrine does not separate politics and religion, the state and its agents are always constrained by the *sharia* (Islamic law based on the *Quran*) and the *Sunnah,* (traditions based on the deeds and sayings of the Prophet). Secular totalitarians have no such limitations.

There Are No Moderate Fundamentalists

In his criticism of current U.S. policy toward Muslim fundamentalists in opposition, Pipes assumes that the policy is based on the bad advice of academics, who downplay the threat of fundamentalists, and even see the phenomenon of fundamentalism as a positive democratic force in the Middle East. One who holds this view is John Esposito, who argues that the Islamic threat to the West is a myth, and that Islam is not antithetical to democracy and the supporting traditions of social and political pluralism.[7] Another is John Williams, who advises that the U.S. "must become aware that . . . [fundamentalists] are not our enemies, but our partners and potential friends, who can be talked to and who can be understood."[8]

Although Pipes acknowledges that there are differences between various fundamentalist Muslim groups, he contends that "the notion of good and bad fundamentalist simply has no basis in fact . . . every one of them is inherently extremist."[9] The principal evidence in support of this premise are statements by public figures who have a stake in the existing *status quo,* or else Iranian defenders of the Shah who would naturally be opposed to the Islamic Republic. What seemingly disturbs Pipes and these critics most are the prospects of a "pure Islamic state," which they conclude would be "bound to be a theocracy and totalitarian." Such a state could not help but commit crimes against its own people, its neighbors, Western civilization, and humanity. We can ignore the so-called moderate fundamentalist Muslims, he contends, for by definition they do not exist. Those professing moderation simply cannot be believed.

The basic ideas of contemporary Islamic fundamentalism can be traced back to concepts formulated in the Nineteenth and Twentieth Centuries by reformers such as Muhammad 'Abduh, Jamal al-Din al-Afghani and Muhammad Rashid Rida. Their ideas were essentially responses to Western colonization and the perception in the Islamic world that Muslim culture, values, and traditions were being challenged by Westernization. What fundamentalist groups, past and present, share in common is the call for the detailed application in society of the *sharia*. Fundamentalist groups, however, differ on how to interpret the *sharia* and how strictly it should be applied.

Since medieval times Islam has given rise to various movements and ideas attempting to please God through the application of the *sharia*.[10] Suffice it to say that fundamentalist Islam has manifested itself in divergent ways. One major tendency has been the *salafiyah* (ancestral movement such as the Wahhabis in Saudi Arabia and the Muslim Brotherhood in Egypt). The Wahhabis have sought an Islamic solution to the challenges of modern life by attempting to rid society of all Western influences. Their aim has been a life based strictly on an exoteric interpretation of the *sharia*—a puritanical society.

Similarly, the Brotherhood has sought to revive the moral teachings of Islam in society but adapt them to the requirements of modern living. In the words of Mustafa Mashhur, deputy general guide of the Muslim Brotherhood: "The Muslim Brothers seek to propagate the divine call. They have no worldly ambitions . . . . The Muslim Brothers have not challenged the rulers, nor have they borne arms to topple or depose a ruler."[11]

The direct interest of these two groups in politics and international relations is marginal; their priorities lie elsewhere. To the extent that the Wahhabis are apolitical, the United States has no important national interest in a dialogue with them. On the other hand, the United States may find it advantageous to engage the Muslim Brothers who, although they advocate change, are not an immediate threat to the friendly Egyptian Government.

The second trend, which is of a more recent vintage, is much more political in orientation. It is to this branch of Islamic fundamentalism that Pipes' generalizations most apply: to groups like Islamic Jihad, Groupe Armée Islamique, and Hizballah, the agendas of which usually include national liberation from Israeli occupation and the eradication of Western political and cultural influences.

In the 1950s the Egyptian Sayyid Qutb, the would-be theoretician of modern fundamentalism, argued passionately for applying the *sharia* to politics. To him, Islam is a comprehensive and all-inclusive system under which state and church, beliefs and deeds, religion and politics, are inseparable.

Ayatollah Khomeini carried this political orientation even further, sparking the 1979 Iranian revolution that ended the regime of the Shah—long considered the agent of the West and especially the United States. Khomeini spoke the language of the ordinary person, who "called for arms to be given to the people: if the young men cannot save the country, it is not worth saving; we have not fought a revolution just for security and economic well being, but for Islam, for a just society. . . ."[12]

Qutb's writings and Khomeini's actions combined to give contemporary fundamentalism its radical bent. Indeed, theirs is a new creed calling for a total revolution to restructure society on a new basis. They view the world in a state of conflict in which Muslims have no choice but to wage *jihad* (holy war) against the forces of Satan (the U.S. and its Western allies), and consequently, they dismiss any possibility of coexistence between the contending forces—the struggle can end only in the triumph of Islam.

Voices of Accommodation and Moderation

Aware of the negative connotations of the term "Islamic fundamentalism," especially in the West, the Muslim Brotherhood issued a recent statement clarifying its position on several questions designed to dispel the negative image associated with fundamentalism. The Brotherhood wanted to explain its position toward contentious contemporary issues, including political pluralism, democracy and women's rights.[13] Its tenor was one of accommodation and moderation.

On the question of pluralism, the Brotherhood acknowledged that their Christian compatriots in Egypt have equal rights and obligations and are "partners in the homeland and our brothers in the long national struggle. They enjoy full citizenship rights, moral and material, civic and political. It is an Islamic obligation to be kind to them and cooperate with them."[14]

As for democracy, the statement noted that Islam does not follow the divine right of rulers. Instead, regimes are legitimate if they please the people, are chosen by them, and allow them to participate in decision-making. The declaration also noted the importance of political opposition since the latter provide "protection against the despotism and tyranny of the majority."[15] And, in the best tradition of liberal democratic norms, it denounced and rejected terrorism and violence as detrimental to the security of the nation and a threat to economic and political progress.

Finally, there was the reassertion that Islam honors man and humanity and rises above differences in race, color or creed, and that the Muslim Brothers respect the human rights of all and seek to facilitate the means by which freedom can be practiced within existing legal and moral frameworks:

> Here we are, holding our book in our right hand; this is the testimony we give ourselves; this is our call for wisdom and good advice for a new chapter in the relations between people and nations, from which evil will be pulled out by the roots and everyone will return to the arena of justice, freedom and peace.[16]

Islam and Progress

The negative image of Islam and fundamentalism in the Western world concerns many Muslims, including some prominent Islamic fundamentalists, who have begun an effort to project Islam in a favorable manner. One such prominent polemicist of Islamic fundamentalism, with influence across the Islamic world, is the Western-educated Dr. Hasan al-Turabi, the leader of the National Islamic Front of Sudan.[17]

A central premise of al-Turabi's thought is a cyclical theory of history: not only do nations and civilizations follow cycles over long stretches of time, but so do ideologies. Therefore, Islam will replace the foreign ideologies of liberalism, communism and nationalism. Among Muslims, Islam is experiencing a renaissance, and will replace secularism and all its ills with the duty of serving God first.

Al-Turabi's vision of Islam and Islamic government is avant-garde, well-reasoned and modernist in tone. He argues, ". . . God wants us to mobilize ourselves for progress . . . Islam is spiritual, it is intellectual, it is material. Islam demands progress."[18] In this sense, al-Turabi sets himself apart from the *salafis*, viewing Islam as fully engaged in the modern world and its issues. For example, he favors a societal role for women on the same footing as men, including the rights to serve in the military, police, and government. He denounces terrorism and violence, and calls for a dialogue among the monotheistic religions whose aim is to support faith, morality, and decency.[19]

The views of many Muslim intellectuals on contemporary topics were issued by a committee at the conclusion of "The Nationalist-Islamist Conference" held in Beirut during October 1994.[20] Among the declared principles included in this document were a recognition of the need for *ijtihad* (judicial interpretation) by qualified jurists to address the needs of the contemporary age. The Islamic nation, it was said, cannot be allowed to stagnate by simply imitating the past. Also, with respect to the West and its civilization, the paper declared that, based on their ideology, culture and traditions, Islamists believe in pluralism and respect for other cultures and traditions just as they respect political pluralism. The declaration calls for a constructive dialogue with the West on issues of mutual concern and condemned all acts of terrorism.

Proof of Moderation

Unfortunately, acts of violence committed by Hamas, Islamic Jihad, Hizballah, and Armé Islamique Du Salut overshadow moderate statements made by leading Islamist thinkers. Pipes would probably say that actions speak louder than words, and that the only acceptable evidence of moderation is a long record of total absence of violence.

But the evidence should also include the stated positions and declarations of leaders, especially religious leaders, who have a major influence on the behavior of followers. The foregoing strongly supports the claim that there are Islamist moderates who are tolerant of opposing viewpoints, recognize the rights of minorities, are forward looking, and above all, abhor and condemn terrorism as a legitimate means to political ends. What the Muslim Brothers, al-Turabi and others are seeking is a dialogue with the West, and their statements are a form of assurance that such a dialogue is both possible and potentially productive.

To be sure, lip-service to Western political ideas on the part of Islamists is not absolute proof of their moderation. Nor does it exonerate those among them for whatever past acts of violence they may have perpetrated or for which they have been responsible. But it does suggest that there is a movement in the right direction that ought to be encouraged. It is precisely because Islamists understand the language of the West that the latter should engage those who clearly and openly denounce terrorism and violence as legitimate means to achieving political ends.

The Growth of Islam

Pipes himself has concluded that "... Islamism's potential grows as do its numbers. Current trends suggest that it will remain a force for some time to come."[21] Because it is a force, it behooves the West to attempt to channel Islamism's political energy toward peaceful and productive ends. The dialogue may well prove to be unproductive; nevertheless, it must be given a chance.

The issue could be viewed from yet another angle. As already noted, Pipes believes that the "clash of civilizations" with fundamental Islam is inevitable, and that the fundamentalists' acquisition of a "Western mind" makes them even more formidable enemies. But as R. K. Ramazani has persuasively argued, the history of the encounter between the West and Islam is not a "clash of civilizations" but a process of mutual adaptation and accommodation—"the truth is that civilizations also blend."[22] Ramazani views the current state of world politics following the collapse of the Soviet Union and the end of the bipolar world as one of uncertainty in all human relations, and notes that "Civilizations will continue to clash and blend at least to the end of the century . . . . although clashes of all kinds characterize our age of uncertainty, this reality must not blind us to the fact that our time is also encouragingly marked by numerous and significant acts of human compromise, accommodation and agreement."[23]

Using the framework of the clash and blending of civilizations, it becomes plausible to argue that the interaction between the West and fundamentalist Islam is such a relationship. The clash lies in the fact that most fundamentalist movements seek to reorder their societies along new lines, which is disruptive of the *status quo* often presided over by pro-Western regimes and rulers. The existence of "moderate" Islamists who understand the political and philosophical concepts of the West is a sign of the blending of civilizations. It does not serve the interests of the West to block that step.

U.S. Policy Toward Islam

Its national interests require that the U.S. must remain engaged in global affairs, not as the world's policeman or its social worker, but as the major catalyst for an emerging new world order in the Information Age. The realization that the U.S. has international responsibilities in the post-Cold War period has shaped the policies of the Bush and the Clinton Administrations toward Islam and fundamentalism.

The U.S. position was first enunciated by then Assistant Secretary of State for Near Eastern and South Asian Affairs Edward P. Djerejian in June 1992. At that time, many "conspiracy" theories had been circulating in the region seeking to explain the "true" causes of the Gulf War, the "real" intentions of the U.S. in the region, and its "obdurate" attitude toward Islam and Muslims. In such an emotionally charged environment, Djerejian sought to dispel fears that the U.S. Government was contributing to the perception of "a widening gap between Western values and those of the Muslim world." He emphasized that the "U.S. Government does not view Islam as the next 'ism' confronting the West or threatening world peace," and noted that "we acknowledge Islam as a historic civilizing force among the many that have influenced and enriched our culture." About Islamic fundamentalist movements, he suggested that "we detect no monolithic or coordinated international effort behind these movements."

The U.S. policy of support for human rights, pluralism, minority rights, and popular participation in government, does not mean that the American model should be imposed on others. Nonetheless,

> Those who are prepared to take specific steps toward free elections, creating independent judiciaries, promoting the rule of law, reducing restrictions on the press, respecting the right of minorities, and guaranteeing individual rights will find us ready to recognize and support their efforts, just as those moving in the opposite direction will find us ready to speak candidly and act accordingly.[24]

Thirteen months later, before the House Foreign Affairs Committee, Djerejian detailed the Clinton Administration's position on the subject. He voiced concern over connections between extremist groups and radical regimes such as Iran and the Sudan, and noted that the U.S. parts company with "those individuals—and governments—who seek to advance their agenda through violence, through terror, through intolerance, through coercion. Our quarrel is with extremism, whether in a religious or secular guise."[25] Similarly, the U.S. does not look with favor on those who use the democratic process as a vehicle to monopolize political power. In other words, "while we support the principle of 'one man, one vote,' we do not support 'one man, one vote, one time'."[26]

The Department of State has devised logical policies for the achievement of U.S. national interests in the region. Those policies clearly reflect our values. The U.S. respects Islam as one of the world's great religions, and acknowledges peoples' rights to aspire and work to improve their political, social and economic circumstances. Also, the U.S. prefers and counsels that the process of social, economic and political change be peaceful and one that will not close the door on subsequent demands for further change.

The statements of several Islamic fundamentalist leaders make it clear that the change to which they aspire should be accomplished peacefully, preserving the broad principles of democracy, rule of law, majority rule, minority rights, freedom of expression, and political participation. A dialogue with such individuals cannot harm U.S. interests.[27] Indeed, if Pipes is right that Islamic fundamentalism is a phenomenon whose popularity is on the increase in the Muslim world, such a dialogue is imperative.

NOTES

1. For a detailed discussion of the views of American scholars on this subject, see the two articles: Peter W. Rodman, "Co-opt or Confront Fundamentalist Islam?" and Norvell B. De Atkine, "Middle East Scholars Strike Out in Washington," *Middle East Quarterly*, Vol. 1, No. 4 (December 1994).
2. Daniel Pipes, "There Are No Moderates—Dealing With Fundamentalist Islam," *The National Interest*, No. 41, (Fall 1995), pp. 48-57. This article is representative of the major arguments by Western scholars against Islamic fundamentalism.
3. Ibid., pp. 52-53.
4. Ibid., p. 48.
5. See J.L. Talmon, *The Origins of Totalitarian Democracy* (New York: Praeger, 1961), pp. 1-13.
6. Ibid., p. 10.
7. This is the thesis of John Esposito's book, *The Islamic Threat: Myth or Reality?* (New York: Oxford University Press, 1992).
8. John A. Williams, "The Revival of Islam in the Modern World," *America*, October 13, 1990, p. 240.
9. Pipes, "There Are No Moderates," p. 54
10. For a detailed discussion of fundamentalist ideas from an Islamic perspective, see John O. Voll, "Renewal and Reform in Islamic History: Tajdid and Islah," in John Esposito, ed., *Voices of Resurgent Islam* (New York: Oxford University Press, 1983).
11. Interview with Mustafa Mashhur in *Cairo Al-Nur*, March 8, 1995, p. 4 (FBIS-NES-95-051, March 16, 1995, p. 12).
12. Michael M. J. Fischer, "Imam Khomeini: Four Levels of Understanding," in John Esposito, ed., *Voices of*

Resurgent Islam, p. 162. For a detailed discussion of Qutb's ideas, see Yvonne Y. Haddad, "Sayyid Qutb: Ideologue of Islamic Revival," in Esposito, *Voices of Resurgent Islam.*
13. Statement to the Public from the Muslim Brotherhood in *Cairo Al-Sha'b*, May 2, 1995 (FBIS-NES-95-090, May 10, 1995).
14. Ibid., pp. 1-2.
15. Ibid., p. 2.
16. Ibid., p. 3. The centrist and moderate positions of the Muslim Brotherhood are fully discussed in Sana Abed Kotob, "The Accommodationist Speak: Goals and Strategies of the Muslim Brotherhood of Egypt," *International Journal of Middle East Studies,* No. 27 (1995), pp. 321-339.
17. For a biography and detailed discussion of the ideas of al-Turabi, see Judith Miller, "Faces of Fundamentalism: Hasan al-Turabi and Muhammad Fadlallah," *Foreign Affairs,* Vol. 73, No. 6, (November/December 1994). I have selected the example of Hasan al-Turabi because of his popularity and influence in the Islamic world compared to other "moderates" such as Abbasi Madani of the Algerian Islamic Salvation Front (FIS), and Rashed al-Ghanouchi of Tunisia's Al-Nahda (Renaissance) Islamic Party. A dialogue with al-Turabi, and with like-minded Islamists, is in the U.S. national interest. On the other hand, the allegation linking Sudan, and by extension al-Turabi, to international terrorism is certainly a point of concern. If evidence is found connecting him directly to terrorism, then any dialogue with him should be ceased and the reasons publicized in the Muslim world.
18. Al-Turabi interview, *Paris Le Figaro,* April 15, 1995 (FBIS-NEA-95-076, April 20, 1995, p. 20).
19. See ibid. Also in *Qira'at Siyasiyyah* (Political Readings, in Arabic) (Tampa, FL: World and Islam Studies Enterprise), Vol. 5, No. 1 (Winter, 1995), p. 151.
20. This conference brought together some 100 major personalities in the Arab and Islamic world representing various Islamic movements, nationalist parties and independent thinkers. Text of all working papers were published in Arabic in *Qira'at Siyasiyyah,* ibid.
21. Pipes, "The Western Mind of Radical Islam," *First Things,* No. 58, (December 1995), p. 23.
22. R. K. Ramazani, "The Blending of Civilization?" *Middle East Insight,* Vol. XI, No.5 (July-August 1995), p. 15.
23. Ibid., p. 17.
24. Edward P. Djerejian, "The U.S. and the Middle East in a Changing World," Address at the Meridian House International, Washington, DC, June 2, 1992, in *U.S. Department of State Dispatch,* June 8, 1992.
25. Edward P. Djerejian, "U.S. Policy on Recent Developments and Other Issues in the Middle East," Statement before the Subcommittee on Europe and the Middle East of the House Foreign Affairs Committee, Washington, DC, July 27, 1993, in *U.S. Department of State Dispatch,* Vol. 4, No. 32, August 9, 1993.
26. Ibid.
27. Michael Hudson argued recently that the U.S. stands today as the dominant power over the Middle East and concluded that, "Instead of mobilizing against a so-called Islamic threat, a vigorous initiative to promote dialogue would reduce mutual fears and antagonisms." See his "To Play the Hegemon: Fifty Years of U.S. Policy Toward the Middle East," *The Middle East Journal,* Vol. 50, No. 3 (Summer 1996), p. 343.

☆ ☆ ☆ ☆

The Domestic Side of American Foreign Policy

The Public, Public Opinion, and the Media (Articles 12 and 13)
The Role of American Values (Articles 14 and 15)

Conventional political wisdom holds that foreign policy and domestic policy are two very different arenas. Not only are the origins and gravity of the problems different, but the political rules for seeking solutions are dissimilar. Where partisan politics, lobbying, and the weight of public opinion are held to play legitimate roles in the formulation of health, education, or welfare policy, they are seen as corrupting influences in the making of foreign policy. An effective foreign policy demands a quiescent public, one that gives knowledgeable professionals the needed leeway to bring their expertise to bear on the problems. It demands a Congress that unites behind presidential foreign policy doctrines rather than one that investigates failures or pursues its own agenda. In brief, if American foreign policy is to succeed, politics must stop "at the water's edge."

This conventional wisdom has never been shared by all who write on American foreign policy. Two very different groups of scholars have dissented from this inclination to neglect the importance of domestic influences on American foreign policy. One group holds that the essence of democracy lies in the ability of the public to hold policymakers accountable for their decisions, and therefore that elections, interest group lobbying, and other forms of political expression are just as central to the study of foreign policy as they are to the study of domestic policy. A second group of scholars sees domestic forces as important because it is the fundamental nature of society that determines a country's foreign policy. These scholars direct their attention to studying the influence on American foreign policy of such forces as capitalism, American national style, and the structure of elite values.

The debate over how much emphasis to accord domestic influences in the study of American foreign policy went largely unresolved during the cold war, with all sides able to maintain the essential correctness of their position. One of the most visible signs that American foreign policy is undergoing important changes in the post–cold war era is the amount of attention now being given to domestic forces. The altered agenda of the post–cold war era breathed new life into this debate and refocused attention on the domestic side of American foreign policy. Today it seems quite natural to include a discussion of interest groups, public opinion, elections, the nature of American values, and the media in any accounting of American foreign policy. This certainly has been the case in the Clinton Administration. Such diverse policy initiatives as security support for the North American Free Trade Agreement (NAFTA), proposing to end the ban on gays in the military, the reluctance to act in Bosnia, and the perceived need to act in Haiti all were influenced by considerations of domestic politics.

What is not yet clear is which of these public voices will be heard loudest or what they will say. Some fear that rather than serving as a check on policymakers or ensuring that their decisions are in accordance with the will of the American people, domestic forces may stampede policymakers into undertaking rash actions, bring about abrupt shifts in the direction of American foreign policy, or forestall any type of change. Because of these uncertainties, debate continues over whether the increased prominence of domestic factors in formulating American foreign policy is to be applauded or condemned.

The readings in this section provide an overview of the ways in which U.S. domestic politics and foreign policy interact. The first set of articles highlights the growing influence of the public voice in making foreign policy. In "The Common Sense," John Mueller presents ten propo-

UNIT 3

sitions regarding public attitudes toward foreign policy. Then, Garrick Utley, in "The Shrinking of Foreign News: From Broadcast to Narrowcast," provides an overview of the nature of foreign news coverage provided by the media and examines the conflict between the needs of good journalism and the need to make a profit.

The second set of readings focuses on the enduring influence of American values on U.S. foreign policy. George Kennan, one of the leading architects of containment, asserts that the best way for the United States to help small states is to lead by the power of example. Finally, Benjamin Schwarz presents a very different view of American values and how they influence foreign policy. Starting from a neo-Marxian perspective, he analyzes the influence of capitalism on American foreign policy and is critical of American attempts to assert international economic and political control.

Looking Ahead: Challenge Questions

Should policymakers listen to the U.S. public in making foreign policy decisions? Why or why not?

What types of issues are the American public most informed about?

In what ways is U.S. foreign policy true to traditional American values? How did these values apply during the cold war? What role should American values play in making foreign policy?

What is the most effective way for Americans to express their views to the makers of foreign policy?

How much influence does the media have on American foreign policy? Does it promote responsible policy making or encourage failures?

Is American foreign policy driven by the needs of capitalism? What is the proper relationship between business interests and American foreign policy?

What are the most important questions that should be asked in a public opinion poll about American foreign policy?

# Article 12

The Common Sense

John Mueller

A FEW YEARS ago international politics experienced the functional equivalent of World War III, only without the bloodshed. In a remarkably short time, virtually all the major problems that haunted international affairs for a half century were solved. The Cold War evaporated, the attendant arms race was reversed, intense disagreement over Eastern Europe and the division of Germany was resolved, and the threat of expansionist international communism simply withered away. In the wake of this quiet cataclysm, we have entered an extraordinary new era: If we apply conventional standards, the leading countries are today presented at the international level with minor, immediate problems and major long-range ones—but no major immediate problems or threats.

Some international relations scholars and writers have been trying, at times a trifle desperately, to refashion constructs and theories originally designed for an era with compelling threats to fit one that lacks them. Despite their efforts, however, a policy consensus seems to be emerging among those who actually carry out international affairs in the leading countries. It stresses as a primary goal economic enrichment through open markets and freer trade (rather than through empire or triumph in war as in days of old); it allows for the inclusion into the club of those less developed countries that are able to get their acts together; and it seeks cooperatively to alleviate troubles in other parts of the world if this can be done at low cost (particularly in lives), and to isolate and contain those troubles that cannot be so alleviated.

In this new world dominated by unthreatened wealth seekers, public opinion will play its role in U.S. foreign policy, and as always it will be an important one. Many have rued this condition, George Kennan famously among them, but looked at over time, the general sense of the American public on core issues of foreign policy has often been rather coherent and reasonable—sometimes more so than that shown by the country's elites.

There is a considerable cache of good data about public opinion on foreign policy, some of it sufficiently consistent in design over time to show reliable patterns.[1] Such data do not, of course, announce their own interpretations, but their meaning can be teased out. Based on extensive analysis of this data—but without drowning the narrative in a half ton of documentary footnotes—I offer here ten proposi-

---

John Mueller is professor of political science at the University of Rochester. Among his books are *Retreat From Doomsday: The Obsolescence of Major War* (Basic Books, 1989), and *Policy and Opinion in the Gulf War* (University of Chicago Press, 1994).

[1] Huge quantities of public opinion survey results—hundreds of thousands of questions going back to the 1930s—are stored, and readily available for research, at such organizations as the Roper Public Opinion Research Center at the University of Connecticut.

tions about American public opinion that bear important implications for the practice of foreign policy in our new era. Some of these propositions will strike many readers as obvious, others may seem counterintuitive—but not necessarily to the same readers.

1. Two facts are central: The public pays little attention to international affairs, and nothing much can be done about it; this, however, does not mean that Americans have become, or are becoming, isolationist.

Even in an age in which international interdependence is supposedly increasing by the minute, Americans principally focus on domestic matters. From time to time their attention can be diverted by major threats, or by explicit, specific, and dramatic dangers to American lives. But once these troubles vanish from the scene, the public returns to domestic concerns with considerable alacrity. So strong is the evidence on this score that it must be accepted as a fact of life that no amount of elite cajoling or uses of the bully pulpit will ever change.

According to the data, over the last sixty years the few events that have notably caused the public to divert its attention from domestic matters include the Second World War, the Korean War, the Vietnam War, and certain Cold War crises before 1963. Also included in this list, fleetingly at least, were the Iran hostage crisis of 1979-80, perhaps embellished by concern over the Soviet invasion of Afghanistan; the apparent prospect in the early to mid-1980s of nuclear war; and the Gulf War. That's about it; at no time since the 1968 Tet Offensive have foreign policy concerns outweighed domestic ones in the public eye—even in the midst of the Gulf War.

Nevertheless, the data suggest that the public has not become newly isolationist—it is about as accepting of involvement in foreign affairs as ever. That the American public has been able to contain its enthusiasm for sending American troops to police such trouble spots as Bosnia and Haiti does not mean that it has turned isolationist. Americans were willing, at least at the outset, to send troops to die in Korea and Vietnam because they subscribed to the view that communism was a genuine and serious threat to the United States that needed to be stopped wherever it was advancing. But polls from the time make clear that they had little interest in risking American lives simply to help out beleaguered South Koreans or South Vietnamese. Moreover, poll questions designed directly to measure isolationism find little change in the wake of the Cold War. In other words, the public does not pay much attention to foreign affairs most of the time, but it seems ready to care about foreign affairs if there is a clear, obvious reason to do so. This trait has been fairly consistent over many years.

2. The public undertakes a fairly sensible cost-benefit accounting when evaluating foreign affairs and, not unreasonably, the key to its definition of cost is the high value it places on American lives.

Public opinion analysis generally supports the proposition that the American people will tolerate a substantial loss of American lives if the enemy is seen to be powerful and set on jeopardizing vital American interests. But the notion that Americans should die to police a small, distant, perennially troubled, and unthreatening place has always proved difficult to sell. Nor has it been possible to generate much support for the notion that American lives should be put at risk in order to encourage democracy abroad.

After Pearl Harbor the American public had no difficulty accepting the necessity, and the human costs, of confronting the threats posed by Germany and Japan. And after the war, it came to accept international communism as a similar source of threat and was willing to support military action to combat it. However, as the Cold War's hot wars progressed in Korea and Vietnam, the data show clearly that the public undertook a continuing reevaluation of these premises, and, as it did, misgivings mounted. The data also suggest that these misgivings were primarily a function of cumulating American casualties, not of television coverage and, in the case of Vietnam, definitely not of antiwar protest.

Policy in the Gulf War was subject to a similar calculus. Many Americans bought George Bush's notion that it was worth some American lives—perhaps one or two thousand, far lower than in Korea or Vietnam—to turn back Saddam Hussein's aggression in Kuwait. But it is clear from poll data that support for the effort would have eroded quickly if significant casualties had been suffered.

While the public's concern about American lives often seems nuanced, there are times when it becomes so obsessive, so unreasonable by some standards, that policy may suffer in consequence. In the case of Vietnam, public opinion essentially supported the war until American prisoners-of-war held by Hanoi were returned; after that burden was eased, the weight of growing misgivings overtook any inclination to press on. Although some might question the wisdom of continuing a war costing thousands of lives to gain the return of a few hundred prisoners, it would be difficult to exaggerate the political potency of this issue. In a May 1971 poll, 68 percent agreed that U.S. troops should be withdrawn from Vietnam by the end of the year. However, when asked if they approved of withdrawal "even if it threatened [not *cost*] the lives or safety of United States POWs held by North Vietnam", support for withdrawal plummeted to 11 percent.

The emotional attachment to prisoners-of-war has been a recurring theme in the politics of U.S. military interventions. It was central to the lengthy and acrimonious peace talks in Korea, and outrage at the fate of American POWs on Bataan probably generated as much hatred for the Japanese during the Second World War as the attack on Pearl Harbor. Saddam Hussein's decision to parade captured American pilots on television early in the Gulf War ranks among his many major blunders. The preoccupation with hostages held by Iran during the crisis of 1979-81, and after that the fate of a few abducted Americans in Lebanon—a concern that helped to generate the Iran-Contra scandal—are also cases in point.

On the other hand, Americans seem quite insensitive to casualties suffered by foreigners, including foreign civilians. During the Gulf War Americans displayed little animosity toward the Iraqi people. However, the available data show that this view did not translate into sympathy for Iraqi casualties. Extensive coverage of civilian deaths in an attack on a Baghdad bomb shelter had no effect on attitudes toward U.S. bombing policy. Similarly, images of the "highway of death", and early postwar reports that 100,000 Iraqi soldiers had died in the war (a figure too high probably by a factor of more than ten), scarcely dampened the enthusiasm of the various "victory" parades and celebrations.[2]

These basic characteristics of American opinion are also illustrated by the public response to the international mission to Somalia in 1992-93. American policy there has been labeled a "failure" because, although tens and probably hundreds of thousands of foreign lives were saved, a few Americans were killed in the process. In essence, when Americans asked themselves how many American lives peace in Somalia was worth, the answer was rather close to zero.

3 The public's attitudes on foreign affairs are set much more by the objective content of the issue and by the position of major policymakers (including the political opposition) than by the media.

The media are not so much agenda setters as purveyors and entrepreneurs of tantalizing information and, like any other entrepreneur, they are susceptible to market forces. If they give an issue big play, it may arrest attention for a while, but this is no guarantee the issue will "take." As with any business enterprise, media moguls follow up on those proffered items that stimulate their customers' interest. In that very important sense, the media does not set the agenda, the public does.

Concern about the Ethiopian famine of the mid-1980s, for example, is often taken to have been media-generated since it was only after the problem received prominent play that it entered the public's agenda. However, the media were at first reluctant to cover the issue because they saw African famine as a dog-bites-man story. Then NBC television decided to buck the consensus and do a three-day sequence on it, and this in turn inspired a huge public response, whereupon NBC gave the crisis extensive follow-up coverage while its television and print competitors scrambled to get on the bandwagon. There is a sense, of course, in which it could be said that NBC put the issue on the public's agenda. But the network is constantly doing three-day stories, and this one just happened to catch on, to strike a responsive chord. It seems more accurate, then, to say that NBC put the item on display—alongside a great many others—and

---

[2] On Iraqi casualties, see my essay, "The Perfect Enemy", *Security Studies* (Autumn 1995).

that it was the public that found it there, picked it out, and took it home.

4 The "CNN effect" is vastly exaggerated. It follows from the above that the argument that television pictures set the public's agenda and policy mood—the so-called CNN effect—is hard to credit. This effect is usually taken to mean that televised images can cause intense interest where there might otherwise be none, and that such interest can have important effects on policy. Sometimes this might be the case, but, on balance, the CNN effect is exaggerated, and some interpretations of it seem well off the mark.

Essentially, believers in the CNN effect contend that people are so unimaginative that they react only when they see something visualized. However, Americans were outraged and quickly mobilized over the Pearl Harbor attack months before they saw any pictures of the event. Less obvious but more important, the Vietnam War was not noticeably more unpopular than the Korean War for the period in which the wars produced comparable American casualties, despite the fact that the later war was a "television war", while the earlier one was fought during that medium's infancy.

The conventional wisdom about the CNN effect amounts to a triumph of myth over matter. After all, for years we were deluged by pictures of horrors in Bosnia and, while these pictures may have influenced the opinion of some editorial writers and columnists, there was remarkably little public demand to send American troops over to fix the problem. Nor did poignant and memorable pictures inspire a surging public demand to do much of anything about Rwanda or Haiti. The reason, it would seem from the data, is disarmingly simple: Whatever the pictures showed, the public saw no serious threat to American security in either of these cases that could justify risking American lives.

On those rare occasions when pictures have—or seem to have—an impact, as over Ethiopia in the mid-1980s, observers eagerly note the fact. But when pictures fail to have an impact, the same observers fail to notice *that* fact—or come up with tortured accountings to explain the media's lack of impact. This slippery process is nicely illustrated by the case of the journalist Jack Germond.

As the Haitian crisis was heating up in 1994, Germond pointedly noted that "We're seeing the coverage of children starving and ill and so forth." When it was pointed out to him that the polls were suggesting that most Americans did not want troops in Haiti because it was not in the country's vital national interest, Germond responded, "The numbers might change if we keep getting all this film about the starving kids there." However, when the numbers didn't change, he later mused, "It's interesting that three or four years ago in Somalia, for example, television film of starving children was enough to make the country act. Now, television film of starving children in Haiti and atrocities is not enough." Groping for an explanation, Germond philosophized, "No one wants to say so, but there's a race factor here. There's no question about that."[3] That the starving children in Haiti happened to be of the same race as those in Somalia did not dampen his punditry in the slightest.

Another example: One explanation offered for the unwillingness of the American public to send troops to Bosnia is that the constant suffering shown on television happened not to "sensitize" the public but rather "inured" it.[4] We are supposed to believe that whether the public, in its collective wisdom, concludes that troops should or should not be sent, television is always somehow the cause. It isn't.

5 Foreign policy has become less important in judging the performance of the president and of presidential contenders.

During the Cold War, foreign policy was often important in presidential elections, but in its wake the general tendency of the American public to ignore foreign policy in national elections has been given free reign. Banking on his Gulf War success and on his opponent's lack of experience in foreign policy, George Bush tried hard to make foreign

---

[3] Quotations taken from transcripts of "The McLaughlin Group", Public Broadcasting Service, July 1 and September 16, 1994.

[4] See Clifford Orwin, "Distant Compassion: CNN and Borrioboola-Gha", *The National Interest* (Spring 1996).

affairs a central issue in the 1992 campaign, but failed. His ratings for handling the economy plummeted within days of the end of the war as the public quickly refocussed its attention on domestic matters. And when candidate Bill Clinton went out of his way to deliver a few serious foreign policy speeches, he found them generating little public or press attention. As suggested by the 1996 campaign, this phenomenon is likely to continue.

6 The advantage to a president of a success in a minor foreign policy venture is marginal; the disadvantage to a president of a failure in such a venture is more than marginal, but still far from devastating unless the failure becomes massively expensive.

If George Bush found little lasting electoral advantage in a large dramatic victory like the Gulf War, smaller accomplishments are likely to be even less rewarding in an era of great foreign policy inattention. America's recent venture into Haiti has been a success by most reasonable standards. Yet, while surely a feather in his cap, this venture has garnered Bill Clinton little credit—though it probably helped to diffuse his reputation for foreign policy ineptitude as a potential Republican campaign issue. Something similar could be said for his successes—possibly of historical importance—on the North American Free Trade Agreement and on the General Agreement on Tariffs and Trade.

Although messing up marginal ventures can be politically damaging by contrast, particularly if seen to fall within a pattern of poor performance, the costs need not be high. This stems from the fact that the public has shown a willingness to abandon an overextended or untenable position after American lives have been lost: The deaths of eighteen U.S. soldiers in Somalia in 1993, for example, led to outraged demands for withdrawal, not for calls to revenge the humiliation.

This episode, as well as the withdrawal from Lebanon after a truck bomb killed 241 U.S. Marines in 1983, suggests that when peacekeeping leads to unacceptable deaths, peacekeepers can be readily removed with little concern for saving face. If a venture is seen to be of little importance in terms of serious American interests, a president can, precisely because of that, cut and run without fear of inordinate electoral costs—though it will hardly be something to brag about. U.S. military interventions, then, need not become "quagmires."

7 If they are not being killed, American troops can remain in peacekeeping ventures virtually indefinitely with little public criticism; it is not important to have an "exit strategy", a "closed-end commitment", or "a time-certain for withdrawal" except for the purpose of selling an intervention in the first place.

Although there is an overwhelming political demand that casualties be extremely low in ventures deemed of minor importance, there seems to be little problem with keeping occupying forces in place as long as they are not being killed. After the deadly Somalia firefight, the Americans stayed on for several months and, since there were no further casualties, little attention was paid or concern voiced. Similarly, although there was scant public or political support for sending U.S. troops to Haiti, there has been almost no protest about keeping them there since none have been killed. And Americans have tolerated—indeed, hardly noticed—the stationing of hundreds of thousands of U.S. troops in Europe, Japan, and South Korea for decades on end. If they are not being killed, it scarcely matters whether the troops are in Macedonia or in Kansas.

On the other hand, if American troops start to take casualties while on peacekeeping missions, there will be demands to get them out quickly, whatever "date-certain" for withdrawal had been previously arranged. Thus, despite calls for knowing in advance what the endgame will look like, the only real "exit strategy" required is the tactical flexibility to yank the troops abruptly from the scene if things go awry.

8 A venture deemed of small importance is best sold not with cosmic internationalist hype, but rather as international social work that can be shrugged off if it goes wrong.

Most of the knotty and dramatic international problems that occupy the headlines are of remarkably little concern to the United States if one applies commonly accepted standards of what constitutes the national interest—and the public seems to be applying exactly those standards. Many problems are, in fact, mainly humanitarian in nature, exercises in what Michael Mandelbaum has called international "social work."[5]

But the notion of the United States doing international social work is not necessarily a non-starter. There is, after all, adequate support for domestic social work. International social work might best be sold in the same way as the domestic variety—as a good faith effort that can be abandoned if the client proves untreatable, rather than wrapped in the false guise of strategic interest. By contrast, in 1995 President Clinton argued that, "If war reignites in Bosnia, it could spark a much wider conflagration. In 1914, a gunshot in Sarajevo launched the first of two world wars"—a historical parallel that was wildly overdrawn, as numerous commentators promptly pointed out. Despite Clinton's claim that a new war in Bosnia "could spread like a cancer throughout the region", the "conflagration" in Bosnia seems, if anything, to have been successfully contained.

In principle, grandiloquent rhetoric can restrict later policy flexibility: If the fate of Europe really does hinge on tiny Bosnia (Clinton: "Europe will not come together with a brutal conflict raging at its heart"), failure there would be disaster. Fortunately, however, the public often seems more sensible on such matters than its leaders. When he sent the Marines to help police Lebanon, Ronald Reagan declared that "in an age of nuclear challenge and economic interdependence, such conflicts are a threat to all the people of the world, not just to the Middle East itself." Despite such an overblown sales pitch, however, the public had no difficulty accepting Reagan's later decision to have the Marines "re-deployed to the sea" after 241 of them were killed by a truck bomb.

The American people clearly do not spend a lot of time musing over public policy issues, particularly international ones. But they *are* grown-ups and, generally, they react as such. Policymakers might do well occasionally to notice this elemental and important fact.

---

[5]Michael Mandelbaum, "Foreign Policy as Social Work", *Foreign Affairs* (January/February 1996).

9 A danger in peacekeeping missions is that Americans might be taken hostage, something that can suddenly and disproportionately magnify the perceived stakes.

Because of the overriding importance Americans place on American lives, policy in low-valued ventures remains vulnerable to hostage-taking. As noted, peacekeeping missions need not become quagmires because the president can still abruptly withdraw troops from an overextended position with little long-lasting political cost. However, this flexibility can be dramatically compromised if American troops are taken hostage.

This is illustrated by some evidence from the Somalia episode. In the debacle of October 1993, a Somali group captured one American soldier. Polls clearly demonstrated that the public was determined that U.S. forces remain until the prisoner was recovered and only then to withdraw. Some opposition to placing U.S. soldiers on the Golan Heights between Israel and Syria has rested in part upon fear that U.S. personnel might be taken hostage by Syrian-supported Shi'a fundamentalists—and perhaps killed as well, as was the fate of Lt. Col. William Higgins in 1989. While such fears may be exaggerated, and sometimes pressed into political service for ulterior reasons, the concern is by no means baseless.

10 Nuclear weapons in the hands of rogue states and international terrorism remain potentially attention-arresting concerns.

In an era free of compelling threats, few concerns can turn the public's attention to foreign affairs. However, polls show that from time to time nuclear weapons do seem to retain some of their legendary attention-arresting aura, and the same may hold for biological and chemical weapons.

While it is not entirely clear what a country like North Korea, Iran, Iraq would actually do with a nuclear weapon or two—confronted as they are by countries that have thousands of them—alarm over such a possibility can rise to notable levels. In 1994, 82 percent of the public (up from 58 percent four years earlier) identified "preventing the spread of nuclear weapons" as a very important foreign policy goal—putting it in third place in the poll's sixteen-item list. (The top two goals were really more of domestic than of foreign policy concern: "stopping the flow of illegal drugs into the U.S." and "protecting the jobs of American workers.") The public also selected "the possibility of unfriendly countries becoming nuclear powers" as the top "critical threat" to the United States.

The public's fear of international terrorism is also quite robust. On average, international terrorism kills fewer Americans each year than lightning, or colliding with a deer. But though terrorism is rather unimportant in that literal sense, it generates fear and concern far out of proportion to its objective significance; it was almost as oft-cited a "critical threat" as nuclear proliferation in the 1994 poll.

IN THE END, it seems, misanthropes and curmudgeons are the only truly happy people: no matter how much things improve, there will always be something to complain about and to worry over. When one problem is solved, another is quickly promoted to take its place. Thus, now that life expectancy has increased to a level that would have tested the credulity of our ancestors a century ago, we, their progeny, worry about the huge budget deficit substantially caused by the fact that people now live so long. Most Americans believe that there has been an increase over the last twenty years in air pollution and in the number of elderly living in poverty, when the reverse is decidedly the case. "Status quo", as Ronald Reagan reportedly liked to put it, "is Latin for 'the mess we're in'", and there is, reliably, always some mess somewhere to be in.

This general phenomenon carries over to international affairs as well. When a peace mission helps peoples in the former Yugoslavia to stop killing each other, pundits are quick to find fault because it is unable to entice them to love each other as well. Thus there is a school of thought that contends that the post-Cold War era is just as dangerous as the one we have left behind, and it counsels keeping commitments and defense spending high, and tolerance for the mischief of others low. So, even in a state of considerable peace the catastrophe quota will always remain comfortably full. Although the chances of a global thermonuclear war—or indeed of any war among major developed countries—have diminished to the point where remarkably few even remember the terror it once inspired, one can concentrate on more vaporous enemies like insecurity, uncertainty, instability, and what one European foreign minister, the late Johan Jørgen Holst of Norway, darkly labeled "unspecified risks and dangers."[6] Or one can declare our new era to be profoundly, even dangerously, "complex" by conveniently forgetting the difficult and painful choices of the Cold War: The United States once had to treat Mobutu Sese Seko of Zaire as a dictator who brought his country to ruin, but who had been on the right side in the Cold War; today it can treat him merely as a dictator who has brought his country to ruin.

In any event, it is clear that alarums about uncertainty and complexity from academics and pensive foreign diplomats will not cure the attention deficit disorder that, as usual, characterizes the American public's approach to international affairs. In an era free of compelling threats, the public is likely to continue happily to focus its ennui and its *Weltschmerz* on parochial matters, not foreign ones—at least until there is good reason for them to do otherwise. Given the record of its generally good sense, that is perhaps not such a tragedy.

---

[6]Johan Jørgen Holst, "European and Atlantic Security in a Period of Ambiguity", *The World Today* (December 1992), p. 218.

The Shrinking of Foreign News

From Broadcast to Narrowcast

Garrick Utley

Television's foreign correspondents do not travel light. Off camera, their distinguishing feature is the small mountain of equipment traveling with them, which sets baggage handlers to dreaming of large tips and airlines to calculating budget-busting excess-weight charges.

The financial burden of that luggage is only one factor making the network television foreign correspondent an endangered species. New technologies in cable and satellite TV have turned the stable, predictable, almost automatically profitable television marketplace into a competitive cauldron in which journalism must increasingly compete with entertainment programming. This has prompted a redefining, or at least a questioning, of the traditional news agenda in the post–Cold War world. Producers and network executives believe the American mass audience's interest in daily events beyond their nation's borders is declining, so little such news is offered—which exacerbates the high cost/low return (or low visibility) nature of international coverage today. On-screen sightings of foreign correspondents grow rarer in the place where the most people would see them—on the networks. According to the *Tyndall Report*, total foreign coverage on network nightly news programs has declined precipitously, from 3,733 minutes in 1989 to 1,838 minutes in 1996 at ABC, the leader, and from 3,351 minutes to 1,175 minutes at third-place NBC.

A PARTNERSHIP WITH THE CAMERA

The image of the correspondent reporting from some troubled land has become firmly imprinted in viewers' imaginations, particularly since 1963. Televised coverage of the assassination of John F. Kennedy bonded viewers to what was beginning to be called a "medium," which could convey human experience and emotions as they could never rise off the printed page. A Roper poll that year found for the first time that television was the main source of news for more Americans than newspapers. Moreover, in 1963 NBC and CBS expanded their nightly news programs from 15 minutes to 30. Some at the networks wondered whether there was an audience—and, therefore, sponsors—for the longer newscasts. More pressing yet, would there be enough news to fill the half-hour? One solution was to build up foreign coverage and the role of foreign correspondents.

From the beginning, a television foreign correspondent performed three functions. First, he—it was a mostly male club—was a journalist reporting the story. He was also the report's producer, deciding what events or visual elements needed to be filmed and what interviews recorded to make the story. In the half-hour for-

---

GARRICK UTLEY, former Chief Foreign Correspondent for NBC News and ABC News, is a Contributor at CNN.

mat, reports initially ran a minimum of two and a half minutes and often three to five minutes, compared with one and a half minutes or even less today. Reports required a narrative line with the reporter as storyteller, which brought up the correspondent's third role, more image-driven than the first two but equally essential: he was a familiar figure who established the news program's "presence" in the story. Merely by being there, the correspondent gave the network credibility, demonstrating to viewers that his organization spared no effort or expense to be on the scene anywhere in the world where important events were taking place.

Almost immediately, however, it became apparent that the correspondent had a partner with a will of its own: the camera. If television's greatest strength was the transmission of human experience rather than facts, analysis, or concepts, the correspondent ran the risk of becoming little more than a caption writer for the moving pictures. Vietnam brought the issue to a head, as sounds and images of Americans at war resonated in living rooms stateside. Even as they enjoyed the status and visibility television bestowed on them, the correspondents in Vietnam found themselves losing editorial autonomy and the pictures' compelling force taking over. Recognizing the immense power of the new visual language, television journalists eventually reached an accommodation with it.

TV COVERS THE EARTH

Then as now, the question facing the foreign correspondent was whether television news, besides offering drama and emotion, could add, if not to viewers' detailed knowledge of the world, at least to their awareness of it. The answer, I believe, is that it has, although the effect is difficult to quantify. Television had an impact on public opinion, which in turn affected the government's formulation of foreign policy, during and after the Tet offensive in Vietnam in 1968, the seizure of the American embassy in Tehran in 1979, the terrorist attack on the Marine Corps barracks in Beirut in 1982, and the killing of American troops in Somalia in 1994. Amid the background noise of the beating of nativist drums and ideologues' declamations, there are few signs that a majority of Americans seek a return to the "splendid isolation" or the Fortress America of the pre-television era. Many factors have contributed to that relative openness to the world, but TV has played a central role.

The growth of network television news coincided with a broadening of the foreign news agenda. Until the 1960s, correspondents (print and electronic) were based primarily in the European capitals and Tokyo. Those covering Latin America, Africa, the Middle East, and the rest of Asia were allotted few column inches and little airtime, regardless of what was going on in those regions. In the 1960s, however, that changed rapidly, not only because of the longer network newscasts but also because of the growing prominence of the Third World and the nonaligned nations movement, both seen in the context of the Cold War rivalry. The 1955 Bandung Conference, trouble in Indochina, the Congo crisis of 1959-62, and armed conflict between India and Pakistan in the 1960s and 1970s meant that correspondents could no longer remain in familiar capitals working their traditional sources. For all the expertise and language skills they had acquired, news was occurring far from London, Paris, or Tokyo.

Travel became a key part of the foreign correspondent's job description. The advent of the Boeing 707 halved the time it took journalists to get to another continent. In the 1970s the routine use of communications satellites made same-day coverage possible, increasing the incentive for reporters and camera crews to race off to breaking stories in remote locations. Newscasts saw a marked shift from overseas feature and background stories to hard news. They gained the immediacy of broadcasting "today's news today," at the cost of the more explanatory coverage that had been part of the evening news of earlier years.

For the foreign correspondent, instant satellite communications left little time for developing expertise in a specific country. Reporters became known as "firemen," flying from one international conflagration to the next. In March 1978 I was based in London, working for NBC News. On a Monday morning of a quiet news period, I had no plans to leave the city. By Saturday, I had covered South Moluccans seizing hostages in the Netherlands, the Israeli incursion to the Litani River in southern Lebanon, and the kidnapping of Prime Minister Aldo Moro in Rome, and had returned home—three stories in three countries on two continents in five days.

COLD WAR CONSUMERS

The mass public in the United States has never shown much sustained interest in what is happening abroad. Throughout the nation's history, the American sense of self-containment has rarely been challenged, and then only by direct threats to U.S. interests. The Barbary pirates' "terrorism," the War of 1812, and the sinking of the *Maine* were international punctuation marks of the nineteenth century. In this century, too, Americans' interest in foreign affairs has generally been limited to war and the threat of war. The longest of these conflicts, the Cold War, coincided with the growth of television, from the late 1940s to the late 1980s.

For those four decades, the East-West conflict was the global environment in which Americans lived. As long as nuclear weapons were aimed at American communities, the question of personal security took on an international dimension. Journalists quickly discovered that they could sell their editors—because their editors could sell the public—almost any story pegged to a Soviet or communist threat, from crises in Berlin to Vietnam to Angola. The dynamics were not unlike those in the defense industry or in politics, where a new weapons system or an anticommunist crusade could always be justified as part of the Cold War struggle.

Afghanistan is a vivid example. In the 1980s the war there received extensive television news coverage so long as the story was about Soviet expansionism. After the Soviet Union's withdrawal in 1989, news coverage in general and network television coverage in particular plummeted, even though Afghan factions were fighting each other with brutal intensity. Not until last October, when Taliban forces occupied Kabul and cameras recorded the excesses of the victors and their vision of Islamic law—hanging bodies and women ordered to stay at home—was the American news appetite whetted again.

The passing of the Cold War era has left many institutions adrift, searching for a new order or definition, and television news is no exception. Without stories from abroad that could be presented as part of an overall threat to American security, newscasts suffered a severe loss in an increasingly competitive medium that thrives—perhaps depends—on drama and conflict to attract and hold an audience's attention. The external threats (say, ICBMs) have been replaced by what many perceive as the threats at home (a mugger on the street corner, drugs, children born out of wedlock).

Paradoxically, broad viewer interest in world affairs is declining from its modest Cold War heights just as U.S. global influence is reaching new levels as the result of several administrations' efforts to expand trade, businesses' need to expand overseas, and the global dominance of American popular culture, all driven by American leadership in the development and exploitation of new technologies. Today more Americans than ever before are working and traveling abroad, from CEOs to sales reps, students, and tourists. International trade is equal to about one-quarter of GDP.

Americans who see themselves as

global players (or are merely curious about foreign affairs) find that more international information is available than ever before, from sources targeting smaller audiences. Satellites transmit daily television programs from Europe, the Middle East, Asia, and Latin America to niche and ethnic markets in the United States. One can choose from among on-line computer services or download volumes of free information and comment from sites on the World Wide Web. Television offers numerous business and financial channels and the all-news channels—CNN, which began broadcasting in 1980; MSNBC; and the fledgling Fox News—many of which operate around the clock. The Public Broadcasting Service's "NewsHour with Jim Lehrer" also maintains a journalistic sensibility attuned to international affairs, although it cannot provide much in the way of on-site coverage. National Public Radio and Public Radio International offer extensive international reporting for a fraction of the production costs required in television.

JOURNALISM'S BAGGAGE

More than the other news media, television is caught between the declining interest in international affairs and rising costs and competition. It is the most expensive medium for news, and production costs for international reporting are particularly high. A correspondent for a newspaper, magazine, press agency, or radio station or network is engaged in what is basically one-person journalism. He or she can travel to the scene of a story alone, cover it alone, write it up alone, and transmit it alone via telephone, fax, or E-mail.

Television is of a different organizational magnitude. The basic working unit in international television news consists of a correspondent, a field producer, a cameraperson, and a sound engineer, plus some 600 pounds of camera and personal equipment. If a report is to be prepared for satellite transmission, an editor and an additional 600 pounds of editing equipment come along. (Because American television's technical standards are incompatible with the systems the rest of the world uses, the networks must bring all their own equipment.) The cost of this journalistic caravan, including hotels, per diem expenses, car rentals, and local support staff, begins at around $3,000 a day. Airfare and excess-baggage charges can easily reach $12,000. Then there are "extras" like satellite fees. New digital technology, including smaller and lighter cameras and editing equipment, will eventually reduce costs, but there is no indication that the networks would use the savings to increase international coverage.

Network news divisions are currently spending up to $50 million a year on foreign coverage. While only a fraction of overall network news costs, this is an extremely exposed part of the budget at a time when the cost of television news is already under scrutiny. Advances in cable and satellite distribution systems have caused the broadcast news and information market to fragment, spawning fierce competition. Each of the new services competes for market share among attentive viewers who in the past had only the networks to watch if they wanted to feel informed. At any given moment each of the new channels may have an audience one-tenth or even one-twentieth that of an evening newscast. But together they have cut the networks' share of the television news market approximately 25 percent from the peak years, at the same time that the networks' overall market share has been eroding.

The decline has pushed network news producers to the apparently logical, if journalistically undesirable, conclusion that foreign news is expendable unless it is of compelling interest to a mass audience. The new litmus test at network news programs is whether viewers (in the producers' opinion) will instinctively "relate" to the story. As in other industries, as choice increases, power shifts from the producer to the consumer.

The drive to reduce overseas expenditures has also led to alliances among broadcasters and the growth of television news agencies. The exchange of news video provides worldwide coverage with greater cost efficiency but sacrifices the depth and perspective that an on-the-scene reporter can provide. It is at this juncture that the new competitive pressures collide with the journalistic ethos of the foreign correspondent as well as the expectations of viewers interested in international affairs.

The network news programs and, indeed, news programs in general ought to consider not only whether their response to market forces can sustain good journalism but whether it is a sound long-term business decision. The programs' producers can claim to be focusing on their customers, or at least the largest portion of them. The editorial downsizing, narrowing of focus, and increasing homogeneity of content, however, give viewers searching for broader exposure to the world even less reason to watch the programs. It is a slippery slope.

These days, a television broadcasting company will maintain a costly worldwide operation only if it has a news service that requires (and can help amortize) its international coverage for its audiences in the United States and abroad. The Cable News Network, with its separate domestic and international news services, falls into this category. The new MSNBC (a joint venture of software power Microsoft and NBC) and the Fox News Channel face the challenge of building major international news operations to match CNN. Among the Big Three networks, only ABC News has kept its overseas operation largely intact.

THEY REAP WHAT THEY SHOW

As a few of the most ambitious television news organizations expand internationally, a new shadow looms over the foreign correspondent. With the 1996 merger of Time-Warner and Turner Broadcasting, the parent of CNN, all the major American news divisions are owned by transnational corporations. The financial benefits are clear: Jack Welch, chairman and chief executive officer of NBC's parent company, General Electric, and Rupert Murdoch, who controls Fox, could provide heavy backing for their start-up news channels. Deep pockets count for a lot in the race to create global television empires. But the drive to penetrate new markets and build media imperia raises serious concerns for international reporting and broadcasting. Authorities in the countries on the receiving end often see the news beamed in as politically or culturally undesirable, even subversive. When interests clash, as they inevitably do, good journalism is likely to be sacrificed. The trend is already established.

Item: Australian media magnate Rupert Murdoch's purchase of the Hong Kong–based Star TV satellite system in July 1993 was the keystone of his strategy for dominating satellite broadcasting from the Pacific to the Middle East. The main attraction was China's booming economy and potential consumers. Star TV, however, carried BBC World, the British international television news service. Chinese authorities did not want the BBC's coverage, or that of any other autonomous television news service, entering China. Murdoch bowed to pressure from Beijing and dropped BBC news from Star.

Item: In July 1995 the Walt Disney Co. stunned the media world by buying Capital Cities/ABC. At the press conference announcing the deal, a reporter asked Disney CEO Michael Eisner how he viewed the synergy between the two companies. Eisner's response took on a global dimension: "There are many places in the world, like China, India, and other places, that do not want to accept programming that has any political content. But they have no problem with sports, and they have no problem with Disney kind of programming." Political content, however, is what much of news coverage is about, at ABC or anywhere else. Politics even enters the sports arena, as NBC discovered, and films, as Disney has been reminded. Last year Disney came under intense pressure from China not to release a Martin Scorsese film about the Dalai Lama that the Chinese government believed would be hostile to its claim to Tibet. Disney announced that it would not back down and abandon the film, but Beijing had fired a shot across the company's bow.

Item: At the opening ceremonies of the Olympic Games in Atlanta last summer, NBC Sports commentator Bob Costas angered the Chinese government with his remarks as the Chinese team marched into the stadium. Costas said, according to an NBC transcript, "Every economic power including the United States wants to tap into that huge potential market, but of course there are problems with human rights, property rights disputes, the threat posed to Taiwan." Costas also mentioned suspicions that performance-enhancing drugs could be behind some of the achievements of Chinese athletes. China's state-run media and its Foreign Ministry attacked Costas' comments. A month later NBC issued a statement apologizing "for any resulting hurt feelings." The statement continued, "The comments were not based on NBC beliefs. Nobody at NBC ever intends to offend anyone." But the Chinese government did not ease its pressure on NBC, whose owner, General Electric, and GE's partner in the MSNBC news channel, Microsoft, both have extensive commercial interests and ambitions in China. The Foreign Ministry declared, "Any news agency in the world should respect and comply with the most fundamental professional ethics and not produce reports which distort facts. It is hoped that NBC will draw lessons and make sure that there will be no recurrence of things like that."

Commercial and other pressures have long been known to have a chilling effect on the independence of reporters and their employers. Increasingly, it will be the foreign correspondent who feels the chill as she or he reports from countries where markets have become free before the flow of information has. Unlike the traditional publisher or owner with whom reporters and editors could discuss a sensitive issue after climbing a flight of stairs, the new owners, because of the vastness of their organizations, are distant physically and in their priorities. Censorship is not a new experience for foreign correspondents. But what they will face in nations whose leaders seek the profits and products of the global market without sacrificing political control can be as effective and more insidious: self-censorship. As GE tries to sell more jet engines to the Chinese, and Microsoft more software, how confident will NBC or MSNBC reporters feel about interviewing dissidents? If Disney builds a Disney World outside Shanghai or Hong Kong, will ABC News producers and reporters have second thoughts about taping an investigative report on corruption in the ranks of Chinese government and party officials? As NBC and Bob Costas can testify, these are no longer hypothetical dilemmas.

EVERYONE IS A REPORTER

The growing tension between journalistic and commercial priorities may never be fully resolved. But whatever direction events may lead journalists, the role of traditional news organizations is likely to shrink further. The flow of information from fax machines to the Internet and through other technologies already developed or still undreamed of will overwhelm efforts to control it. Today and in the future, anyone sending information from one country to another is a de facto foreign corespondent. The number of correspondents, accredited or not, will rapidly increase. Equipped with camcorders and computers, they will send out and receive more and more foreign dispatches. Even in countries where governments try to control the availability of video on the Internet, ingenuity and ever smaller satellite dishes will enable some, perhaps much, news and information to get through.

Given the global commercial and technological changes facing television news, in a world where almost anyone can be a foreign correspondent, what will be the role of the traditional bearer of that name? When the Internet and on-line services offer full-motion video, network newscasts will feel even less compelled to provide coverage of foreign events to a mass audience. But those interested in what is happening abroad will find a selection of information even broader and deeper than cable news channels now offer. Layering of information—video, sound, text, and graphics—will give the news consumer unprecedented choice, as well as editorial control. And the person providing that information could be a new type of foreign correspondent, or perhaps the old type with new means of communication.

Rather than dashing around the world to provide an on-screen presence, the correspondent will be judged on the quality and depth of knowledge he or she possesses. Foreign correspondents will have to be versatile and informed journalists who can write commentary for videotape as well as for print, knowledgeable specialists who closely follow a country, region, or topic and can appear on camera or on line to talk about it and respond to questions and comments. They will have to be able to communicate interactively with an audience whose members will be informed, engaged, and more demanding than the passive television viewers of today.

Those Americans who actively seek more knowledge about the rest of the world and how their country or business fits into it will be better served. Since they will likely be opinion makers—and voters—public discussion of foreign affairs could conceivably improve. Unfortunately, the debate would not include the broader public that is not plugged into the wider world.

What is being lost, or at least weakened, has long been forecast: the role of a few television network news organizations as a unifying central nervous system of information for the nation, and the communal benefits associated with that. Some may mourn the loss, especially those who grew up with network news. (More than half the audience for the evening network news programs is 50 or older.) Viewers and social critics may debate whether the gains accompanying the growing diversity and flexibility of news and information delivery outweigh the losses. But quite aside from the fact that nothing can be done to stop the technological advances, the benefits in choice and content are clear.

It is always tempting to ascribe a utopian future to societies that are being profoundly altered by new technologies. Still, for the fraternity of foreign correspondents, the forces of change could offer a road back to their traditional craft. The foreign correspondent of the future may wear the obligatory trench coat or safari jacket of yesteryear. But underneath it, she or he will have to possess a depth of expertise to satisfy the increasingly demanding, informed, and technologically equipped consumer of the information age.

On American Principles

George F. Kennan

George F. Kennan is Professor Emeritus in the School of Historical Studies at the Institute for Advanced Study in Princeton, N.J. This is his nineteenth article for Foreign Affairs. *His first, "The Sources of Soviet Conduct," appeared in July 1947 under the pseudonym X.*

THE HISTORICAL EXPERIENCE

AT A LARGE dinner given in New York in recognition of his ninetieth birthday, the author of these lines ventured to say that what our country needed at this point was not primarily policies, "much less a single policy." What we needed, he argued, were principles—sound principles—"principles that accorded with the nature, the needs, the interests, and the limitations of our country." This rather cryptic statement could surely benefit from a few words of elucidation.

The place that principle has taken in the conduct of American foreign policy in past years and decades can perhaps best be explained by a single example from American history. In the aftermath of the Napoleonic wars, and particularly in the period beginning about 1815–25, there set in a weakening of the ties that had previously held the Spanish empire together, and demands were raised by certain of the American colonies for complete independence. Pressure was brought on Washington to take the lead not only in recognizing their independence at an early stage, but also in giving them political and presumably military aid in their efforts to consolidate their independence in the face of whatever resistance might be put up by the Spanish government.

These questions presented themselves with particular intensity when James Monroe was president (1817–25). At that time the office of secretary of state was occupied by John Quincy Adams. In view of his exceptional qualities and experience, and the high respect with which he was held in Washington and throughout the country, much of the burden of designing the U.S. response to those pressures rested on him.

Adams realized that the U.S. historical experience left no choice but to welcome and give moral support to these South American peoples in their struggle for the recognition and consolidation of their independence. But he had little confidence in the ability of the new revolutionary leaders to shape these communities at any early date into mature, orderly, and firmly established states.

For this reason, he was determined that America not be drawn too deeply into their armed conflicts with Spain, domestic political squabbles, or sometimes complicated relationships with their neighbors. Adams took this position, incidentally, not just with regard to the emerging South American countries, but also in relation to similar conflicts in Europe, particularly the efforts of Greek patriots to break away from the Turkish empire and establish an independent state.

These attitudes on Adams' part did not fail to meet with opposition in portions of the American political establishment. Some people, including the influential speaker of the House, Henry Clay, remembering America's own recent struggle for independence, felt strongly that the United States should take an active part in the similar struggles of other peoples. This, of course, was directly opposed to Adams' views. For this reason, Adams felt the need to take the problem to a wider audience and enlist public support for his views. In 1823, when he was invited by a committee of citizens to deliver a Fourth of July address in the nation's capital, he promptly agreed. The address was delivered in the premises of the House of Representatives, although not before a formal session of that body. The talk was presented as a personal statement, not an official one; and Adams took care to see that the text was printed and made widely available to the public.

A considerable part of the address was devoted to the questions I have just mentioned. On this subject Adams had some firm views. America, he said, had always extended to these new candidates for statehood "the hand of honest friendship, of equal freedom, and of generous reciprocity." It had spoken to them in "the language of equal liberty, of equal justice, and of equal rights." It had respected their independence. It had abstained from interference with their undertakings even when these were being conducted "for principles to which she [America] clings, as to the last vital drop that visits the heart." Why? Because, he explained, "America goes not abroad in search of monsters to destroy. She is the well-wisher to the freedom and independence of all. She is the champion and vindicator only of her own. She will recommend the general cause by the countenance of her voice, and the benignant sympathy of her example. She well knows that by once enlisting under other banners than her own, were they even the banners of foreign independence, she would involve herself beyond the power of extrication, in all the wars of interest and intrigue, of individual avarice, envy, and ambition, which assumed the colors and usurped the standards of freedom.... She might become the dictatress of the world. She would be no longer the ruler of her own spirit."

The relevance of this statement to many current problems—in such places as Iraq, Lebanon, Somalia, Bosnia, Rwanda, and even Haiti—is obvious. But that is not the reason why attention is being drawn to the statement at this point. What Adams was doing in those passages of his address was enunciating a principle of American foreign policy: namely, that, while it was "the well-wisher to the freedom and independence of all," America was also "the champion and vindicator only of her own." Those words seem to provide as clear an example as any of what the term "principle" might mean in relation to the diplomacy of this country or any other.

THE IDEAL VS. REALITY

HOW, THEN, using Adams' statement as a model, would the term "principle" be defined? One might say that a principle is a general rule of conduct by which a given country chooses to abide in the conduct of its relations with other countries. There are several aspects of the term, one or two of them touched on in this definition, others not, that require elucidation.

A principle was just defined as a general rule of conduct. That means that whoever adopts a principle does not specify any particular situation, problem, or bilateral relationship to which this rule should apply. It is designed to cover the entirety of possible or presumptive situations. It merely defines certain limits, positive and negative, within which policy, when those situations present themselves, ought to operate.

A government cannot play fast and loose with the interests of its people.

A principle, then, is a rule of conduct. But it is not an absolute one. The possibility is not precluded that situations might arise—unforeseeable situations, in particular—to which the adopted principle might not seem applicable or to the meeting of which the resources of the government in question were clearly inadequate. In such cases, exceptions might have to be made. This is not, after all, a perfect world. People make mistakes in judgment. And there is always the unforeseeable and unexpected.

But as new situations and challenges present themselves, and as government is confronted with the necessity of devising actions or policies with which to meet them, established principle is something that should have the first and the most authoritative claim on the attention and respect of the policymaker. Barring special circumstances, principle should be automatically applied, and whoever proposes to set it aside or violate it should explain why such violation seems unavoidable.

Second, a principle is, by definition, self-engendered. It is not something that requires, or would even admit of, any sort of communication, negotiation, or formal agreement with another government. In the case of the individual person (because individuals have principles, just as governments do), the principles that guide his life are a matter of conscience and self-respect. They flow from the individual's view of himself; the nature of his inner commitments, and his concept of the way he ought to behave if he is to be at peace with himself.

Now, the principles of a government are not entirely the same as those of an individual. The individual, in choosing his principles, engages only himself. He is at liberty to sacrifice his own practical interests in the service of some higher and more unselfish ideal. But this sort of sacrifice is one that a responsible government, and a democratic government in particular, is unable to take upon itself. It is an agent, not a principal. It is only a representative of others.

When a government speaks, it speaks not only for itself but for the people of the country. It cannot play fast and loose with their interests. Yet a country, too, can have a predominant collective sense of itself—what sort of a country it conceives itself or would like itself to be—and what sort of behavior would fit that concept. The place where this self-image finds its most natural reflection is in the principles that a country chooses to adopt and, to the extent possible, to follow. Principle represents, in other words, the ideal, if not always, alas, the reality, of the rules and restraints a country adopts. Once established, those rules and restraints require no explanation or defense to others. They are one's own business.

A drawing that appeared in *The New Yorker* magazine many years ago showed a cringing subordinate standing before the desk of an irate officer, presumably a colonel, who was banging the desk with his fist and saying: "There is no reason, damn it; it's just our policy."

Well, as a statement about policy, this was ridiculous. But had the colonel been referring to a principle instead of a policy, the statement might not have been so out of place. It would not be unusual, for example, for someone in authority in Washington today to say to the representative of a foreign government, when the situation warranted it, "I am sorry, but for us, this is a matter of principle, and I am afraid we will have to go on from there."

Let me also point out that principles can have negative as well as positive aspects. There can be certain things that a country can make it a matter of principle not to do. In many instances these negative aspects of principle

3 ❖ DOMESTIC SIDE: The Role of American Values

may be more important than the positive ones. The positive ones normally suggest or involve action; actions have a way of carrying over almost imperceptibly from the realm of principle into that of policy, where they develop a momentum of their own in which the original considerations of principle either are forgotten or are compelled to yield to what appear to be necessities of the moment. In other words, it is sometimes clearer and simpler to define on principle the kinds of things a country will not go in for—the things that would fit with neither its standards nor its pretensions—than it is to define ways in which it will act positively, whatever the circumstances. The basic function of principles is, after all, to establish the parameters within which the policies of a country may be normally conducted. This is essentially a negative, rather than a positive, determination.

Another quality of a principle that deserves notice is that it is not, and cannot be, the product of the normal workings of the political process in any democratic country. It could not be decided by a plebiscite or even by legislative action. You would never get agreement on it if it came under that sort of debate, and whatever results might be achieved would deprive the concept of the degree of flexibility it requires to serve its purpose.

A principle is something that can only be declared, and then only by a political leader. It represents, of necessity, his own view of what sort of a country his is, and how it should conduct itself in the international arena. But the principle finds its reality, if it finds it at all, in the degree of acceptance, tacit or otherwise, that its proclamation ultimately receives from the remainder of the political establishment and from the populace at large. If that acceptance and support are not forthcoming in sufficient degree, a principle ceases to have reality. The statesman who proclaims it, therefore, has to be reasonably confident that, in putting it forward, he is interpreting, appealing to, and expressing the sentiment of a large proportion of the people for whom he speaks. This task of defining a principle must be seen as not just a privilege, but also a duty of political leadership.

Adams' statement certainly had this quality. The concept was indeed his own. But his formulation of it met wide and enthusiastic support among the people of his time, as he probably thought it would. The same could be said of similar declarations of principle from a number of other American statesmen, then and later. One has only to think, for example, of George Washington's statements in his farewell address, Thomas Jefferson's language in the Declaration of Independence, or Abraham Lincoln's in his Gettysburg speech. In each of those instances, the leaders, in putting forward their idea of principle, were speaking from their own estimate—a well-informed estimate—of what would find a sufficient response on the part of a large body, and not just a partisan body, of American opinion.

In no way other than by advocacy or proclamation from high office could such professions of principle be usefully formulated and brought forward. The rest of us may have our thoughts from time to time about the principles America ought to follow in its relations with the world, but none of us could state these principles in a manner that would give them significance for the behavior of the country at large.

THE POWER OF EXAMPLE

SO MUCH, then, for the essential characteristics of a principle and the manner in which it can be established. But there are those who will not be content with this abstract description of what a principle is, and who will want an example of what a principle valid for adoption by the United States of our day might look like.

The principle cited from Secretary Adams' Fourth of July speech was one that was applicable, in his view, to the situation then. The world now is, of course, different from his in many respects. There are those who will hold the gloomy view that such is the variety of our population and such are the differences among its various components, racial, social, and political, that it is idle to suppose that there could be any consensus among them on matters of principle. They have too little in common. There is much to be said for that view. This writer has at times been inclined to it himself. But further reflection suggests that there are certain feelings that we Americans or the great majority of us share, living as we do under the same political system and enjoying the same national consciousness, even though we are not always aware of having them. One may further suspect that if the translation of these feelings into principles of American behavior on the world scene were to be put forward from the highest governmental levels and adequately explained to the people at large, it might evoke a surprisingly strong response.

But this understanding and support cannot be expected to come spontaneously from below. It will not be likely to emerge from a public media dominated by advertisers and the entertainment industry. It will not be likely to emerge from legislative bodies extensively beholden to special interests, precisely because what would be at stake here would be the feelings and interests of the nation as a whole and not those of any particular and limited bodies of the citizenry. An adequate consensus on principles, in other words, could come from below only by way of response to suggestions from above, brought forward by a leadership that would take responsibility for educating and forming popular opinion, rather than merely trying to assess its existing moods and prejudices and play up to them.

Now, coming back to the model of Adams' Fourth of July speech, the problems now facing this country show a strong resemblance to ones Adams had in mind when he gave that address in 1823. At that time the dissolution of the great empires was only just beginning, and few—

at the most half a dozen—of the newly emerging states were looking to us for assistance. In the period between Adams' time and our own, and particularly in the wake of the Second World War, the process of decolonization has preceded at a dizzying pace, casting onto the surface of international life dozens of new states, many of them poorly prepared, as were those of Adams' time, for the responsibilities of independent statehood. This has led to many situations of instability, including civil wars and armed conflicts with neighbors, and there have been, accordingly, a great many appeals to us for political, economic, or military support.

To what extent, then, could Adams' principle of nonintervention, as set forth in 1823, be relevant to our situation today?

One cannot ignore the many respects in which our present situation differs from that which Adams was obliged to face. This writer is well aware of the increasingly global nature of our problems and the myriad involvements connecting our people and government with foreign countries. I do not mean to suggest a great reduction in those minor involvements. But what is at stake here are major political-military interventions by our government in the affairs of smaller countries. These are very different things.

First of all, we do not approach these questions with entirely free hands. We have conducted a number of such interventions in recent years, and at least three of these—Korea, Iraq, and Haiti—have led to new commitments that are still weighty and active.

There are several things to note about these interventions and commitments. First, while some may well have helped preserve peace or promote stability in local military relationships, this has not always been their stated purpose; in a number of instances, in particular, where we have portrayed them as efforts to promote democracy or human rights, they seem to have had little enduring success.

Second, lest there be any misunderstanding about this, the interventions in which we are now engaged or committed represent serious responsibilities. Any abrupt withdrawal from them would be a violation of these responsibilities; and there is no intention here to recommend anything of that sort. On the contrary, it should be a matter of principle for this government to meet to the best of its ability any responsibilities it has already incurred. Only when we have succeeded in extracting ourselves from the existing ones with dignity and honor will the question of further interventions present itself to us in the way that it did to Mr. Adams.

Third, instances where we have undertaken or committed ourselves to intervene represent only a small proportion of the demands and expectations that have come to rest on us. This is a great and confused world, and there are many other peoples and countries clamoring for our assistance. Yet it is clear that even these involvements stretch to the limit our economic and military resources, not to mention the goodwill of our people. And even if this were not a compelling limitation, there would still be the question of consistency. Are there any considerations being presented as justifications for our present involvements that would not, if consistently applied, be found to be relevant to many other situations as well? And if not, the question arises: If we cannot meet all the demands of this sort coming to rest upon us, should we attempt to meet any at all? The answer many would give to this question would be: yes, but only when our vital national interests are clearly threatened.

And last, beyond all these considerations, we have the general proposition that clearly underlay John Quincy Adams' response to similar problems so many years ago—his recognition that it is very difficult for one country to help another by intervening directly in its domestic affairs or in its conflicts with its neighbors. It is particularly difficult to do this without creating new and unwelcome embarrassments and burdens for the country endeavoring to help. The best way for a larger country to help smaller ones is surely by the power of example. Adams made this clear in the address cited above. One will recall his urging that the best response we could give to those appealing to us for support would be to give them what he called "the benign sympathy of our example." To go further, he warned, and try to give direct assistance would be to involve ourselves beyond the power of extrication "in all the wars of interest and intrigue, of individual avarice, envy, and ambition, which assumed the colors and usurped the standards of freedom." Who, today, looking at our involvements of recent years, could maintain that the fears these words expressed were any less applicable in our time than in his?

The best way for a larger country to help smaller ones is by the power of example.

These, then, are some of the considerations bearing on the relevance of Adams' principle to the present problems of our country. This writer, for one, finds Adams' principle, albeit with certain adjustments to meet our present circumstances and commitments, entirely suitable and indeed greatly needed as a guide for American policy in the coming period. This examination of what Adams said, and its relevance to the problems of our own age, will in any case have served to illustrate what the word "principle" meant in his time and what it could, in this case or others, mean in our own.

One last word: the example offered above of what a principle might be revolved primarily around our relations with smaller countries that felt, or professed to feel, the need for our help in furthering their places in the modern world. These demands have indeed taken a leading place in our diplomacy of this post-Cold War era. But one should not be left with the impression that these relationships were all that counted in our present problems with diplomacy. Also at stake are our relations with the other great powers, and these place even more important demands on our attention, policies, and resources.

The present moment is marked, most happily, by the fact that there are no great conflicts among the great powers. This situation is without precedent in recent centuries, and it is essential that it be cherished, nurtured, and preserved. Such is the destructive potential of advanced modern weapons that another great conflict between any of the leading powers could well do irreparable damage to the entire structure of modern civilization.

Intimately connected with those problems, of course, is the necessity of restraining, and eventually halting, the proliferation of weapons of mass destruction and of achieving their eventual total removal from national arsenals. And finally, also connected with these problems but going beyond them in many respects, there is the great environmental crisis our world is entering. To this crisis, too, adequate answers must be found if modern civilization is to have a future.

All of these challenges stand before us. Until they are met, even the many smaller and weaker countries can have no happy future. Our priorities must be shaped accordingly. Only when these wider problems have found their answers will any efforts we make to solve the problems of humane and civil government in the rest of the world have hopes of success.

WHY AMERICA THINKS IT HAS TO RUN THE WORLD

by BENJAMIN SCHWARZ

The Cold War is over, and America is staggering under a colossal debt and an accumulation of frightening social problems. Yet it continues to spend billions to protect Germany and Japan—two rich nations whose freedom is in no apparent danger. Why? Here is the answer that the foreign-policy elite would give if it dared to speak frankly about the delicate matter of American efforts to assert international economic and political control

THREE years ago, in light of the end of the Cold War, the Clinton Administration undertook a "fundamental reassessment" of America's national-security requirements. But after six months of analysis Administration officials concluded that the defense of U.S. global interests still demanded military spending of more than $1.3 trillion over the following five years and the permanent commitment of more than 200,000 U.S. soldiers in East Asia and Europe—in other words, a strategy remarkably similar to that which America pursued during the Cold War. Moreover, rather than relinquish America's costly and risky responsibilities by dissolving Cold War alliances, defense strategists now plan to expand NATO's responsibilities eastward. Those who call for a more modest plan argue that U.S. strategy seems to be extravagance born of paranoia, or of the defense establishment's anxiety to protect its budget. In fact, given the way the makers of U.S. foreign policy have defined American interests since the late 1940s, these plans are quite prudent. And that is the problem.

If many Americans had been asked ten years ago why U.S. troops were deployed in East Asia and Europe, they would have answered, To keep the Soviets out. They may have wondered, however, why the United States persisted in its strategy long after Japan, South Korea, and Western Europe had become capable of defending themselves. Now that the USSR itself has disappeared, why does Washington continue to insist that U.S. "leadership" in East Asia and Europe is still indispensable?

Ask National Security Council staff members, think-tank analysts, or State Department policy planners about America's globe-girdling security commitments and they will deliver very different answers—ones that have not changed in forty-five years. They will justify the Pax Americana by invoking "the imperative of continued U.S. world leadership," the need to "shape a favorable international environment," "reassurance of allies," and the ongoing need for "stability" and "continuing engagement." Even during the Cold War the "Soviet threat" might not have been mentioned.

The question that all this justification ignores is What, exactly, is "leadership," and why has it been the mantra of foreign-policy cognoscenti for nearly fifty years? What have we been doing around the globe, and why?

Most Americans misunderstand their country's foreign policy. It seems to operate only when "danger" looms—when Iraq invades Kuwait, when Russian "imperialism" threatens to resurface, when China rattles its sabers at Taiwan. Even people who religiously read the newspapers fail to grasp that U.S. foreign policy is far more than simply a series of responses to crises.

For instance, media coverage of recurring tensions on the Korean Peninsula has focused on speculation about North Korea's nuclear program and the prospect of a new Korean war. But when foreign-policy officials and experts discuss the Korean crisis among themselves, they rapidly leave the Koreas behind to focus on the real players in the region: China and Japan. As far as national-security experts are concerned, almost any immediate crisis is subsumed by a larger threat—in this case no less than East Asia's role in the potential collapse of the international economy that U.S. power has sustained since the late 1940s.

3 ❖ DOMESTIC SIDE: The Role of American Values

It's now an axiom of the U.S. foreign-policy establishment that economic, technological, and demographic changes are making East Asia the world's most dynamic arena, a driving force—increasingly the dominant force—in the international economy. The Pacific Century, we are told ad nauseam, has dawned. This transformation also means a shift in the international distribution of political and military power. In a typical evaluation of East Asia's strategic future the foreign-policy expert Aaron Friedberg states darkly in the journal *International Security*,

> In the long run, it is Asia [rather than Europe] that seems far more likely to be the cockpit of great power conflict. The half millennium during which Europe was the world's primary generator of war (as well as of wealth and knowledge) is coming to a close. But, for better and for worse, Europe's past could be Asia's future.

Friedberg's assertion nicely illustrates the ambivalence with which the U.S. national-security community views East Asia's future. He both prophesies an exhilarating Pacific Century and warns the West that the East may once again be up to no good.

East Asia has never been a terribly successful field for American diplomacy. There are undoubtedly many reasons for this, and surely that shortcoming for which the United States is continually indicted—cultural and historical myopia—has contributed enormously to its failures in the region. Americans have always seen East Asia not for what it is but for what it can do to them or for them: the region is either danger or opportunity—either a new "ground war in Asia" or a new China market. American understanding of Japan, for instance, is, in the words of the historian Bruce Cumings, caught within the conflicting views of Japan as "miracle and menace, docile and aggressive, fragile blossom and Tokyo Rose." As Friedberg's analysis attests, the U.S. foreign-policy community worries that the fragile blossom may again bloom into a Tokyo Rose.

Pacific Century rhetoric usually describes the new era in a "post–Cold War" context. This is misleading, because it starts at the wrong place. First, the shift of economic activity has not been sudden. Even if East Asia rose in the American consciousness just as the Soviet Union receded, to define the economic and geopolitical transformation of East Asia as a post–Cold War phenomenon Americanizes and trivializes a development in international (not American) politics of far greater impact than the Cold War itself. Although Vietnam, China, and North Korea were for forty years able to contain America's Cold War ambition to "roll back" communism, they are proving utterly unable to contain the juggernaut of East Asia's capitalist political economy. Most important, to imply that the end of the Cold War is of primary significance to U.S. policy in East Asia is to wrench that policy out of its most important context and to distort its underlying aims and challenges.

What we think of as the Cold War was merely instrumental in America's larger "Cold War" strategy. In "scaring hell out of the American people," as Senator Arthur Vandenberg said in 1947, the U.S.-Soviet rivalry helped to secure domestic support for Washington's ambition to create a U.S.-dominated world order. That same year one of Vandenberg's colleagues, the fervently anti-Communist Senator Robert Taft, expressed a strong suspicion that the supposed dangers to the nation from the USSR failed to explain America's new foreign policy. He complained that he was "more than a bit tired of having the Russian menace invoked as a reason for doing any—and every—thing that might or might not be desirable or necessary on its own merits." The former Secretary of State Dean Acheson put things in proper perspective: describing how Washington overcame domestic opposition to its internationalist policies in 1950, he recalled in 1954 that at that critical moment the crisis in Korea "came along and saved us."

MAKING THE WORLD SAFE FOR CAPITALISM

A FUNDAMENTAL aim of America's Cold War strategy was to create and maintain what the former Secretary of State James Baker has called "a global liberal economic regime"—a capitalist world order. After the Second World War, American statesmen believed that the United States, standing alone and strong in a world of weary nations, had a remarkable opportunity, as Acheson said, to "grab hold of history and make it conform." American statesmen seized that opportunity by creating a complex strategy to reify Adam Smith's dream. Washington envisioned a world economy in which trade and capital would flow across national boundaries in response to the laws of comparative advantage and supply and demand—an economy in which production and finance would be integrated on a global scale. The constricted national markets that were emerging in the immediate aftermath of the Second World War in Europe and East Asia would be combined, eliminating the inefficiencies of statism and self-sufficiency. Large-scale regional economies would in turn be integrated into an interdependent world economy. U.S. policymakers knew that building this multinational capitalist community required the United States to provide Western Europe and Japan with enormous amounts of economic aid (through such schemes as the Marshall Plan, for Europe, and the Dodge Plan, its equivalent for Japan), so that those areas would not retreat into closed economies. They also knew that an open world economy demanded an even more ambitious American project: transforming international relations.

The greatest danger to U.S. democracy and prosperity came, they believed, not from the Soviet Union but from Germany and Japan, whose potential strength amounted to a sort of Catch-22. Without a flourishing international economy, Under Secretary of State Will Clayton warned in 1947, "our democratic free enterprise system" could not function. As late as 1960 exports accounted for only 3.8 percent and imports for 4.8 percent of GDP. The health of the international economy, in this disputable view, depended on Germany's and Japan's economic revitalization. Germany, if its economy was resurrected, would once again be Europe's most efficient producer and most avid consumer. Its very economic potential, however, made Germany a threat to the other Western European states, which, as the future Secretary of State John Foster Dulles explained to a closed Senate panel in 1949, were "afraid to bring that strong, powerful, highly concentrated group of people into unity with them." Similarly, as Dulles, Acheson, and other policymakers understood, a strong Japan was both necessary for a prosperous international order and intolerable to its neighbors. The problem lay in the inherent contradiction between capitalism and international politics.

Capitalist economies prosper most when labor, technology, and capital are fluid, so that they are driven toward international integration and interdependence. But whereas all states benefit absolutely in an open international economy, some states benefit more than others. In the normal course of world politics, in which states are driven to compete for their security, the relative distribution of power is a country's principal concern, discouraging economic interdependence. Thus 250 years ago the philosopher David Hume bemoaned the lack of economic cooperation among countries, blaming the "narrow malignity and envy of nations, which can never bear to see their neighbors thriving, but continually repine at any new efforts towards industry made by any other nation." In its efforts to ensure the distribution of power in its favor and at the expense of actual or potential rivals, a state will "nationalize"—that is, pursue autarkic policies, practicing capitalism only within its borders or among countries in a trading bloc. This circumscribes both production factors and markets, and thereby fragments an international economy.

A truly global economy is probably impossible to achieve. In fact, as the Princeton political economist Robert Gilpin has said, "what today we call international economic interdependence runs so counter to the great bulk of human experience that only extraordinary changes and novel circumstances could have led to its innovation and triumph over other means of economic exchange." Historically, to secure international capitalism a dominant power must guarantee the security of other states, so that they need not pursue autarkic policies or form trading blocs to improve their relative positions. This suspension of international politics through hegemony has been the fundamental aim of U.S. foreign policy since the 1940s. The real story of that policy is not the thwarting of and triumph over the Soviet threat but the effort to impose an ambitious economic vision on a recalcitrant world.

15. America Thinks It Has to Run the World

NURTURING—AND CONSTRAINING— THE FRAGILE BLOSSOM

THE overriding objective of U.S. postwar policy toward East Asia was restoring Japanese economic power. To be sure, this would help to immunize the region against Communist expansion; but Acheson and the other creators of the American Century thought the goal itself vital, regardless of the Soviet threat. As the historians William Borden, Bruce Cumings, Ronald McGlothlen, and Michael Schaller have argued, in attempting to create a global economic system Washington pursued a course designed in essence to restore the Greater East Asian Co-Prosperity Sphere—imperial Japan's regional economy, which the United States had just destroyed in the Second World War. If Japan was to help fuel the world economy, it would have to be, in Acheson's words, "the workshop of Asia." American postwar planners viewed the political economy that had developed in Northeast Asia from about 1900 to 1945 as the region's natural economy—a tripartite system in which Japan, given access to continental markets and raw materials, formed the industrial core and its neighbors formed the economic semi-periphery and periphery. As Japan advanced in the product cycle, climbing up the technological ladder, it spun off its low-technology and low-wage industries to its neighbors.

In the late 1940s and the 1950s the United States essentially restored this system; but the machine could not run by itself. Washington had to ensure that Japan's neighbors would feel secure politically in the regional hierarchy atop which Japan stood. Washington also had to ensure that the hierarchy did not develop—as it had in the past—into a Japanese-led closed economic bloc, which would threaten the world economy. NSC 48, the National Security Council's 1949 blueprint for America's Cold War strategy in East Asia, summed up the chief difficulty facing Washington's economic goals in the region—and around the globe. Starting with the premise that "the economic life of the modern world is geared to expansion," requiring "the establishment of conditions favorable to the export of technology and capital and to a liberal trade policy throughout the world," NSC 48's authors went on to warn that "the complexity of international trade makes it well to bear in mind that such ephemeral matters as national pride and ambition can inhibit or prevent the necessary degree of international cooperation, or the development of a favorable atmosphere and conditions to promote economic expansion."

The distinguished historian and diplomat George Kennan, then the head of the State Department's policy-planning staff, saw only one solution to what he described as the "terrible dilemma" confronting U.S. ambitions in East Asia. Forty-seven years later Washington continues to pursue that course.

3 ❖ DOMESTIC SIDE: The Role of American Values

You have the terrific problem of how then the Japanese are going to get along unless they reopen some sort of Empire toward the South. Clearly we have got . . . to achieve opening up of trade possibilities, commercial possibilities for Japan on a scale very far greater than anything Japan knew before. It is a formidable task. On the other hand, it seems to me absolutely inevitable that we must keep completely the maritime and air controls as a means . . . of keeping control of the situation with respect to [the] Japanese in all eventualities. . . . [It is] all the more imperative that we retain the ability to control their situation by controlling the overseas sources of supply and the naval power and air power without which [Japan] cannot become again aggressive. . . .

If we really in the Western world could work out controls, I suppose, adept enough and foolproof enough and cleverly enough exercised really to have power over what Japan imports in the way of oil and such other things as she has got to get from overseas, we would have veto power on what she does need in the military and industrial field.

By providing for Japan's security and by enmeshing its foreign and military policies in a U.S.-controlled alliance, Americans have contained their erstwhile enemy, preventing their "partner" from embarking upon independent—and, so the thinking goes, dangerous—political and military policies. By restraining its powerful ally, Washington has, to use a euphemism favored in policymaking circles, "reassured" Japan's neighbors and stabilized relations among the states of East Asia. The United States played the decisive role in promoting Tokyo's integration with its former colonies in Japan-centered regional trade networks that have been the foundation of East Asia's economic "miracle." South Korea and Taiwan, for example, overcame their fear and resentment of Japan and opened their doors to Japanese investment and trade.

In a series of revealing interviews published in 1970 the former undersecretary of state Eugene Rostow was pressed to explain the motivations underlying U.S. foreign policy generally and U.S. policy toward Vietnam specifically. In doing so he betrayed the lingering and profound distrust that U.S. policymakers feel toward any powerful state that could play a role in world politics more independent than the one the United States has assigned to it. At a time when America was involved in Southeast Asia ostensibly to draw a line against international communism, Rostow admitted, "I think the major concern—at least my major concern—in this miserable affair is the long-range impact a [U.S.] withdrawal would have on Japanese policy." He explained, "After the Japanese lost the war they reached certain conclusions, the principal one being that it was infinitely better to cooperate with the United States than to follow a hostile, militaristic line. Now, it's greatly to our interest to have that judgment proved correct." If the United States abruptly pulled out of Vietnam, Rostow went on, "I think the Japanese will draw certain conclusions. And I think their policy will take on a much more nationalistic cast. . . . I think the first thing that would happen would be that they wouldn't ratify the nuclear-non-proliferation treaty. They would feel compelled to become a nuclear power." This would endanger the imperative that America preserve "a world of wide horizons in which we can move around and trade and travel on a large scale."

AMERICA AS "ADULT SUPERVISOR"

AMERICA'S Cold War policy is best understood not by its communism-containing words but by its ally-containing deeds. Washington committed itself to building and maintaining an international economic and political order based on what officials at the time termed a U.S. "preponderance of power." By banishing power politics and nationalist rivalries, America's Cold War alliances in East Asia and Europe in effect protected the states of those regions from themselves.

The United States has not subjugated colonies but, like Great Britain in the nineteenth century, has built and benefited economically from a stable international political order. In this way Lenin was right: imperialism is, or allows for, "the highest stage of capitalism"—an open economy among the industrialized nations.

By building this global economy the United States has realized what Lenin called "[the German socialist Karl] Kautsky's silly little fable about ultraimperialism." In the celebrated debate between Lenin and Kautsky, Lenin held that any international capitalist order was inherently temporary, since the political order among competing states would shift over time. Whereas Lenin argued that international capitalism thus could not transcend the Hobbesian reality of international politics, Kautsky maintained that capitalists were much too rational to destroy themselves in internecine conflicts. An international class of enlightened capitalists, recognizing that international political and military competition would upset the orderly processes of world finance and trade, would instead seek peace, free trade, and the cooperative development of backward areas.

But Lenin and Kautsky were talking past each other, since Kautsky believed that the common interest of what he called the "inter-capitalist class" determined international relations, whereas in Lenin's analysis international relations were founded not in social classes but in competition among states. Lenin argued that there was an irreconcilable contradiction between capitalism and the international system; Kautsky didn't recognize the division in the first place.

America's foreign policy has been based on a hybrid of Lenin's and Kautsky's analyses. It has aimed at the unified,

15. America Thinks It Has to Run the World

After the Second World War, American statesmen believed that the United States, standing alone and strong in a world of weary nations, had a remarkable opportunity, as Dean Acheson said, to "grab hold of history and make it conform." Washington's dream of a world economy in which trade and capital flowed freely across national boundaries demanded the transformation of international relations.

liberalized international capitalist community Kautsky envisioned. But the global role that the United States has undertaken to sustain that community is determined by a worldview very close to Lenin's. To Washington, Baker's "global liberal economic regime" cannot be maintained simply by an internationalized economic elite's desire for it to exist; it can be maintained only by American power. Thus, in explaining its global strategy in 1993, in its "post–Cold War" defense strategy, the Pentagon defined the creation of "a prosperous, largely democratic, market-oriented zone of peace and prosperity that encompasses more than two-thirds of the world's economy" as "perhaps our nation's most significant achievement since the Second World War"—not the victory over Moscow. And it declared that this global capitalist order required the "stability" that only American "leadership" could provide. Ultimately, of course, U.S. policymakers and Lenin diverge. Although Lenin recognized that any given international political order was by its nature impermanent, America's foreign-policy strategists have hoped to keep the reality of international politics permanently at bay.

Although the Cold War has ended, what National Security Advisor Anthony Lake calls the "imperative of continued U.S. world leadership"—as exercised, for instance, in America's dominance of its alliances in East Asia and of NATO—remains necessary to maintain a global economy. The now-infamous draft of the Pentagon's defense plan, or the Defense Planning Guidance, which was leaked to *The New York Times* in 1992, gave the public an unprecedented glimpse of the thinking that informs Washington's security strategy, merely stating in somewhat undiplomatic language the logic behind America's Cold War strategy. The United States, it argued, must continue to dominate the international system and thus "discourage" the "advanced industrial nations from challenging our leadership or . . . even aspiring to a larger regional or global role." To accomplish this, America must do nothing less than "retain the pre-eminent responsibility for addressing . . . those wrongs which threaten not only our interests, but those of our allies or friends, or which could seriously unsettle international relations."

The United States, in other words, must provide what one of the Planning Guidance's authors termed "adult supervision." It must not only dominate regions composed of wealthy and technologically sophisticated states but also take care of such nuisances as Saddam Hussein, Slobodan Milosevic, and North Korea's dictator Kim Jong Il, to protect the interests of virtually all potential great powers so that they need not acquire the capability to protect themselves—that is, so that those powers need not act like great powers. Thus, for instance, Washington must protect Germany's and Japan's access to Persian Gulf oil, because if these countries were to protect their own interests in the Gulf, they would develop military forces capable of global "power projection." No wonder the United States must spend more on its "national security" than the rest of the world's countries combined. This post–Cold War strategy reflects what the historian Melvyn Leffler defined as an imperative of America's Cold War national-security policy: that "neither an integrated Europe nor a united Germany nor an independent Japan must be permitted to emerge as a third force."

Only in this context can Washington's concerns regarding current developments in East Asia be properly understood. For instance, in 1993 Alberto Coll, then a deputy assistant secretary of defense, clarified U.S. aims in East Asia. "In the future," Coll declared in the *Washington Quarterly*,

> the stability of the Pacific Basin and a strong US-Japanese relationship will be more important to the United States than ever before. The US economy needs the vast markets of the Pacific Rim, and it benefits enormously from Japanese investment capital and technology and the impetus toward greater productivity provided by Japanese competition.

All these benefits would be lost, according to Coll, if the "traditional rivalries among Asian powers . . . unravel into unrestrained military competition, conflict and aggression." In the same vein the author of the Clinton Administration's security strategy for East Asia, Joseph Nye, then the assistant secretary of defense, asserted last year that the U.S. military protectorate is "the basis for stability and prosperity in the region"; if the United States were to forsake its "leadership role" in East Asia, "the stable expectations of entrepreneurs and investors [would] be subverted." Although the United States committed forces to Japan ostensibly to protect it from the Soviets, and to South Korea to protect it from the North, in 1993 the deputy defense secretary, William Perry (now the Secretary of Defense), declared that America would continue to reassure and stabilize East Asia by maintaining troops "permanently" in Japan and even in a future unified Korea.

3 ❖ DOMESTIC SIDE: The Role of American Values

THE DOMINO THEORY REVIVED

To Washington, East Asia is still composed of dominoes ready to fall. "Renationalization," a term used by the cognoscenti to mean the resumption of international politics, could start virtually anywhere and spread rapidly. In one of Aaron Friedberg's many nightmare scenarios one can almost hear the click of the falling dominoes:

> The nuclearization of Korea (North, South, or whether through reunification or competitive arms programs both together) could lead to a similar development in Japan, which might cause China to accelerate and expand its nuclear programs, which could then have an impact on the defense policies of Taiwan, India (and through it, Pakistan) and Russia (which would also be affected by events in Japan and Korea). . . . similar shock waves could also travel through the system in different directions (for example, from India to China to Japan to Korea).

Friedberg and other national-security analysts paint a similarly gloomy picture in Southeast Asia if, for example, Japan should undertake a military buildup in response to Korean reunification. Japan's reaction would alarm China—the emerging colossus, which U.S. defense planners now regard as the most serious potential long-term threat to America's global position. China would speed up the development of its "power projection" forces. This would alarm Korea, Taiwan, and Japan—and also Indonesia, Malaysia, Singapore, and Vietnam. Their defensive response would further alarm China.

Such developments, from Washington's perspective, would have one of two results, either of which would shatter the global economy: international anarchy, or regional dominance by China or Japan, which policymakers believe would lead inevitably to a regional trading bloc. Arguing in 1992 for the maintenance of America's leadership of its Cold War alliances, a high-ranking Pentagon official asked, "If we pull out, who knows what nervousness will result?" The problem, of course, is that America can never know. According to this logic, it must always stay.

To the United States, the best change in East Asia is no change at all, because any alteration in the status quo could start the dominoes falling. And if there is to be change, Washington—not Tokyo or Beijing—must manage it. To permit otherwise would send a dangerous signal about America's diminishing ability to regulate, calibrate, and manipulate international politics in East Asia. Of course, Washington appreciates that change is inevitable, and its frustration comes from being unable to square the circle—to manage an increasingly unmanageable world.

Although the United States remains committed to preserving the Pax Americana in East Asia, the states in the region see U.S. influence inexorably declining, and they are planning accordingly. South Korea, for example, is reorienting its military away from an emphasis on the threat from the North and toward projecting power against a future threat from Japan by means of naval and air forces, submarines, spy planes, and satellites. The problem is that in prudently preparing for similar eventualities the East Asian states may indeed, as Washington fears, precipitate renationalization.

At a loss for what to do, U.S. policymakers propose two contradictory solutions. On the assumption that democracies are inherently peaceful toward one another, one solution goes, the United States should tranquilize East Asia by democratizing it. At the same time, the second solution has it, because only American dominance can ensure stability in the region (as in Europe), the United States should maintain its hegemony indefinitely. Leaving aside the question of whether either goal can be achieved, it should be clear that proposing these solutions is as inconsistent as simultaneously asserting, as do most in the U.S. national-security community, that although democracies pose no danger to other democracies, America must continue to contain Germany and Japan.

The hope and fear with which policymakers view economic change in East Asia illustrates the contradictory convictions that animate U.S. policy. Washington both heralds the economic dynamism of the Pacific Rim, hoping it will bring democracy and peace and worldwide economic growth, and dreads the Asian miracle. It knows that just as economic change engenders a shift in political and military power, so a particular economic order is jeopardized as the foundation upon which it rests—U.S. hegemony—weakens. In the oxymoronic vocabulary of U.S. diplomacy, strong "partners" are economically welcome and indeed necessary, but U.S. "leadership" is indispensable. Zbigniew Brzezinski, who developed the idea of a trilateral division of responsibility among the United States, Japan, and Europe, calls for Washington to develop "a more cooperative partnership" with Tokyo even as he asserts that America must continue to control Japan militarily.

LOSING GROUND

There is something at once poignant and obtuse in James Baker's comment that because President Clinton's foreign policy lacks consistency and firmness, "for the first time since the Second World War, Japan is not delivering an automatic vote for the US position." Sticking his head in the sand, the former Secretary of State claimed that such problems could be obviated "as long as America leads. . . . We have to lead." Japan's actions are certainly related to a decline in U.S. leadership, but that decline is not the fault of what Baker would characterize as Clinton's weak foreign policy. No matter who is in charge of U.S. foreign policy, America is less and less able to lead. Baker seems to have forgotten that America's leadership in the Gulf War was possible only because its allies agreed to pick up the tab. Given such leadership, it is no surprise that once-subservient "partners" are increasingly going their own way. Preponderance cannot simply be asserted; it must reflect a position based on power. When that position shifts enough, preponderance—"leadership"—is lost.

Lenin argued seventy-eight years ago that international capitalism would be economically successful but, by growing in a world of competitive states, would plant the seeds of its own destruction. Ironically, the worldwide economic system that the United States has fostered has itself largely determined America's relative decline even as it has contributed to the country's economic growth. Through trade, foreign investment, and the spread of technology and managerial expertise, economic power has diffused from the United States to new centers of growth, thus undermining American hegemony and ultimately jeopardizing the world economy.

Nearly everyone applauds today's complex web of global trade, production, and finance as the highest stage of capitalism. But international capitalism may be approaching a crisis just as it is reaching its fullest flower. A genuinely interdependent world market is extraordinarily fragile. The emergent high-technology industries, for instance, are the most powerful engines of world economic growth, but they require a level of specialization and a breadth of markets that are possible only in an integrated global economy. As U.S. hegemony continues to weaken, renationalized foreign and economic policies among the industrialized powers could fragment that economy.

The future of a foreign policy designed to strengthen what the United States must contain and, at the same time, to maintain an economic order that weakens the very foundation of that order seems evident: it will collapse under the weight of its own contradictions. The United States remains caught in the dilemma Kennan discerned more than forty years ago: "To what end 'security'? For the continuation of our economic expansion? But our economic expansion . . . cannot proceed much further without . . . creating new problems of national security much more rapidly than we can ever hope to solve them." To escape this dilemma, Americans will have to understand the foreign policy that is conducted in their name and re-examine the requirements for their own security and prosperity.

Benjamin Schwarz is a senior fellow at the World Policy Institute, in New York. He is at work on a book about U.S. foreign policy.

The Institutional Context of American Foreign Policy

Law and the Courts (Article 16)
State and Local Governments (Article 17)
Congress (Article 18)
The Bureaucracy (Articles 19 and 20)

Central to any study of American foreign policy are the institutions responsible for its content and conduct. In fact, institutions and policy are so tightly intertwined that it often becomes impossible to talk about one without the other. Vietnam quickly brings to mind images of the "imperial presidency"; Pearl Harbor is associated forever with the need for more coordination among the national security bureaucracies; the isolationist and protectionist trade policies of the 1930s can only be discussed within the context of congressional politics; and references to the Central Intelligence Agency (CIA) abound in any study of U.S. foreign policy toward Cuba, Angola, Chile, Iran, and Guatemala.

This close linkage between institutions and policies suggests that if American foreign policy is to adapt successfully to the challenges of the post-cold war era, American policy-making institutions must also change their ways. Many find it unreasonable to expect that institutions that built a political or budgetary power base around policies designed to contain Communism can provide a hospitable environment for policies designed to further human rights, engage in multilateral peacemaking operations, protect the environment, or open markets to American products.

The process of bringing about institutional reform thus promises to be a long and difficult one, and one that proceeds forward on many levels. It may be little more than renaming congressional committees (i.e. from the House Armed Services Committee to the National Security Committee). In other places it may involve potentially significant organizational changes such as those proposed for the State Department and the absorption of the Arms Control and Disarmament Agency, the Agency for International Development, and the U.S. Information Agency. In still other places, it may involve the formation of new organizational units such as the creation of economic development and trade offices in the 50 states.

The historical record regarding institutional change in the United States also suggests a point of caution to those seeking reform. Once put into place, institutional reforms often have unintended consequences that thwart the purposes of the reform initiative or create new, unimagined problems.

It will not be enough to reform any one institution if changes in American foreign policy are to be realized, because no one institution is capable of bringing about substantive changes by itself. Rather, as has long been noted, when it comes to foreign policy, the Constitution of the United States amounts to little more than an "invitation to struggle." Thinking about the institutions of American foreign policy making in terms of the need to change, and their ability to do so, thus requires us to look at a wide range of institutions.

In prioritizing institutions for change, Congress and the presidency must come first, because these two bodies are the lead protagonists in the struggle to control the content and conduct of American foreign policy. The relationship between them has varied over time, with such phrases as the "imperial presidency," "bipartisanship," and "divided government" being used to describe it. The Republican victory in the 1994 congressional elections brought a new intensity to the battle of wills between Congress and the presidency and a new prominence for Congress in the policy process. Jennifer Washburn, in her article "When Money Talks, Congress Listens," examines the influence of the arms industry on American foreign policy.

A second set of institutions thought to be in need of change are the bureaucracies that play influential roles in making foreign policy by supplying policymakers with information, defining problems, and implementing the selected policies. The end of the cold war presents foreign policy bureaucracies with a special challenge. Old threats and enemies have declined in importance or disappeared entirely. To remain effective players in post-cold war foreign policy making, these institutions must adjust their organizational structures and ways of thinking or risk being seen by policymakers as irrelevant anachronisms. The three leading foreign policy bureaucracies of the cold war were the State Department, the Defense Department, and the Central Intelligence Agency (CIA). What the future holds for each of these institutions is the subject of two

UNIT 4

articles in this subsection. The future of the CIA is examined by Melvin Goodman in the report "Ending the CIA's Cold War Legacy." Then, Steven Metz, in "Racing toward the Future: The Revolution in Military Affairs," looks at the prospects for meaningful reform in the military.

A final set of institutions demands our attention not because they need reform, but because the altered agenda of world politics raises the possibility that they might become more important players in making policy. The first of these are the state and local governments. Their increased importance is tied to the greater attention being paid to international economic issues in American foreign policy and what that means for states. James Garcia and Dave McNeely, in "The Politics of NAFTA: Why Is Texas So Much Hotter for NAFTA than California?" examine the differing impact that this agreement has on these states.

The courts may also play a greater role in American foreign policy due to the increased involvement of the United States in multilateral efforts. Particularly controversial is the relationship between the American legal system and international law. In the first unit article, "International Judicial Intervention," David Scheffer examines the argument for establishing an international court of justice to deal with war crimes and discusses the relationship between international law and domestic law.

Looking Ahead: Challenge Questions

How relevant is the Constitution to the conduct of American foreign policy? Do courts have a legitimate role to play in determining the content of U.S. foreign policy? Explain. What role should international law play in making policy?

Why do some states respond positively to NAFTA while others do not? Define the positive and negative aspects of NAFTA.

Is Congress best seen as an obstacle course that presidents must navigate successfully in making foreign policy? What is the proper role of Congress in making foreign policy? Is it the same for military and economic policy?

Which of the foreign affairs bureaucracies discussed in this unit is most important? Which is in the most need of reform? Which is most incapable of being reformed?

Given the growing influence of competing organizations, what is left for the president to do in making foreign policy? What is the proper role of the president?

International Judicial Intervention

David J. Scheffer

David J. Scheffer is senior adviser and counsel to the U.S. permanent representative to the United Nations. The views expressed here are the author's own and do not necessarily represent those of the U.S. government.

A dominant feature of the post-Cold War years has been the perpetuation of atrocities during times of war, ethnic violence, and social upheaval. This ageless practice has recently cast dark shadows over whatever "order" the new world was supposed to embrace. Amazingly, genocide has become a growth industry.

But in response, international judicial intervention is taking hold. Fifty years after the Nuremberg and Tokyo war-crimes trials, opportunities are emerging to hold individuals accountable for crimes of gross inhumanity. We are finally learning that the pursuit of peace can coexist with the search for justice and that the pursuit of justice is often a prerequisite for lasting peace.

The number of war crimes—genocide, crimes against humanity, and violations of the laws and customs of war—that have occurred in our time is depressingly large: the Iraqi assault against its own Kurdish and Shiite populations and against Kuwait; ethnic cleansing in Bosnia and Croatia; genocide in Burundi and Rwanda; widespread terror and murder in Angola, Chechnya, Ethiopia, Haiti, Liberia, Somalia, and Sri Lanka; the human depravity of recent decades echoed in the courtrooms and public arenas of Argentina, Chile, Ethiopia, Guatemala, and Honduras; and the unforgettable genocide in Cambodia. Together they have sparked global indignation and prompted calls for national or international remedies.

These crimes involve issues of morality, national reconciliation, the rule of both domestic and international law, and the deterrence of future atrocities, Lingering on the horizon are rogue horsemen seemingly liberated from the rule of international law: Individuals acting with impunity, sometimes shielded by governments that embrace violations of international humanitarian law, are threats to the peace and security of their own peoples and, inevitably, to the international community.

A half-century ago, two major events helped lay the foundation for the rule of law in the postwar world. The first was the signing of the United Nations Charter, a state-oriented document: Nothing in the Charter focuses explicitly on the responsibility of individuals. The other event was an agreement among the victorious Allies on how to bring Nazi war criminals to trial.

The United States took the lead in crafting a plan for prosecuting these men. That plan, which became the International Military Tribunal at Nuremberg, was presented to America's allies in San Francisco at the same time that the U.N. Charter was signed. Within a year, a similar plan was adopted for the prosecution of top Japanese war criminals. The justice of those trials has largely withstood the test of time, although the legitimacy and fairness of the trial in Manila of Japanese general Tomoyuki Yamashita remain in question.

In recent years we have, to some extent, repeated the historical experience of judging the Holocaust. The international community's initially limited knowledge about atrocities in Bosnia, Croatia, and Rwanda—and its response to them—is reminiscent of the Allies' response to Nazi atrocities during World War II. Government officials and scholars have debated theories of law and prosecution just as their predecessors did in the 1940s. U.S. federal agencies have had to struggle to coordinate their war-crimes work just as they did during World War II. Then, as now, the United States led the creation of a process for investigating and prosecuting war criminals. Then, as now, the United States and its allies have not agreed on every aspect of the process. A hobbled U.N. War Crimes Commission preceded the establishment of the Nuremberg tribunal, and an underfunded U.N. Commission of Experts preceded the International Criminal Tribunal for the Former Yugoslavia.

There are contrasts, as well. In Bosnia, information about atrocities was obtained more rapidly. The United States and Europe launched a massive humanitarian effort and accepted (instead of turning away) refugees. The ad hoc criminal tribunal was created long before the end of the war. The U.S. peace initiative in 1995 was driven to a great extent by the desire to stop atrocities.

Although many of the constitutive documents underpinning Nuremberg originated with the young United Nations, the Nuremberg trials themselves occurred largely outside the fledgling organization. Victors' justice prevailed. The major powers prosecuted war criminals in a way that bears little relevance to the challenges we face today. Nuremberg was a coalition effort unconstrained by a U.N. mired in bureaucratic and financial woes. Funding and staffing levels did not present ob-

Amazingly, genocide has become a growth industry.

stacles and, in the end, the necessary political will was mustered. But the Nuremberg and Tokyo tribunals came too late to deter the murder of millions. Years of deliberation and fighting passed before World War II was won and ad hoc military tribunals could be created to try German and Japanese war criminals.

Today, we are compelled to practice victims' justice, for interethnic conflicts often slog on with no clear victor and no party immune from culpability for atrocities. The result is judicial intervention without the threat or use of military force. The legal endeavor is sometimes distant from the scene of the crime. The arsenal of judicial weapons ranges from truth commissions to ad hoc tribunals to the prospect of a permanent international criminal court.

Some countries have employed innovative mechanisms in recent years to address widespread human rights abuses with strictly domestic remedies. Argentina and Chile are examples of societies where a mixture of truth-finding, public accountability, and amnesty have paved the way for a return to a relatively civil and humane life. In Honduras, a civilian court has charged military officers with committing human rights violations during the 1980s. Ethiopia, with some assistance from the United States, has undertaken domestic criminal proceedings against the architects of the Mengistu regime, which conducted a Stalinesque reign of terror against its opponents in the 1970s and 1980s. South Africa is absorbed with an internal judicial process intended to try to help the country move beyond the crimes committed under apartheid.

These national instruments of accountability typically seek to overcome years of internal human rights abuses so that a society can move forward. Some reformist governments choose to offer amnesty liberally in an effort to promote internal peace rather than relying on a strict enforcement of the law. Despite the hard hits human rights standards take in these cases and the risk of never breaking the cycle of retribution and violence, the choice of "peace over justice" is sometimes the most effective means of reconciliation.

But when domestic transgressions have regional consequences and involve significant violations of international humanitarian law, there is a growing trend to explore international remedies. The United Nations, and the will of the international community that it embodies, is usually the source of such responses. Issues of sovereignty remain problematic when the U.N. seeks to protect the victims of war crimes. Nonetheless, international humanitarian-law and the law of the United Nations have developed enough that a solid foundation upon which to consider options for judicial intervention now exists.

Some observers contend that the U.N. Charter prohibits intervention in the internal affairs of states unless the Security Council is acting under the provisions of Chapter VII to intervene militarily or through the imposition of sanctions. Article 2(7) of the Charter speaks more specifically about noninterference in "matters which are essentially within the domestic jurisdiction of any state" and outlines more broadly the overriding exception to that rule for any "enforcement measures under Chapter VII."

When the Security Council created the Bosnia and Rwanda criminal tribunals under the authority of Chapter VII, it rejected conservative notions about "matters of domestic jurisdiction." But in 1945, many of the Charter's creators understood that "domestic jurisdiction" was a relative term that would evolve according to the conduct of states and international law itself.

Thus international humanitarian law can now trump "domestic jurisdiction." If atrocities remain common, then the judicial weapons that the international community—often working through the United Nations—employs to combat these atrocities are likely to increase if the present ad hoc tribunals work. Like human rights law in general, international humanitarian law can reach deep into societies—into detention camps and remote villages—where systematic torture or crimes against humanity are the sordid business of the day.

The maturing of these legal norms thus has changed the face of "domestic jurisdiction" and opened the door to judicial intervention. And the U.N. is the key actor legitimizing judicial intervention.

4 ❖ INSTITUTIONAL CONTEXT: Law and the Courts

Above: Hermann Goering (left) uses a paper to cover a wide grin as he exchanges jovialities with Rudolf Hess (center) and Joachim von Ribbentrop (right) before the start of a session of the war crimes trial at Nuremburg in February 1946. Karl Doenitz, in dark glasses, sits in the background. UPI/Bettman

AD HOC TRIBUNALS

The clearest manifestations of an emerging trend toward international judicial intervention are the two ad hoc criminal tribunals recently established by the Security Council—one in early 1993 for the former Yugoslavia and the other in late 1994 for Rwanda. The United States was at the forefront in creating both tribunals and continues to be their leading source of political, financial, personnel, logistical, and information-sharing support.

In each case, the Security Council created an independent tribunal before any final resolution of the internal struggle and before the emergence of any unchallenged victor or any guarantee of gaining custody of war criminals. The Council recognized the enforcement of international law as an immediate priority, subordinate to neither political nor military imperatives.

Each tribunal was created by the Security Council as a Chapter VII U.N. entity; thus, either all the states involved agree to cooperate, or the Security Council can enact stiff enforcement measures. The Council regarded the Bosnian and Rwandan conflicts as threats to international peace and security. Each tribunal, in turn, is regarded as a means of rendering justice *and* enhancing the peace by identifying, from within the larger population, those specific individuals responsible for war crimes.

The two ad hoc tribunals both represent and help define a new era of international judicial intervention. The ethnic and religious struggles addressed by each tribunal do not easily identify victor and vanquished. Are there victors after the General Framework Agreement for Peace in Bosnia and Herzegovina (GFA) or simply parties that have settled for what they can? Are the Tutsis victors in Rwanda despite the genocide of their people and the lingering threat of renewed war with the Hutus?

International judicial intervention can never be completely isolated from politics. For example, the Security Council was delayed many weeks by the government of Rwanda, which at the time was a Council member, in establishing the International Criminal Tribunal for Rwanda. Although Rwanda had originally requested the immediate establishment of an ad hoc tribunal, the ruling Tutsi government sought to influence the text of the tribunal's statute, particularly its jurisdiction. It also sought to impose its control over the selection of the judges and the chief prosecutor. But the Council prevailed in creating an independent tribunal.

The appointment of a chief prosecutor for the International Criminal Tribunal for the Former Yugoslavia proved to be highly contentious as well, taking more than 14 months. After stumbling through many candidates (and even formally appointing one of them for a short time), the Security Council finally selected South African justice Richard Goldstone. Given Goldstone's stellar performance, he has proved to be worth the wait. But the politically charged process leading to his appointment should never be repeated.

The tribunals have the opportunity to promote accountability for the way that officials of any rank treat their own citizens. Such accountability is necessary in order to encourage long-term reconciliation and peace. Ambassador Madeleine Albright, the U.S. permanent representative to the United Nations, often remarks that the search for individual accountability is essential if the people of these strife-torn lands are to have any chance of living together peacefully.

In the future, persons responsible for violations of international humanitarian law will not be able to hide easily behind the screen of national sovereignty. The international commu-

Above: Bosnian Serb leader Radovan Karadžić (right) and General Ratko Mladić (left) speak to reporters in Pale, Bosnia, in November 1994. Both have been indicted as war criminals by the United Nations–created International Criminal Tribunal for the former Yugoslavia. Reuter/Bettman

nity will have the ability and right and, finally, a modern precedent for judging and punishing them.

We know from experience in Bosnia that local authorities—camp commanders and temporary local "officials"—sometimes do what they can to improve the circumstances of those under their care once they know that the international community will investigate and punish those who fail to respect human rights standards. Uncompromising indictments by the Yugoslav tribunal have crippled the political and military authority of Bosnian Serb leaders Radovan Karadzic and Ratko Mladić and deprived them of legitimate standing in the international community.

The law will have to develop further before all persons are adequately protected from such acts as genocide, other crimes against humanity, and war crimes. This should be an accelerating process, but it will still take many years and perhaps several more tribunals.

The Yugoslav and Rwanda tribunals are seizing the opportunity to take the first steps. They have jurisdiction over crimes against humanity, including "ethnic cleansing." The International Military Tribunals that sat at Nuremberg and Tokyo had jurisdiction over crimes against humanity only if they were connected to either crimes against peace or war crimes. As a result, atrocities committed in Germany during the 1930s were not redressed (except possibly for some that might have been strongly linked to the war effort).

The judges of the Yugoslav tribunal have delivered several decisions that strengthen the jurisprudence of international humanitarian law. The distinction between a civil and an interstate war had long been significant in international law. The Yugoslav tribunal has weakened this distinction considerably. The judges determined that the tribunal has jurisdiction over crimes against humanity and war crimes whether they occur in an internal or an international armed conflict. In fact, the judges confirmed that customary international law no longer requires any connection between crimes against humanity and armed conflict of any character. (Of course, indictment for the most extreme treaty-based crime against humanity—genocide—has never required the existence of an armed conflict.)

The Yugoslav tribunal also has upheld its own lawful establishment by the Security Council, the primacy of its rulings over those of domestic courts, and unique protective measures for witnesses (including victims of rape). The judges thus have answered some of defense counsels' more potent arguments.

The statute of the Rwanda tribunal expressly isolates the jurisdiction for crimes against humanity from any causal connection with armed conflict. This historic step will soon be tested as the first indictments are prosecuted before the tribunal. An authoritative body of international law stands poised to hold officials accountable for the way they have treated persons under their control without regard to whether or not the acts occurred during armed conflict. Significantly, the Yugoslav tribunal will hold even officials of separatist movements accountable for their crimes against humanity.

THE DAYTON AGREEMENT

A crucial test for international judicial intervention occurred last November in Dayton, Ohio, during the negotiations leading to the GFA. The stakes were high. Journalists, commentators, human rights groups, and even Justice Goldstone speculated before and throughout the negotiations that the United States was prepared to sacrifice justice for peace. Some outside observers worried in particular that amnesty would be granted to indicted war criminals Karadžić and Mladić and guaranteed to Serbian president Slobodan Milosevic, who has not been charged. Many also expected that the Dayton team would not insist that the parties cooperate with the Yugoslav tribunal and its orders to arrest indicted war criminals and transfer them to the Hague.

There was not a shred of truth to this speculation. In fact, the U.S. negotiators incorporated the Yugoslav tribunal into the GFA and eight of its 11 annexes, thus creating a powerful mosaic of obligations that confirm—at least on paper—the tribunal's powers in Bosnia, Croatia, and Serbia. The GFA proves that peace negotiations can be compatible with the investigation and prosecution of international crimes. Neither was compromised at Dayton. Weeks before the signing of the agreement, President Bill Clinton said, "Some people are concerned that pursuing peace in Bosnia and prosecuting war criminals are incompatible goals. But I believe they are wrong. There must be peace for justice to prevail, but there must be justice when peace prevails."

Amnesty was never proposed at the Dayton talks and was thus a nonissue. The administration's clear message for years has been "no amnesty." President Clinton had made clear that the tribunal's "indictments are not negotiable," and, of course, the administration's Dayton negotiators could not have reversed that position. Ambassador Albright has said of both tribunals that "the United States supports strongly the commitment... to pursue any suspect, regardless of his or her rank, position, or stature, wherever the evidence leads. There is not, and there should never be, any statute of limitations on the force and effect of the tribunals' indictments." Only the Security Council can entertain granting amnesty to an indicted war criminal, and the likelihood of its doing so is nil.

Those who wanted the GFA to *guarantee* the enforcement of full cooperation with the tribunal had unrealistic goals. Short of completely occupying the Balkans and launching search-and-arrest missions against indicted war criminals, the United States and other law-abiding member states have to approach tribunal enforcement as pragmatically and effectively as possible.

Eight weapons of enforcement are embodied in or otherwise buttress the GFA and the Yugoslav tribunal:

- Under the new constitution of Bosnia and Herzegovina, no sentenced or indicted war criminal can hold any public office (if indicted but cooperating with the tribunal, the criminal is exempted prior to sentencing). The deteriorating power of Karadžić and Mladić reflects the ultimate use of this weapon.

4 ❖ INSTITUTIONAL CONTEXT: Law and the Courts

- The NATO-commanded Implementation Force (IFOR) has the authority to detain indicted war criminals and transfer them to the custody of the tribunal if the opportunity arises or if any such individual threatens the IFOR mission. NATO approved this authority on December 16, 1995.
- Without the GFA, there would be far less likelihood of tribunal access to witnesses and mass gravesites—and far greater likelihood of more war crimes. On January 22, 1996, IFOR commander Admiral Leighton Smith and Justice Goldstone issued a joint statement that confirmed IFOR's support for tribunal investigators, but also noted IFOR's limitations due to its mandate and available resources.
- The Security Council agreed that suspended economic sanctions against Serbia and Montenegro will be automatically reimposed if the IFOR commander or the high representative for civilian matters determines that either the Federal Republic of Yugoslavia or the Bosnian Serb authorities "are failing significantly to meet their obligations under the Peace Agreement." Compliance with the requests and orders of the tribunal "constitutes an essential aspect of implementing the Peace Agreement." In addition, the Bosnian Serbs are subject to a strict regime of sanctions suspension that depends upon the withdrawal of their troops behind the Zone of Separation on their side of the agreed ceasefire line.
- The Clinton administration seeks to maintain international support for an "outer wall" of restraints on Serbia and Montenegro that will remain standing until Belgrade cooperates with the tribunal, permits effective human rights monitoring of Kosovo by the Organization for Security and Cooperation in Europe, restores effective autonomy for Kosovo, and renounces its claim to be the only successor state of the former Yugoslavia. The outer wall includes membership in international organizations, access to financing by international financial institutions, and bilateral diplomatic relations.
- General U.S. policy is to deny U.S. bilateral economic assistance to jurisdictions whose authorities have the ability to turn over indicted war criminals but refuse to do so within a reasonable period of time.
- For all intents and purposes, indicted war criminals are prisoners in their own territory; they are subject to arrest if they travel anywhere outside their borders.
- No statute of limitations exists on the indictments of the tribunal.

This final weapon of enforcement requires patience by all who are frustrated by the paucity of indicted individuals in the tribunal's custody to date. There are years and probably decades of work ahead to apprehend and bring to justice all those indicted by both the Yugoslav tribunal (52 by January 1996) and the Rwanda tribunal (the ringleaders of the genocide may number more than 100). That is the nature of the beast. The experience with Nazi war criminals shows how long and difficult it can be to track them down and bring them to justice. But the United States has made a long-term commitment to the tribunals.

The mere fact that top Bosnian Serb leaders and others had been, or were about to be, indicted kept them from influencing the Dayton peace talks. The indictments helped to pave the way for Milosevic to take over the Serbian side of the negotiations and, essentially, represent the Bosnian Serbs.

Justice Goldstone and the president of the Yugoslav tribunal, Judge Antonio Cassese, welcomed the GFA shortly after it had been signed. They regarded it as "entirely in keeping with the Security Council resolutions concerning the Tribunal" and concluded that the tribunal had been fortified by it.

There were, however, setbacks during the negotiations and immediately following the signing. Bosnian Croat general Tihomir Blaskic, indicted by the tribunal for crimes against humanity, was appointed as inspector general of the Croatian army. The Bosnian Croat administration in Mostar, rather than transferring to the custody of the tribunal the already arrested commander of the notorious Stupni Do detention camp, Ivica Rajic, instead released him from prison after he was conveniently acquitted in a local court on war-crimes charges. The first Bosnian Muslim apprehended for war crimes and held in the tribunal's prison in the Hague had to be freed in December 1995 because of the failure by Serb authorities to cooperate with tribunal investigators, who needed to collect evidence. Belgrade has persisted in its uncooperative ways despite Milosevic's assurances to U.S. officials and his own signing of the GFA.

The Clinton administration has always been mindful of the fact that getting all parties to comply with tribunal orders will take time, and there may be frequent setbacks. Progress will have to be measured over time. To try and speed the process somewhat, Judge Goldstone has begun to publicly air the evidence against indicted individuals who evade apprehension through a special "Rule 61 proceeding." Such action is then followed by the issuance of an international arrest warrant.

In addition to the challenge of arresting those it indicts, the tribunals face several other issues. First, governments and private beneficiaries have little enthusiasm for voluntarily contributing funds to support the fees accrued by the defense counsel. Yet the independence and integrity of the tribunals depend upon their ability to accord the right of due process to defendants. A special appeal by the United States helped unlock from U.N. budget controls about $80,000 in the Yugoslav tribunal's voluntary fund. The money helped restart the Dusan Tadic case, which had been delayed by the defense counsel due to a shortage of funds available to mount an adequate defense.

Second, there is the perpetual need to adequately fund and staff the Yugoslav and Rwanda tribunals. The U.N. budget crisis threatens the viability of these institutions. With U.S. political support, the Yugoslav tribunal succeeded in 1995 in obtaining an exemption from the overall U.N. freeze on travel expenses for the tribunals, thereby enabling investigators to continue their fieldwork. The United States paid its assessments for both tribunals and also made large voluntary contributions. But such temporary support does not ensure the long-term operation of the tribunals. Importantly, the Security Council resolutions establishing the tribunals encourage voluntary contributions from governmental and nongovernmental sources—provisions the Clinton administration insisted upon. Private support for the tribunals will be critical in the years ahead.

Adequate and timely funding facilitates the hiring of expert staff for the tribunals. From the outset, the administration filled critical gaps in staffing by detailing U.S. prosecutors and investigators to the Hague and to Kigali. Justice Goldstone often remarks that without the hard work of this exceptionally talented group of U.S. personnel, the Yugoslav tribunal would have been crippled, and the number of indictments would be far smaller. But as the staffs of both tribunals grow and diversify, a more systematic approach to hiring will have to be supported by a stable source of funding.

Third, in the aftermath of the fall of the Srebrenica and Zepa enclaves in eastern Bosnia last summer, many speculated that the United States was not sharing all of the information it could with the Yugoslav tribunal and the public about Serb military planning and the atrocities that resulted. Even Justice Goldstone raised concerns about the speed and sufficiency of American responses to his requests for information. The speculation was unfortunate and, in many cases, simply false. It led to fantastic presumptions about what the U.S. government knew and fueled accusations that it was "withholding" information from the Yugoslav tribunal.

Such rhetoric misrepresented the administration's efforts

International humanitarian law can now trump domestic jurisdiction.

since early 1993 to provide as much information as it could, first to the U.N. Commission of Experts on the former Yugoslavia and then to the Yugoslav tribunal. The United States essentially stood alone in assisting the tribunal in this respect. The provision of sensitive information is necessarily conditioned by the protection of sources and methods, the labor-intensive character of such work, the need to ensure that information be conveyed in a secure manner to the tribunal, and whether the prosecutor's requests for support are specific enough to facilitate a timely response.

Nonetheless, last November the administration pledged to speed the flow of information to the Yugoslav tribunal and to give such work higher priority within the U.S. government. Likewise, tribunal staff now better understand the need to prioritize their own requests for information. The integrity of the judicial process, including the protection of witnesses and mass gravesites, necessitates that much of the information—no matter how quickly it is conveyed to the prosecutor—should not be disclosed publicly. Daily, government officials and the tribunal prosecutor must make judgments between, on the one hand, keeping information secret to protect sources and the integrity of the prosecution effort and, on the other hand, informing the public about atrocities and those who commit them.

A PERMANENT COURT

While the two ad hoc international criminal tribunals serve as the most prominent examples of international judicial intervention, there are other recent precedents. With strong congressional support, the Clinton administration has launched a wide-ranging investigation into the genocide in Cambodia and the prospects for holding accountable before a court of law those who are responsible.

The administration supports efforts to create an international commission to investigate the government of Iraq for the war crimes and atrocities it committed against the Kurds during the "Anfal" campaign of the late 1980s, against the Kuwaitis during the Persian Gulf war, and against the Kurds and Shiites afterward. The U.S. government holds or has access to a large amount of incriminating evidence against Iraq. It could be usefully reviewed by a U.N. commission of experts that could be established by the Security Council in a manner similar to the commissions created for the former Yugoslavia and Rwanda.

The administration has also supported an effort to encourage other governments to bring a genocide case against Iraq in the International Court of Justice (ICJ) in connection with the "Anfal" campaign. (Because the United states has taken a number of reservations and understandings to the Genocide Convention that would complicate any case, it is not a preferred claimant against Iraq in this court.) Exposing Saddam Hussein's butchery of his own people and of the Kuwaitis during the Gulf war is the least such judicial efforts could accomplish.

The United States was instrumental in the Security Council's 1995 creation of the International Commission of Inquiry to examine the 1993 massacres in Burundi, which left an estimated 50,000 people dead. One reason genocidal acts of violence have continued in Burundi is that individual accountability for the 1993 atrocities has not been established. An international commission, created by the Security Council, can go a long way toward establishing the facts and identifying suspects: This has been true in Rwanda and the former Yugoslavia, where initial investigatory commissions, having provided enough preliminary information to justify criminal investigations and prosecutions, helped legitimize the establishment of ad hoc tribunals.

In Haiti, the creation of the National Commission for Truth and Justice, following the return of President Jean-Bertrand Aristide in October 1994, has been an important component of restoring democratic rule. Severe human rights abuses during the years of military rule under General Raoul Cédras need to be accounted for if there is to be any hope of healing the deep wounds among Haitians. Though created by the government of Haiti, the commission receives support from the U.S.

government and various international nongovernmental organizations.

Options such as national prosecutions, truth commissions, bodies of inquiry, and ad hoc international criminal tribunals will need to be examined and possibly applied in various countries—such as the would-be breakaway republic of Chechnya, Liberia, and Sri Lanka—where atrocities have been committed in recent years.

The ultimate weapon of international judicial intervention would be a permanent international criminal court (ICC). The Nuremberg and Tokyo tribunals inspired serious efforts after World War II to create an ICC. But those efforts soon got bogged down with the endless task of selecting and defining the crimes that would form the jurisdiction of the court. It took the United Nations almost two decades to reach a definition for the crime of aggression, and even that has proven too imprecise. And the protracted effort to create a Code of Crimes Against the Peace and Security of Mankind, which would define crimes indictable by an international criminal court, continues within the U.N.'s International Law Commission.

Fifty years of difficulty notwithstanding, the proposal for a permanent tribunal is gaining ground. Governments recognize that international crimes that threaten peace and security are increasing. The high costs associated with each ad hoc measure simply cannot continue to be absorbed by national governments, unless at the expense of other priorities.

Indeed, Security Council members already complain of "tribunal fatigue." Having created the International Criminal Tribunals for the Former Yugoslavia and Rwanda as well as their predecessor commissions, Council members are unenthusiastic about the prospect of reinventing the wheel—and financing it—every time an outrage against humanity merits judicial intervention. New prosecutors, investigators, judges, and secure courtrooms are required for novel judicial systems, which take months to conceive and may cost many millions of dollars per year to operate.

Fortunately, for the past few years international lawyers and diplomats have been laboring over a draft statute for a permanent international court. The International Law Commission produced a "final draft statute" in 1994, but its deficiencies prompted many governments, including the United States, to call for further work.

In 1995 two "ad hoc committee" sessions were held at the United Nations to examine the draft statute. The discussions between governments were exceptionally productive. The United States put considerable effort into preparing for and participating in those sessions, consulting bilaterally with more than 25 governments.

In 1996 the U.N. will convene two three-week sessions to try to resolve some outstanding issues and to begin drafting alternative text. By the opening of the 51st General Assembly in September 1996, the U.N. will determine whether the work has advanced far enough to justify convening a diplomatic conference aimed at attracting global support for a treaty to create a permanent court.

Advocates for an international criminal court often misconstrue the U.S. position on the issue as too cautious and even obstructionist. From the Clinton administration's earliest days, the government established a far more positive approach to the concept of an international criminal court than had the previous administration. The guiding principle has been "get it right," not "get it now." The administration also knew that the success or failure of the ad hoc war-crimes tribunals in Rwanda and the former Yugoslavia would deeply influence the prospects for a permanent tribunal. Therefore, the administration has been determined to do all it can to help the ad hoc tribunals succeed and thereby build more confidence in the idea of a permanent court.

A permanent court with jurisdiction over serious violations of international humanitarian law—such as genocide, crimes against humanity, and war crimes—is needed and should be created. On October 15, 1995, President Clinton declared that "nations all around the world who value freedom and tolerance [should] establish a permanent international court to prosecute, with the support of the U.N. Security Council, serious violations of humanitarian law." He said that such a permanent international court "would be the ultimate tribute to the people who did such important work at Nuremberg."

There is also considerable merit in the proposition that the new Torture Convention and the new Convention on the Safety of United Nations and Associated Personnel should be incorporated into the court's jurisdiction. This arrangement would largely eliminate the need to create ad hoc tribunals to investigate and prosecute new atrocities. Thus, over the long run it should save money and act as a more effective deterrent than the haphazard and politically charged complex of ad hoc measures.

The permanent court should begin with limited jurisdiction. The United States has resisted efforts to include drug trafficking in the court's jurisdiction. Likewise, the United States has expressed serious concerns about the ability of a permanent court to judge crimes of international terrorism. Crimes such as these are extremely expensive and difficult to investigate and prosecute. Years of fieldwork—often using highly classified information—are required to develop credible legal cases. National governments bear a special responsibility to handle these cases domestically. The U.S. Department of Justice, for instance, assists many governments directly to enhance their domestic capabilities.

The United States believes that the Security Council's responsibility to promote international peace and security requires that its interests be protected in cases that have security dimensions. In the absence of prior Council approval, the permanent court should not hear a case that clearly pertains to an ongoing Council operation under Chapter VI (peacekeeping) or Chapter VII (peace enforcement). The stakes are too high; the primary U.N. body empowered to handle issues of international peace and security must not be handcuffed by the prosecutor investigating a particular suspect. In most cases the judicial process will not conflict with or threaten to undermine the Council's responsibilities, and Council approval will be granted; but the exceptional case must be covered.

It is equally important that the Security Council be empowered to refer cases and situations, large and small, to a permanent court and to require, if necessary, judicial enforcement under Chapter VII. For example, if genocide were to recur in Rwanda, the Council could consider the matter formally and then refer the entire conflict or atrocity to the permanent court. That court would determine individual accountability without requiring Security Council involvement in the tens or hundreds of cases that might be developed. In effect, the Council would be using the permanent court for the same purpose as it has the ad hoc tribunals, but with less start-up cost and greater dispatch.

It would be ironic indeed if a permanent court exercised fewer powers than the ad hoc tribunals. The Security Council would have to ensure that such is not the case. If the proposed court were weak, then individual governments would likely try to manipulate the court's indictment powers in order to further their own agendas.

A permanent international criminal court would prosecute individuals. The ICJ, the long-standing judicial arm of the U.N., adjudicates only cases arising between states. But, the ICJ is underutilized, and its potential as an instrument of judicial intervention could be improved. The U.S. withdrawal from the compulsory jurisdiction of the ICJ during the Reagan administration does not prevent the United States from seizing opportunities to take interstate disputes to the ICJ or to support other governments that choose to do so.

International judicial intervention will continue to be less common than conventional means of politico-military intervention. But in a world of ethnic violence and dissonant voices, where violence against innocent civilians is common, the rule of law must be rooted firmly in order to protect individual and group rights and to hold evil people accountable for their crimes.

The ad hoc war crimes tribunals and the proposal for a permanent international criminal court are significant steps toward creating the capacity for international judicial intervention. In the civilized world's box of foreign policy tools, this will be the shiny new hammer to swing in the years ahead.

The Politics of NAFTA

Why is Texas so much hotter for NAFTA than California?

By James E. Garcia and Dave McNeely

David Dean, a Dallas-based international trade consultant, makes a living convincing people he is right. And he has a prediction: "The next president of the United States will be a free-trader."

That is to say, a North-American-Free-Trader.

And commerce department officials in at least Texas, California, Arizona, Illinois, Michigan and New York hope that Dean is right.

Those states have the most to gain under the North American Free Trade Agreement—NAFTA. The multi-billion dollar pact was approved by the United States, Mexico and Canada in 1993, creating the world's largest trading bloc. Its backers said the agreement would enable the hemisphere to compete with the colossal trading blocs of Europe and the Far East. Since both President Clinton and (former) Senator Bob Dole backed approval of the trade agreement during a tight congressional vote in 1993, the election in November of a so-called free-trader is certain, barring a third-party surge. (Dallas billionaire Ross Perot, who got 19 percent in his 1992 presidential race, was a vehement opponent of NAFTA, but is considered an even longer shot for the presidency in 1996.)

What's at stake for those trading with Mexico under NAFTA?

For Texas, about $22 billion in exports and 450,000 jobs, according to the U.S. Department of Commerce.

For California, the No. 2 NAFTA state, the figure is more than $7 billion in export-related earnings and 140,000 jobs. Ranking next are Arizona, Illinois, Michigan and New York, in that order. And even far-off New York sends just over $1 billion in goods to our southern neighbor—and employs 18,000 to 20,000 people doing it.

James E. Garcia reports on Mexican and border issues for The Austin American-Statesman. Dave McNeely is the paper's columnist on state and national politics and government.

TRADING WITH MEXICO

Although free trade with Canada has been a long-standing U.S. policy, expanding cross-border economic ties with Mexico has not been easy.

Mexico's recent economic crash, sparked by a massive peso devaluation in 1994, rocked the hemisphere's markets. The peso lost more than 50 percent of its value against the dollar, and inflation and interest rates jumped dramatically. In some cases, interest rates increased to 100 percent. More than 1 million workers—some say as many as 2 million—have lost their jobs. This in a nation where underemployment has always been a serious problem, and economists have stated the economy needed to add 1 million jobs a year simply to keep pace with population growth.

Experts think the Mexican economy has begun a slow recovery, but the balance of trade between the two nations has shifted Mexico's recession. In 1994, the United States was running a large trade surplus with Mexico. That trade surplus and the promise of jobs helped win approval for the trade agreement in the U.S. Congress, political analysts say. But the peso's crash and a related drop in labor and other production costs have made the country's goods less expensive, tipping the trade balance in Mexico's favor.

That trend is beginning to turn around, but Mexican economist Jesus Vargas, who now works for Dean International, says it could be the turn of the century before the United States is again selling more to Mexico than it buys.

The United States still has a lot to gain, says Vargas. He estimates that based on current trends, U.S. exports to Mexico will grow by about 19 percent by the end of the decade. And Mexican exports to the United States will increase by 9 percent during the same period.

In Texas, Governor George W. Bush agrees. Bush, who supported President Clinton in sending $20 billion to Mexico to shore up the peso, is doing everything he can to ensure that his state gets a big chunk of the growth in U.S. exports. Texas sales to Mexico, led by a strong expansion in the Long Star State's computer and electronics industries, could top $26 billion by 2000, says Vargas.

> "Business links with Mexico will likely grow at a faster pace than with Canada."
> —ERIC JAMES
> OKLAHOMA DEPARTMENT OF COMMERCE

California's exports to Mexico could grow to about $8 billion by the end of the decade. And other states, such as Florida and Oklahoma, believe trade with Mexico will pick up the pace as well.

Oklahoma sends about $750 million in exports to Canada and $250 million in goods to Mexico, says Eric James of the Oklahoma Department of Commerce. Yet, James notes, "We expect a tilt." In other words, business links with Mexico will likely grow at a faster pace than with Canada.

EXEMPLARY RELATIONSHIP

The business of doing business with Mexico, say many observers, has best been exemplified by the relationship cultivated by recent Texas governors and the Mexican leadership.

The philosophy of Governor Bush, who took office the month NAFTA was implemented, is expressed in the age-old saying: "Remember who your friends are."

It was with those words, in fact, that Bush began an editorial for the *New York Times* last year.

"Across our country," he wrote, "Mexico is proving to be a strong economic friend.... Not only will free trade help [the United States], it will provide a much-needed boost for Mexico."

And referring to what he called the "bright red bull's eye" Mexico has borne in the wake of its economic crisis and claims by some that immigrants from that country are harming the U.S. economy, Bush pointed out that Texas and Mexico are inextricably linked.

"You cannot wall Mexico away from Texas," Bush recently told *Mexico Business* magazine. With Latinos accounting for 25 percent of Texas' population, up from 18 percent just a decade earlier, and a growing percentage of its voters, it is perhaps no accident that the personable governor appointed as his secretary of state Tony Garza, an equally personable former county judge from the Texas border town of Brownsville.

Garza, a lawyer who dealt with many Texas-Mexico issues in his bilingual/bicultural home town, notes that Texas accounts for almost half of the exports from the United States to Mexico. And three-fourths of the trade between the two countries either travels from Texas or through it.

Bush is the eldest son of former President George Bush, who began NAFTA negotiations with Mexico. President Bush, like President Clinton, predicted NAFTA would lead to freer trade throughout the hemisphere.

A looming problem for NAFTA supporters has been the nation's growing antipathy toward illegal immigrants. NAFTA critics say the trade pact may have actually increased illegal immigration, especially from Mexico.

But for Governor Bush, the formula is simple: Improve the Mexican economy and the Mexican middle class will grow. Grow the Mexican middle class—meaning, reduce poverty—and illegal immigration will slow.

Bush is critical of so-called Mexico bashers—such as Perot and former TV commentator Pat Buchanan—who say signing the North American Free Trade Agreement was a mistake.

"We mustn't allow isolationist rhetoric or bad trade policy to alienate our trading partners," says Bush.

Exports to Mexico

State	'95 Exports ($ billions)	Related jobs*
Texas	$21.9	438,000
California	7.4	148,000
Arizona	2.6	52,000
Illinois	1.7	34,000
Michigan	1.5	30,000
New York	1	20,000

* Based on 20,000 jobs per $1 billion in exports.
Source: U.S. Department of Commerce

It is this positive attitude by Texans, say analysts, that accounts in part for the close diplomatic and rapidly expanding economic ties between Texas and Mexico.

Texas, simply put, treats Mexico like a friend. And that friendship, along with an intense lobbying effort by former Texas Governor Ann Richards and other Texas-based NAFTA backers, has reaped rewards for the state.

For instance, Dallas is headquarters to NAFTA's labor secretariat, a commission set up under a related accord to monitor violations of labor rights in Mexico, Canada and the United States. San Antonio is home to the North American Development Bank, which helps provide funding for environmental and infrastructure projects along the Southwest border.

And Ciudad Juarez, just across the border from El Paso, is where the Border Environment Cooperation Commission has been located. It will monitor environmental practices related to the trilateral pact. Van Whiting, a trade expert at the Center for U.S.-Mexican Studies at the University of California at San Diego, says Texas has a long geographic and even historic advantage in competing for a piece of the Mexican trade pie.

For instance, Texas, the easternmost of the states that border Mexico, shares a 1,248-mile border with Mexico—more than all the other states combined. It has several well-developed and sizable border towns. The state's highway and rail links provide direct and relatively easy access to Mexico City, Monterrey and Guadalajara, which economists refer to as the country's industrial golden triangle. In the other direction, Texas highways and rail links head for the Northeast and Middle West in the United States.

CALIFORNIA CONTRAST

California, by comparison, has only 140 miles of border with Mexico. And Tijuana, about 20 miles south of San Diego, is the only major city on the California-Mexico border. (Tijuana, however, is home to the largest single concentration of so-called maquiladoras, mostly foreign-owned factories that export primarily to the United States.) Interstate 35, which begins in Laredo, Texas, stretches all the way to Canada. States along the I-35 corridor are lobbying Congress to have it designated the official NAFTA highway, bringing with it potentially hundreds of millions in federal funding for infrastructure improvements. Californians face other obstacles in trying to develop trade ties with Mexico. Among them, say some, is their own governor. While Mexico considers Governor Bush a friend, it has had little good to say about California Governor Pete Wilson. And Wilson has reciprocated.

Wilson served in the U.S. Senate for eight years before becoming governor in 1990. He was reelected in 1994. He based a significant portion of his reelection effort on an aggressive campaign against illegal immigration, especially from Mexico. Most of California's estimated 1.5 million illegal immigrants are from Mexico. Wilson's stance against illegal immigration—he backed Proposition 187, a voter-approved referendum to bar illegal immigrants from receiving most forms of public assistance—angered Mexico. But Wilson's hard-line position won him votes in California.

Still, some believe Wilson's position on immigration could have long-term economic consequences for California. As one California trade official recently noted, "You could remove all of the tariffs tomorrow, but if somebody doesn't want to do business with you they're not going to." On the other hand, Whiting believes Wilson's hostile attitude toward immigrants may be softening. "The immigration issue is still a live issue," he says. "But we haven't heard as much rhetoric coming out of Sacramento."

Whiting noted that U.S. Senator Diane Feinstein of California now publicly opposes a controversial provision in the federal immigration reform bill that would allow states to decide if they want to kick the children of illegal immigrants out of public schools. That, Whiting suggests, may be a sign that the state's strident anti-immigrant sentiment may be changing.

While Texas Governor Bush also opposes kicking illegal immigrant children out of public schools, Wilson wants states to have the capability to be able to turn them away. Wilson's approach was included in Proposition 187, which is on hold pending court action.

Nevertheless, Whiting predicts that relations between California and Mexico will improve.

"California is strong not only in manufacturing and the seemingly invisible areas of electronic commerce, but a lot of joint venturing and partnering with Mexico is happening," Whiting says.

Even so, it will be a long time before California closes the trade gap, says Whiting, who cautions against expecting anything having to do with NAFTA to happen quickly. "This is not a one-year program," he says. "It's a 20-year program." And like many long-term initiatives, there are often short-term political consequences. Early in the presidential campaign, especially during the primary elections, NAFTA and Mexico became a lightning rod for what Buchanan and others contend is wrong with U.S. economic domestic and international policy. Free trade, Buchanan claims, is destroying the U.S. economy. Sending jobs overseas hurts the American middle class, he says. Buchanan may not have won the Republican nomination, but his antitrade message has resonated, says James.

"It's still an issue, because of the flight of some jobs to Mexico," James said. "Even if the (presidential) candidates aren't talking about it, the public is."

Critics of the trade agreement, meanwhile, say it has not lived up to the many promises of its backers.

Consumer activist Ralph Nader claims hundreds of thousands of jobs have been lost to Mexico and Canada as a result of NAFTA.

Most economists dispute that claim, noting that only about 50,000 to 60,000 lost jobs are tied to the enactment of the trade pact, while a strong U.S. economy in recent years has created millions of new jobs, many of them export-related.

BORDER FACTORIES

A report issued earlier this year by Nader's Public Citizen group stated that the more than 2,000 factories that dot the U.S.-Mexican border, many owned by U.S. companies, continue to pollute the environment from Brownsville to Tijuana. NAFTA backers had predicted that the number of maquiladoras, most of them foreign-owned, would decrease after the agreement was passed as the plants' owners rushed to supply goods to Mexico's middle class. As a result, they said, pollution would be reduced. But the economic collapse and a subsequent drop in the cost of labor has made it more attractive for foreign companies to produce products in Mexico—convincing many companies to expand or open new facilities along the border. More plants have opened in Mexico's interior. But a hold on highway construction and other infrastructure development means it is still far easier to move goods bound for the United States and other markets if plants are located along the border.

Trading Partners

**Total trade in 1994 between
United States and Canada:**
$243 billion

**Total trade in 1994 between
United States and Mexico:**
$109 billion

**Total trade in 1995 between
United States and Canada:**
$272 billion

**Total trade in 1995 between
United States and Mexico:**
$108 billion

Source: U.S. Department of Commerce:

Nader wants the agreement scrapped. He claims that now that Buchanan is more or less out of the picture, Clinton and Dole are downplaying NAFTA because they are ashamed of its track record.

Whiting disputes that. "I don't think they're ashamed of it," he says. Clinton and Dole aren't talking much about it simply because they both support it, and because other news coming out of Mexico—much of it focusing on high level corruption and international drug trafficking—hasn't been all that good. (The brother of former President Carlos Salinas de Gotari has been jailed, and opposition political movements continue to protest the ruling party's lock on power. In addition, a second rebel movement has surfaced in the state of Guerrero, home to Acapulco.)

"There seems to be a tacit agreement to let [NAFTA] be a post-election issue," says Whiting. As far as Dean is concerned—and keep in mind that he is paid to say this—the economic future of free trade with Mexico is bright. More than 80 percent of Mexico's imports come from the United States. "The fact is we produce more in this country than we consume," says Dean. "Exporting makes sense."

When money talks, Congress listens

By Jennifer Washburn

DID FOREIGN CAMPAIGN CONTRIbutions distort U.S. policy? An investigation into that possibility is under way, drawing unprecedented attention to the corrosive influence of money in politics. Strangely absent from investigation, however, is the much more pervasive influence that domestic interests—like the U.S. arms industry—exert over the political process.

The arms industry, dominated by a few mega-corporations like Lockheed Martin, McDonnell Douglas, and Boeing, is one of the most powerful of U.S. special interest groups. Using its formidable financial and political clout, the industry has grown expert in slanting U.S. policy decisions for its own financial gain—often to the detriment of human rights and global security. As Lora Lumpe of the Federation of American Scientists explains: "Increasingly, U.S. foreign policy and arms sales decisions have become captive to the narrow economic interests of the weapons industry."

To make sure it gets its way, the arms industry is pouring more money into political coffers than ever before. In the 1995–96 election cycle, according to a study by my colleague William Hartung of the World Policy Institute, the top 25 U.S. weapons-exporting firms doled out a record $10.8 million in political action committee (PAC) and soft money contributions—a 56 percent increase over the industry's previous high in 1991–92.[1]

The jump in contributions in the 1990s represents a concerted industry effort to offset post–Cold War reductions in military outlays. "The arms industry wants to keep defense spending and subsidies as high as possible," says Hartung. "Weapons manufacturers [have] worked to elect a Republican Congress that is helping them to do just that, together with Democrats who have defense plants in their districts."

The industry's lobbying efforts seem to have paid off.[2] With budgets remaining at average Cold War levels, in 1995 Congress added an additional $7 billion to the Pentagon's already bloated request, and last year it added $9 billion more.

Still, from the arms industry's perspective, Pentagon spending for new weapons has plummeted—as compared with the peak Reagan years, that is. Faced with this shortfall, weapons makers were confronted with a choice: convert to civilian production or increase exports. Most companies prefer the export option.

Only one problem remained: the world weapons market was already saturated. Arms makers quickly realized that if the export push were to succeed, they would need substantial U.S. government assistance in the form of federal subsidies to promote and finance overseas sales, relaxed policies on high technology exports, and reduced restrictions in regional markets like Eastern Europe and Latin America.

And that's pretty much what arms makers got. As John Mikels, the vice president of Hughes's missile division, told *Boston Globe* reporter Charles Sennott for a February 1996 special issue on the arms trade: "We've all been pretty pleasantly surprised by Clinton. We have seen . . . a realization that in order to keep production alive they are going to have to actively help the industry in seeking out export markets. I would say it's a dramatic turn."

Others, like Lawrence Korb, an assistant secretary of defense under Reagan, argue that the Clinton administration's pro-export policies are dangerous: "The brakes are off the system. . . . It has become a money game: an absurd spiral in which we export arms only to develop more sophisticated ones to counter those spread out all over the world."

Today, nearly 6,400 Pentagon, State, and Commerce Department employees are assigned full time to help arms makers promote, broker, negotiate, and close foreign sales. The government spends an estimated $7.5 billion

---

Jennifer Washburn is a research associate at the World Policy Institute's Arms Trade Resource Center, which is based at the New School for Social Research in New York City.

a year to support weapons merchants through a mixture of grants, subsidized loans, tax breaks, and promotional activities. This assistance calls into question the arms industry's claim—repeated like a mantra on Capitol Hill—that dollars from overseas weapons sales save American jobs. With international sales likely to hold steady at approximately $12–16 billion a year, more than half of all U.S. arms exports through the end of the decade will be paid for by the U.S. taxpayer, not by foreign weapons buyers. Arms exporters' subsidies are now second only to agricultural price supports.[3]

Targeting Congress

In 1995, the arms industry scored big, winning two major victories that were at the top of their lobbying wish list: a $15 billion arms export loan program, guaranteed by the U.S. government, and a $200 million annual tax break.

In both cases, industry lobbyists benefited from the unusual access they have to the highest echelons of government, through groups like the Defense Policy Advisory Committee on Trade, a panel of industry executives that gives the defense secretary confidential advice on arms sales policy. In November 1988, the committee (led by Norman Augustine, head of Lockheed Martin, the Pentagon's largest defense contractor and leading weapons exporter) began recommending the new loan fund and special tax exemptions. Lockheed Martin, described by Hartung as the "the leader of the PACs," made $2.3 million in political contributions in the last election cycle.

Augustine himself played a critical role in winning both victories. Early in the Clinton administration, Augustine and the Aerospace Industries Association wrote an industry letter to Defense Secretary Les Aspin on behalf of the loan fund, and later Augustine personally wrote every member of the House Armed Services Committee praising both the fund and the tax break proposals.

In the case of the $200 million annual tax break, the Clinton administration supported industry's position from the start, submitting legislation each year until it passed. The break allows the president to waive the "recoupment fees" normally attached to foreign arms sales. The fees, which had generated anywhere from $200 to $500 million in taxes each year, were designed to partially reimburse the government for its investment in research and development on weapon systems that were later sold for profit.

With regard to the $15 billion loan fund, industry lobbyists acted without administration support. Most of their efforts were directed at Congress. Jane Harman, a California Democrat and major recipient of arms industry largesse, spearheaded the legislative effort in the House; Idaho Republican Dirk Kempthorne, a former vice president of the FMC Corporation, served as chief sponsor in the Senate. In addition, moderate to liberal Democrats like Sens. Dianne Feinstein of California and Christopher Dodd of Connecticut were enlisted in support of the fund, in large part because they believed that weapons-exporting companies based in their states would benefit from increased financing for foreign arms sales.

In an August 1995 floor debate over the loan guarantees, Dodd touted similar loans he had earlier helped to secure for the $1 billion sale of Sikorsky Blackhawk helicopters to Turkey, saying that they "enabled some people in my state to remain employed who might otherwise have lost their jobs." Then, in support of the new $15 billion loan program, he proclaimed: "The time has come to stop treating workers in the defense industry like second-class citizens." Opponents of the loan program argued that it was both costly and unnecessary, because the government already provides an estimated $3 billion a year through the Foreign Military Financing Program as well as hundreds of millions more in government-guaranteed loans through the Export-Import Bank.

CATCH F-22

Why do we need the F-22 jet fighter?

To keep ahead of other countries.

How will we pay for it?

By selling it to other countries.

In the Senate, the opposition was led by Arkansas Democrat Dale Bumpers, who introduced an amendment that would have stripped the loan fund from the Defense authorization bill. The Bumpers amendment failed, 58–41. While campaign spending by arms exporters may not be the only reason a majority of legislators voted with industry, an analysis of the vote on the Bumpers amendment reveals that those who favored the fund received twice as much PAC money from arms exporters as those who voted against it.

The new loan program allows the Pentagon to offer U.S.-backed loans to any of 37 countries in Europe and Asia, ranging from Romania and Hungary to Singapore and Indonesia. If arms buyers default on these loans, the guarantee means that U.S. taxpayers will almost certainly pick up the bill. Since 1990, the United States has written off nearly $10 billion in arms-related loans.

What's good for industry ...

In addition to lobbying for greater subsidies, weapons-producers have also pushed hard since the end of the Cold War to lift restrictions on the sale of the most advanced U.S. weapons systems. The battle over Lockheed Martin's next generation F-22 fighter illustrates how quickly the aerospace industry adjusts its arguments to the times.

Initially, the company said that the $74 billion F-22 program was needed to preserve U.S. superiority over other countries' advanced fighters, and Lockheed lobbyists circulated literature that featured a menacing map blackened with the world's fighter planes—failing to mention that most had been obtained from the United States.[4]

But after several government assessments concluded that the F-22 was too expensive, over budget, or not needed, the company shifted its strategy in late 1996. The company began arguing that the plane's per-unit cost (the F-22 is the most expensive fighter plane ever built) could be reduced if it were also sold abroad. A spokesman for the air force, which appears to be close to approving the company's plan to export the plane, told *Defense News* on January 21: "We've been feeling the heat from Lockheed. . . . We also need to keep costs down. . . . So I'd expect the recommendation to come out in favor of qualified exports."

The air force's willingness to sanction weapons exports as a way to help defense contractors is nothing new. But making the commercialization of arms export decisions official policy is. In February 1995, as part of a policy review, the Clinton administration declared that the financial impact on the arms industry should be an explicit consideration in the weapons-export approval process.

In March, the aerospace lobby succeeded in penetrating the Latin American arms market—a long-time goal. Reversing a two-decade-long U.S. policy of denying the sale of sophisticated combat planes to Latin American countries, the administration granted approval for U.S. manufacturers to market advanced fighter aircraft to Chile. As of late May, the administration had not yet announced a formal policy change, but the government did release technical data on U.S. fighter planes to potential Latin American customers. It is very rare for the government to release such data unless it is willing to allow a sale to go through.

Opponents argue that lifting the ban may spark an arms race at a time when Latin America's fledgling democracies are still struggling to impose full civilian control over their militaries. As former Secretary of State Warren Christopher said last year, "We should show restraint in introducing new or higher levels of weapons where they don't presently have them. We should try to encourage countries to put their money into things that are of greater benefit to their citizens."

But arms makers continued to beat the drum, calling for an end to all restrictions. A year ago, aerospace lobbyists helped circulate letters in both houses of Congress that urged Christopher to reverse his position. In the last election cycle, the 78 representatives and 38 senators who signed those letters received more than $1 million from PACs controlled by Lockheed Martin, McDonnell Douglas, and the major subcontractors for the F-16 and F-18, planes that are contenders for any Latin American sale.

Industry lobbyists also got a boost from various government agencies that were more than willing to help. First, according to Douglas Waller of *Time* magazine, the Pentagon discreetly arranged for Puerto Rican Air National Guard pilots to fly Brazilian generals in F-16s—presumably, just for the thrill. Then, at a March 1996 weapons exhibition held in Santiago, Chile, the Commerce Department orchestrated an impressive display of military prowess. Flying overhead, U.S. Air Force personnel staged a demonstration flight of the B-2 Stealth bomber and performed dramatic dives with F-16 fighters for all of Latin America's military brass to see.

"The State Department was furious with the stunts," wrote Waller, "but the

More blessed to give?

	Campaign contributions*	Major export items
Lockheed Martin	$2,351,400	F-16 fighters, C-130 transports
General Motors/Hughes	$1,047,200	Saudi Peace Shield, AMRAAM missiles
Northrop Grumman	$ 864,600	F-18, F-5 subcontractor
General Electric	$ 816,500	F-110, F-108 engines
Boeing	$ 796,600	AWACS, Chinook helicopters
United Technologies	$ 737,900	Blackhawk helicopters, F-100 engines
General Dynamics	$ 615,100	M-1 tanks
Raytheon	$ 526,900	Patriot, Hawk, and AMRAAM missiles
McDonnell Douglas	$ 505,500	F-15, F-18 fighters, Apache helicopters
Rockwell	$ 413,800	C-130, Hellfire missiles, cluster bombs

*During 1995–96 election cycle.

air show accomplished exactly what the Pentagon had wanted." Within six months, Chile and Brazil were both requesting information on buying F-16s and F/A-18s, information that the government has since supplied.

Former Defense Secretary William Perry did little to hide his support for lifting the ban. He told journalists at the show that after the administration's review of the Latin American arms ban was complete, he hoped "the new policy . . . will be more liberal."[5] William Cohen, Perry's successor, also signed a letter in favor of lifting the Latin American ban when he served in the Senate, and this year he personally lobbied the president to release marketing data to Chile. In his last year in the Senate, Cohen received $42,600 from top arms exporters.

With little thought for tomorrow

In their rush to please companies like McDonnell Douglas and Lockheed Martin, neither Congress nor the administration appears to have given much thought to the consequences of making weapons exports a major post–Cold War activity.

Despite government assurances that exports are carefully vetted, over the last four years 84 percent of U.S. arms transfers to the developing world have gone to countries the State Department considers undemocratic.[6] In addition, U.S. weapons are involved in 45 of the world's 50 largest ethnic and territorial conflicts. Not only do these weapons increase global insecurity, they can turn around and become a threat to U.S. forces stationed overseas.[7]

As Oscar Arias, a Nobel Peace Prize Laureate and champion of arms export controls, has often said, countries beset with poverty deprive their citizens of basic human and civil rights when they spend precious resources on deadly weapons. Turkey, for instance, has a weak economy and a bloated military, and gets many weapons from the United States—either as giveaways or purchases made with U.S. taxpayer-backed loan guarantees. It has turned those weapons against the Kurdish population of southeastern Turkey, where 3,000 villages have been bombed.

One effort to reverse the legacy of U.S. weapons exports involves "Code of Conduct" legislation sponsored by Georgia Democrat Cynthia McKinney and California Republican Dana Rohrabacher. The code would prohibit military assistance and arms transfers to non-democratic regimes and human rights violators. A tally of last year's Senate vote shows that those senators who voted to defeat the bill received five times more in campaign donations from arms exporters during the 1995–96 election cycle than those who voted for it.

However you look at it, arms export policy is being driven by the demands of weapons manufacturers as never before. Special interest money may not be the only culprit, but reform of campaign finance laws and passage of the "Code of Conduct" offer the best hope for curbing runaway foreign arms sales.

. . . Or to receive?

House member	Contributions from top arms exporters*
Robert Livingston, Louisiana Republican Chairman, Appropriations	$ 86,000
John Murtha, Pennsylvania, Ranking Democrat, National Security Subcommittee, Appropriations	$ 81,500
Norm Dicks, Washington Democrat, Member National Security Subcommittee, Appropriations	$ 67,750
Jane Harman, California Democrat, Member, National Security Committee	$ 66,750
Ike Skelton, Missouri, Ranking Democrat, Military Procurement Subcommittee, National Security Committee	$ 62,000
Senate member	
John Warner, Virginia Republican, Chairman, Airland Forces Subcommittee, Armed Services	$117,300
Ted Stevens, Alaska Republican, Chairman, Defense Subcommittee, Appropriations	$103,500
James M. Inhofe, Oklahoma Republican, Member, Armed Services Committee	$ 91,500
Strom Thurmond, South Carolina Republican, Chairman, Armed Services Committee	$ 82,500
Mitch McConnell, Kentucky Republican, Chairman Foreign Operations Subcommittee, Appropriations	$ 73,305

*1995–96 election cycle contributions by top 25 arms-exporting firms only. Source: The Center for Responsive Politics.

1. William D. Hartung, "Peddling Arms, Peddling Influence Update," World Policy Institute, April 1997.
2. The FY 1998 budget request for military spending of $265 billion is comparable to spending levels of the late 1970s. Under the Clinton five-year defense plan, spending on new weapons procurement is slated to go from $44 billion this year to $68 billion in 2002, an increase of more than 50 percent.
3. William D. Hartung, "Welfare for Weapons Dealers: The Hidden Costs of the Arms Trade," World Policy Institute, 1996.
4. *The F-22 Air Superiority Fighter: Peace Through Conventional Deterrence*, Lockheed Corporation, Marietta, Georgia, March 1994, pp. 5, 7–8.
5. *Arms Trade News*, Aug./Sept. 1996 (Council for a Livable World).
6. "Dictators or Democracies: U.S. Arms Transfers to Developing Countries 1991–1995, Project for Demilitarization and Democracy," Washington, D.C., August 1996.
7. William D. Hartung, "U.S. Weapons at War," World Policy Institute, June 1995.

Article 19

> "Decisions made in Washington in the coming years will determine whether the revolution in military affairs stokes future arms races and proliferation problems... So far the American approach, while a logical response to vexing strategic problems, has not been shaped by concern for long-term political implications."

Racing Toward the Future: The Revolution in Military Affairs

STEVEN METZ

The Persian Gulf War may have signaled a historic change in the nature of armed conflict. By most indicators the Iraqi military that occupied Kuwait was proficient and well equipped with modern weaponry, especially tanks, artillery, and air defense systems. Battle-tested in a long war with Iran, it should have been a fearsome enemy for the United States–led coalition. Pundits and political leaders expected a bloody struggle. But once the war began, Saddam Hussein's forces were brushed aside with stunning suddenness and minimal human cost to the United States and its allies, leaving the world to ponder the war's meaning.

Initially, American military leaders saw Desert Storm as the payoff for years of accumulated improvement in training, personnel quality, doctrine, leadership, and equipment. Some analysts unearthed deeper lessons. Rather than attributing the outcome to evolutionary advancements in the United States military, they saw Desert Storm as the prologue to a fundamental transformation in the nature of warfare—a "revolution in military affairs," or RMA. This idea had such immense strategic and political implications that American military leaders, defense policymakers, and strategic analysts soon adopted it, changing the RMA concept from a theoretical construct to a blueprint for the armed forces of the twenty-first century.

Today the RMA has become the basis of most long-term thinking in the Defense Department and, increasingly, for the militaries of other advanced states. But the full implication of this is not yet clear; many dimensions of the RMA await analysis. For example, little thought has been given to how the RMA might affect arms races and weapons proliferation—a serious oversight. If armed conflict is undergoing historic and significant change, "traditional" arms races will persist into the next century even as new and very different ones take shape. The more these new problems are anticipated, the easier they will be to deal with. To assess the proliferation and arms control issues that will challenge world leaders 10 years from now requires tracing the evolution of thinking on the RMA and its effect on military strategy in the United States and around the world.

THE EVOLUTION OF AN IDEA

The concept of military revolutions grew from Soviet writing of the 1970s and 1980s, particularly a series of papers by Marshal Nikolai Ogarkov. When American defense analysts initially considered this idea, they focused on the technological dimension. One of the first major study groups in the United States labeled its final report *The Military Technical Revolution*.[1] But it quickly became clear that this was an overly narrow approach that understated the importance of concepts and organizations. The idea of a "military-technical revolution" soon evolved into the more holistic concept of a revolution in military affairs.

There is now a loose consensus among scholars, policymakers, and military strategists on the most salient aspects of RMAs. In simple terms, an RMA is a rapid and radical increase in the effectiveness of

---

STEVEN METZ *is Henry L. Stimson Professor of Military Affairs at the United States Army War College and a research professor at the college's Strategic Studies Institute, where he specializes in future warfare and changes in military technology. The views expressed in this essay are those of the author.*

[1] Michael J. Mazarr, et al., *The Military Technical Revolution: A Structural Framework* (Washington, D.C.: Center for Strategic and International Studies, March 1993).

military units that alters the nature of warfare and changes the strategic environment. RMAs result from mutually supportive changes in technology, concepts, and organizations; technological advancement alone does not make an RMA. Analysts also agree that RMAs are, by definition, strategically significant. States that understand and exploit them accrue geopolitical benefits; those that do not slide into military weakness.

Even given this simple conceptual base, writers differ on when RMAs have occurred in the past. Ironically, there is greater agreement on the nature of the current RMA. Scholars, military strategists, and defense policymakers acknowledge that what drives it is a vast improvement in the quality and quantity of information made available to military commanders by improvements in computers and other devices for collecting, analyzing, storing, and transmitting data. The United States Army, for instance, talks of "digitized" battle in which a commander would use an array of sensors and data-fusion technologies to obtain a near-perfect picture of the battlefield that would provide the location and status of all friendly and most enemy units, thus dispersing what has been called the "fog of war." Such a development would certainly represent a sea change in the nature of armed conflict. The presence (or absence) of accurate information has long shaped the conduct of warfare. If the RMA does lift the "fog of war," the results will be stunning, giving those armed forces that master the changes immense advantages.

The increasing quality and quantity of military information will have a number of corollary effects. One is an alteration of the traditional relationship between operational complexity and effective control. Accurate, real-time information and advanced, computer-based training and simulation models will allow more complex military operations than in the past. Simultaneous operations across one or more military theaters might soon be possible. At the same time, the relationship between accuracy and distance in the application of military force might change as extremely precise, standoff strikes become the method preferred by advanced militaries. The RMA could relegate the close-quarters clash of troops to history.

The RMA might change military strategy as well. Futurists Alvin and Heidi Toffler have argued that information is becoming the basis of economic strength, especially in what they call "Third Wave" states. During the "First Wave" of human development, production was primarily agricultural, so military strategies were designed to seize and hold territory or steal portable wealth. During the "Second Wave" industrial production dominated, which meant that war was often a struggle of attrition where belligerents wore down their enemies' capacity to feed, clothe, and equip armies. Following this logic, "Third Wave" warfare will seek to erode or destroy the enemy's means of collecting, processing, storing, and disseminating information.[2] Instead of using explosives to kill and destroy, the warrior of the future might fight with a laptop computer from a motel room, attacking digital targets with strikes launched through fiber-optic webs in order to damage or alter enemy information infrastructure and data resources. The opening words of the next global war might be "Log-on successful" rather than "Tora, Tora, Tora." From the perspective of arms control, it is a chilling thought that something as uncontrollable as a few thousand lines of computer code could become a dangerous weapon.

THE AMERICAN ORTHODOXY

No organization undertakes a revolution without a pressing incentive. This certainly holds for the United States military. The Defense Department is pursuing the RMA in response to two important post–cold war strategic trends. One is a decline in the American military force structure and budget without a concomitant decline in responsibilities and missions, which has generated a growing mismatch between means and ends. The other is what military and civilian leaders see as the American public's limited tolerance for the human toll of armed conflict. These two issues form the core dilemma of current United States national security strategy and drive the quest for the RMA.

During the wide-ranging reassessment of national security strategy in the early 1990s, people like Andrew Marshall, director of the Defense Department's Office of Net Assessment, and Admiral William A. Owens, former vice chairman of the Joint Chiefs of Staff, concluded that an American military built along the principles of the RMA could be smaller yet more powerful than the present one. To use jargon that has become a mantra within the military, the goal was to "leverage technology" to solve strategic dilemmas. By the mid-1990s the RMA had moved from the realm of theorists and military historians to the world of force structure planning and programming.

---

[2] Alvin and Heidi Toffler, *War and Anti-War: Survival at the Dawn of the 21st Century* (Boston: Little, Brown, 1993).

4 ❖ INSTITUTIONAL CONTEXT: The Bureaucracy

The RMA quickly entered the mainstream thinking of the American armed forces. Courses appeared at war colleges and staff schools, RMA-related articles became common in military journals, and military think tanks began to produce studies, reports, exercises, and war games. Institutions designed to develop, test, and refine RMA-related concepts emerged throughout the Department of Defense. Government labs explored technologies to make the RMA possible, especially in areas such as information gathering, assessment, and dissemination, nonlethal weapons, robotics, unmanned military systems, new materials, and new energy sources.

Other nations quickly joined the bandwagon. The Australian military hosted one of the first major RMA conferences outside the United States in Canberra, Australia, in February 1996. At the National Institute for Defense Studies in Tokyo, a series of RMA seminars attracted the attention of senior policymakers. The French have also begun exploration of the RMA.

Still, the United States military is clearly the leader in RMA thinking and continues to define the "orthodoxy." In 1996 this was codified in Chairman of the Joint Chiefs of Staff General John Shalikashvili's Joint Vision 2010, which is the best distillation of official United States thinking on the RMA and the future security environment. Joint Vision 2010 projects no revolutionary change in the global strategic environment over the next decade. The primary task of American armed forces, Shalikashvili contends, will continue to be to deter conflict and, if that fails, to fight and win the nation's wars. Power projection enabled by an overseas presence will remain the fundamental strategic concept, and the military forces of other nations still the primary foe.

Joint Vision 2010 does, however, anticipate great strides in the adoption of new technology, concepts, and organizations. It predicts that technology will allow even more emphasis on long-range precision strikes. New weapons based on directed energy will appear. Advances in low observable ("stealth") technologies will augment the ability to mask friendly forces from enemies. And improvements in information and systems integration technologies will provide decision makers with fast and accurate information. In combination, these technologies will allow increased stealth, mobility, and dispersion, and a higher tempo of operations, all under the shield of information superiority.

> *The opening words of the next global war might be "Log-on successful" rather than "Tora, Tora, Tora."*

Four operational concepts form the heart of Joint Vision 2010. The first, *dominant maneuver,* would allow overwhelming force against an opponent by conducting synchronized operations from dispersed locations rather than from a few large bases or camps. The second key concept is *precision engagement*. This would be based on a "system of systems" that would allow United States forces to locate a target, attack it with great accuracy, assess the effectiveness of the attack, and strike again when necessary. In many cases, the strike systems themselves would be "stealthy." The third operational concept, *full-dimension protection,* entails protecting friendly forces from enemy information warfare, missile attacks, and other threats. The final concept is *focused logistics,* which fuses information, logistics, and transportation technology to deliver tailored logistics packages at all levels of military operations. If attained, these four concepts would give American forces full spectrum dominance over anticipated enemies in the first two decades of the twenty-first century, assuming such enemies cannot develop effective responses to American advances.

While largely excluded from Joint Vision 2010, there is one other important component of current American thinking on the RMA: a desire to use technology to make warfare "cleaner" by reducing the casualties and collateral damage normally associated with combat operations. To a great extent, this is a response to the global communications explosion that has expanded the audience for armed conflict beyond the participants. To be politically acceptable, military operations must minimize casualties. Precision conventional strikes are part of this, but even more radical change may be possible through explicitly nonlethal weapons such as acoustic, laser, and high-power microwaves; nonnuclear electromagnetic pulses; high-power jamming; obscurants, foams, glues, and slicks; supercaustics that erode enemy equipment; magnetohydrodynamics; information warfare; and soldier protection. The American military's interest in nonlethality has increased dramatically, but the full implications—especially for human rights and ethical limits on the use of force—await exploration.

STOKING A NEW ARMS RACE?

The military described in Joint Vision 2010 will be able to counter a traditional enemy relying on massed, armor-heavy formations in relatively open terrain. But, since Desert Storm showed the futility of pitting an old-fashioned military against a cutting-edge one in maneuver warfare, future opponents are unlikely to repeat Iraq's mistakes. Indeed, the world is unlikely to cede permanent military superiority to the United States. A few advanced nations may emulate the American version of the RMA, but those with the technological capacity to do so do not have the political incentive.

Most potential enemies will not have the scientific and technological resources to emulate the United States military and will instead seek asymmetric counterweights. Like guerrilla warfare in Vietnam, these may not give American enemies the ability to win battlefield victories, but they will allow them to raise the cost of the conflict, possibly to the point of paralyzing American policymakers. One example is the "Somali strategy," in which small groups of warriors armed with relatively low-cost weapons operate among civilians in an urban environment. The United States military envisioned in Joint Vision 2010 would have more trouble with such an opponent than with an Iraq- or North Korea-style enemy. Even more ominously, potential enemies may turn to terrorism against "soft" targets in the United States, perhaps using weapons of mass destruction, in order to deter American military action. Even though terrorism may not be the preferred method of fighting, enemies of the United States may feel that its military power leaves them no alternative.

Finally, information warfare is likely to stoke an arms race of its own. Even today there is sharp competition between computer hackers and virus-writers and businesses, networks, and law-abiding individuals. As armed forces become more information- and computer-dependent, this competition may shift to the military realm. Hacking, virus-writing, and crashing data information systems—as well as defending against enemy hackers and virus writers—may become core military skills, as important as the ability to shoot. In this particular arena, the American armed services are less clearly superior to potential enemies than in traditional military functions, so the spiral of response and counter-response is likely to be intense.

Marching toward the fringe

The RMA described in Joint Vision 2010 does not represent a fundamental transformation of armed conflict; it is more "hyper-evolutionary" than revolutionary. But it is possible to use existing trends to speculate on the direction armed combat may take beyond 2010 and imagine the problems that could emerge. For example, future armed conflict may involve little or no direct human contact. Advances in robotics and nanotechnology—the ability to manipulate and manufacture individual molecules—may soon allow the construction of tiny but "brilliant" military machines capable of complex decision making. This could turn warfare into a machine-on-machine struggle, with humans on the sidelines. Machines may become self-repairing, self-replicating, even self-improving. At some point, cyborgs—complex machines with some attributes of living organisms—may become feasible and the proliferation of militarily relevant genetic material a key issue for arms control.

Even more ominously, technology to manipulate human thoughts, perceptions, attitudes, and beliefs using electronic or chemical means might become feasible. This could entail direct "mind control," holograms, and "morphing" an individual by creating, manipulating, and transmitting a computer-generated image indistinguishable from a real one. It is easy to imagine the horror of such developments, but it is equally easy to understand how a beleaguered leader might decide that the immorality of psychotechnology is justified by a serious security threat (especially if the public has already become accustomed to such techniques through the entertainment and advertising industries). If one nation opens this Pandora's box and demonstrates substantial progress in psychotechnology, others will surely follow, unleashing another kind of arms race.

Finally, future warfare may also see changes in who fights, with the "privatization" of warfare made possible, perhaps even likely. If the current RMA allows the development of small but effective armed forces, powerful transnational mercenary corporations may arise. The same factors that led to the proliferation of mercenaries in the past—the expense of training and sustaining a military force, the sporadic need for one, and a moral disdain for the profession of arms—show signs of rebirth. In coming decades, high-tech, transnational mercenary corporations or the private armies of other transnational corporations may be able to challenge or defeat the armed forces of less advanced states.

Distant rumblings

Only the historians of the future will know whether a full-scale RMA was under way in the 1990s. But for those living through these times—especially policymakers who must deal with arms control and proliferation—there is little doubt that there is at least a revolution in weaponry. This can be seen in the shifting valuation of weapons systems. In the past, valuation was based on the ratio of cost to destructiveness. Now what might be called "discernment"—accuracy and, increasingly, decision-making capacity—is equally important. To some extent, availability and usability will still structure the arms races of the early twenty-first century, but the technology-driven global dispersion of information, the advent of "brilliant" systems requiring less training, the development of highly realistic computer-based training systems, and the declining distinction between weaponry and other types of information technology will encourage proliferation and arms races. At the same time, information-based weapons systems will erode the concept of national arms industries, again complicating traditional state-centric arms control regimes.

Decisions made in Washington in the coming years will determine whether the RMA stokes future arms races and proliferation problems. Other nations are interested in the RMA, but only the United States has the money, technological prowess, and strategic incentive to embrace it. So far the American approach, while a logical response to vexing strategic problems, has not been shaped by concern for long-term political implications. Pursuit of an RMA is not the wrong policy, but pursuit of the RMA described in Joint Vision 2010 may generate unintended political and diplomatic side effects and lead to a more dangerous world rather than a more stable one.

In part, this problem is structural. Within the United States government, responsibility for military strategy and arms control policy is split. The Defense Department is charged with the former while the State Department and the Arms Control and Disarmament Agency oversee the latter. In terms of political power and influence, this is an uneven match. The architects of American military strategy are not oblivious to political and diplomatic concerns, but they must respond primarily to the nation's strategic dilemma. Their attention to the diplomatic and political impact of military strategy is minimal. (The National Security Council was designed to synchronize and integrate the disparate dimensions of United States national security strategy but has shown little inclination to shape long-term military strategy.)

Still, the American approach to the RMA could be recast so that long-term political and diplomatic considerations would receive greater emphasis. This would require redirecting the RMA from simply improving power projection. Seeking a radical improvement in the American military while the United States faces no powerful enemy raises suspicions. To many other states, the only logical reason for the United States to augment its military power in the current security environment is to pursue hegemony. So long as United States military strategy seeks power projection, other states will develop countermeasures to American military prowess, thus sparking arms races, whether symmetric or asymmetric. While this may be an acceptable risk, American policymakers and military strategists should at least explore the possibility of a less provocative variant of the RMA.

In addition, the United States should develop a coherent strategy to defend national information assets. Information systems are daily becoming more central to national life (and thus national security), but no government agency has clear responsibility for coordinating efforts to protect them. Enemies will recognize this vulnerability and attempt to use it to counter the American military, unleashing a spiral of escalation. The United States should also publicly eschew and condemn the development of any technology designed to manipulate human thoughts, beliefs, or perceptions. However alluring this "nonlethal" technology might appear at first glance, its danger is immense. Finally, the United States should expand the time horizons of its efforts to control arms races and proliferation. This would entail crafting regimes to control forms of military technology that, although technologically feasible, are not yet fielded. It is much easier to manage the development of a new form of technology than to control one that has matured to the point that powerful organizations have a vested interest in it.

The political difficulties of altering the current trajectory of the RMA should not be underestimated. In the short term, the RMA will benefit the United States by easing or alleviating some key strategic problems. The United States military of 2010 will be smaller than the current military, but it will also be more effective. In the long term, however, the RMA will create new problems for the United States by provoking asymmetric responses and fueling arms races. The record of the United States at forgoing short-term benefits for long-term gains offers little ground for optimism.

Ending the CIA's Cold War Legacy

by Melvin A. Goodman

"The question is, said Alice, whether you can make words mean so many different things. The question is, said Humpty Dumpty, which is to be master—that's all."
—Lewis Carroll
Through the Looking Glass, 1872

"Facts can confuse."
—CIA director William Casey, 1985

The next Central Intelligence Agency director has a unique opportunity to return the CIA to Harry Truman's original concept of an independent and objective interpreter of foreign events. To do so, the new director—who at this writing is likely to be Anthony Lake, the president's nominee—must address head-on the legacy of the CIA's failure to see the magnitude of the crisis in the Soviet Union in the 1980s. His predecessors have refused to do so. The costs of this failure include the huge defense budgets of the Reagan-Bush years, with their damaging expansion of the deficit; a needlessly prolonged confrontation with Moscow that delayed arms control agreements and conflict resolution in the Third World; and a lost opportunity to influence developments in the Russian Federation.

Recent CIA directors even ignored the impact of this legacy on the CIA itself, perhaps because those who contributed directly to the failure remain in positions of authority. The CIA's leaders in the 1980s, particularly William Casey and Robert Gates, advocated a confrontational policy toward Moscow and slanted intelligence to support their views. Rather than "telling it like it is" with detachment and objectivity, Casey wanted access to policymakers and a position in the president's cabinet. If the new director does not correct these problems, the institutional temptation for politicization will remain.

Lake, who would be the fifth director of central intelligence (DCI) in the past six years, has obvious strengths and weaknesses that will help him to deal with this legacy. As a scholar and former professor, Lake is in a strong position to manage the CIA's intelligence analysis in an environment free of political interference. But as a cabinet member and former national security adviser, he will have to sponsor National Intelligence Estimates (NIES) that from time to time will challenge policies that he helped to create. He will also have to inform Congress of clandestine operations that may embarrass the White House.

THE PROCESS OF POLITICIZATION

The collapse of the Warsaw Pact and the Soviet Union surprised U.S. policymakers, in part because the CIA provided no warning. Former president George Bush said he had no idea the Berlin Wall was going to come down and his national security adviser, Brent Scowcroft, could not recall any CIA warning about the Soviet demise. General Colin Powell, President Ronald Reagan's last national security adviser, has written that CIA specialists could not "anticipate events much better than a layman watching television." Former CIA director Stansfield Turner charges that the agency's "corporate view missed by a mile" and that it "should not gloss over the enor-

---

MELVIN A. GOODMAN, *coauthor of* The Wars of Eduard Shevardnadze *(Penn State Press, 1997), is a professor of international security at the National War College and a senior fellow at the Center for International Policy. He was a senior analyst on Soviet policy at the CIA from 1966 to 1986.*

mity of this failure to forecast the magnitude of the Soviet crisis."

Turmoil and Triumph, the memoir of former secretary of state George Shultz, offers the best description of the CIA's failure to track the Soviet decline. Shultz believed that "CIA analysis was distorted by strong views about policy" and accused Casey of providing "bum dope" to the president. He warned the White House that the agency was "unable to perceive that change was coming in the Soviet Union." He charged that acting CIA director Gates was trying to "manipulate" him and reminded Gates that the CIA was "usually wrong" about Moscow, having dismissed Mikhail Gorbachev's policies as "just another Soviet attempt to deceive us." He noted that even "when it became evident that the Soviet Union was, in fact, changing, the CIA line was that the changes wouldn't really make a difference."

The CIA's failure in the 1980s was in part the result of a deliberate effort by Casey and Gates to slant intelligence to support their view of a Soviet threat and the need for a U.S. policy of confrontation with Moscow. They used many methods to politicize intelligence on the Soviet Union. Occasionally, they forced a particular line of analysis on assessments (as they did on Soviet involvement in international terrorism, the attempted assassination of the pope, and U.S. policy toward Iran). They rejected intelligence papers that were incompatible with their beliefs and encouraged assessments that reinforced their views on arms control and the Third World. When Gates killed a paper that concluded (correctly) that Moscow would not deliver MiG-29 fighter planes to Nicaragua, he said the CIA should not "go out on a limb" on this issue.

At his confirmation hearings in 1991, Gates denied any personal role in politicizing intelligence. Nevertheless he left little doubt that the intelligence process had been corrupted during the Casey era. Eventually, he acknowledged that he had watched Casey "on issue after issue sit in meetings and present intelligence framed in terms of the policy he wanted pursued." In his memoir, *From the Shadows* (see Loch Johnson's review in FOREIGN POLICY 105, Winter 1996–97), Gates conceded that he had underestimated the dramatic change of course in Soviet policy and had not anticipated Gorbachev's strategic retreat abroad or destruction of the Soviet system at home. In other words, Gates and the CIA were wrong on the biggest intelligence issues of the Cold War: the strength of the Soviet Union and the intentions of its leaders.

Instead of attempting to determine what went wrong, however, the CIA has tried to exonerate itself. Determined to gloss over the Agency's analytical failures, Gates proclaimed in 1992 that the CIA had looked into the matter with care and found little to fault in its performance. His successors, James Woolsey and John Deutch, never understood the issue and accepted his verdict.

For the past several years, moreover, the CIA has waged a campaign to show that it did in fact anticipate the Soviet collapse. The agency has declassified selected documents that suggest it had provided warning of the Soviet demise. Then deputy director of intelligence Douglas MacEachin, the senior office director for the Soviet Union during much of the 1980s, led the campaign. According to my interview with a CIA official, MacEachin made

Gates's immediate successors have recycled those high-level officials who contributed to the politicization of intelligence in the first place.

sure that the documents went to a journalist from the *Los Angeles Times* as background for an article to demonstrate that the CIA "got it right" and to consultants with close ties to the agency. Former agency consultant Abraham Becker defended the CIA's analysis of the Soviet economy and dismissed the notion that the agency had "cooked the books." Jeffrey Richelson and former agency analyst Bruce Berkowitz cited the CIA documents in a *National Interest* article concluding that the agency had been vindicated.

As part of this effort, the CIA entered into a cooperative venture with Harvard University's John F. Kennedy School of Government in 1993, financing a case study that concluded the CIA "got it right." The study was written by a former wire-service reporter, Kirsten Lundberg, who in an interview with me said she had no experience in Soviet politics. Her methodology consisted of reviewing the declassified documents and interviewing selected CIA officials who were eager to defend their own analytical records. The case study indicates that she made no attempt to talk to agency critics and made no use of the critical commentary on the CIA offered during the Gates hearings in 1991—standard stuff even for reporters.

Both the CIA and the Kennedy School have benefited from this ethically questionable collaboration. The CIA received high marks from Harvard, and the Kennedy School continued to receive millions in research contracts from the CIA. MacEachin, now on a sabbatical at the Kennedy School, completed a monograph there praising the CIA's track record; not surprisingly, the agency published it.

The agency's defenders have focused much of their commentary on the narrow issue of whether the agency predicted the coup attempt against Gorbachev in 1991, obfuscating more important questions. But the CIA should be judged on whether it provided U.S. leaders with accurate assessments of Moscow's weakness and vulnerability and whether it recognized that Gorbachev's stated intentions were genuine. The CIA failed on both counts. It issued only limited warnings of Soviet weakness and no warning that the strategic relationship between the United States and the Soviet Union was about to change radically. It therefore could not predict, anticipate, or even imagine the convulsions that accompanied the Soviet decline. Indeed, CIA estimates in the mid-1980s concluded that Gorbachev endorsed "well-established goals for expanded Soviet power and influence" and that Soviet leaders were "attempting to prepare their military forces for the possibility of having to fight a nuclear war."

A History of Pressure

The CIA was created in 1947 to serve as an unbiased "honest broker" that would deliver objective intelligence reporting to policymakers. Prior to the Casey-Gates era, the CIA had a good record on sensitive military issues and resisted pressures to slant intelligence to support policy. The CIA demonstrated that Soviet surface-to-air missiles could not be upgraded to an anti-ballistic missile defense, which led to the Anti-Ballistic Missile treaty in 1972. The CIA maintained that because the Soviet SS-9 intercontinental ballistic missile (ICBM) was inaccurate and was not equipped with multiple independently targetable reentry vehicles, it could not threaten the U.S. ICBM force. This analysis led to the 1972 strategic arms treaty.

CIA assessments on the Soviet military provided early warning of new weapon systems. With the exception of Soviet nuclear testing in the late 1940s and early 1950s, few Soviet military developments surprised U.S. policymakers. While the CIA exaggerated the operational dates and rates of deployment of many Soviet weapon systems, its track record was better than that of any other institution, particularly the Pentagon's Defense Intelligence Agency (DIA), which resorted to worst-case assessments to justify higher defense spending.

CIA scientists contributed to the development of the U-2 and SR-71 reconnaissance aircraft and satellite reconnaissance vehicles, which have played a major role in U.S. intelligence collection capabilities and have given the United States a decided advantage in flash points involving the Soviet Union since the Cuban missile crisis. Using data from these systems, the CIA provided the Eisenhower administration with evidence that there was no bomber gap and convinced the Kennedy administration that there was no missile gap.

CIA data collection and analysis enabled the United States to verify arms control agreements and supported the Coordinating Committee for Multilateral Export Controls, which limited the economic development of communist states during the Cold War. Currently CIA data collection efforts enable the United Nations and the International Atomic Energy Agency to monitor developments in Iraq and North Korea, and they contribute to peacekeeping in Bosnia. The Clinton administration, thanks to CIA analysis, was aware of violations of embargo arrangements in the former Yugoslavia and of Serbian crimes against Muslims in Bosnia.

The CIA's objectivity on the Soviet Union ended abruptly in 1981, when Casey became the DCI—and the first one to be a member of the president's cabinet. Gates became Casey's deputy director for intelligence (DDI) in 1982 and chaired the National Intelligence Council. For the first time, one individual had the last word on all NIEs and current intelligence. Gates appointed MacEachin (who eventually became DDI) and then George Kolt (who is currently the national intelligence officer for Russia) to head the office of Soviet analysis from 1984 to 1992; they were in command of Soviet assessments during the period of politicization.

4 ❖ INSTITUTIONAL CONTEXT: The Bureaucracy

CIA Directors: 1947 to present

Harry S Truman — 1945–1953
Sidney William Souers (first official DCI, 1946)
Hoyt Sanford Vandenberg (1946–47)
Roscoe Henry Hillenkoetter (1947–50)
Walter Bedell Smith (1950–53)

Dwight D. Eisenhower — 1953–1961
Allen Welsh Dulles (1953–61)

John F. Kennedy — 1961–1963
Allen Welsh Dulles (1953–61)
John Alex McCone (1961–65)

Lyndon B. Johnson — 1963–1969
John Alex McCone (1961–65)
William Francis Raborn, Jr. (1965–66)
Richard McGarrah Helms (1966–73)

Richard M. Nixon — 1969–1974
Richard McGarrah Helms (1966–73)
James Rodney Schlesinger (1973)
William Egan Colby (1973–76)

Jimmy Carter — 1977–1981
George Bush (appointed by Gerald Ford, 1976–77)
Stansfield Turner (1977–81)

Ronald Reagan — 1981–1989
William Joseph Casey (1981–87)
William Hedgock Webster (1987–91)

George Bush — 1989–1993
William Hedgock Webster (1987–91)
Robert Michael Gates (1991–93)

Bill Clinton — 1993 to present
R. James Woolsey (1993–95)
John M. Deutch (1995–96)
Anthony Lake (designated, 1997)

Source: Directors and Deputy Directors of Central Intelligence (Washington, D.C.: CIA, 1994).

The USSR and International Terrorism. Casey cooked the books in his very first NIE, which dealt with the Soviet Union and international terrorism. The day after Reagan's inauguration, Secretary of State Alexander Haig, believing that Moscow had tried to assassinate him in Europe while he served as supreme allied commander, linked the Soviet Union to all acts of international terrorism. There was no evidence to support such a sweeping charge, but Casey had read the late Claire Sterling's *The Terror Network* and—like Haig—was convinced that a Soviet conspiracy was behind global terrorism. Casey pushed this line in order to justify more U.S. covert action in the Third World. But specialists at the CIA dismissed the Sterling book, knowing that much of it was based on the CIA's own "black propaganda"—anticommunist allegations planted in the European press.

State Department officials requested an NIE on terrorism to convince Haig that Moscow was not the coordinator of all international terrorism. Haig had support from State Department counselor Robert MacFarlane and director of policy planning Paul Wolfowitz, who believed that an NIE that contradicted the views of the secretary would be embarrassing.

Few people in intelligence shared Haig's view, and one official at the CIA told me that, with regard to the estimate, "we will have to let Haig down, but we must do it gently."

The draft NIE, coordinated by the entire intelligence community, was the first on the Soviets and terrorism and became the most contentious intelligence document produced since the Vietnam War. It asserted that Moscow provided arms and training to such groups as the Palestine Liberation Organization and that Moscow's East European allies provided haven to terrorists from a variety of groups. But it stated that there was no evidence that Moscow encouraged or directed these groups to commit terrorism nor was there evidence of Soviet links to such terrorist groups as the Red Brigades in Italy, Baader-Meinhof in West Germany, or the Provisional Irish Republican Army. In fact, the bulk of evidence was to the contrary.

The State Department gave the draft NIE to Haig, who accused its creators of "naiveté." The CIA gave it to Casey, who exercised the first ideological veto of an NIE. The drafters did not know that Casey had already told a skeptical Senate Select Committee on Intelligence that Moscow directed international terrorism; his briefings had convinced Senator Barry Goldwater that he was a loose cannon who should be replaced.

Having rejected the draft NIE, Casey turned to the DIA, whose former director, the late lieutenant general Eugene Tighe, argued in 1981 that the lack of evidence of Soviet support for terrorism actually demonstrated how clever the Soviets were. The DIA draft was a worst-case document that even Casey would not release. Eventually, the estimate on terrorism was completed by a visiting scholar on loan from Rutgers University who did not review the voluminous files on Soviet activities. Casey had succeeded in "judge shopping in the courthouse," finding a sympathetic scholar to substantiate his (and Gates's) desired verdict that Moscow was "deeply engaged in support of revolutionary violence worldwide."

The NIE on terrorism was repudiated in the policy and intelligence communities, contributing to a decline in the CIA's credibility. Secretary Shultz, Haig's successor, disagreed with the NIE and shelved it. William Webster, Casey's successor, repudiated it publicly. No intelligence service in Western Europe supported the CIA view on terrorism, and even Israel's spy service, the Mossad, was incredulous. The exercise created distrust and suspicion at the CIA; the agency that had been created to search for truth had been unable to protect itself from Casey's manipulation.

The Papal Canard. Gates used similar techniques in 1985 when he ordered an intelligence assessment of a supposed Soviet plot against the pope, citing another Sterling book—*The Time of the Assassins*—which traced the 1981 assassination attempt to the KGB. When the CIA produced a specious assessment in 1985, charging the Kremlin with the attempt against Pope John Paul II, its politicization of intelligence on the Soviet Union reached rock bottom. Earlier assessments—and Gates's 1983 testimony to the Senate Select Committee on Intelligence—had concluded that Moscow had no role in the papal plot. Officials at the CIA's directorate of operations had informed Casey and Gates that Moscow had stopped political assassinations and that neither the Soviets nor the Bulgarians had been involved.

But Casey wanted a document that would undermine Shultz's efforts to improve relations with Moscow, and Gates made sure that carefully selected CIA analysts worked in camera to prevent proper vetting and coordination. An internal CIA postmortem concluded that the assessment had "stacked the deck" and "circumvented" the coordination process; the authors of the postmortem—a panel of CIA managers—described the assessment as "deliberately skewed" and stated that they could find "no one at the working level in either the [directorates of intelligence] or [operations]—other than the two primary authors of the paper—who agreed with the thrust" of the assessment.

That assessment, *Agca's Attempt to Kill the Pope: The Case for Soviet Involvement*, "read like a novelist's fantasy of Red conspiracy," according to *New York Times* columnist Anthony Lewis, but Gates's covering note to the vice president described the report as a "comprehensive examination" that the CIA "feel[s] able to present ... with some confidence." The character of the still-classified report is revealed in its reasoning: "The Soviets were reluctant to invade Poland" in 1981 "so they decided to demoralize [the Polish] opposition" by killing the Polish Pope. Casey was not one to let the facts stand in his way, and Gates pandered to the Casey agenda, making sure that the draft document was reviewed in less than 24 hours and was not seen by officials familiar with the issue, according to testimony at Gates's confirmation hearings.

Arms to Iran. The CIA provided an intelligence rationale for arms sales to Iran in 1985. For several years, the CIA and other intelligence agencies agreed that Moscow had failed to gain influence in Tehran, that Soviet-Iranian relations were strained, and that Moscow was unlikely to consider military intervention. In May 1985, however, the CIA's national intelligence officer for the Middle East and South Asia, Graham Fuller, who was collaborating with National Security Council (NSC) officials, prepared an NIE that described Iran as a promising target for the Soviet Union and predicted a resumption of Soviet arms sales. No documents were cited in support of these judgments. Fuller distributed his own memorandum to policymakers, encouraging Washington to play up to so-called moderates in the Ayatollah Ruhollah Khomeini's regime. There were none.

THE SOVIET THREAT

Casey and Gates did their greatest damage by influencing the CIA's estimates of Soviet military strength. Exaggerated estimates of the Red Army's military power were used to justify increased U.S. defense spending and led to the most significant U.S. intelligence failure since Pearl Harbor—the failure to chart the weakness and collapse of the Soviet Union.

The CIA issued only limited warnings of Soviet weakness and no warning that the strategic relationship between the United States and the Soviet Union was about to change radically.

The CIA's most important series of NIEs was titled *Soviet Capabilities for Strategic Nuclear Conflict*. As late as 1983, six years after Leonid Brezhnev signaled reduced growth in Soviet defense spending, the annual NIE in the series concluded that the Soviets sought "superior capabilities to fight and win a nuclear war with the United States, and have been working to improve their chances of prevailing in such a conflict." Ignoring dissent from the State Department, CIA analysts used language that catered to Casey's notions of threatening communist intentions: "[The Soviets] have seriously addressed many of the problems of conducting military operations in a nuclear war, thereby improving their ability to deal with the many contingencies of such a conflict, and raising the probability of outcomes favorable to the USSR."

Gates, as deputy and acting director of the CIA from 1986 to 1989, slanted NIES on Soviet strategic defense programs to buttress the Reagan administration's case for the Strategic Defense Initiative. In a 1986 speech, Gates claimed that the USSR had spent more than $150 billion on its "Star Wars" programs; he failed to mention that most of this money was for air defense, not antimissile defense—a fact he must have known. He charged incorrectly that the Soviets were preparing an anti-ballistic missile defense of their national territory.

The CIA depiction of a Soviet military Goliath with global reach bolstered the Reagan administration's portrayal of an "evil empire." The CIA exaggerated both the flight range of the TU-22 Backfire bomber (which justified counting the airplane as a strategic intercontinental bomber) and the accuracy of the SS-19 ICBM (which contributed to the myth of a "window of vulnerability"). Although these errors were acknowledged by the CIA in congressional testimony in 1989, after Gates left the agency to join the NSC, they continued to appear in the unclassified DIA publication, *Soviet Military Power*, a propaganda vehicle for the Department of Defense. The CIA, created as an independent agency, had failed in its role as "honest broker" between intelligence and policy.

CIA assessments and NIEs overstated every aspect of the Soviet military and provided no warning of the Soviet withdrawal from Afghanistan, Cam Ranh Bay in Vietnam, or the littoral states of Africa. The CIA even rejected Moscow's claims that it would withdraw from Afghanistan—the first major step in its strategic retreat. That withdrawal helped to set the stage for anticommunist revolutions in Eastern Europe and the reunification of Germany. The CIA completely missed the greatest triumph of political liberalism in modern history.

The CIA distorted the military power of Warsaw Pact forces and never anticipated that the pact would dissolve. As late as 1990, only months before the Warsaw Pact's collapse, the CIA concluded that the pact had matched or exceeded NATO's capabilities in all groundforce weapons and would keep pace with NATO's nodernization programs. CIA assessments and NIES ignored Moscow's concerns about U.S. modernization, particularly the presence of Pershing II and ground-launched cruise missiles in Europe.

CIA errors on military issues delayed arms control negotiations with the Soviet Union. Estimates of Soviet military manpower in Europe, a key issue in negotiations for mutual and balanced force reductions, assumed 95 per cent staffing levels when the actual average was much less. The CIA overestimated Soviet chemical warfare stocks, and Gates delayed the release of an assessment demonstrating a change in Soviet thinking about chemical warfare. This assessment would have supported an earlier decision by U.S. policymakers to seek a chemical weapons ban.

THE GORBACHEV FIASCO

Casey and Gates were dead wrong on the most important intelligence question of our time. Was Gorbachev serious? As a consequence, the CIA missed virtually every sign of change during the Gorbachev era, beginning with the significance of his accession to power and the political impact of the unexpected appointment of Eduard Shevardnadze as foreign minister. Gorbachev and Shevardnadze implemented a revolution in Soviet national security policy, but in 1985 the CIA still argued that Gorbachev gave "every indication of endorsing well-established Soviet goals for expanded power and influence."

Soviet commentators had been engaged in a public debate on the backwardness of the Soviet system since the 1960s, but as late as 1985 an NIE (*Domestic Stresses on the Soviet System*) described a "very stable country" that was a "powerful and acquisitive actor on the international scene." According to this NIE, the Soviet Union would use

> assertive diplomacy backed by a combination of military power, propaganda, and subversive tactics to advance its interests. Its ruling elite, now and for the *foreseeable future*, sees its mission in history, its security, and its legitimacy in maximizing its ability to control political life within and outside Soviet borders. The domestic problems of the USSR are unlikely to alter this quality of the Soviet system and the *international appetites* that spring from it. [Emphasis added.]

In fact, Moscow's severe domestic problems already had produced the policies of strategic retreat.

Missing the Revolution in Soviet Security Policy. Shultz's memoir documents the CIA's failure to track the revolution in Moscow's disarmament policy, which included Gorbachev's willingness to accept intrusive on-site inspections, asymmetric agreements, and unilateral reductions. American negotiators, according to Shultz, were unprepared for Gorbachev's flexibility.

NIES on arms control became highly politicized documents that ignored changes in Soviet negotiating positions and missed Moscow's motives for conciliation. In January 1977, Brezhnev stated that nuclear war would be suicidal for both sides and that no victory was possible. His speech signaled a decisive shift: Soviet cuts in the procurement of weapon systems and a decline in the growth of military spending. Brezhnev elaborated on this message at the 26th Communist Party Congress in 1981, and Gorbachev expanded it at the 27th Congress in 1986. But the CIA, as late as 1988, dismissed the Soviet statements as self-serving. Gates argued that Moscow was merely exploiting the disarmament issue in order to weaken the West. The State Department disputed this view, accepting Moscow's interest in disarmament, but the CIA redacted State's dissent by releasing the declassified NIES.

As a result of the CIA's errors, U.S. policymakers were unprepared. Gorbachev's dramatic announcement of a unilateral reduction of forces at the U.N. on December 7, 1988—the 47th anniversary of the Japanese attack on Pearl Harbor—was a seminal statement of Soviet policy. It came as a shock to the Reagan administration. The resignation of the chief of the Soviet general staff Marshal Sergei Akhromeyev, on the day of Gorbachev's speech, was a clear demonstration of the military's opposition to these cuts. The CIA attributed Akhromeyev's resignation to poor health.

Missing the Soviet Economic Failure. The Soviet economy had fallen into the early stages of collapse from 1976 to 1986, and economists such as Sweden's Anders Aslund, the Soviet Union's Abel Aganbegyan, and Soviet émigré Igor Birman have pointed out fissures in the Soviet economy and flaws in the

CIA analysis. In the early 1980s, Birman predicted a Soviet economic collapse by decade's end. Swedish and British analysts had long regarded the Soviet economy as functionally Third World—an Upper Volta with a nuclear arsenal—but CIA economists continued to exaggerate the size of the Soviet economy and to underestimate the economic burden of maintaining a large military. As a result, the CIA ignored Moscow's pleas for "breathing space" in the international arena.

CIA analysts estimated the size of the Soviet economy in 1986 to be 57 per cent that of the U.S. economy. Aslund's figures suggest that estimate was inflated by nearly 20 percentage points. The CIA finally began to report lower growth rates for the Soviet economy in the mid-1980s, but by then Aganbegyan concluded that there had been "practically no economic growth" in the Soviet Union between 1981 and 1985, the very years during which the Reagan administration was using CIA data to refute arguments against record defense spending. The agency failed to assess correctly the burden of the military on the economy, placing the share of Soviet gross national product (GNP) between 15 and 17 per cent, while critics argued that it was 25 to 35 per cent.

These arguments were not academic. The CIA analysis describing a Soviet economy that could grow and fuel military expansion encouraged higher U.S. defense spending. In the late 1980s, the CIA argued incorrectly that Soviet growth in industrial investment and GNP would allow for increased military procurement and influence abroad. The CIA predicted no significant shifts in military production in the near future. Several months before Gorbachev announced unilateral cuts in Soviet ground forces, the CIA predicted that Soviet forces would be modernized and argued that Gorbachev would place a "new emphasis on organizing and planning sustained conventional theater offensive operations."

The CIA completely misread the qualitative and comparative economic picture and provided no warning to policymakers of the dramatic economic decline of the 1980s. Fortunately, in 1990 Shevardnadze's top aides briefed Secretary of State James Baker and others about the plight of the Soviet economy. This information allowed the chairman of the U.S. Council of Economic Advisers, Michael Boskin, to tell a congressional committee in 1990 that "Soviet GNP is probably... only about one-third of the GNP of the U.S." He ignored assessments that—as late as the 1980s—estimated Soviet GNP to be at three-quarters of the American level.

The CIA also failed to predict the economic collapse in Eastern Europe, which diminished the effectiveness of Warsaw Pact forces and hurt Soviet industrial production. The Soviet military-industrial complex was dependent on Eastern Europe, particularly for machine tools denied by the West. Production problems in Eastern Europe presaged the reduced procurement of key weapon systems in the Soviet Union, which began in 1976. But as late as 1986 the CIA still believed that East Germany was ahead of West Germany in per capita output.

The urgency of Gorbachev's efforts to reform the system and reach accommodation with the United States on arms control should have been a clue to CIA economists, but the agency overstated the value of the ruble, the volume of Soviet investment relative to the United States, and the rate of growth of the Soviet economy. It made errors in estimating Soviet investment in fixed capital, particularly machinery and equipment, which contributed to overly alarming accounts of the size and capability of Moscow's military-industrial complex. CIA analysts totally missed the qualitative disparities between the two countries, arguing that the rate of growth of personal consumption in the Soviet Union from 1951 to 1988 exceeded growth rates in the United States. As a result, they concluded that the "USSR was much less constrained than the United States by domestic considerations." On balance, the inflated estimates of Soviet consumption and investment contributed to the CIA's misunderstanding of the defense burden on the economy, the critical need for reform, and the imminent economic crisis. These errors led to an unwillingness to accept Gorbachev's commitment to change.

Responding to Failure

When director Deutch told graduates of the National Defense University in 1995 that the primary mission of intelligence was to provide the president with the best possible information: "We have to maintain an unassailable reputation for unvarnished treatment of the facts, never allowing ourselves to tailor our analysis to meet some policy conclusion that may be of convenience to one of our leaders at one time or another. If we do so, it will quickly destroy [our] credibility." The CIA's credibility was virtually destroyed, however, when Casey and Gates distorted intelligence on Soviet military and economic power and the political intentions of Soviet leaders.

Gates's immediate successors, moreover, have compounded the problem by refusing to face and deal with it. Rather, they have condoned the efforts of CIA officers seeking to obfuscate the record and have recycled those high-level officials who contributed to the politicization of intelligence in the first place. Two senior officials who were responsible for corrupting intelligence on the Soviet Union later became the national intelligence officer for Russia and the deputy director for intelligence, respectively. The project manager of the papal plot assessment is now one of the agency's highest-ranking officers, the deputy director for operations. The coauthor of the papal assessment is the CIA historian. Deutch even named Gates to head a panel to determine whether a recent NIE on strategic threats to the United States had been politicized, as its critics had charged. The rewarding of these officials and the CIA's refusal to confront past abuses contributes to institutional cynicism and prevents systemic reform.

As a scholar and former professor, Lake would be in a strong position to restore the integrity and credibility of the CIA and to confront its Cold War legacy. That task is overdue, coming seven years after the collapse of the Berlin Wall. The new DCI must return the CIA to its original role as an honest broker, detached from specific policy positions and dedicated to providing both the bad news and the good to policymakers. He must take a hard look at the agency's senior leadership and remove those connected with the abuses of the past. He must review current policies at the CIA, particularly the merger of analysis and operations, which undermines the credibility and objectivity of analysis. And he must reverse the image of the CIA as an espionage organization and a producer of tactical intelligence for the military, which makes it more difficult for the agency to act as an independent interpreter of strategic events.

It is almost a cliché to repeat philosopher George Santayana's words: "Those who cannot remember the past are condemned to repeat it." But if the CIA is unwilling to learn from its mistakes, it will undoubtedly make similarly fundamental errors in the future.

The Foreign Policy-Making Process

In thinking about how to bring a halt to the fighting in Bosnia, bring about peace in the Middle East, respond to the refugee crisis in Rwanda, or stop human rights violations in China while at the same time improving trade relations with that country, we often slip into the habit of assuming that an underlying rationality is at work. Goals are established, policy options listed, the implications of competing courses of action are assessed, a conscious choice made as to which policy to adopt, and then the policy is implemented correctly. This assumption is comforting because it implies that policymakers are in control of events and that solutions do exist. Moreover, it allows us to assign responsibility for policy decisions and hold policymakers accountable for the success or failure of their actions.

Comforting as this assumption is, it is also false. Driven by domestic, international, and institutional forces, as well as by chance and accident, perfect rationality is elusive. Often policymakers are knowingly forced to settle for a satisfactory or sufficient solution to a problem rather than the optimum one. At other times, the most pressing task may not be solving the problem but getting all the involved parties to agree on a course of action—any course of action. This retreat from rationality has been evident as the Clinton administration struggled to formulate a policy toward China. Rather than proceeding in orderly steps of identifying goals and weighing options, the policymaking process lurched back and forth as conditions in China changed and political pressures for action on the part of the Clinton administration rose and fell.

While most Americans are willing to acknowledge that the give and take of the political process can have a negative effect on the quality of decisions arrived at, even when decisions are made out of the public spotlight, rationality can be difficult to achieve. This is true regardless of whether the decision is made in a small group setting or by large bureaucracies. Small groups are created when the scope of the foreign policy problem appears to lie beyond the expertise of any single individual. This is frequently the case in crisis situations. The essence of the decision-making problem here lies in the overriding desire of group members to get along. Determined to be productive members of the team and not to rock the boat, individual group members suppress personal doubts about the wisdom of what is being considered and become less critical of the information before them than they would be if they alone were responsible for the decision. They may stereotype the enemy, assume that the policy cannot fail, or believe that all members of the group are in agreement on what must be done.

The absence of rationality in decision making by large bureaucracies stems from their dual nature. On the one hand, bureaucracies are politically neutral institutions that exist to serve the president and other senior officials by providing them with information and implementing their policies. On the other hand, they have goals and interests of their own that may not only conflict with the positions taken by other bureaucracies but may be inconsistent with the official position taken by policymakers. Because not every bureaucracy sees a foreign policy problem the same way, policies must be negotiated into existence, and implementation becomes anything but automatic. While essential for building a foreign policy consensus, this exercise in bureaucratic politics robs the policy process of much of the rationality that we look for in government decision making.

The readings in this unit provide insight into the process by which foreign policy decisions are made in Washington. David Ignatius, in "The Curse of the Merit Class," gives an intellectual overview of the Clinton administration's foreign policy brain trust. He is particularly concerned with how the notion of rationality impedes the decision-making process. In "How the Warlord Outwitted Clinton's Spooks," Patrick Sloyan takes us into the decision-making process that was in operation during the 1993 U.S. military presence in Somalia. He finds that the Clinton administration repeated many of the mistakes made by its predecessors when confronted by failed diplomatic initiatives.

Amy Smithson, in "Playing Politics with the Chemical Weapons Convention," sees the Clinton administration's 1993 efforts to secure passage of the Chemical Weapons Treaty as perfunctory and provides an account of congressional-executive interaction in the ratification process.

UNIT 5

In the essay "Inside the White House Situation Room," an insider's account of how the National Security Council is organized to respond to international crises is provided. Written for senior- and middle-level intelligence professionals, this report provides insight into a little-studied facet of the foreign policy-making process.

Looking Ahead: Challenge Questions

Construct an ideal foreign policy-making process. How close does the United States come to this ideal? Is it possible for the United States to act in the ideal manner? If not, is the failing due to individuals who make foreign policy or the institutions in which they work?

What is the single largest failing of the foreign policy-making process? How can it be corrected?

What is the single largest strength of the foreign policy-making process?

Does a good policy-making process ensure that good decisions will be made? Why or why not?

Does the foreign policy-making process operate the same way in all policy areas (human rights, foreign aid, military intervention, etc.)? Should it? Explain.

What changes, if any, are necessary in the U.S. foreign policy-making process if the United States is to act effectively with other countries in multilateral efforts?

Should the United States try to be more like other countries in the way it makes foreign policy decisions? If so, what countries should serve as a model?

Does the bureaucracy have too much influence in making foreign policy decisions? Why, or why not?

What role, if any, should domestic political considerations play in making foreign policy decisions?

The Curse of the Merit Class

Can the Clinton Generation's Best and Brightest Learn How to Make Smart Foreign Policy?

David Ignatius

David Ignatius is an assistant managing editor to The Post. His new novel [is] "The Bank of Fear."

A story is told about a prominent young lawyer who was being considered for a senior post in the Clinton administration. The lawyer went to Little Rock a few weeks after the election for an interview with the president-elect. They talked about NAFTA and other issues, but some of the conversation was about the many talented people they knew in common.

Bill Clinton was impressed and later offered the lawyer a job. But as the interview was ending, he asked a final question of this latest recruit to his 1990s' version of the Best and the Brightest. "How is it that we've never met before?" wondered the president-elect. It was the sort of question that, several generations ago, George Bush's father might have asked an aspiring young man at the yacht club at Kennebunkport. But it's different now. The club is a meritocracy.

Perhaps more than any in our history, Clinton's is a government of smart people. The president has put the nation's business in the hands of a diverse group of men and women who have been sifted by the great universities and validated as the best. There are at least 15 Rhodes scholars in the Clinton administration, six of them on the White House staff. There are scores of graduates of Harvard and Yale.

And as Clinton's comment suggests, they all seem to know each other. For in addition to being the most credentialed administration in our history, this is also the most networked. Friendships formed at elite colleges and law schools have been sustained through an archipelago of think tanks, foundations, councils and associations. Consider, for example, that eight members of Clinton's Cabinet, including the president, are members of the Council on Foreign Relations.

So a question arises, one year into the life of this extraordinarily talented new administration: Why are these smart people having so much trouble, especially in foreign affairs? What is it about the process that has shaped this meritocratic elite that is contributing to its difficulties in power?

One answer is that for all its degrees and credentials, the meritocratic education is deficient in certain respects. Meritocrats are taught to reason their way through conflicts, and to rely on other bright men and women to solve problems. This may be good training for future lawyers or university professors, but less so for people who now find themselves confronting adversaries who are less susceptible to reason, such as Bosnian Serbs or the health insurance lobby.

An intellectual profile of the Clinton administration's foreign policy team might begin at the Aspen Institute's conference center at Wye Plantation on Maryland's Eastern Shore. For it is here that the Aspen Strategy Group held its annual March meeting. Although the small, 26-person group has received little publicity, it is a fact that nearly every senior member of the Clinton administration's foreign policy team has been a member.

The roster of former Aspen Strategy Group members includes: Vice president Al Gore; former secretary of defense Les Aspin; William J. Perry, who succeeded Aspin in the top Pentagon post; Bobby Ray Inman, the retired admiral who was briefly Clinton's choice to succeed Aspin; John Deutch, initially undersecretary of defense and now Perry's successor in the second-ranking job; James Woolsey, director of Central Intelligence; Joseph Nye, chairman of the National Intelligence Council; Strobe Talbott, just confirmed as deputy secretary of state; David Gergen, the peripatetic presidential counselor.

If ever there was a Cabinet-in-waiting, it was here at the Aspen Strategy Group. So what did the members do, in all those years of waiting?

The Aspen group was established in 1983 to discuss the contentious arms control issues of that time. Its politics tended toward the sensible center; a stance well described by one of Nye's books, which recommended that arms controllers be neither hawks nor doves, but *owls*. A broader goal was to rebuild, through regular social and intellectual exchanges, the kind of bipartisan foreign policy elite that steered the nation during the early Cold War years. It was, in that sense, a social club for smart people.

The gatherings at Wye typically took place over two days. The members of the group would convene Friday evening for

21. Curse of the Merit Class

cocktails and dinner in a lavishly decorated new building called the River House. The atmosphere was convivial; members and guests asked the sorts of questions friends typically ask each other: about jobs and children, vacations recently taken, movies recently seen. After dinner, the group would repair to a large living room with comfy couches and chairs to begin discussing the topic for that weekend's conference. One member of the group usually would present a paper, and then others would jump in.

The next morning, the discussions would begin in earnest in the River House's basement conference room. It is the sort of room in which you could imagine the nation's leaders planning how to fight a nuclear war. The lighting is soft and artificial; the chairs are like first-class airline seats, except bigger. The normal world, though just outside, feels very far away.

I can describe this Inner Temple because I was lucky enough to be invited to join two sessions of the Aspen Strategy Group as a guest. One, in March 1992, debated a paper on nuclear strategy for the post-cold War world that was presented by Les Aspin. The second session held in March 1993, focused on how to deal with the new problem of ethnic conflict, as seen in the Balkans.

The ground rules ban direct quotation of the participants, so I can't give you verbatim details. But suffice it to say that, with occasional exceptions, the tone was that of a high-level bull session. It was a roomful of bright people discussing an important topic.

And yet, in the two sessions I observed, there was something unsatisfying about the discussion. The problem was that it never really led anywhere. One was left at the end of the two days with the same muddle as before about how to prevent North Korea from acquiring nuclear weapons, or how to stop the war in Bosnia. The discussion led right up to those hard moral and political choices—and then stopped.

At first I thought this inability to achieve consensus might be because the people who really knew things—the ones in the group with code-word clearances and access to all the real secrets—couldn't say what they really thought with journalists present. But on reflection, I don't think that was the problem. The discussions weren't supposed to settle anything. That isn't the name of the game in conference-land. The goal is to discuss issues, not resolve them. And for most of the participants, this is a forum for making debating points, rather than expressing deeply held convictions. Indeed, strong beliefs are almost a liability in this setting. They get in the way. They make for awkward moments at cocktail hour.

Adding to the delicious obscurity of the Aspen discussions was the fact that they so often focused on arms control issues. It's hard to remember now the extent to which the grammar of arms control—"throw weight," "window of vulnerability," "counterforce strategy"—came to dominate foreign policy discussions during the 1980s. But learning that strange language was the price of admission to places like the Wye Plantation. And for the regular participants, it made for a lopsided education.

The Aspen gatherings are modeled on similar retreats in Britain that have been held for many years at Ditchley House, the estate where Winston Churchill spent weekends during World War II. Not surprisingly, the style of these discussions remains very British. The premium is on being clever. A bit of substance is all right, so long as it isn't too boring. The British literary critic George Steiner once distinguished between the grand theorists of the Continental tradition and the "steely trimmers" that British academic life had tended to produce—who could demonstrate the logical fallacies and pomposities of the Big Thinkers but would never think of offering a competing grand vision of their own. Too easily deflated. Too embarrassing.

The Aspen Strategy Group, while it had no grand theorists, at least had a few position-paper-theorists like Les Aspin. But the soul of the group, it seemed to me, lay with the steely trimmers. And that is the first of the points to make about the intellectual background shared by so many of the Clinton foreign policy team. Their experience in conference-land has taught them to make clever interventions, but not how to weave a broader tapestry. Unfortunately, this is a moment when the nation needs a new grand design to replace the Cold War. But we have a foreign-policy elite that has been trained in the art of steely trimming, at the finest country houses in the land.

The surfeit of Rhodes scholars within the Clinton administration has been widely noted. But there has been less discussion of what difference it makes in the life of the nation that so many of its top officials shared this same experience.

The most obvious fact is that Cecil Rhodes, the man who established the scholarships, would be pleased with what his bequest has wrought. His aim, in endowing the Rhodes Trust, was to create a system for educating an international elite to share the burden of leadership with the British Empire. The age of High Imperialism has long since passed, and the Rhodes mission is now explained in terms of fostering such things as the Atlantic Alliance and the Future of the West. But the vision of rule by an enlightened, meritocratic elite persists.

Here in Washington we have living proof of the power of Rhodes' vision: A young man from a broken family in Arkansas (Bill Clinton) goes to Oxford, where he meets a patrician Russia scholar from Yale (Strobe Talbott), a diminutive social scientist from Dartmouth (Robert Reich) and a gangly social engineer from Brown (Ira Magaziner). Twenty years later, they are running the country. To help them stay in touch with the younger generation, they recruit an Oxonian in his thirties (George Stephanopoulos).

The common denominator among all these people is the selection process that punched the Rhodes ticket in the first place. Michael Kinsley, another member of the brethren, described how it works: "The way you get a Rhodes scholarship is to solicit eight recommendations, compose a personal essay and then submit to a series of intense interviews by a selection committee. The committee is composed of local dignitaries, mostly former Rhodes scholars, in your state and region. The whole procedure is an institutionalized Horatio Alger story, an orgy of mentoring."

The Rhodes ideal was embodied by the scholar-journalist Strobe Talbott, who was described in the years after he left Oxford as "the young man the older men trust." In the 1980s, he was the informal biographer of the establishmentarian arms controller, Paul Nitze. By 1994 he had, in a very real sense, *become* Paul Nitze, which is no small accomplishment.

People who manage institutions like the Rhodes Scholarships and the Ditchley Foundation and the Aspen Institute used to worry, a few years ago, about what they called "the successor generation." This was the term used for younger people from America and Europe who hadn't gone through World War II and thus hadn't been tempered by the same harsh lessons as their elders. The fear was that the successor generation would be weak-willed and confused when it came to dealing with the Soviets. "Wet," as the British like to say. The unstated purpose of all these fellowships and conferences was to create the next generation of Cold Warriors.

Nobody gave much thought back then to the set of circumstances that would actually prevail when the successor generation finally took center stage, in the person of Bill Clinton. The Cold War was over, ended under the last of the World War II presidents, George Bush. The old communist world was fragmenting into dozens of warring ethnic states and mini-states. The world wasn't anguishing about throw weight anymore. It had a new set of worries, for which the successor generation was ill-prepared.

And that is the second point about the meritocrats. Like most elites, they were trained to fight the last war, not the next.

The other great intellectual spawning ground of the Clinton foreign policy team has been the Council on Foreign Relations. Over the years, this group has come to symbolize the ruling elite known as the "Establishment." This was certainly true in the old days of the WASP ascendancy, when the council was headed by John J. McCloy and David Rockefeller. But the council is equally representative today of the new meritocratic elite. The current chairman is Peter G. Peterson, a son of Greek immigrant parents who made a fortune on Wall Street as an investment banker. The current president is Leslie Gelb, a Jewish ex-newspaperman from the New York Times.

The council, in many ways, illustrates what is best about the networking chain that sustains the new meritocrats. It has opened its doors to a wider and more diverse membership, making itself a kind of Re-Establishment. It has become the Big Tent for people who care about America's connection to the rest of the world.

The council's ranks in 1992 included: a former governor of Arkansas and now president (Clinton); a former governor of Arizona and now interior secretary (Bruce Babbitt); a Lebanese-American former university president and now HHS secretary (Donna Shalala); a Mexican-American former mayor of Houston and now Housing secretary (Henry Cisneros); an Italian-American economics professor and now chairman of the Council of Economic Advisers (Laura D'Andrea Tyson).

Perhaps the clearest sign of the council's ascendancy is the fact that its former president, Peter Tarnoff, is now serving as undersecretary of state. His two immediate superiors, Strobe Talbott and Warren Christopher, both served until recently on the council's board of directors. One can only praise their work to sustain and expand the council in recent years. This is no longer a narrowly Protestant, patrician institution.

And yet, a steady diet of Council on Foreign Relations meetings is hardly a balanced diet. It is a series of intellectual snacks—formal visits at which the world comes calling to present its cards and say a few words. As a member of the council, I confess that the procession of visitors often seems endless: Arabs and Israelis; Uzbeks and Latvians; Chinese and Kenyans; every flavor of European—all coming for breakfast, lunch, dinner, tea and coffee.

There is something about this parade of nationalities that induces, at least in me, a kind of world-weary cosmopolitanism. If it's Thursday afternoon, it must be the Sri Lankans. It's the kind of deformation that often afflicts journalists. You've heard so many earnest speeches over the years that you honestly don't believe any of them any more. The part of you that believes in things—that would take action to deal with them—gets worn down. That may be good training for journalists, who are supposed to be independent and skeptical observers—but not so good for the people who are actually running the country. They need to be engaged, in ways that meritocrats rarely are.

Nicholas Lemann of the Atlantic Monthly, who has written wisely about what he calls the Meritocratic Upper Class, fears that this group is "more Darwinian, more convinced of its own superiority, than the Protestant Establishment was," and is thus increasingly "isolated from the rest of the country."

That was, in fact, the concern expressed by the lawyer who went to see Clinton in Little Rock. Hearing Clinton's "Why don't I know you?" comment, the lawyer thought a moment and replied: "You may think you know everybody, and you do know a lot of people. But this is a big country."

And that leads to a final observation about the meritocrats. For all their deficiencies, they're smart. They know it's a big world out there, and they want to do well. Their experience may be limited, but they learn from it. And over time, the Clinton meritocrats are doing better. Foreign policy appears to be far better managed today than it was six months ago. The threat of force in Bosnia, which for so long was obviously posturing, seems finally to have become credible to the Russians and the Bosnian Serbs. And for the moment, it seems to be working. That's the thing about smart people. They have the capacity to learn, especially when their reputations are on the line.

How the Warlord Outwitted Clinton's Spooks

Patrick J. Sloyan

Patrick Sloyan is senior correspondent for Newsday's *Washington bureau.*

It seemed odd. Bill Clinton ignored the vaunted traveling White House communications system. Instead, he left the fairway on the Martha's Vineyard golf course to use the pay phone in the clubhouse. It was one in a series of calls that fateful day. The first real vacation for the young president was suddenly overwhelmed by events in Somalia.

It was Sunday, Aug. 22. Clinton was informed that six more U.S. soldiers had been wounded by a land mine in Mogadishu. It was detonated by a Somali spotter using a remote-controlled trigger—the same method used in two earlier attacks. One of those, on Aug. 8, killed four U.S. Army military policemen.

For Clinton, the Aug. 22 attack was the final straw. He launched a bitterly debated secret operation that would end in a bloodbath seven weeks later and begin an American retreat from Somalia completed on March 25. . . . At almost the same time, the Senate Armed Services Committee completed an investigation that tracked the secret operations by the CIA and the Special Operations Command.

"I hope we can get out a sanitized version of what really happened," said Chairman Sam Nunn (D-Ga.). The Senate study was spearheaded by Democratic Sen. Carl Levin (Mich.) and Republican Sen. John Warner (Va.) who conducted extensive interviews in Mogadishu and at CIA headquarters in Langley. "There's still a lot of confusion and unanswered questions," said Warner.

When made public, the facts will put a stain on Clinton's foreign policy record, as the president has privately acknowledged. "It was my low point," Clinton later told Mark Gearan, White House communications director. "Somalia was the one thing where we were really responsible for what went wrong," said another Clinton confidante.

On that night back in August, on orders from Clinton in Martha's Vineyard, Delta Force commandos from Ft. Bragg, N.C., a helicopter detachment from Ft. Campbell, Ky., and Army Rangers from Ft. Benning, Ga., were en route to Somalia. Once there, the clandestine Special Operations force would coordinate with a CIA team that had been in place for more than a month.

Their mission: Capture Mohamed Farah Aideed, the dominant political leader in one of the world's poorest countries. Once Aideed was in custody, Delta Force would whisk him to a third-country ship off the coast of Kenya. A tribunal of African judges assembled by the CIA would then conduct a shipboard trial of Aideed on a charge of murder.

"We were going to set Aideed aside," said one senior Clinton adviser, using the White House euphemism for what was more commonly known as the "snatch" operation.

But the seventh and final effort by the Special Operations team on Oct. 3 ended in the most costly firefight for U.S. forces since the Vietnam War. Eighteen American soldiers died and 77 were wounded. An estimated 300 Aideed followers were killed and another 700 wounded. U.S. officials later conceded that a third of the 1,000 Somali casualties were women and children.

The disaster was symbolized by television broadcasts of a U.S. soldier's body dragged through the dusty streets of Mogadishu. Clinton quickly laid the blame on the United Nations. "We cannot let a charge we got under a U.N. resolution to do some police work—which is essentially what it is, to arrest suspects—turn into a military mission," Clinton told reporters.

The line was echoed by White House Press Secretary Dee Dee Myers but was more specific from the mouth of Pentagon spokeswoman Kathleen deLaski. "The search-and-seizure missions are U.N. operations," deLaski told reporters.

But a closer examination of events leading up to the U.S. debacle shows Clinton followed in the missteps of his predecessors. Once more, a president frustrated by diplomacy resorted to the quick-and-dirty solution offered by the CIA and the Mission Impossible men of Delta Force. And, once again, it produced a grisly fiasco.

5 ❖ FOREIGN POLICY-MAKING PROCESS

It began with all the best intentions shortly after Clinton's inauguration. As a candidate, Clinton pledged to avoid future Vietnams by requiring other nations to share the dirty work in places such as Bosnia, where an international authority would call the shots. Somalia would be the test case. Secretary of State Warren Christopher's trip to the U.N. in February was given the utmost priority. "We wanted to get this one right," said a Christopher aide. With U.S. support, the U.N. mission in Somalia would shift from famine relief and peacekeeping to peace enforcement.

Because the United States had the largest force in Somalia, U.N. Secretary General Boutros Boutros-Ghali offered Christopher the choice of the person to direct the U.N. mission. The selection was later made by Anthony Lake, Clinton's adviser on national security affairs, who picked retired U.S. Navy admiral Jonathan Howe. According to a Lake deputy, Howe, as deputy to former National Security Adviser Brent Scowcroft, was intimately involved in President Bush's decision to deploy U.S. troops in Somalia in December 1992. While Howe was certain to be responsive to American wishes, Clinton officials also insisted on retaining direct control of its troops in Somalia, although they were nominally under the command of a Turkish general in charge of all U.N. troops.

To Americans wary of foreign entanglements, it seemed a good plan. Clinton spotlighted the withdrawal of the bulk—25,000—of U.S. combat troops from Somalia. They would be replaced by forces from other countries joining the U.N. contingent. But that withdrawal would bedevil Clinton in the coming months as dwindling American troops became targets for Aideed's reprisals.

In May, the U.N. would take over a relatively peaceful Somalia. U.N. envoy Robert Oakley, a former U.S. ambassador there, and Marine Lt. Gen. Robert Johnston, the senior U.S. representative, had won Aideed's support for an end to clan warfare. The U.S.-sponsored agreement worked out in Addis Ababa included a disarmament conference to be sponsored by Aideed in Mogadishu. But the agreement was scrapped with the arrival of the new U.S. envoy, Robert Gosende, who, with the support of Christopher and Peter Tarnoff, undersecretary of state for political affairs, viewed Aideed as the cause, not the solution to violence. Gosende recommended that disarmament be under U.N. control, a plan also supported by Howe. And bad blood between Oakley and Howe served to undercut a Somali-controlled peace plan. "They couldn't stand each other," said an observer of their meetings in Mogadishu.

To Aideed, Gosende and Howe were merely fronting for his old enemy, Boutros-Ghali who, while in the Egyptian government, had supported Siad Barre, the dictator ousted by Aideed. Also, the U.N. presence was becoming a threat to Aideed's clan in an East African country where fighting for clan survival is as basic as fighting to protect water wells.

Within weeks, the political stand-off erupted into violence. On June 5, 24 Pakistani peacekeepers were killed in an ambush. Aideed denied responsibility. There was the possibility that an Aideed clan member, acting on his own, staged the ambush. But within 24 hours, Clinton backed a U.N. Security Council resolution calling for the arrest and trial of those responsible.

Howe offered a $25,000 reward for information leading to Aideed's arrest and within a week, U.S. gunships and hundreds of U.N. troops began four days of attacks on Aideed's stronghold.

"We didn't plan to kill him, but the president knew that if something fell on Aideed and killed him, no tears would be shed," said one senior official who participated in Clinton's June decision.

"We're striking a blow against lawlessness and killing," Clinton said the day of the first attack. At a news conference later, he said: "We cannot have a situation where one of these warlords, while everybody else is cooperating, decides he can go out and slaughter 20 peacekeepers."

But the attacks on Aideed produced bipartisan objections in Congress to a deeper military commitment in Somalia. The congressional opposition effectively ruled out Clinton consideration of sending additional conventional troops to capture Aideed. Only 1,200 American combat soldiers remained in Somalia with 3,000 support troops.

In hindsight, one senior administration official said, after the June attacks by U.S. gunships, there was an ideal interlude to resume negotiations with Aideed.

"He sent us a message and we sent him a message," the Pentagon official said. "Then we should have invited Aideed to lunch and talk things over." Instead, the State Department wanted Aideed out. Gosende, through official cables, and Howe, using Navy connections at the Pentagon, pushed for removing Aideed. "Howe knew Delta Force had the ideal capability," a senior Pentagon official said of Howe's back-channel forays.

But Gosende's approach came under fire from Marine Gen. Joseph Hoar, head of U.S. Central Command with responsibility for Somalia. Hoar argued chances were one in four of catching Aideed, a former Mogadishu police chief who knew every twist and turn of the old city's warrens. And, even if Aideed was captured, Hoar argued, it would make no difference. Aideed's clan members would take up the challenge to U.N. threats.

One Hoar objection, however, triggered CIA intervention. With the withdrawal of U.S. forces, Hoar pointed out, the Americans had effectively eliminated the intelligence capability needed by Delta Force to locate Aideed. By late June, senior officials from the White House, Pentagon, State Department and CIA began plans to track Aideed in Mogadishu—without deploying Delta Force. "But the CIA said there was no point going into Mogadishu unless that snatch team was there," said one participant. "It went on like that."

At the same time, an interagency task force was organized to decide what would be done once Aideed was captured. The U.N. had no authority to try Aideed, and Ethiopia and other countries in the region refused to take him in custody. "Using a ship for an offshore trial was a solution to the legal problems," said one task force participant. "The CIA would provide the judges."

22. Warlord Outwitted Clinton's Spooks

But a stalemate remained over the issue of Delta Force. Defense Secretary Les Aspin and Army Gen. Colin Powell, chairman of the Joint Chiefs of Staff, had embraced Hoar's arguments against the move. At the White House, Clinton was confronted by appeals to capture Aideed by Christopher, Tarnoff and David Shinn, special coordinator for Somalia.

But Lake had misgivings. As a young foreign service officer, the national security adviser served in the U.S. Embassy in Saigon in 1963 when President Kennedy "set aside" another political problem, South Vietnam President Ngo Dinh Diem. A coup tacitly encouraged in Washington resulted in Diem's death and almost a decade of American puppet governments in Saigon. Instead of using U.S. forces, Lake sought to have the British government deploy a contingent of commandos. "London said no thanks," a White House official said.

As a compromise, Clinton approved the dispatch in July of a CIA team expert in intercepting communications and building a network of informers to locate Aideed. But Aideed avoided satellite phone calls and used antique walkie-talkies and a mobile radio transmitter—both too low-powered for the sophisticated CIA systems. "Aideed went into deep cover," said a Pentagon official.

Shinn gave a candid assessment on Aug. 10 after returning from a fact-finding mission in Somalia. "We have been trying to arrest Aideed for some period of time," the special coordinator said. "The fact of the matter is that it's not easy" with conventional U.S. and U.N. troops.

Shinn spoke two days after Aideed had upped the ante. For the first time, U.S. soldiers were the target of a remote-controlled land mine; four MPs were killed. By the third such attack on Aug. 22, Powell's opposition to the snatch mission crumbled. "We have to do something or we are going to be nibbled to death," the general told Clinton, according to insiders. "The decision was driven by the circumstances of the attacks in Somalia," a Powell aide said.

Powell's change of heart was a major shift. He had developed a personal relationship with Clinton and had come to dominate NSC deliberations. When Clinton called Lake from Martha's Vineyard, Lake in turn called Powell.

"It looks like we are going to send them in," Powell told Hoar that Sunday afternoon, according to aides who heard the conversation. Hoar's response was a long silence that effectively restated his belief that the snatch mission was certain to fail.

Hoar's predictions came true eight days later when Delta Force captured—then released with a red face—a U.N. official who vaguely resembled Aideed. At the Pentagon, Aspin fumed over the embarrassment. "We look like the gang that can't shoot straight," Aspin complained.

Veteran journalists who witnessed Rangers cascading from helicopters in Mogadishu knew instinctively a not-so-covert operation was underway. Rangers are used almost exclusively as the muscle for U.S. Army Special Forces who conduct Delta Force operations. But at the White House and the Pentagon, the cover story sought to hide the truth from the public.

"This is not an effort to go after one man," deLaski said in assuring reporters that the Rangers were merely a conventional light infantry force. "It's an effort to improve the overall situation."

Instead, it quickly worsened. Reacting to the hunt for their leader, Aideed supporters and their families took to the streets to confront an outnumbered American contingent. On Sept. 9, a crowd attacked U.S. and Pakistani soldiers trying to clear a roadblock. U.S. Army Cobra helicopters responded and fired 20mm cannon into the crowd. Women and children were among the scores of Somalis killed.

"In an ambush, there are no sidelines or spectator seats," Army Maj. David Stockwell said in defending the gunship attack. But the incident appalled Hoar, who was in Mogadishu that day. A week earlier, U.S. envoy Gosende had cabled Washington that thousands of additional U.S. troops were needed to gain control in the worsening Somalia violence. Hoar attacked Gosende in what became known as the "Mission Creep" memo. According to a senior Pentagon official, "Hoar said we had lost control in Mogadishu. He argued if more troops were necessary, it was time to reassess our entire policy."

Hoar's memo deepened second-thoughts at the White House and State Department. And, according to aides, Clinton was disturbed by the Sept. 9 gunship attack. As a young anti-vietnam activist, Clinton had written that he "loathed" American Army tactics that often killed women and children in Vietnam. "Now, he felt responsible" for the same tactics, a Clinton adviser said.

But to some aides, Clinton's most important change of heart came after a meeting with former president Jimmy Carter three days after the gunship attack. Carter also had tried to use Delta Force to get him out of difficulty in Iran. But it had ended in the 1980s disaster of Desert One.

Carter spent the night of Sept. 12 at the White House before taking part in the peace signing ceremony between Israel and the PLO. Carter had met Aideed and had received letters from the Somali leader since the violence flared, protesting his innocence. According to Carter aides, the former president told Clinton that the key to success in Somalia was a political settlement. Long past midnight, Carter drove home the point that without Aideed, no political settlement was possible.

In Congress, Sen. Robert Byrd (D-W. Va.) reacted to the abortive hunt for Aideed by pushing for a vote to sustain U.S. involvement or leave Somalia. "My vote is for the latter," Byrd said.

By late September, the worsening violence in Mogadishu, congressional pressures and Carter's appeal caused Aspin, Christopher and Lake to recommend another shift in policy. "It was a consensus by his advisers that caused the president to change direction," a Clinton adviser said.

The new policy: an initiative aimed at a political settlement that would include Aideed but, at the same time, continue to hunt him down as a means of keeping pressure on the Somali leader. This "two-track" plan, revealed during Clinton's trip to the U.N. Sept. 27, remains a source of controversy within the administration. To State Department veterans, Clinton was covering his political bets. "There was still an outside chance to bring Aideed to justice and score some points on the domestic political front," said one career diplomat.

Six days later, Clinton and Delta Force ran out of luck in Mogadishu. In the aftermath of the Oct. 3 disaster, an elaborate damage-limitation program managed to fog the public perception of Clinton's responsibility. One key facet was David Gergen's counsel to Clinton to avoid public appearances with the survivors of the firefight.

But three weeks after the battle, a doctor at Walter Reed Army Medical Center called the White House to complain about the official cold shoulder for his patients who had been wounded in Mogadishu. "He [the Army doctor] said these men have been here for three weeks and no one had paid any attention to them," said a source informed of the exchange. "The White House called back and said, 'The president will be there tomorrow morning.'"

Clinton showed up with Lake on Oct. 24. The media was banned from a two-hour tour of the Somali wounded that shocked Clinton. One soldier had lost his right hand, right leg, sight and hearing. Another had his hand grafted to his stomach so a shattered arm could heal. Bullets, shrapnel and fire had maimed a young private. A sergeant had his leg in a steel bird cage after the first of a series of bone grafts.

"Clinton was visibly moved," said one hospital official. "He didn't know what to say."

Article 23

> "Unless the Senate ratifies the Chemical Weapons Convention before it enters into force at the end of April, Washington will have abandoned a sturdy ship of its own making... America's elected officials have the opportunity to rectify their undistinguished track record in addressing the problem of chemical weapons proliferation."

Playing Politics with the Chemical Weapons Convention

AMY E. SMITHSON

In June 1989, a bipartisan group of 73 senators wrote President George Bush, urging him to conclude international negotiations for a "total, verifiable" chemical weapons ban. Bush did so, leaving newly elected President Bill Clinton an accord that had been sought by his five predecessors. For the first two years of his administration, Clinton had ideal conditions to quickly ratify the Chemical Weapons Convention (CWC): the president was presenting a Republican-negotiated treaty for approval, and he could presumably count on the cooperation of Democrats, who formed a majority in the Senate. Clinton dallied, however, not submitting the treaty to the Senate until November 23, 1993, minutes before Congress adjourned for the holidays.

The administration's initial campaign to secure the Senate's approval of the Convention was perfunctory at best. Clinton mentioned the treaty infrequently when he listed foreign and defense policy objectives. Cabinet members testified before relevant congressional committees, but rarely worked the issue at other times. Few senators aside from the upper chamber's resident duo of arms control experts, Richard Lugar (R-IN) and Sam Nunn (D-GA), regularly appeared at hearings to learn the basic facts about the Convention. In short, the administration was going through the motions of a ratification campaign, and the Senate was almost sleepwalking through its constitutional responsibility to provide advice on and consent to international agreements.

At the close of the 103d Congress in 1994, the administration could have pushed for committee and floor votes, but there was little White House action to back up Clinton's rhetorical embrace of the Convention. Senators, sensing that the treaty was not a White House priority, instead focused on domestic issues that were more meaningful to the midterm elections.

The 1994 Republican revolution elevated archconservative Senator Jesse Helms (R-NC) to the chairmanship of the Foreign Relations Committee. Helms did not wait long before taking the CWC, other treaties, and ambassadorial nominations hostage to his quest to revamp the foreign policy bureaucracy and gut the foreign aid budget. No hearings were held on the Convention in 1995, but during the December bartering to resolve the impasse over the Department of State authorization bill, Senator John Kerry (D-MA) managed to secure an agreement requiring committee action on the treaty by April 30, 1996.

At a committee business meeting on April 25, 1996, Helms planned to offer a resolution of ratification with 20 conditions that would have required renegotiation of the Convention or America's abrogation of it. In the face of Helms's scorched-earth legislation, Senator Lugar deftly assembled a bipartisan coalition to substitute a more reasonable bill, which the committee approved by a 13-5 vote. Many in the administration were ready to declare victory, especially after Democratic legislators pressed the new Senate majority leader, Trent Lott (R-MS), to set a September 14 deadline for a floor debate and vote. Meanwhile, a small but vocal band of treaty opponents, underestimated by most in Washington, began executing their plot to sink the Convention.

AMY E. SMITHSON *is director of the chemical and biological weapons project at the Henry L. Stimson Center in Washington, D.C. She has written widely on issues associated with the control and elimination of chemical and biological weapons.*

Torpedoing a Treaty

The first salvos fired against the CWC took advantage of a paradox that is inseparable from efforts to abolish chemical weapons. Many chemicals found in ordinary commercial products, such as flame-retardant materials, pharmaceuticals, and fertilizers, can also be used in chemical weapons. With the ubiquity of such products in modern life, the negotiators could hardly have decreed their elimination in order to get at the chemical weapons problem. The treaty instead contains extensive verification provisions to guard against commercial facilities serving as a facade for covert chemical weapons production.

The Convention's data declarations will for the first time enable the tracking of global trade in chemicals that could pose a proliferation risk. Routine inspections will confirm the accuracy of these declarations and the absence of chemical weapons-related activities in the industrial sector. The treaty also breaks new ground with challenge inspections, which will be launched on short notice to investigate charges of cheating, whether at commercial or government sites. Both routine and challenge inspections may involve questioning personnel, reviewing records, sampling and analyzing chemical compounds, and obtaining access to various areas of a facility. When the United States proposed these tough verification measures in 1984, few believed that the Soviet Union or other countries at the negotiating table would ever agree to routine, much less challenge, inspections. Yet over 160 governments have signed the Convention.

The treaty's verification provisions were devised in cooperation with American industry, which began working with negotiators in the late 1970s to fashion treaty provisions that would enable verification but protect confidential business information. The United States Chemical Manufacturers Association, which represents more than 90 percent of America's chemical manufacturing capacity and the majority of facilities that would be involved in treaty-monitoring activities, spearheaded the industry's coalition effort. Chemical companies tested the data declaration forms, helped the government draft the treaty's implementing legislation, and allowed trial inspections at their facilities to evaluate the verification provisions.

Early in June 1996, Helms warned his Senate colleagues that the Convention "may compromise trade secrets," circulating a confidential list of American companies possibly affected by the treaty. At the end of July, Helms distributed press releases across the country to alert the states where he asserted private industry would be "hardest hit" by the Convention. Analysis prepared by two conservative Washington, D.C., think tanks fueled Helms's efforts. Senator John Kyl (R-AZ) joined Helms's crusade against the treaty, and the myth that the Convention would ravage United States industry began to transform into political reality within the halls of the Senate. In particular, treaty opponents asserted that small businesses would be overwhelmed by the burdens the Convention would place on them.

Appalled, chemical industry representatives repeatedly told the Senate that the treaty's verification requirements were reasonable and acceptable. Moreover, they explained that without ratification the treaty's automatic economic sanctions, which United States negotiators had pushed to put pressure on hold-out states, would backfire on the United States chemical industry. If the treaty were not ratified, United States chemical trade would decline by at least $600 million and many American jobs would be lost.

Normally, when an industry with $65 billion in exports makes the rounds on Capitol Hill, senators pay close attention. In this case, many Republican senators turned a deaf ear to the industry's arguments for the Convention, listening instead to a handful of former Reagan officials claiming to represent industry's interests. Endorsements poured in from the Pharmaceutical Research and Manufacturers of America, the Synthetic Organic Chemical Manufacturers Association of America, the Biotechnology Industry Organization, the Business Executives for National Security, and other business groups. Even when an organization representing more than 600,000 small businesses, the National Federation of Independent Business, later announced that "it is 100 percent incorrect...that NFIB opposes" the treaty, rumors that the CWC would harm American companies continued to circulate.

Treaty opponents launched another line of argument, asserting that the Convention's verification provisions would breach Fourth Amendment rights prohibiting unlawful searches and seizures and Fifth Amendment protections against self-incrimination. Article VII of the treaty, however, calls for its implementation "in accordance with [each state's] constitutional processes." Legal scholars Abram Chayes and Louis Henkin note that the treaty allows alternative means of inspection to be used if inspectors' requests for information, samples, or other forms of access are deemed unreasonable. The Convention's "managed access" inspection procedures and United States implementing legislation provide numerous mechanisms to protect sensitive and proprietary information. Chayes has concluded that the "convention in its final form is thus fully consistent with United States constitutional requirements."

Intervention by Clinton and his cabinet might have reversed the tide against the treaty, but instead the White House counted on senators to follow Lugar's lead and left the treaty in the hands of staffers. As the summer waned, treaty adversaries also revived a tried-and-true battle cry against arms control: the Convention was unverifiable. "Verifiability"—a measure of how well cheating can be detected—has long been a key litmus test for arms control accords. The Convention's opponents insisted that the treaty would not detect violations with high confidence. This argument appeared to clash with a frequent refrain of treaty advocates that the Convention contained novel and very intrusive verification provisions. Both statements, however, are correct.

For decades, United States reconnaissance satellites have been able to detect missile silos, mobile missiles, nuclear test preparations, and other nuclear activities. However, the signs of chemical weapons proliferation are not readily picked up by satellites, partly because many chemical companies use modern environmental safeguards that make it difficult to pinpoint possible covert weapons sites. Given the large number of chemical facilities worldwide, even the Convention's rigorous verification measures cannot provide an ironclad guarantee that all instances of small-scale cheating would be detected.

Conceding this fact, former CIA director James Woolsey nonetheless testified that the Convention would bring "a new tool to [the intelligence community's] collection tool kit [that could] help resolve a wide variety of problems." Writing in the February 11, 1997, *Washington Post,* two other distinguished national security authorities, Brent Scowcroft and John Deutch, observed that "debates about various definitions of 'effectively verifiable' miss the point. The limits imposed by the CWC surely are imperfect, but since we are unilaterally abandoning chemical weapons in any case, it is hard to see how its imperfect constraints are worse than no constraints at all."

Treaty opponents also dusted off the "universal adherence" argument, noting that chemical proliferators such as Libya, North Korea, and Syria would simply ignore the Convention. They forgot to mention, however, that approximately two-thirds of the countries on the intelligence community's proliferation watch list have already signed the Convention. The treaty will gradually deny any remaining holdout states supplies of chemical weapons ingredients, making it more difficult for them to augment their arsenals. In short, the Convention will contain and eventually reverse the proliferation problem as holdout states succumb to the added economic and political isolation brought about by it.

POLITICAL UNDERTOW

In a radio address days before the Senate's scheduled debate on the treaty, Clinton observed that ratification of the Convention would reduce the threat of chemical weapons. While the press overlooked Clinton's remarks, conservative columnists filled newspaper op-ed pages with dire warnings against the Convention. In addition, the opposition enlisted former Defense Secretaries Caspar Weinberger and Richard Cheney, as well as several other Reagan and Bush officials. Two Clinton cabinet members published a lone riposte, but otherwise the administration was publicly silent. As the hours passed and Clinton's cavalry did not saddle up, the hopes of the Convention's advocates began to flag.

Whether the convention was sidelined by politics or neglect, both reasons are unacceptable.

The death blow was dealt by Republican presidential candidate Bob Dole, who on September 11 declined to support the Convention unless it was "effectively verifiable and genuinely global." By the next morning even Lugar could not assemble the needed two-thirds majority. Approximately 35 Republicans had indicated they would vote against the Convention. Facing defeat, the White House agreed to postpone a vote indefinitely.

What happened? Perhaps the most obvious explanation of this outcome is that the Convention was a victim of election-year politics. The Republicans were just as eager to deny Clinton a foreign policy victory as Clinton was to avoid a foreign policy defeat. Such political calculations may have spurred the Republicans to scuttle a Republican-negotiated treaty and the White House to favor the easy road over the more politically assertive one.

Another possible explanation of this outcome is a regrettable combination of neglect and ignorance of a serious problem. Far too few in Washington have recognized the changing nature of post–cold war security threats. A quick glance at history reveals that while nuclear weapons are held in reserve, chemical weapons are used—as recently as the Iran-Iraq War in the 1980s. The number of suspected chemical weapons possessors—more than 20—is roughly triple the membership of the nuclear weapons club. Given the relative availability and inexpensiveness of chemical weapons ingredients, poison gas has become a favored weapon of governments and, perhaps more ominously, terrorists. In March 1995, the religious cult Aum Shinrikyo released the nerve agent sarin in a crowded Tokyo subway, killing a dozen people and injuring more than 5,500. This act broke a taboo against the terrorist use of weapons of mass destruction and provided a horrifying example for other terrorists to follow.

Chemical terrorism may already have surfaced in the United States. Evidence indicates that the 1993 World Trade Center bomb also included cyanide gas. Only a mistake on the part of the bombers saved the thousands of people in the building. In other words, so far Americans have been lucky. Were Washington policymakers paying better attention, they would understand that the security dilemmas of the future are less about mutual assured destruction and more about mutual vulnerability to poison gases and deliberately spread diseases.

ABANDONING SHIP

One of the oldest gambits used to defeat a proposed policy or program is to play both ends against the middle. In this instance, treaty opponents have simultaneously described the Convention's verification measures as so tough that they would breach United States constitutional rights and not tough enough to catch violations elsewhere. As noted earlier, the treaty has ample mechanisms to protect constitutional rights. Moreover, monitoring a chemical weapons prohibition is at least an order of magnitude more difficult than monitoring a nuclear weapons treaty. The Convention's verification provisions are designed to detect militarily significant violations. Inspection procedures capable of exposing each and every small violation would not only shred the United States Constitution, but would result in the loss of confidential business and national security information. As drafted, the Convention balances the need for intrusive verification with the need to protect property and privacy. Assuming that the United States and other participating countries remain vigilant about exercising their right to conduct challenge inspections, senators can be reasonably confident that inspectors will uncover militarily significant cheating in a timely fashion.

With some reflection, senators might also realize the absurdity of the opponents' argument that adherence to the Convention must be immediate and universal. Foreign and defense policy goals are not achieved overnight; they are articulated and pursued over the long term. Those who insist on instant universal adherence to the Convention are in effect ceding the role of setting the standards of acceptable international behavior to Muammar Qaddafi and Saddam Hussein. United States national interests would be much better served by establishing the illegality of chemical weapons development and possession and working persistently thereafter to eliminate poison gas.

Unless the Senate ratifies the Convention before it enters into force at the end of April, Washington will have abandoned a sturdy ship of its own making. Consequently, the Convention's debut will be somewhat hollow: Russia, which outranks the United States as the world's largest chemical weapons possessor, will not ratify before the United States does.

At a time when important precedents will be set, not ratifying the treaty means that the United States will lose its vote on how the treaty operates. No Americans will be hired at the international inspectorate, and Washington will be denied formal access to the information this agency gathers about chemical activities in other countries. In short, not ratifying the treaty will marginalize the United States; Washington's absence will undermine the nascent chemical weapons nonproliferation regime and may jeopardize its long-term legitimacy.

Whether the Convention was sidelined by politics or neglect, both reasons are unacceptable, especially in the area of the stewardship of United States defense and foreign policy. At the beginning of the second Clinton administration and the 105th Congress, America's elected officials have the opportunity to rectify their undistinguished track record in addressing the problem of chemical weapons proliferation.

THE ELEVENTH HOUR

On October 31, Hungary became the sixty-fifth nation to deposit its instrument of ratification with the United Nations, triggering a countdown of six months until the treaty's entry into force. The Clinton administration faced a considerable challenge—albeit one partly of its own making—in gaining

Senate approval before the April 29, 1997, deadline. So early in a new Congress, members are loath to make major decisions. The Republican majority would be more inclined to inaugurate the session with its own agenda. Finally, Helms, having been reelected, was sure to resort to his familiar tactics. Unless Clinton wanted to begin his second term with an undeniable security and foreign policy failure, he had no choice but to step up the intensity of his administration's campaign to secure the Senate's advice and consent to ratification.

Clinton began by personally telephoning Majority Leader Lott to ask that a vote be scheduled and sending his new national security adviser, Samuel Berger, to discuss the issue further with Lott. The senior Mississippi senator then decided that he would appoint a task force of nine Republicans to weigh the issue. Among Lott's appointees were three treaty supporters; the other six were moderately or adamantly against the Convention. Lott's decision to create a task force could be read either as a way to find compromises suitable to the treaty's most entrenched Senate opponents or as a way to insulate himself from the matter and delay action on the treaty. As for Helms, his recommendation to Lott was that the Senate not take up the Convention until other Republican priorities had been addressed, including the restructuring of the State Department and the comprehensive reform of the United Nations. In other words, Helms took the treaty hostage again.

Meanwhile, Clinton's new secretary of state, Madeleine Albright, and secretary of defense, former Republican Senator William Cohen, began actively promoting the Convention. After meeting with Albright in early February, former President Bush declared that a vote on the Convention "should be beyond partisanship... We don't need chemical weapons, and we ought to get out front and make clear that we are opposed to others having them." Endorsements also began to appear from such prominent individuals as former Secretary of State James Baker 3d, General Norman Schwarzkopf, and Admiral Elmo Zumwalt, Jr.

The situation is nearing critical mass. Lott is hearing two crucial messages with increasing frequency. First, the Convention is, on balance, in United States interests. Second, this matter is a test of his leadership because the Convention is so widely endorsed and has enjoyed bipartisan support. If Lott does not soon pry the treaty from Helms and schedule a vote, Clinton himself can be expected to step up to the presidential bully pulpit on behalf of the treaty, further escalating the pressure.

Although the outcome of this saga will directly alter the effectiveness of chemical weapons nonproliferation efforts, the manner in which Washington has handled the Convention has more far-reaching implications. Unless the Senate logjam is broken, the paralysis that has suspended the Convention threatens to engulf other arms control accords, such as the recently concluded Comprehensive Test Ban Treaty. During the last two Congresses, more than 15 other environmental, trade, and criminal justice treaties have also stacked up in the Foreign Relations Committee. America's leaders need to break the post-Vietnam habit whereby both ends of Pennsylvania Avenue continually jostle for control of the ship of state. Especially on essential security issues, the White House and Congress must rise above politics and work together.

The consensus view is that United States foreign policy should seek to reduce security threats, improve trade relationships, and foster cooperation on such matters as the environment and human rights. As the vestiges of the cold war and the accompanying restraints of bipolarity dissolve into an increasingly unruly world, strategies for achieving these goals remain unarticulated. Most agree, however, that the economic and political costs of being a full-time international policeman would bankrupt America.

A sensible alternative to global hegemony is for Washington to invest seriously in creating and strengthening new rules of positive international behavior. Though sometimes difficult to orchestrate, multilateral mechanisms can be a cost-effective route to reducing security threats and inducing cooperation in other areas. The Chemical Weapons Convention, one of many treaties that would help to set and reinforce positive behavioral norms, is an obvious step in the right direction. Surely Washington can find the determination to outlaw chemical weapons. If not, United States foreign policy is definitely adrift.

Article 24

A National Nerve Center

Inside The White House Situation Room

Michael Donley, Cornelius O'Leary, and John Montgomery

> **"** Just remember that there are many important people who work in the White House, and you're not one of them. **"**

Michael Donley was Deputy Executive Secretary of the National Security Council, 1987-89.
Cornelius O'Leary is a former Director of the White House Situation Room. **John Montgomery** is a former intelligence analyst at the National Security Council.

Go to the southwest gate of the White House complex, present the guard with identification, and state your business. If you are on the appointment list, an escort will be called. Walk up West Executive Avenue and turn right into the West Basement entrance; another guard will check your pass for White House access. Take the first right, down a few stairs. To the left is the White House Mess; on the right is a locked door.

Behind these layers of security is the White House Situation Room (WHSR), a conference room surrounded on three sides by two small offices, multiple workstations, computers, and communications equipment. The conference room is soundproofed and well appointed but small and slightly cramped. The technical equipment is up to date, though not necessarily "leading edge"; every square foot of space is functional. Visitors typically are impressed by the location and technology, but they are often surprised at the small size.

While it is widely known that important meetings are held here, the importance of the WHSR in the daily life of the National Security Council (NSC) and White House staff and its critical role in Washington's network of key national security operations and intelligence centers are less understood. This paper is intended to fill that void. We believe there is a longstanding need within middle and senior levels of the Intelligence Community (IC) for a basic understanding of NSC and White House functions and how current intelligence information is provided to key decisionmakers, including the President.

Mission, Organization, Functions

The WHSR was established by President Kennedy after the Bay of Pigs disaster in 1961. That crisis revealed a need for rapid and secure presidential communications and for White House coordination of the many external communications channels of national security information which led to the President.[1] Since then, the mission of the "Sit Room" has been to provide current intelligence and crisis support to the NSC staff, the National Security Adviser, and the President. The Sit Room staff is composed of approximately 30 personnel, organized around five Watch Teams that provide 7-day, 24-hour monitoring of international events. A generic Watch Team includes three Duty Officers, a communications assistant, and an intelligence analyst. The number and composition of personnel varies, depending on shift requirements and workload.

Sit Room personnel are handpicked from nominations made by military and civilian intelligence agencies for approximately two-year tours. This is a close, high-visibility work environment. Egos are checked at the door, as captured in the admonition of a former Sit Room Director to incoming Duty Officers: "Just remember that there are many important people who work in the White House, and you're not one of them." Personal characteristics count: an even

From *Studies in Intelligence*, No. 1, 1997, pp. 7-13. Reprinted by permission of *Studies in Intelligence*, a publication of the Central Intelligence Agency (CIA), United States of America.

24. Inside the White House Situation Room

temperament, coolness under pressure, and the ability to have a coherent, professional, no-advance-notice conversation with the President of the United States.

Sit Room functions are perhaps described best in the daily routine of activities. The day begins with the Watch Team's preparation of the Morning Book. Prepared for the President, Vice President, and most senior White House staff, the Morning Book contains a copy of the *National Intelligence Daily*, the *State Department's Morning Summary*, and diplomatic cables and intelligence reports. These cables and reports are selected based on their relevance to ongoing diplomatic initiatives and/or specific subject matter on the President's schedule. The Morning Book is usually in the car when the National Security Adviser is picked up for work. The morning routine also includes the *President's Daily Brief*, which is prepared by CIA, hand-delivered, and briefed by a CIA officer to the President and other NSC principals.[2]

In addition, the Watch Teams produce morning and evening summaries of highly selective material. These summaries, targeted on current interagency issues, are transmitted electronically to the NSC staff. Such summaries, which draw on a number of finished interagency products, field reports, and newswires, may also elicit requests for the original products. The Sit Room staff does not perform intelligence analysis or render the kind of formal interagency judgments found in National Intelligence Estimates. But it is important to recognize that, especially at the White House, there is always more intelligence information available than there is time for senior decisionmakers to read, and it falls to the Sit Room to boil that information down to its essential elements.

In a typical 24-hour day, the Sit Room will provide alerts on breaking events to NSC and White House personnel. Triggered by specific events

> **In all situations other than nuclear war or physical threats against the President, the Sit Room is in effect the 24-hour, one-stop shop for the White House staff.**

and followed with consultations among operations and intelligence centers, the alert notification process results in a rapid series of phone calls to key officials. Responsibility for informing the President belongs to the National Security Adviser. Later, a written "Sit Room Note" will be prepared, summarizing the event with up-to-the-minute reports from other centers, perhaps including a photo, diagram, or map. At the direction of the National Security Adviser, such a note might be delivered by a Duty Officer directly to the Oval Office or the President's residential quarters. After hours, depending on their personal style or interest, the President or Vice President might call the Sit Room directly or drop by unannounced for a quick update.

The advent of 24-hour-a-day television news broadcasting as well as radio has added a new dynamic to warning and alert operations. Not only do Duty Officers pour over hundreds of incoming cables, but they also are constantly bombarded by on-site television broadcasts from the crisis area and newswire services pumping a steady volume of information destined for the morning front pages. The Duty Officer's task is to ensure that the President and National Security Adviser are informed not only of the current situation but also how the situation is being portrayed by the media. Less-than-objective images can sometimes place the Duty Officer in a position of having to produce "negative" intelligence to put the event into context. Occasionally, it may even prove necessary to tell the principal that the events as portrayed by the press are incorrect.

While the advancements in telecommunications have placed more pressure on the watch standers, they have also simplified the exchange of information among participating agencies. The same satellites that allow news reporting from the field also enable crisis-support elements to extract information from remote databases, provide for timely reporting, and, in some cases, engage in video teleconferencing.

Another typical Sit Room activity is arranging the President's phone calls and other sensitive communications with foreign heads of state. This includes coordinating the timing of such calls at each end, providing interpreters where necessary, and ensuring appropriate security and recordkeeping. In this function, the Sit Room coordinates closely with the White House Communications Agency, which supplies communications technicians to the Watch Teams.

The importance of the Sit Room's communications function cannot be overstated. In all situations other than nuclear war or physical threats against the President, the Sit Room is in effect the 24-hour, one-stop shop for the White House staff. It is also the funnel through which most communications, especially classified information, will pass when the President is not in residence. It is an essential link, providing the traveling White House with access to all the information available from Washington's national security community.

Essential Relationships

There are two essential relationships that the Situation Room has to maintain if it is to be successful in providing timely information to the Oval Office. The most important relationship is with the NSC's Executive Secretary, who reports directly

153

to the National Security Adviser and the Deputy.

As statutory head of the NSC staff, the Executive Secretary is the primary point of contact for the White House Staff Secretary and is the key player in moving national security information to and from the Oval Office.[3] National-security-related memorandums from departments and agencies to the President are transmitted through the NSC's Executive Secretary for staffing to the appropriate office. When staffing is complete, finished packages for the National Security Adviser or the President are sent back up the chain through the Executive Secretary. When the President makes a decision or approves a course of action, the Executive Secretary formally communicates the decision to affected departments and agencies. Thus, virtually all national security correspondence passes through the Executive Secretary.

> **This intimate knowledge of the President's schedule makes the Sit Room unique among Washington-area operations and intelligence centers.**

For this reason, the Sit Room has often been administratively assigned to the Office of the Executive Secretary. With inclusion of the Sit Room, the Executive Secretary becomes the focal point for all information going to the National Security Adviser, from the deliberative ("slow paper") policy process to fast-moving perishable intelligence and crisis information. As coordinator of the President's national security schedule, the Office of the Executive Secretary also has an enormous reservoir of policy and operational information at its fingertips. It is through this key relationship that the Sit Room will first hear of a proposed Presidential trip abroad or a potential call to a foreign head of state.

A second essential connection for the WHSR is its relationship with the National Security Adviser, formally known as the Assistant to the President for National Security Affairs. He and the Deputy are the officials most "in the know," and they are in frequent and direct contact with NSC principals and key subordinates. Because of the Sit Room's role in the alert process, its position as the funnel for national security information when the President is traveling, and its 24-hour capability, a close working relationship with the National Security Adviser usually develops. For the system to work at its best, a special trust has to be established among the National Security Adviser, the Executive Secretary, and the Sit Room Director.

This trust is especially important in establishing the thresholds for warning and alert after hours and providing advance notice of future events. Upon the death of a foreign head of state, for example, it may not be necessary to awaken the National Security Adviser or the President in the middle of the night. If there are no threats to American citizens involved and no action for the President to take, perhaps a "wake-up" notification at 5 a.m. would suffice. Similarly, it is not unusual for the Sit Room Director to be included in sensitive interagency meetings before initiation of military operations or for the National Security Adviser to instruct the Sit Room that a special "Eyes Only" message should be brought directly upstairs. Establishing such trust can be developed only through close and routine personal interactions.

Through daily interaction with the Executive Secretary and National Security Adviser (including the Deputy), and routine access to the schedules and agendas of interagency meetings, the Sit Room Director is able to provide effective operational guidance to Watch Teams. The teams are then in a better position to assess the value and importance of incoming cables and newswires in the context of long-range policy issues under discussion at the highest levels, as well as fast-breaking crises that will demand Presidential attention. This intimate knowledge of the President's schedule makes the Sit Room unique among Washington-area operations and intelligence centers.

Support to the NSC Staff

The NSC staff is organized into regional and functional directorates located in the Old Executive Office Building (OEOB). A directorate is headed by a Senior Director, who is appointed by the President to coordinate and oversee Presidential policy in a particular area. A Senior Director's counterpart at State or Defense would be at the Assistant Secretary level. The Senior Director supports the National Security Adviser, in effect coordinating the interagency policy agenda in a given area. The directorates are best described as a mile wide and an inch deep because they usually consist only of a Senior Director assisted by two to four directors. On a day-to-day basis, the Sit Room supports the NSC directorates by electronically routing nearly 1,000 messages to staff members; scanning cables, newswires, and press reports; and monitoring CNN for fast-breaking events.

It is important that the NSC's Directorate for Intelligence Programs not be confused with Sit Room operations. The Intelligence Directorate oversees interagency intelligence policies and programs such as covert action Findings, counterintelligence, major procurement projects, and the interagency intelligence budget; it has no responsibility for production, dissemination, or coordination of current intelligence.[4]

Direct Sit Room contact with the NSC staff increases markedly during crises. In some cases, such as Iraq's invasion of Kuwait and the 1991 coup attempt against President Gorbachev, it is not unusual for the Senior Director to move into the Sit Room to be closer to the crisis and take advantage of the on-duty staff and its communications services. This approach, however, has limitations: Sit Room Watch Teams may lack the specific regional expertise appropriate to the crisis; Sit Room spaces are cramped and not suited physically to accommodate longer term crisis operations; and Watch Teams have a continuing responsibility to monitor other global events.

Intelligence Support to Policymakers

Efforts to strengthen intelligence support to policymakers have a long history. Every administration seems to reach its own modus vivendi, squaring expectations with realities between the policy and intelligence communities. As in the creation of the Sit Room itself, postcrisis evaluations often are catalysts for change. Many adjustments in organization, process, and personnel have been made over the years in response to the problems perceived at the time. We describe below a model that was used successfully in the late 1980s to strengthen intelligence support at the NSC Senior Director and Interagency Working Group level.

In the late 1980s, the connectivity of the Sit Room to the NSC staff benefited from the assignment of several regional and functional intelligence analysts to the Sit Room staff. These analysts worked for the Sit Room Director but had offices in the OEOB and were assigned to the NSC's regional and functional directorates. Their job was to provide tailored current intelligence support to the staff and to serve as a focal point for Sit Room support in the directorates. Though a recent casualty of personnel cutbacks, this approach was developed after several years of trial and error focused on improving internal and external intelligence support for the National Security Adviser and the NSC staff.

Use of intelligence analysts to provide daily intelligence augmentation to NSC directorates was previously considered necessary to keep up with even the normal volume of relevant intelligence and cable traffic. At the same time, resulting from their close association with the policy staff, intelligence analysts also garnered an insider's perspective on interagency policy deliberations. This perspective strengthened the Sit Room's ability to anticipate specific intelligence requirements. During crises, the Senior Director would have a familiar face who would coordinate intelligence support in the Sit Room and who would know where to find key information in the IC. In turn, the Sit Room Watch Team would be augmented by appropriate functional or regional expertise from an intelligence analyst familiar with current interagency policy deliberations. It proved on many occasions to be a useful marriage.

Use of on-scene intelligence analysts was also a valuable means for the IC to enhance its support to the White House. With insights gained through daily interaction with the NSC directors, the analysts communicated the precise current needs of the directorates to the IC's production elements. The analysts served as a soundingboard for IC-initiated studies and would discuss with NSC directors the gist of draft or just-published studies, often resulting in requests for deskside briefings. Finally, the analysts were responsible for framing the bulk of the issues included in the Sit Room's *Weekly Emphasis List,* which was often exchanged with other agencies.

Again, it is important not to confuse the role of the Sit Room Watch Team or intelligence analysts with the role of other, more senior players in the interagency intelligence process. The interagency process includes National Intelligence Officers (NIOs), who are responsible for coordinating the preparation and adjudication of formal interagency National Intelligence Estimates in support of the policy community. NIOs are often included in senior-level interagency meetings and provide feedback and tasking to the IC. Whereas the NIO is focused on *future* (although sometimes near-term) requirements for collection, production, and analysis, the Sit Room analyst was focused on ensuring access to *today's* information already available in the Community, and on effecting close coordination at the working level.

This model worked for several reasons: It supported (rather than competed with) the senior policymakers' role as crisis managers; the Sit Room's role as the NSC focal point for current intelligence was reinforced; midcareer analysts were careful not to intrude on NIO responsibilities; and the process worked the same way with the same people in both routine and crisis environments.

Interagency Connections

In addition to providing current intelligence support to the NSC staff in important regional and functional areas, the Sit Room has a more independent role to play as an operations and intelligence center. There is a constant need for daily coordination on

> "Perhaps the most distinguishing feature of the Sit Room is its proximity to the President. As in real estate, the operative principles are location, location, and location."

current issues with other centers, especially at the Defense and State Departments and CIA. This coordination takes place largely out of view of the NSC staff and leadership, but is nonetheless critical to the effectiveness of the interagency system. When less formal coordination has been found inadequate, formal interagency groups have been chartered by the President or National Security Adviser to strengthen connectivity among operations and intelligence centers, improve the flow of information, develop common practices and procedures where possible, and coordinate hardware and software decisions concerning interagency communications systems.

Sit Room responsibilities sometimes extend beyond intelligence and national security functions. Maintaining connectivity with the Federal Emergency Management Agency, the Departments of Justice, Transportation, Commerce, and other agencies, the Sit Room is frequently the initial point of White House notification for domestic disasters, including everything from earthquakes, fires, and floods to Haitian refugees and Federal prison riots. The periodic inclusion of Coast Guard and other Federal agency personnel as Sit Room Duty Officers has sometimes proved helpful in these crises, because the Sit Room may be called upon to facilitate initial coordination of crisis response within the White House until an appropriate interagency task force is formed.

Comparisons With Other Washington-Area Centers

Perhaps the most distinguishing feature of the Sit Room is its proximity to the President. As in real estate, the operative principles are location, location, and location. To be sure, the President gets most important intelligence advice and inputs from the Director of Central Intelligence, NIOs, and other key officials. But these officials cannot be at the White House 24 hours a day. The Sit Room often is the "first phone call" when senior White House officials are looking for the latest intelligence information, and it plays a key role in synthesizing cables and intelligence products originated by other agencies.[5]

A second feature is that the Sit Room is both an operations and intelligence center for the White House. These activities are divided in most departments and agencies. In the Department of Defense, for example, the National Military Command Center is colocated but separate from the National Military Joint Intelligence Center. Likewise, in the State Department and at CIA headquarters, operations and intelligence activities are separated. In the White House, this means that the relationship between policy development and current intelligence can be extremely close.

The close connectivity between intelligence and policy also means that the White House is not a passive consumer of intelligence. Even at the national level, information has an "operational" and sometimes "tactical" dimension. Diplomatic and intelligence cables may be closely correlated with Presidential events, perhaps allowing a glimpse of the talking points of a foreign head of state only hours or minutes before he meets with the President.

A third feature is the small size of the Sit Room staff. By all measures, the Sit Room is the smallest of the Washington-area operations and intelligence centers. This has come to mean a relatively junior staff. Senior Duty Officers are perhaps O-3, or GS-12 or 13 equivalents, as compared to O-6 or GS-15 equivalents elsewhere. Limitations of size and depth, however, can in part be offset by quality personnel, high standards of performance, the Sit Room's interagency character, excellent technical support, and the motivation that comes with working inside the White House.

In addition to the Sit Room's inherent limitations stemming from the small size of its staff, it lacks many advantages of a large intelligence agency. But the Sit Room does not need such advantages to fulfill its mission, and it should not be considered a peer competitor for influence in the IC. The implications of the Sit Room's proximity to the President, moreover, should not be underrated. Despite its limitations, the Sit Room by virtue of its location has greater access and potential impact on White House officials than any of

> **Sit Room personnel provide some of what little continuity exists within the NSC staff, and they are often able to observe potential gaps in the complex, fast-moving crisis management process.**

Washington's other operations and intelligence centers.

Implications for Leadership

A better understanding of the role of the WHSR has important implications for NSC leadership and for the intelligence agencies which supply both information and personnel to the NSC staff, including the Sit Room.

There is a need within the NSC for continuing education and dialogue among staff and leadership about the role and potential of the Sit Room in support of NSC activities. An orientation to Sit Room operations should be mandatory for incoming NSC staff officers. Likewise, an orientation to the NSC and interagency process should be mandatory for incoming Sit Room Duty Officers.

In addition, the National Security Adviser, Executive Secretary, and Sit Room Director should nurture in their personal interactions a routine concept of operations for crisis management. The enemy in crises is confusion and "ad hocracy"; responsibilities and expectations need to be as clear as possible. Sit Room personnel provide some of what little continuity exists within the NSC staff, and they are often able to observe potential gaps in the complex, fast-moving crisis management process. Routine and open dialogue with key NSC officials is essential for getting the most from the Sit Room staff.

The messages for the IC are equally clear. First, departmental and agency Watch Teams should be better educated about who works at the Sit Room and what they do. Operations and intelligence center personnel need to know that access is sometimes more important than rank. When a Sit Room Duty Officer phones, even though he or she may be junior in rank or grade, take the call and get the answer. Do not view the Sit Room as an institutional threat; support the White House in any attempt to find information and accept that the deadlines imposed, however unreasonable, will be for good reason. The IC should be confident that Sit Room information requests are for legitimate purposes and will not be mishandled.

Second, send your best people and treat them well when they return. Personnel nominated to serve as Sit Room duty officers should have operations/intelligence center experience. These are junior-to-midlevel personnel going to an outside assignment—not always regarded as a career-enhancing move. But the destination is crucial; these junior personnel may have more contact with senior officials than certain agency directors. Personal screening of nominations by the leadership of supporting agencies is called for, as well as personal debriefings. In addition, look for opportunities to augment the Sit Room staff or NSC directorates with mid- to senior-level intelligence analysts during periods of intense activity or crisis.

When Sit Room Duty Officers return to your agency for their next assignment, ensure that the personnel system makes the most of their experience. Promotion boards do not always recognize the signature of the National Security Adviser or his Deputy on personnel evaluation or promotion recommendation forms. Take a close look at planned career progression, and concentrate on placement that takes advantage of the White House experience and enlarges the individual's Sit Room-attained knowledge of the IC.

Conclusion

Greater knowledge about the role of the WHSR has the potential for several beneficial effects within the IC. These include strengthening current intelligence support within the NSC staff and the White House; improving the timeliness of intelligence support during crises; enhancing the quality of individual agency products in support of national leadership; and better internal use of department and agency personnel with White House experience. In current intelligence and crisis support, the Situation Room is well positioned at the working level to assist in bridging the needs of the policy and intelligence communities. IC effectiveness would be improved with better understanding of how the White House works, how the President gets information, and how decisions are made.

NOTES

1. Bromley Smith, "Organizational History of the National Security Council During the Kennedy and Johnson Administrations," p. 51. Unpublished monograph, courtesy of the NSC staff.

2. Further unclassified background on the *President's Daily Brief* can be found in: "PDB, the Only News Not Fit for Anyone Else To Read," *The Washington Post*, 27 August 94, p. 7.

3. 50 U.S.C. 402, Sec. 101(c)

4. An example of the coordination and oversight functions performed by the NSC's Intelligence Directorate may be found in David G. Major's article, "Operation 'Famish': The Integration of Counterintelligence into the National Strategic Decisionmaking Process," *Defense Intelligence Journal*, Vol. 4, No. 1, spring 1995.

5. For a broader and fuller treatment of the White House–CIA relationship, see Robert M. Gates, "An Opportunity Unfulfilled: The Use and Perceptions of Intelligence at the White House," *Washington Quarterly*, winter 1989.

U.S. International Economic Strategy

As in so many areas of American foreign policy, the selection of U.S. international economic strategies during the cold war seems to have been a rather straightforward process and the accompanying policy rebates fairly minor compared to the situation that exists today. At the most fundamental level, it was taken for granted that the American economy would best be served by the existence of a global free trade system. The lengthy Depression of the 1930s and the accompanying rise to power of extremist governments in Germany, Italy, and elsewhere had discredited the competing policy of protectionism. A consensus also existed that for a free trade system to work, America's active involvement and leadership were essential. To that end, international organizations were set up whose collective task it was to oversee the operation of the postwar international economic order. Foremost among them were the General Agreement on Tariffs and Trade (GATT), the International Monetary Fund (IMF), and the International Bank for Reconstruction and Development (the World Bank).

It was also widely accepted that many states would not be able to resist pressures from the Soviet Union or from domestic communist parties, due to the weak state of their economies and military establishments. Thus, containing Communism would require foreign aid programs designed to transfer American economic and military expertise, goods and services, and financial resources to key states. Finally, containing Communism was seen as requiring economic strategies of denial. Lists were drawn up of goods that U.S. firms were prohibited from selling to communist states because they could contribute to the strength of communist military establishments.

Over time, problems arose in all of these areas. Events of the 1960s and 1970s shook the international economic system at its political and economic foundations. Among the most prominent were the growing U.S. balance of payments deficits growing out of the Vietnam War; the completed economic recoveries of Germany and Japan; President Richard Nixon's decision to take the United States off the gold standard and allow the exchange rate to fluctuate; and oil price hikes led by the Organization of Petroleum Exporting Countries (OPEC). It was now clear that there was nothing automatic about the operation of a free trade system. The institutions created after World War II have struggled to meet the challenges presented by the increased attractiveness of regional trading blocks, the recognition that economic issues intersect with environmental and democratization problems, and the lingering effects of large-scale developing world debt.

Foreign aid programs also became controversial. Unable to foster economic growth and development that would remove the need for continued U.S. foreign aid, these programs increasingly came to be seen as entitlement programs. Moreover, many began to question America's ability to pay for such programs, given the declining health of the American economy. A concern for the state of the American economy also led to disenchantment with policies denying American products to the Soviet Union and its allies. With many U.S. allies selling "denied" technology to the Soviet Union, these policies were costing American companies access to markets and costing American workers jobs.

The end of the cold war, then, did not in a single stroke undermine America's international economic strategy. It did bring into sharp relief the strategy's growing ineffectiveness and open up the policy process to the possibility of new solutions. As the debates over the North American Free Trade Agreement (NAFTA), foreign aid to the former Soviet Union countries, and establishing the World Trade Organization make clear, a consensus has not yet taken hold within the American political system on what type of international economic strategy to pursue. For some, the solution lies in reaffirming the commitment to making a global free trade system work. For others, the solution lies with a policy centered on the creation of a system of regional trading blocs. Also at issue is the degree to which the government should allow market forces to dictate the direction of the American economy and the extent to which it should intervene to promote certain economic sectors and protect others from foreign competition.

The readings in this unit highlight several important dimensions to U.S. international economic policy. Carol Graham, in "Foreign Aid," directs our attention to one of the perennial problem areas in American foreign eco-

UNIT 6

nomic policy. She asserts that it is time to ask some hard questions about the effectiveness of foreign aid, particularly: would economic performance in recipient states have been worse without aid; how is the United States allocating aid; do economic aid policies produce growth; and do better economic conditions facilitate the implementation of better policies?

In "A U.S.–Japan Trade Agenda," Edward Lincoln asserts that we are in danger of treating Japan as "yesterday's problem." Lincoln identifies a series of issues, including World Trade Organization negotiations, Japanese firms, and monitoring trade agreements, as issues that need to be skillfully negotiated if U.S. interests are to be served.

Economic sanctions are a favorite foreign policy tool. In "Adjusting to Sanctions," Jahangir Amuzegar examines the reasons why Iran has not responded as expected to American economic sanctions. His article sheds light both on the general problems involved in using sanctions and the nature of U.S.–Iranian relations. Amuzegar concludes by examining U.S. options toward Iran.

Looking Ahead: Challenge Questions

What weight should be given to economic factors in making American foreign policy?

Rank in order of importance the major international economic powers in the world today. Where does the United States stand? How does this compare to 5 and 10 years ago? Where do you expect it to rank in another 5 years? If the U.S. ranking has changed, explain why.

Which type of international system, global free trade or regional trading blocs, is in America's national interest?

Should the United States pursue a policy of managed trade? If so, what sectors of the economy should the government try to protect? How should it go about doing this?

Which is the most important trading partner for the United States: Japan, Europe, or Mexico? Defend your answer.

What is the proper balance among environmental, human rights, and economic concerns in making U.S. foreign policy?

Select a country in need of foreign aid. What type of foreign aid strategy should the United States pursue toward it? How does this compare with current U.S. foreign aid programs?

Should membership in NAFTA be expanded to include all of the countries in Latin and Central America? Why, or why not? Should any other states be permitted to join?

What types of foreign policy goals can be advanced using economic means?

Should the United States continue to rely on economic sanctions as a way of furthering its foreign policy goals?

FOREIGN AID

CAROL GRAHAM

At a time when the entire foreign affairs budget is under fire, it is more important than ever to address the question of whether foreign aid is effective. Official development assistance, or ODA, as the foreign assistance component of the foreign affairs budget is called, is roughly half of that budget, and is arguably the part about which the public is most skeptical.

The United States, once the world leader in global aid, is now in fourth place after Japan, Germany, and France in terms of absolute amounts. In terms of percentage of GDP with 0.1 percent of American GDP allocated to ODA, the United States is well at the bottom of all industrialized nation donors. This clearly imperils U.S. leadership not only in international financial institutions such as the World Bank, but also in the aid debate more generally. Washington is increasingly being seen as unwilling to pay its global dues.

It is time to ask some hard questions about foreign aid. What do we know about it? Does it work? Is it effective? There has been much debate in recent years. I'd like to try to sum up what we know about aid effectiveness—and what we don't.

One reason for the extensive debate over aid is that so many diverse objectives drive its allocation that it is hard to evaluate how effective it is. While economic growth is clearly not the sole objective of foreign assistance, it's one of the few areas where empirical evidence permits evaluation. Growth is also important because without growth it is difficult, if not impossible, to achieve all the other goals—security, human rights, democracy—attributed to aid.

Recently the debate has been heightened by a series of studies that have found a negative relationship between conditioned aid flows and economic growth, particularly in low-income countries in Africa. These same studies, however, are also finding that the broader policy orientation that aid seeks to promote—market-friendly, open economic policies with prudent macroeconomic management—is producing strong results in countries worldwide. And the experience of many Asian countries and, more recently, many Latin American countries confirms that appropriate policies do yield good results.

These findings raise three questions about aid flows. First, is aid ineffective, or would poor economic performers have fared worse without aid? Second, how effective is conditionality in its current form? How are we allocating aid, and how is it working? And third, what is the causal relationship? Do policies produce growth, or do better initial economic conditions facilitate the implementation of better policies?

CAN AID SLOW GROWTH?

What accounts for the negative correlation between aid flows and growth performance? Africa, for example, receives 10 times more aid per capita than Latin America or East Asia and yet performs far worse by most or all economic measures. There are several explanations, and I don't want to oversimplify the issue, but one point is clear. By removing a hard budget constraint, aid inflows to a country can impede formation of a domestic consensus on the need for difficult economic reforms. Recent research on economic crisis undertaken at the World Bank suggests that countries that enter high-inflation crises tend to implement more complete reforms and then enjoy higher average growth rates than countries that just muddle along at "medium" inflation rates. What happens is that aid flows are often cut off in countries with very high inflation rates but continue in countries with medium inflation rates. These aid flows protect countries from the full costs of bad economic policies, often preventing the onset of deeper crisis and the important policy learning experience that is often critical to successful economic reform. Countries often have to hit bottom to get a domestic consensus on the need for economic reforms. Of course, allowing countries to enter acute crisis is hardly an acceptable policy recommendation. And to complicate the issue further, it's also important to note that in some cases aid has actually helped develop a consensus in favor of market reforms. For example, in Poland in 1989 the promise of foreign aid as something that the reform team could deliver was critical to the election of that team and the undertaking of market reform.

Carol Graham is a visiting fellow in the Brookings Foreign Policy Studies program. She is the author, with Michael O'Hanlon, of "Foreign Aid: Paved with Good Intentions," to appear in the May–June issue of Foreign Affairs.

Both the timing and the role of aid flows in the implementation of policy reforms is still being widely debated. But what we clearly do know is that financial aid to countries where there is no consensus at all in favor of reform has a negative impact.

STOPPING THE FLOW OF INEFFECTIVE AID

How and why has so much aid continued to flow under such conditions? Conditionality, which is how aid is appropriated for the most part, is usually applied "ex ante," that is, borrowing countries must meet certain conditions to be eligible for a loan and then must continue to meet those conditions along the way as aid is disbursed. But despite a marked increase in conditional lending in the past decade, and also an increase in the number of conditions on each loan, conditionality has not been particularly effective in attaining borrower compliance. The higher number of conditions actually seems to decrease borrower ownership of reforms. It creates a vicious cycle: weak compliance with conditions prompts donors to impose more conditions, increased conditions make it yet harder for the recipient to comply, thus increasing the incentive not to comply, and so on. On the donor side, meanwhile, the incentive structure rewards continued lending rather than halting financial flows in response to breaches in compliance. Ultimately multilateral institutions are lending institutions, and they must lend to remain operational. It's their raison d'être. So the average loan officer at the World Bank or the Interamerican Development Bank has a lot more incentives to disburse loans on time than to enforce strict compliance among recipients of those loans.

As a result, many countries continue to receive loans even though they have bad records at both compliance and policy reform. It's increasingly evident, at least to those who observe it closely, that we have to move to more selective lending, with less focus on detailed conditions and more focus on building overall agreement on a policy package. At the very least we really have to stop lending to countries with major slippage on conditions.

While the shift to more selective lending makes intuitive sense, it also entails substantial risk. For example, withdrawing funds, particularly from many poor countries in Africa, may well spur the adoption of policy reforms in some, but in others it will cause performance to deteriorate even further, and at a relatively high human cost. At the least, one would need to maintain humanitarian and technical assistance. There could also be other costs to lending more selectively. A lot of the lending that takes place now is undertaken to enable debtor countries to pay back loans. For example, when heavily indebted countries default on loans, somebody is going to have to pay the cost. So a shift to selective lending must be taken with care, and while budget cutters would like to see it as a way of saving money, in the short term a shift toward more selective and more effective lending would actually increase costs.

THE CHICKEN OR THE EGG?

The final question is whether policies or initial conditions determine a country's economic performance. One school of thought is that poor countries perform badly on the macroeconomic front because of their weak initial conditions: a very poor country's performance is almost predetermined regardless of the level of aid. But some recent research refutes this view. Jeffrey Sachs and Andrew Warner of Harvard University did a study of the effects of policy as against those of initial economic conditions on economic performance. Using a sample of more than 100 countries, they found that countries that follow standard, market-oriented policies, and in particular maintain open trading regimes, have an overwhelming tendency to grow faster and converge with wealthier countries, regardless of initial conditions. Indeed, they had trouble finding a single case where a poor country

> Uncertainty about foreign aid effectiveness, uncomfortable enough at any time, is particularly worrisome when the foreign affairs budget is under fire.

that protected property rights and maintained economic openness did not grow. Very few of the countries that pursued poor policies, meanwhile, grew at equivalent rates. One that did was China. In fact, one reason why China is growing is that half of its economy actually functions with the market policies that produce growth in all the other countries. In any event, we have increasing evidence besides the Sachs and Warner study that good policies produce growth performance and poor policies do not, and that initial conditions are not a predetermining factor.

We need to know more about how aid can better support the adoption of appropriate policies. We have a sense that the answer lies in a more selective aid strategy, but the debate over the appropriate timing and level of aid flows is unresolved. Such uncertainty about aid effectiveness, uncomfortable enough at any time, is particularly worrisome when the foreign affairs budget is under fire.

A U.S.–Japan TRADE AGENDA

Despite Recent Reverses, Japan Is Still A Huge Market That Needs To Be More Open

BY EDWARD J. LINCOLN

Edward J. Lincoln is a senior fellow in the Brookings Foreign Policy Studies program. He was special economic advisor to Ambassador Walter Mondale in Japan during 1994–96.

Judging from the American press, Japan has become yesterday's problem. With the collapse of Japanese stock and real estate prices in the early 1990s, very slow economic growth from 1992 to 1995, and revelations of large amounts of bad debt in the banking sector, longstanding U.S. concerns about trade with Japan seem simply to have slipped the minds of many Americans. Even the Clinton administration, which pursued a high-profile and active stance on trade issues with Japan in its first term, shows little inclination to continue a high-pressure campaign now.

But though Japan no longer seems an unstoppable juggernaut, it nevertheless remains one of the world's leading industrial nations. Its economy is recovering: growth was 3.6 percent in 1996 (outpacing the United States) and is likely to be at least 2 percent this year. Japan also remains a big part of U.S. trade. In 1995, Japan was the second largest U.S. export market, taking 11 percent of all U.S. exports, and was the source of 15 percent of U.S. imports. And leading Japanese corporations are still the chief global competitors in many industries for American firms. Japanese markets are large, affluent, and growing—all reasons for American firms to be involved in them.

To be sure, these individual trade problems are not linked in any major way to macroeconomic balances. Solving market access problems will not materially alter Japan's global trade surplus or the bilateral imbalance between Japan and the United States. Large declines in the value of the yen against the dollar in the past two years will result in sharp increases in Japanese trade surpluses this year and next. But those surpluses should not be the reason for increasing pressure on trade issues. Market access issues have a separate justification, growing out of the intellectual concept of free trade and the official support that notion has garnered from major nations—including Japan.

An active market-access approach to trade with Japan will involve disputes and tension. But more open markets increase economic flows of trade and investment and ultimately strengthen the U.S.-Japan relationship. Temporary antagonisms that flare during trade disputes are less dangerous than long-term ill will engendered by a lack of access to many Japanese markets. Though the Clinton administration shows a certain amount of fatigue on Japan after four active and contentious years, it should nevertheless persevere. The following modest agenda would keep trade issues moving forward.

Running through these suggestions is an implicit theme—the need for more fiscal and human resources. Only a handful of people work actively on these issues within the U.S. government. Too often in the past the U.S. government has been at a disadvantage when negotiating with the many, well-prepared officials representing the Japanese government. Reinforcing the U.S. team is not a major financial issue. The size and importance of Japanese markets to American businesses and the seriousness of some of the problems justify the added expense and effort.

WTO

In June 1996, the United States Trade Representative (USTR) chose to take a dispute over access to the color film market to the World Trade Organization. The dispute, a landmark case, raises fundamental questions about the nature of industrial policy in Japan, the continuing existence of opaque and unusual regulatory controls over the distribution sector, and the ability of the WTO to handle such complex issues. In essence the case argues that Japanese industrial policy operated informally to keep the color film market closed despite agreements to eliminate quotas and reduce tariffs. It also argues that regulations in Japan were not designed or administered in a manner to guarantee national treatment for foreign firms, and that administrative processes were not transparent. The Japanese government will probably settle with the United States before the final decision in October rather than risk losing and thereby setting a precedent. But even if a definitive decision on the case is unlikely, the U.S. government should pursue it vigorously and bring more cases to the WTO that challenge the impact of industrial policy in Japan on market access.

The WTO provides additional advantages. If or when Japan loses a case, the demand for change (or authorization of U.S. retaliation) comes from a multilateral source, helping to diffuse Japanese rancor, which is usually directed solely against the United States. The WTO also promotes useful coalition-building (for example, European Union cooperation on the current color film case). Convincing a multilateral panel in Geneva of the legitimacy of U.S. complaints about market access in Japan is obviously harder than simply convincing U.S. government agencies in Washington. But the detailed exposure of Japanese trade barriers in a public forum, as is happening with the color film case, is critical to gaining international understanding and support for American trade policy toward Japan. Therefore, a key aspect of policy should be to make more active use of the WTO to pursue trade problems with Japan.

BILATERAL

Not all problems concerning market access in Japan fit within the framework of the WTO. Sometimes the industries or the behavior involved are not covered by WTO rules. Sometimes the dispute concerns creating new rules for market access rather than disagreement over behavior under past commitments. Except when large multilateral negotiating rounds are under way, the WTO assumes that nations will engage in such negotiations bilaterally, with the stipulation that the results be applied on a most-favored-nation basis to other WTO members. U.S.-Japan bilateral negotiations meet this requirement.

In bilateral cases the key is finding and applying leverage in the form of costs to Japanese commercial interests that can be imposed when negotiations fail. Why should a sovereign nation comply with requests for market liberalization in the absence of international rules? Sometimes governments agree because they, too, desire to sweep away market impediments, to satisfy domestic consumer and business pressure for lower costs and greater efficiency. Rarely, however, do matters happen this way in Japan. There the voice of consumers is weak. Even businesses harmed by protection often fail to press hard for liberalization with their own government—as has been the case in the current dispute over harbor services, where the collusive system raises costs to Japanese shipping companies as well as American ones. Japan's government does, however, respond when faced with a realistic probability of American retaliation in the form of punitive actions against Japanese economic interests in the United States. An early step in any non-WTO bilateral issue must be to determine what leverage of this sort can be brought to bear. Among potential sources of leverage are section 301 (although its use is problematic in the wake of the GATT Uruguay round agreement), regulatory authority, federal contracting rules, and even antitrust prosecution. If these tools are to be effective, they must be used on occasion. The recent decision of the Federal Maritime Commission to impose fees on Japanese shipping lines using U.S. ports, for example, spurred the Japanese government to address the question of restrictive practices at Japanese ports.

MONITORING

Results matter. Trade agreements need to be fully implemented after they are negotiated, and they should lead to increased market opportunities for foreign firms. Setting targets for foreign penetration, as in the case of semiconductors, may be unavoidable when all other approaches fail, though adopting managed trade as a general principle is neither desirable economically nor feasible politically. As a general principle, vigorously monitoring implementation and outcomes without preconditions can help convince the Japanese government that implementation must occur in good faith.

Monitoring does not require a commitment written into bilateral agreements. The Clinton administration spent too much negotiating time in the first term haggling over the terminology for these commitments, especially over language expressing the goal of increased sales and market share for foreign products. What matters most is that implementation be watched closely, statistical data collected, and analysis done on the causes of market outcomes. Should the statistical evidence suggest that problems still exist, the government can determine what approach is needed, such as negotiations to strip away other impediments.

ON TRADE

The public message on bilateral trade issues, especially in a vigorous market-access campaign, should remain low-key. There is no need to portray the trade relationship in dramatic terms, nor to tout successful negotiations as great victories. Even restrained rhetoric, of course, will garner considerable unfavorable attention in the Japanese media. But there is no need to contribute unnecessarily to the Japanese perception of excessive pressure.

Accompanying the low-key rhetoric should be a steady stream of factual information. Simply responding to media questions or holding (infrequent) formal press conferences leaves U.S. policymakers on the defensive. In the color film case, release of the brief filed in Geneva last February provided the media and public with great detail on American allegations, carefully documenting factual evidence and how the Japanese government and industry worked to impede market access. That approach should be the model for all trade disputes.

JAPANESE FIRMS

Continued Japanese direct investment abroad raises new issues for U.S. government scrutiny. Are collusive patterns of behavior at home being replicated abroad? To what extent do large amounts of bilateral foreign aid grease the way for Japanese firms investing in developing countries in Asia? Are American firms disadvantaged by such behavior? To what extent does the increase in Japanese imports represent purchases from manufacturing subsidiaries abroad rather than from independent foreign firms (implying that Japanese markets are not really more open despite rising imports)? These questions do not yet have clear answers, but they will become increasingly important. Focusing exclusively on the bilateral context will miss many of these issues, ranging from questions of preferential access in developing country markets to the rather unrestrained movement of Japanese firms into the Burmese market (in contrast to both Japan's official stance on human rights in Burma and U.S. policy objectives). These issues are particularly salient in Asia, which is now absorbing a rising share of the foreign direct investment of Japanese firms.

THEMES

Large overarching themes, such as the Market-Oriented Sector Selective (MOSS) talks of 1985–86, the Structural Impediments (SI) talks of 1989–90, and the Framework Agreement of 1993–96, are to be avoided. They lead the Japanese government to assume that the Americans have been gripped by another short-term enthusiasm—one that they can ride out with minimal concessions. They also oversimplify U.S. policy, which should be just as complex and multifaceted as the relationship itself.

One particular organizing theme to avoid is deregulation. The two governments have already agreed to upgrade the level of dialogue on deregulation. In theory, this will engage both sides in discussing an issue that has public support in Japan. But deregulation is unlikely to proceed with any vigor in Japan, and a primary focus on it would trap the administration in a discussion of an extraordinarily broad topic, which the Japanese government would try to keep at a high level of generality. The administration should certainly remain engaged on this issue, but not as the central, high-profile focus of policy. Most deregulation issues are better pursued when they arise in the context of particular trade issues, as with the color film dispute (which challenges the existence of the Large Scale Retail Store Law). At least the administration appears to have chosen to discuss only a few issues under the rubric of deregulation, based on existing sectoral access problems.

SHORT-TERM TENSION, LONG-TERM

The approach sketched above would continue or accelerate progress in lowering trade barriers in Japan. It will certainly yield further tension, since it proposes an active pursuit of market access problems that the Japanese government will vigorously oppose at the negotiating table and in the media. Tension is unavoidable, but it can be managed with greater attention to the public message. The long-run gain to the bilateral relationship from greater market openness is a compelling reason to accept the short-term perceptions of tension (and any temporary harm to other aspects of the bilateral relationship) that this active agenda would bring about.

Adjusting to Sanctions

Jahangir Amuzegar

THE TOLL IN IRAN

THE AMERICAN-DRIVEN sanctions against Iran were meant to transform the "backlash state" into a law-abiding, cooperative, and constructive member of the world community. Washington expected trade and investment restrictions to cripple the productive base of the economy and curtail Iran's ability to support international terrorism or acquire sophisticated military hardware. Economic hardship and fiscal austerity would demoralize the population and turn it against the regime. And domestic popular discontent and external political isolation, Washington hoped, would bring the clerical leadership to its senses.

Inadequate hard data make an objective assessment of the sanctions difficult. Supporters of the policy claim that the cost to Iran has been immense, even greater than expected; critics dismiss the policy as self-defeating and divisive. What is certain, however, is that the economic, psychological, and political impact of the American sanctions has not produced the anticipated results or transformed the regime. Although the comparison may seem invidious, the Iranian economy under sanctions is in certain respects healthier and more stable than many developing economies the United States has assisted. Militarily, Iran appears to be stronger now than in 1989, and is certainly less vulnerable than some U.S. allies in the region. The embargo has isolated Washington rather than Tehran.

Iranian officials concede that the boycotts have caused some economic "difficulties" but do not give details of their nature or magnitude. The affected areas, however, are not hard to identify. Finding non-U.S. buyers for Iranian oil and non-Americans to invest in Iran's offshore oil and gas fields has not been cost-free. Banned imports from the United States have been obtained through third parties at extra cost or substituted for from lower-quality sources. Replacing or renovating defense, industrial, and oil equipment based on American components has been more expensive or less satisfactory. Rescheduling of short-term arrears on debt to other countries has taken place under less favorable terms. Some foreign investors have shied away from lucrative projects in Iran under the threat of U.S. retaliation. Normal credits

---

The embargo has isolated Washington rather than Tehran.

---

from international financial organizations have been delayed or canceled. Scheduled long-term foreign loans have been postponed. Foreign technological assistance in some sensitive areas has been withheld. Business confidence in Iran has been shaken, and the climate for foreign and domestic investment in the country has cooled.

There is no doubt that Iran would be in better shape had the United States not resolved to ostracize and cripple it. American economic and political pressures have hurt the Iranian economy, but they have not inflicted irreparable damage. Iran continues to produce its quota for oil set by the Organization of Petroleum Exporting Countries (OPEC), remains solvent, and maintains normal levels of trade and investment with the rest of the world. In fact, various international organizations and foreign media outlets report that economic indicators are healthier than at any time since the early 1990s. High surpluses have been registered in the current account, hard currency reserves are at record highs, and foreign debt payments are being made on schedule. Iran has had some success in raising medium- and long-term financing in Europe, the rial's official exchange rate has been kept stable, import cutbacks have slowed, and the Qeshm and Kish free trade zones have attracted some private foreign investment. Where sanctions were expected to be particularly damaging, their effect has been surprisingly

---

JAHANGIR AMUZEGAR, an international economic consultant, was minister of finance in Iran's pre-1979 government.

Reprinted with permission from *Foreign Affairs*, May/June 1997, pp. 31-41. © 1997 by the Council of Foreign Relations, Inc.

6 ❖ U.S. INTERNATIONAL ECONOMIC STRATEGY

Still contemplating American sanctions, Iranian President Hashemi Rafsanjani

benign. Daily crude oil production in 1996–97 was *higher* than in 1993–94. So were oil export receipts and net foreign assets. As a percentage of GDP, domestic investment was greater, and the budget deficit, external debt, and trade arrears smaller, after the sanctions, thanks in part to higher oil prices and appreciation of the U.S. dollar.

To be sure, the Iranian economy is not trouble-free. Inflation is unacceptably high. Unemployment and underemployment, particularly among the ever-growing numbers of graduates of the mushrooming diploma mills, combined with severe restrictions on normal social outlets for the youth, are economically debilitating and politically explosive. Cost and price distortions are enormous. Labor and capital productivity are low. There will be more turbulence ahead if the global oil market becomes depressed again. Yet American sanctions have not appreciably worsened any of these ills. And whatever their adverse effects, they have not been strong enough to induce a noticeable change in Tehran's behavior.

The psychological effects of the sanctions have been mixed. There are signs that despite their defiance of the United States, President Hashemi Rafsanjani and his government are wary of the costs of American enmity. They prefer compromise to confrontation and abhor the sanctions even as they claim immunity to them.[1] As a sign of America's displeasure with the Tehran regime, the boycotts have also brought psychological comfort to discontented but passive groups inside Iran as well as the boisterous but ineffective opposition forces abroad, which both long for escalating American pressure that might lead to the eventual overthrow of the revolutionary regime.

On the other hand, U.S. sanctions have created a siege mentality; the regime's remaining supporters have become determined to rely on their own resources and ingenuity. The determination to become self-sufficient in most of their needs heralded a shift to other sources of equipment for exporting oil and stronger ties with Asia, Africa, and Latin America. The kinds of sophisticated goods and services now designed and produced in Iran—increasingly for export abroad—did not exist ten or even five years ago. Supreme Leader Ayatollah Sayed Ali Khamenei has publicly welcomed the U.S. ban as a boon to popular mobilization and self-reliance.

The political impact of U.S. pressure has, if anything, also worked in Tehran's favor. When the United States first imposed sanctions on Iran in the mid-1980s, the Islamic Republic's loyal friends around the world could be counted on one hand. In the mid-1990s, the regime's declared enemies were only two: the United States and Israel. Despite the sanctions—or perhaps because of them—Tehran now has close ties to Russia, China, India, Indonesia, and Brazil, which together account for nearly half the world's population. Relations with most countries in Asia and Africa are friendly, and with the European Community they are businesslike, despite recurrent verbal duels concerning Salman Rushdie and other high-profile human rights cases. There are hundreds of treaties of friendship, cooperation, trade, and cultural exchange with both developing and developed countries on six continents.[2] A regime that some American high officials have called an "outlaw state" has been invited to lend its good offices to resolving disputes between Azerbaijan and Armenia, Sudan and Uganda, and other sovereign nations. Tehran has also been active in mediating between ethnic factions in Afghanistan, Tajikistan, Iraq, Bosnia, and elsewhere. Islamic government repre-

---

[1] Many interpret Iran's decision to award the Sirri oil fields contract to the American oil company Conoco, for which President Clinton denied approval in 1995, as an olive branch to Washington.

---

[2] The inauguration in May 1996 of a rail link between Sarakhs, Iran, and Ashkhabad, Turkmenistan, which included representatives from 40 countries (including 12 heads of state or government), has been trumpeted by Tehran as a "triumph" over U.S. efforts to isolate Iran. So has the participation of 1,500 companies from 54 countries in the 1996 Tehran International Trade Fair.

sentatives have won important committee seats in the United Nations and its affiliate organizations in spite of Washington's objections. Last December the International Court of Justice in The Hague voted 14 to 2 to reject Washington's plea for dismissal and to hear Tehran's case against the United States for the deliberate destruction of three Iranian offshore oil platforms in the Persian Gulf in 1987. The Tehran government now feels confident enough about its economy to consider membership in the World Trade Organization.

The Islamic Republic still has festering quarrels with Iraq and is embroiled in political conflicts with Algeria, Bahrain, Egypt, Saudi Arabia, the United Arab Emirates, and the Taliban in Afghanistan. Relations with the U.N. Human Rights Commission are also tense; Maurice Copithorne may join Reynaldo Galindo Pol as the second U.N. rapporteur to be declared persona non grata in Iran because of reports critical of the country's human rights record. Nevertheless, its "isolation index" is now the lowest since the revolution.

WHY THE SETBACKS?

THE REASONS for the evident lack of success of Washington's containment policy are not difficult to fathom. Historically, economic sanctions have worked only when they have been universal and comprehensive, consistent and credible—in short, leakproof. In this case, none of those conditions has held.

Except with respect to transfers of sophisticated military weapons, the American policy toward Iran has been essentially unilateral. Since 1993, and culminating in the Group of Seven Halifax summit in June 1995 and the Sharm al-Sheikh antiterrorism summit in March 1996, Washington has tried and failed to enlist its major allies in its campaign against Iran. Reactions to American initiatives have been negative or, at best, noncommittal. The allies regard the U.S. stance of ignoring Iran's legitimate role in the region as unrealistic and the sanctions' uncompromising message of "redeem yourself or be damned" a non-starter. Defying the U.S. secondary boycott legislation under the Iran and Libya Sanctions Act of 1996, the European Union has lodged a formal complaint with the World Trade Organization and even warned Washington of retaliatory measures if it tries to act under the law. American allies like Turkey, Kuwait, and the United Arab Emirates have now expanded commercial links with Iran. Oil and natural gas deals with the countries of the Commonwealth of Independent States have proceeded as planned. Japan, Russia, China, Canada, and others have largely ignored American requests for trade sanctions. Only Israel and a wavering Uzbekistan have answered Washington's call.

American allies may have their own ulterior motives for opposing the containment strategy—desires to safeguard their historical ties with Iran, expand their commercial interests in a lucrative market, or simply assert their political independence from Washington. But their reservations reflect a second flaw of U.S. sanctions: inconsistency, which saps their credibility. The sanctions have sometimes been selective and arbitrary in their targets, and the United States has frequently breached the policy when it suited its interests. Syria has been on the same list of "terrorist states" as Iran, yet high U.S. officials have often courted Damascus. Sudan and Iran were both barred by the Antiterrorist Act of April 1996 from engaging in any financial transactions with U.S. companies; yet Occidental Petroleum was granted a special exemption to enter into a major oil deal with the Khartoum government soon after the bill was signed. On nuclear weapons, North Korea has pursued a development program similar to Iran's, yet Iran has been denied the same right accorded to Pyongyang, under the Nuclear Nonproliferation Treaty, to develop peaceful uses of nuclear energy. On human rights, China and some U.S. friends in the Middle East—Egypt, Pakistan, Saudi Arabia, and Turkey—have been cited by the State Department as some of the world's worst violators, yet they have enjoyed thriving trade and normal diplomatic relations with the United States.[3] Finally, Washington bitterly declared secondary boycotts to be illegal when the Arab League applied them to Israel, but it now urges its partners to honor them against Iran.

The containment policy has also lacked credibility because of Washington's repeated departures from stated principles. The secret arms deal with Tehran during President Reagan's administration, an aborted attempt at diplomatic rapprochement under President Bush during the release of American hostages in Lebanon in 1991, and the decision under President Clinton to allow Iran to send clandestine arms shipments to Bosnia are flagrant examples. Furthermore, until 1995, the U.S. embargo applied only to a handful of dual-use items and conspicuously excluded oil. Thus, while Washington was exhorting its allies to stop trading with Iran, the United States had become Iran's fourth-largest trading partner.

The final reason U.S. sanctions have been ineffective is that they have not been airtight. Companies and contractors from other Western countries have served as proxies for U.S. subsidiaries abroad. Countries that were not even among the top 25 nations

---

[3]In extending most-favored-nation privileges to Beijing in 1996, the Clinton administration argued that it had a better chance of influencing Chinese behavior through dialogue and trade than through economic pressure. That is precisely what the European Union has suggested with Iran, but Washington has steadfastly rejected the reasoning in Iran's case.

trading with Iran prior to the sanctions now rank fifth and sixth. Shops in Iran are stocked with American goods of every description—many smuggled in, but others imported legally through neighboring countries. Some Iranian exports also have found their way into the American market through third parties and legal loopholes.

WILL TEHRAN CRY UNCLE?

SANCTIONS MATTER not because they can, in their present configuration, bring the Islamic regime to its knees, but because they may handicap it in the race to rapid economic growth. The current U.S. policy is likely to remain largely ineffective, if not counterproductive, unless it is backed by a U.N. Security Council resolution specifically banning exports of oil from Iran and gaining the compliance of all major petroleum-importing countries. Without oil revenues, Iran's economy would quickly be paralyzed. However, judging from the European Union's reaction to the U.S. secondary boycott law—the one issue, incidentally, on which the EU membership has unanimously agreed—and given the fierce opposition that Russia, France, and China would likely raise in the Security Council, no such resolution is in sight at the United Nations. Furthermore, an embargo against Iranian oil would likely push crude prices through the roof for a while, another reason all oil-importing nations would resist it. Washington, therefore, may have to go it alone unless its allies and the world community are presented with irrefutable evidence of Tehran's direct involvement in a dastardly terrorist act, such as the June 1996 truck bombing of a housing complex in Dhahran that took the lives of 19 American military personnel. For its part, Iran can live with U.S. sanctions for a long time with much less difficulty than Cuba or Vietnam, although it cannot prosper without Washington's blessing.

In dealing with the Tehran regime Washington has four distinct, and familiar, policy options. At one end of the spectrum, it can discontinue sanctions and follow the easy route of "silence tinged with indifference or disdain," as an old U.S. intelligence hand has suggested. But while attractive, such a policy may be neither practical nor prudent; Iran's multifaceted activities and machinations in the region cannot be ignored, and the regime may not go out without a bang. At the other extreme, Washington may choose a military confrontation with Tehran, as anti-Iran hawks advocate, to roll back the regime. But this option is fraught with incalculable risks, would be internationally insupportable if launched without clear provocation, and would probably be domestically unpopular, particularly if it involved U.S. troop deployments and American casualties.

The third choice is to tighten comprehensive unilateral sanctions. Persistent advocates of the U.S. boycott still argue that Iran is currently weak and vulnerable economically and financially, that it needs a bailout from the West in the form of credits, technology, and management, and that sanctions will work most effectively if other major industrial powers follow—but even unilateral American sanctions can make a big difference. Patience and perseverance are all that is needed.

Assuming this assessment is correct, the get-tough policy is still not risk-free. Enhanced U.S. sanctions may hasten the day of reckoning, but they run the risk of arousing formidable nationalist resistance in Iran. Serious imbalances and deficiencies plaguing the

> Iran is economically healthier than many countries the United States has assisted.

Iranian economy pose a latent threat to the regime's survival because they give rise to sociopolitical tensions that weaken the rulers' grip on power. With or without the U.S. embargo, the regime is likely to implode eventually unless there is a dramatic change in its domestic Islamic rule and its anti-Western worldview. Therein lies the reason for the regime's survival somewhat beyond its time: not in spite of sanctions, but because of them.

Already sensing a general anxiety across the land about further U.S. economic pressure, the clerical leadership, in a series of smart public relations maneuvers, has blamed the country's economic shortcomings and setbacks on undisguised American hostility toward Islamic rule. Washington's frequent demonization of the government in Tehran has been seized on to demonstrate Iran's unique importance as the defender of the faith and supporter of the oppressed against an arrogant superpower. Taking advantage of the Shiites' historical glorification of martyrdom, the leadership portrays Iran as the victim of a cruel and hostile hegemon. The sanctions themselves are shrugged off as insignificant, but they are highlighted as proof of American hostility.

The regime's appeal to Iranian nationalism, particularly the clever hints that enhanced U.S. sanctions and continued hostility threaten Iran's sovereignty and territorial integrity, has been an effective ploy. Not a single group in the vast array of current opposition to the Islamic government, no matter how hostile to theocratic rule—including diehard monarchists—wants to see sanctions topple the regime if that means Iran's Balkanization. On no other issue have the disparate groups been so united for so long.

The remaining option is to seek a prudent modus vivendi with the rogue state. The regime is a religious oligarchy related by blood and financial ties to the bazaar merchant class. Bazaaris' passion is not policy, but profit. For their partners in the leadership, the overarching goal is not ideological rigor but power. Ayatollah Khomeini in 1988 ingloriously accepted the cease-fire in the eight-year war with Iraq that he had vowed to pursue to total victory. His sole motive was to preserve Islamic rule and keep the clergy in power. Any proposal that could strengthen the economy and give the regime a better chance of survival is likely to get a positive response. The reason that this option, despite its many advocates within the foreign policy establishments on both sides of the Atlantic, has not been actively pursued is because its supporters are looked upon as accommodationsists, appeasers, or opportunists. In neither country is the leadership anxious to take the initiative for fear of being labeled sellouts by the opposition.

SHARED INTERESTS

THE OUTSTANDING differences on many matters of legitimate national concern—including each country's self-proclaimed manifest destiny (Iran to propagate Islam, America to promote democracy)—may rule out relations of the sort that prevailed between Iran and the United States before 1979. But they cannot mask the significant interests that the two *countries*—as distinct from their *governments*—still share. In spite of mutual assertions to the contrary, regional instability, chaos, and tension are in neither country's political or economic interest. Both countries have a vital interest in the free flow of oil through the Persian Gulf and the avoidance of maritime incidents. Both need each other geopolitically, as the twin pillars of a regional counterbalance to Russia's potentially expansionist aspirations within the Commonwealth of Independent States and toward the warm waters of the Persian Gulf. And, finally, both countries can fruitfully cooperate in developing and transporting the energy resources of the Central Asian states and the Caucasus, reducing those nations' dependence on Russia.

For the moment, these mutual interests may not seem impressive to Washington. After the breakup of the Soviet Union, the defeat of Saddam Hussein and Iraq, and the increase in the supply of non-OPEC oil, Iran may have lost its geostrategic, military, and economic cachet for the United States. Washington may perceive no need to make concessions to establish a dialogue with Tehran, hoping instead to force the regime's hand through comprehensive new sanctions. But the current phase may be transitory. Before long the Russian Federation may again be a superpower, and a post-Saddam Iraq may be just as menacing to its neighbors. Iran, regardless of its governing regime, will remain the Middle East's most populous and second-largest country, surrounded by 15 neighbors with which it shares land borders or bodies of water, a major global energy source with 10 percent of the world's oil and 15 percent of its natural gas, a pivotal player both in the region and within OPEC, and a gateway to Central Asia. In a region where national interests are increasingly defined in terms of shifting national alliances and coalitions, a strong, integral Iran may be sorely needed as a constructive force if there is to be stability and progress. The ultimate effects of the U.S. containment policy must be regarded in that light.

Assuming that Iran's territorial integrity and political independence are in the United States' own long-term national interests, a change in the containment policy may be a reasonable insurance premium. Washington may wish to reactivate the long-standing offer of a dialogue between duly authorized representatives, in a confidential manner, without preconditions. Should this option be chosen, a strategic reassessment would be in order. To be effective and credible, the dialogue must avoid going into a long wish list of expected changes in bilateral behavior and instead single out one or two issues of crucial importance to both parties, such as nuclear proliferation, the Arab-Israeli peace process, and the U.S. military presence in the Persian Gulf. The United States should give the Islamic Republic some reasonable incentives for cooperation, such as the release of frozen assets or new loans from the World Bank, and clear disincentives for intransigence, including intensified political pressure or even more drastic action. Under this policy of *reciprocal response*, each offending behavior may be dealt with through quid pro quo, without bestowing a seal of approval on or resorting to a blanket condemnation of either party's overall position.

Should Washington decide that its containment policy is the right course and Tehran continue its anti-American belligerence, the current stalemate will continue. Without a strong consensus among U.S. allies and a tacit understanding with Russia and China not to help Iran, and without convincing the regime's opponents that Iran's territorial integrity will not be jeopardized by U.S. sanctions—that the end of the Islamic Republic will not be the end of Iran—the boycott might still not reach its goal by the year 2010 or even 2020, if the Chinese, Vietnamese, and Cuban experiences serve as precedents.

U.S. Post–Cold War Military Strategy

The Use of Military Power (Articles 28 and 29)
Arms Control (Articles 30 and 31)

During the height of the cold war American defense planners often thought in terms of needing a two-and-a-half-war capacity: the simultaneous ability to fight major wars in Europe and Asia plus a smaller conflict elsewhere. The principal protagonists in this drama were well known: the Soviet Union, China, and their developing world allies. The stakes were also clear. Communism represented a global threat to American political democracy and economic prosperity. It was a conflict in which both sides publicly proclaimed that there could be but one winner. The means for deterring and fighting such challenges included strategic, tactical, and battlefield nuclear weapons; large numbers of conventional forces; alliance systems; arms transfers; and the development of a guerrilla-war capability.

The political-military landscape of the post–cold war world presents defense strategists with a far different set of challenges than did that of the cold war. However, the extent to which the new international order requires rethinking the basic premises and assumptions that produced American cold war military strategy is only now beginning to be fully realized. The influence of cold war thinking and traditional American national security concerns was very much in evidence in the Pentagon's Defense Planning Guidance Report of 1992, which described seven paths to war that might be traveled by the end of the decade. These included an Iraqi invasion of Kuwait and Saudi Arabia, a Russian invasion of Lithuania, a North Korean attack on South Korea, coups in Panama and the Philippines, and the reemergence of a hostile superpower. For each of these paths, the Pentagon study identified a U.S. response force and projected the amount of time it would take U.S. (and Allied) forces to secure a military victory.

Absent from the Pentagon's list was any reference to war emerging from conditions in Africa, Eastern Europe, Central Asia, the Indian subcontinent, or Latin America. Yet these are the areas (Bosnia, Somalia, Rwanda, Haiti, Cuba) where calls for the use of American force have been heard or where U.S. forces have actually found themselves pressed into service. Moreover, the manner in which they have been used bears little resemblance to that anticipated by cold war military planners.

Change is present, however. Military planners now speak of a two-war capacity, meaning, for instance, the ability to conduct Bosnia and Somalia operations simultaneously. The summer of 1994 saw "peace maneuvers" held at the Joint Readiness Training Center at Fort Polk where infantry troops undertook a large-scale field exercise designed to resemble a real-life peace enforcement operation. Even with this new sensitivity to the altered conditions under which U.S. military forces will be placed in combat, the "hows" and "whys" that will govern this process will continue to provoke controversy.

Catherine Kelleher, in "Soldiering On: U.S. Public Opinion on the Use of Force," provides one perspective on the question of using military force in the post–cold war era. She examines public attitudes toward the use of military force and concludes that Americans favor a case-by-case approach in judging the merits of this type of action. The final essay in this subsection, "Deliberate and Inadvertent War in the Post–Cold War World" by Wallace Thies, is critical of defense cutbacks made in the name of realizing a "peace dividend." He argues that recent trends suggest that the greatest threat to regional stability in the future will be inadvertent wars.

With changes in the nature of the military threats confronting the United States has come a change in the arms control agenda. The old agenda was dominated by a concern for reducing the size of U.S. and Soviet nuclear inventories. A much broader agenda exists today, one with many more players.

Two readings contribute to our understanding of the arms control issues now confronting the international community. Focusing on the very existence of nuclear weapons, Frank von Hippel calls for taking U.S. missiles off high-alert status and making deep cuts in U.S. nuclear stockpiles. Then, Michael Klare speaks to a new

UNIT 7

phenomenon in world politics in his report, "The New Arms Race: Light Weapons and International Security." No longer does the transfer of large-scale and sophisticated weapons represent the sole conventional weapons arms control problem. The growth of ethnic conflict has created situations where the transfer of small and light weapons now has the potential for altering regional balances of power.

Looking Ahead: Challenge Questions

List the five most serious national security threats that could face the United States in the next five years. How likely is each to happen? How prepared is the United States military for dealing with each of them?

What lessons do Vietnam, the Persian Gulf War, and the humanitarian intervention in Somalia hold for the future use of military force by the United States?

Under what conditions should U.S. military forces be sent into combat situations? Under what conditions should they be withdrawn?

To what extent should the United States engage in multilateral military operations? Should these be the exception or the rule? How should such operations be organized?

Does arms control have a future? Has arms control contributed to making the United States more secure, or has it weakened U.S. security?

How should we think about nuclear weapons in the post–cold war world? What is their purpose? Who should they be targeted against? What dangers must we guard against?

Construct a scenario of inadvertent war that might lead the United States to consider using military force. What types of forces would be needed? How should they be used? Construct an arms control proposal that would lessen the likelihood of this scenario coming into existence or that would reduce the likelihood that the United States would have to get involved.

SOLDIERING ON

U.S. Public Opinion on the Use of Force

Catherine M. Kelleher

Catherine M. Kelleher is a senior fellow in the Brookings Foreign Policy Studies program. This article draws on an essay published in Beyond the Beltway: Engaging the Public in U.S. Foreign Policy, *edited by Daniel Yankelovich and I. M. Destler (Norton, for the American Assembly, 1994).*

Crises in Bosnia and in Somalia have raised anew a debate that reaches back to the first days of the American republic: under what conditions will and should the United States use military force?

During the Cold War, the answers to these questions seemed fairly straightforward. The United States must be prepared to use force whenever and wherever an implacable ideological foe challenged its fundamental interests and those it shared with its Free World partners. But Vietnam and its aftermath, the debate over American military intervention and the legitimacy of both service and protest, divided the nation and ultimately marked a generation. Throughout the 1970s, the issues—military, political, ethical—involving the use of force were left undiscussed or unresolved. The 1980s, too, yielded few answers as arguments raged over whether to use American force in Nicaragua and Libya and over the impact of military victories and defeats in Lebanon, Grenada, and Panama. In 1991, however, the United States-led coalition's success in ousting Iraq from Kuwait during the Gulf War went a long way toward moderating public trepidation about American military involvement. The conflicting legacies are weighing heavily on the Clinton administration now as it tries to define the role of U.S. military intervention in the new world order.

The debate goes to the heart of American assumptions about the utility of force and about the factors that must now shape American foreign and defense policy. What, in this post–Cold War era, are the appropriate yardsticks and instruments for American national interest? How narrowly can or should we choose to interpret this concept? Regarding both Bosnia and Somalia, how do we now choose between what some portray as our moral responsibility to intervene to prevent further atrocities and protect the innocent and what others argue should be our principled avoidance of an involvement in an uncertain quagmire?

THE POST–COLD WAR CONTEXT

Understanding current attitudes toward the use of force requires s step backward to more theoretical debates about American public opinion toward foreign policy. Immediately after World War II, most analysts agree, Americans tended to be uninformed and uninterested in international issues, their views disproportionately shaped by domestic conditions rather than by adherence to coherent world views. Like most democratic populations, they were slow to anger and generally noninterventionist. But once mobilized by their political leadership, they were prone to rash or "moralistic" action or the "spasm" use of force. They wanted immediate action to "get the job done" and the fastest possible return at the lowest cost of life to the "normal" status of domestic tranquility.

This is clearly no longer the case. Almost every general foreign policy survey in the past five years shows that the American public is increasingly well-informed about global issues, devotes attention to evolving international events, and has opinions on most major foreign and defense policy questions. Americans do take more account of moral issues in evaluating foreign policy choices than some other nationalities. But they are overwhelmingly pragmatic in finally deciding on support for overseas initiatives, including the use of force. Costs and risks count; case-by-case decisions outnumber the invocation of universal principles; short-term actions with a high probability of success are preferred to longer-term involvements with uncertain prospects for achievement. Americans are, in Bruce Jentleson's apt phrase, "the pretty prudent public."

This change reflects less the passing of the Communist threat than a gradual evolution of post-Vietnam thinking about America's role. Americans remain resistant to a new "Vietnam"—military involvement intended to enforce nation building or to intervene in civil wars. But they are more willing to use force for humanitarian ends or to counter blatantly aggressive behavior.

CURRENT OPINION ON THE USE OF FORCE

In the abstract, Americans view direct U.S. military involvement only as a last resort, reserved for the most desperate and extreme circumstances. There is an enduring reservoir of support for the traditional American commitment to NATO and to the use of force to defend our allies in Western Europe. But Americans exhibit an overwhelming reluctance, if not a fundamental aversion to the use of force for what are perceived as less immediate or indirect threats to national security. Nonetheless, they are almost always responsive to presidential leadership that explains why blood and treasure must be risked to defend the national interest.

Polls in 1993 by Times Mirror and Gallup showed that Americans favor a case-by-case approach to the use of force. A majority would approve of American military involvement if Iraq invaded Saudi Arabia, but would disapprove of an American defense of South Korea against North Korea (63 percent), of Ukraine against Russia (91 percent), or of Mexico or any third world government against domestic revolt (more than 50 percent). In general terms, however, Americans are willing to send military forces for humanitarian and famine assistance (56 percent) or to demonstrate American commitment to its allies against aggressive dictators (63 percent).

The end of the Cold War allows new room for concerns about the severity of the budget deficit and heightened pressure to divert badly needed resources from defense to domestic programs. Public support for increasing the defense budget fell from a high of 72 percent at the end of 1981, Ronald Reagan's first year in office, to 39 percent by December 1982, and then continued declining gradually through the mid-1980s. Last September a majority felt defense spending was now "just about right" (52 percent), with only 10 percent wanting an increase. Some 36 percent, indeed, agreed with elites polled that it was now time to cut back.

Most of the American public objects to providing military aid overseas, and support for military assistance even to traditional allies such as Israel and Egypt has suffered since the Cold War ended. Humanitarian assistance clearly outranks all other international initiatives in popular support, as it does in most European countries. Americans consistently support nonmilitary international involvement, even though they continue to express reservations about a blanket intervention policy.

There is indeed an increasing trend supporting an interventionist, engaged America. As Chicago Council of Foreign Relations surveys reveal, public support for an active U.S. world role reached an all-time high in 1956 (71 percent), fell to an all-time low in 1982 (54 percent), and then began growing again. In the most recent poll (1990) the figure was 62 percent. Similarly, the 1993 Times Mirror General Survey found that 91 percent of those questioned agreed that the United States should take a leadership role in world affairs. About two-thirds believed it to be a role of at least equal importance and power to that of 10 years ago. Only a minority believed the United States should be the single leader (10 percent), or the most active nation (27 percent); most believed the role should be shared with other leading nations (51 percent) on a more or less equal basis.

A key factor shaping the American public's attitude toward the use of force is whether the military action is unilateral or multilateral. Throughout most of the Cold War, the American public supported a strong leadership role of the United States to balance the Soviet Union. But Americans now are more likely to support U.S. military involvement as a part of a coalition than when the United States is acting independently. The public has often been somewhat more supportive when the United States is acting as part of a United Nations–sanctioned effort. A December 3–4, 1992, Gallup Poll found that 87 percent of those surveyed agreed that the United States "should commit its troops only as part of a United Nations operation," while 73 percent felt that the United States should commit "only with other allies."

Disillusionment with the United Nations framework, as indeed with the concept of peacekeeping in general, has grown since the beginning of 1993. While a majority of Americans (64 percent) still believes the United States should cooperate fully with the United Nations, most Americans are reluctant to place U.S. troops under permanent UN command. Americans are more comfortable having U.S. troops under the command of NATO allies or in UN missions for only limited periods.

CHANGING THREATS AND INTERESTS

The end of the Cold War changed U.S. public attitudes toward many countries. At the height of the East-West struggle, many countries had a strategic significance for the United States. Now, however, only a few nations are felt to be of special or vital interest; most are regarded as relatively insignificant in terms of U.S. security.

A July 1980 Harris poll found that 84 percent of those surveyed regarded the Soviet Union as "a threat to the security and well-being of the United States." (Some 56 percent so regarded Iran, and 41 percent, Communist China. No other countries were mentioned by more than 17 percent of those polled.) By 1990, 83 percent saw the Soviet Union, instead, as a nation of vital U.S. interest. Times Mirror polls of 1990 and 1993 found that the perception of a Russian threat fell from 32 percent to 8 percent. Japan as an economic competitor, by contrast, was cited as the greatest threat to the United States by 31 percent in 1992, but only by 11 percent (equal to those mentioning China) in 1993. By far the greatest focus of fear was Iraq, still seen by 18 percent in 1993 as a continuing danger.

Chicago Council polls in 1986 and 1990 reflected other changes in how Americans view specific political-military relationships. Only four countries—Saudi Arabia, Japan, Iran, and Poland—were perceived to have become more vital to the United States. All other countries considered in the survey were thought to be less vital to the United States in 1990 than they were in 1986. Most notably, the percentage of Americans viewing the countries of Western Europe as vital continued to fall, although half of those questioned in the 1993 Times Mirror poll still saw Europe as more important to the United States than Asia.

BOSNIA AND SOMALIA

U.S. attitudes about military intervention are evolving as events in Somalia and Bosnia unfold. Presidential leadership remains the essential element in molding popular opinion. What public debate awaits is a cogent case for participation or non-involvement based on the national interests at stake and the risks to be run.

> *U.S. attitudes about military intervention are evolving as events in Somalia and Bosnia unfold. Presidential leadership remains the essential element in molding popular opinion.*

The American public is by no means unconditionally opposed to military engagement. Not surprisingly, public confidence was badly shaken last October when Somalis dragged a U.S. soldier's body through the streets of Mogadishu following a fire fight in which 18 Americans on a "humanitarian mission" were killed. According to an ABC poll immediately following the fire fight, 52 percent of Americans did not approve of President Clinton's handling of the situation, and two out of three respondents favored withdrawal of U.S. troops. Even at that point, however, half of those who favored withdrawal believed it should be carried out gradually, over six months, and with concern for a final peaceful settlement. Comparable polling results taken days and weeks later—after President Clinton's speech to the nation—demonstrated support for gradual disengagement and continued international monitoring of political outcomes. The avalanche of demands for withdrawal, feared by some in Congress, never materialized; the principal public concern seemed to have been with policy drift and the confusion about the limits of American engagement.

Although Bosnia is more complex, U.S. public opinion has registered consistent support for U.S. participation in a multilateral peacekeeping force there once the warring parties come to a final agreement. Between May and October last year, support ranged from 40 percent to 77 percent, with the average hovering around 54.5 percent. American opinion on direct military involvement to secure a cease-fire or a final agreement has primarily stressed caution and the participation of other allies. Lacking a clear presidential appeal for an expanded U.S. role, support has been fairly divided.

Reaction to the February NATO ultimatum to conduct air strikes in retaliation against the shelling of Sarajevo demonstrates this complexity. While 47 percent of Americans polled by CNN/Gallup believed the United States had a moral obligation to use air strikes against the Serbs and 48 percent favored the decision to do so, 57 percent opposed sending in ground troops in the event that air strikes failed to hasten an acceptable peace settlement. Equally important, 65 percent said that regardless of their present feelings, they would approve of air strikes if President Clinton ordered them. A related PIPA poll asking whether Americans would still support U.S. involvement in a multilateral peacekeeping force if an agreement could be reached found that 72 percent either strongly favored or somewhat favored such action.

Moral and political ambiguity in these conflicts poses difficult challenges to U.S. leadership. Thus far, some in the Clinton administration and many in Congress have been reluctant to face these challenges, fearing that foreign policy ventures will interfere or compete with the ambitious domestic agenda. But success at home and leadership abroad are not mutually exclusive, and building a new post–Cold War consensus may be easier than it is often portrayed. An increasingly well-informed public values preserving U.S. interests overseas, whether they be centered on economic stability or human rights, whether they involve the assumption of international obligations or national sacrifice.

ASSESSMENT AND PERSPECTIVE

The sudden dismantling of an international system in place for more than 40 years may have left Americans unsure about what precise role they wish to assume in the post–Cold War world. The desire to curtail defense spending and to limit military involvement overseas clashes with the claim to global leadership. Americans in great numbers do feel a moral compulsion to help countries in need and to defend the weak, but are reluctant to be drawn into unpredictable and open-ended conflicts. They give new recognition to the economic dimensions of security, and they realize the importance of transnational relationships in an increasingly global economy. But they also struggle with how to balance international interests and responsibilities with domestic priorities.

Americans are clear, however, about the general strategy they believe the president and the nation should pursue in international military involvement. The use of military force is to be the exception in U.S. foreign policy. The approach is usually to be multilateral and cooperative, with support and contributions of allies and other countries. The costs and risks involved in any overseas military option should be explained, and there can no longer be blanket approval for military preparation against a range of unlikely threats. Many view the loss of American life, even when counted in the tens and not the hundreds, as intolerable, but most also recognize there are international commitments and national interests beyond simple self defense for which the risk of war is justifiable.

Forty years after the defeat of traditional American isolationism, this should not be surprising. In many respects, it puts the burden of persuasion and leadership in foreign policy where the Founding Fathers wanted it, with a committed president and a questioning, yet patriotic Congress. The public is sensitive both to the lessons of the Vietnam experience and to the "halo effect" of the Gulf War on the American capacity for coalition-building. They are deferential to presidential decisions, yet await a careful assessment of probable outcomes and foreseeable risks. And they are far more attentive to the demands of the new international order and the range of roles the United States can and should play than many pundits and practitioners are willing to credit.

These trends will almost certainly continue and perhaps intensify over the next decade. A reversal of direction in Russia, of course, may strengthen the allure of isolationism and bolster the proponents of both higher defense spending and lessened international involvement. More predictable turbulence will result from the debate about a smaller military at a lower cost and with fewer overseas deployments, especially if the threat of war on the scale assumed in the Cold War or even in Desert Storm continues to recede.

Whatever his domestic imperatives, President Clinton stands at the beginning of a new debate about the use of force in American foreign policy. At stake are not just the skills and the political fortunes of this president, but also the articulation of a national consensus on choices and costs of international military involvement that may last well into the next century. The challenge in many respects parallels that faced by Franklin Roosevelt and Harry Truman. The crucial difference is the state of the public—more informed, more internationalist, and more open to presidential leadership and persuasion.

DELIBERATE AND INADVERTENT WAR IN THE POST-COLD WAR WORLD

WALLACE J. THIES

Wallace J. Thies is Associate Professor of Politics at the Catholic University of America in Washington, DC. He is a graduate of Marquette University and holds an M.A. in International Relations and M.Phil. and Ph.D. degrees from Yale University. He is the author of *When Governments Collide: Coercion and Diplomacy in the Vietnam Conflict* (1980) and *The Atlantic Alliance, Nuclear Weapons and European Attitudes: Re-examining the Conventional Wisdom* (1983).

IN BRIEF

After previous conflicts, the U.S. has cut expenditures for defense in the hope of reaping a "peace dividend." In every case, any savings proved merely transient; the actual result was eroded readiness and capability necessitating a rush to rearm in response to a new emerging threat. Will this pattern repeat itself now? Recent trends suggest that the greatest threat to regional stability and therefore global peace is inadvertent war. This implies that as defense budgets continue to decline, the U.S. should give priority to those forces that can help to prevent wars among regional powers.

Four rounds of military base closings and a decade of stagnant or declining defense budgets have focused public attention on the job losses and economic dislocation caused by downsizing the military. There is, however, a larger issue at stake. Americans responded to the end of World War II and the wars in Korea and Vietnam with high hopes that cutting defense spending would yield a huge peace dividend. But in each case the savings proved only temporary, as declining defense budgets eroded military readiness and necessitated a rush to rearm in the face of new dangers abroad.

This pattern is important, in part, because there were real costs to be paid for overestimating the cuts that could safely be made once "war" was replaced by "peace." The woefully unprepared army units that were thrown into the Korean War in July 1950 took heavy casualties because of years of skimping on maintenance, and supplies. The cuts made after the Korean War left the United States ill-prepared for the crises that erupted during the 1950s over Berlin, Quemoy, and Lebanon. The post-Vietnam decade of neglect necessitated the hugely expensive Carter-Reagan rearmament effort that began at the end of the 1970s.

More important is the question of whether the pattern is repeating itself once again. Since the end of the Cold War, the number of active-duty military personnel has declined by one-third. The 330-ship Navy planned for the rest of this decade will be one-third smaller than the 480-ship Navy that was severely stressed by the Iran and Afghanistan crises in 1979–1980. These cuts are being made even though two dozen less developed states either possess ballistic missiles or are trying to acquire them. Israel, India, Pakistan and South Africa already know how to build nuclear weapons; Iraq, Iran, Libya and North Korea have attempted to acquire them. About twenty less developed states have chemical weapons programs; about ten have biological weapons programs.

As more countries acquire unconventional weaponry, will the danger of war increase, decrease, or remain the same? The U.S.-Soviet rivalry during the Cold War suggests that new weapons do not lead inevitably to war. But the U.S. and the Soviet Union were superpowers with huge armed forces dispersed over entire continents, protected by multiple warning systems, and controlled by authoritative governments that kept a tight grip on the chain of command.

In the post-Cold War world, many regional powers have relatively small missile and air forces, often concentrated on a handful of bases, protected by limited and unreliable warning systems, and controlled by unstable governments vulnerable to coups. These differences suggest that post-Cold War rivalries between regional powers will be played out in ways that accentuate their vulnerability to surprise attack and heighten the danger of war. To see why, it is helpful to consider the kinds of wars likely to occur in the post-Cold War world and the causes associated with each type.

What Kind of War?

So much has been written about war, with such divergent conclusions, that any attempt to discuss the causes of war might seem an impossible and misguided undertaking. The sheer number and variety of wars fought throughout recorded history suggests that, rather than focusing on the reasons behind a particular war, we should ask instead if there are conditions that make it easier for wars to start and thus more likely to occur. One such approach is the distinction between preventive and preemptive wars. In both cases the attacker strikes first because of a belief that war now is better than war later—in the former case, because the balance of power is shifting in an adversary's favor; in the latter, because striking first is preferred to waiting and absorbing an opponent's first strike.[1]

The preventive/preemptive typology is a very useful way of discussing how wars begin, but it begs the question of why and how statesmen become convinced that war, with all its dangers, risks and unknowns, is preferable to peace. More important, it obscures the possibility that certain background conditions might be the source of both preventive and preemptive wars. Preemptive attacks, for example, are often associated with rash behavior and a rush to get in the first blow, but a preemptive war can also be the product of a carefully planned, deliberately timed surprise attack (e.g., Israel's attack on Egypt in 1967). For the purposes of this essay, a broader and more useful distinction is between wars that are begun deliberately (Japan's attack on Pearl Harbor) and wars that begin inadvertently, as a result of hasty decisionmaking, miscalculation, or loss of control over events (the outbreak of the First World War).

Consider, first, wars that are the result of deliberate choice. The recurrence of war is often attributed to a lack of foresight or a failure to think through a line of policy, but it is well to remember that statesmen have marched to the brink of the abyss, gauged its depths, and then jumped in knowing full well what they were doing. Napoleon, Bismarck, and Hitler come readily to mind; in more recent times Kim Il-Sung, Anwar Sadat, and Saddam Hussein have all chosen war over the status quo. How will the spread of ballistic missiles, modern strike aircraft, and the ability to arm both with nuclear, chemical, or biological weapons affect the likelihood of premeditated war, of either the preemptive or preventive variety? A review of recent military trends suggests that the spread of unconventional weaponry and sophisticated delivery systems is increasing the danger of premeditated war, in four ways.

Recent Military Trends

First, ballistic missiles and modern strike aircraft are high-speed weapons that are almost unstoppable once launched but vulnerable if caught on the ground. In the hands of regional rivals with contiguous borders—like Israel and Syria, Iraq and Iran, or India and Pakistan—weapons with these characteristics increase the danger of short-warning or even no-warning surprise attacks. This has important consequences for the calculations of both attackers and defenders. The greater the imbalance between offense and defense, the greater the danger that an aggressive power will see an opportunity to overwhelm or even eliminate a rival. Conversely, the wider the gap between the outcomes associated with striking first and striking second, the greater the likelihood that even status quo powers will conclude that war is inevitable and thus that they must choose between attacking or absorbing the attack that their opponent is about to launch.

Second, the acquisition of new weaponry by regional powers creates the appearance, if not the reality, of sudden changes in the power positions of rival states. Modern military forces are extraordinarily complex, requiring hundreds of types of weapons, ammunition, and related equipment.[2] Ballistic missiles, especially if armed with unconventional warheads, can destroy or neutralize many kinds of weapons owned by a rival power. Rather than try to match a rival across the full spectrum of military capabilities, ballistic missiles offer the promise of a shortcut to equality or even superiority. Sudden changes in the power of rival states increase the danger of preventive wars in two ways. The greater the advantage secured by the state acquiring new weaponry, the greater the temptation to strike before a rival can catch up. Conversely, the greater the apparent change in a neighbor's ability to strike first, the greater the insecurity of the potential target, and the greater the appeal of striking first rather than be struck first.[3]

Third, new weapons affect not only the current offense-defense balance but also create expectations of greater peril in the future. Ballistic missiles, for example, can be upgraded to improve range and accuracy, and they can also be fitted with new and more lethal warheads as the latter become available. Hence the acquisition of short-range and/or inaccurate missiles can be interpreted as an ominous portent of things to come, as suggested by a senior Indian official's comment in 1992 that "within the next five years both [India and Pakistan] will have medium range missiles. Each side will have to assume the worst of each other."[4] This style of thinking suggests that even small missile forces can be a cause of both preventive and preemptive wars, depending on the accuracy of the missiles involved.

Missiles and Other Technology

Missiles such as the Chinese CSS-2 (purchased by Saudi Arabia in 1988) or the ubiquitous Scud, when armed with a high-explosive warhead, lack the explosive power to destroy concentrations of troops, tanks, or aircraft and the accuracy to destroy runways, hangars, or weapons storage bunkers. Moreover, since aircraft can deliver larger payloads over longer ranges, with greater accuracy, and are reusable, the acquisition of inaccurate missiles fuels suspicions that the acquiring power must have some other purpose in mind. "'Anybody who develops such missiles,' an unnamed Israeli officer told *Yediot Aharonot,* an Israeli newspaper, 'will want them to carry chemical, biological, and even nuclear warheads at some point'."[5]

Accurate missiles, in contrast, engender fears of surprise attack and thus encourage thoughts of preemption on the part of the potential victim. The SS-21s acquired by Syria during the 1980s were deemed particularly threatening by Israel because Syria possessed an indigenous chemical weapons capability, which the Israelis feared might make possible a Syrian chemical attack on Israeli air bases, followed by a ground attack to recapture the Golan Heights. Hence the Israelis responded with warnings of a preemptive strike on Syria's chemical weapons facility, although not on the SS-21s themselves, which were mobile and thus more difficult to target.[6]

Finally, technologies that facilitated mutual deterrence and thus reduced the risk of war during the Cold War may be destabilizing in the hands of regional powers. Reconnaissance satellites were one of the foundations of the long peace between the United States and the Soviet Union after the Second World War, making it possible for both sides "to evaluate each other's capabilities to a degree that is totally unprecedented in the history of relations between the great powers."[7] In the hands of regional powers, whose forces are generally smaller and more vulnerable to surprise attack than those of the United States or the former Soviet Union, the ability to orbit reconnaissance satellites may have the pernicious effect of making surprise attacks easier by pinpointing the location of an opponent's forces. States whose forces are being targeted by a foe's satellite(s) will be encouraged to strike first rather than risk being struck themselves, while states with access to satellite intelligence will become more aware of opportunities to strike first and encouraged to do so by their awareness of their opponent's heightened incentives to strike first.

Inadvertent War

In similar fashion, the spread of ballistic missiles and advanced strike aircraft, and the ability to arm both with nuclear, chemical, or biological warheads, is increasing the danger of wars that begin inadvertently, again in four ways. The first is suggested by the history of warfare in the Middle East. The geographical proximity of Israel and its Arab rivals, the lack of strategic depth, and the fast pace of modern warfare have combined to narrow the margins of safety of the states in the region. The narrower the margin between disaster and triumph, the stronger the belief that striking first is preferable to being victimized by an opponent's sneak attack vulnerability; in other words, makes it easier for statesmen to convince themselves that war is inevitable and thus that their preemptive strike is merely a response to their opponent's choice of war, rather than the first shot in a war that has yet to begin and that might not begin at all if restraint prevailed over recklessness. "To Israelis, . . . a preemptive strike is a tactic for winning a war that is about to begin. It isn't the same thing as starting a war."[8]

Second, the geographical compactness and continuity of many regional rivals mean that decision-time will be very short, and that statesmen will feel pressured to choose between peace or war without adequate time for reflection. This is bad enough, but time pressures imposed by geography are often exacerbated by vulnerable command systems and unreliable radars and sensors for detecting an attack. Vulnerable command systems, for example, decrease crisis stability by creating incentives for both the stronger and the weaker of two rival states to strike at the first, often-ambiguous sign that the other is about to strike first. The stronger side can strike much more effectively if its command system is intact rather than in ruins; while the weaker power feels pressured to strike first to degrade the superior power's strength. The greater the preemptive urge, the greater the danger that accidents, false alarms, and the day-to-day mischief-making of rival border patrols or intelligence agencies will trigger a war that both sides would prefer to avoid.[9]

Survivability vs. Control

Third, while potential target states can take heart from the Gulf War, which suggests that Scud-type missiles can be hidden even in a desert, defenders face difficult trade-offs between enhancing survivability and maintaining central control. Mobile missiles are more survivable but also more difficult to control, especially if war seems imminent. The more numerous the safeguards against accidental or unauthorized launch, the more time-consuming the procedures for nuclear release and the less the likelihood that an opponent's first strike can be countered by a policy of launch on warning or launch under attack. The harder it is to launch quickly in the face of an actual or anticipated surprise attack, the greater the danger that field commanders will attempt to by-pass established procedures in order to ensure that they can launch at the first (possibly mistaken) sign of an attack.[10] The greater the danger of being caught by surprise, the greater the psychological pressures on central decision-makers to loosen the restraints on their weapons in order to avoid losing them to an opponent's first strike and thus the greater the danger of a mutual rush to get in the first blow.

Fourth, the growing vulnerability of population centers to no-warning or short-warning attacks by ballistic missiles armed with unconventional warheads exacerbates the danger of a mutual rush to get in the first blow. The 1956 Sinai campaign, the Six-Day War in 1967, the Yom Kippur War in 1973, and the wars between India and Pakistan in 1965 and 1971 were essentially clashes between armies and air forces; cities were for the most part spared direct attack. The spread of ballistic missiles armed with unconventional warheads means that regional powers will no longer have to fight their way through each other's armed forces to inflict massive destruction on urban centers (a development foreshadowed by ballistic missile attacks on cities during both the Iran/Iraq and Persian Gulf wars). In the absence of effective anti-missile defenses, target states are likely to conclude, in the words of an Israeli officer, that "It is better to preempt than to wait for a missile to fall. We have the right to attack if we are sure [Saddam Hussein] is going to."[11]

The growing vulnerability of cities is especially alarming in view of the reluctance of many Third World leaders to share power with subordinates who might use it to topple them via a *coup d'état*. "Decapitation" was not an inviting tactic during the Cold War because both the United States and the Soviet Union possessed authoritative governments and detailed procedures for maintaining the military chain of command. Nor would it be effective for a state armed only with conventional weapons, because of the difficulty of destroying every bunker or command post used by the leader of a rival state. Nuclear weapons, however, make it possible to destroy whole cities in a surprise attack; the absence of legitimacy in a state like Saddam Hussein's Iraq makes such a tactic inviting because potential successors might well mobilize against each other rather than the external foe.

The Danger of Future Wars

How serious is the danger of future wars of either the deliberate or inadvertent variety? Three kinds of evidence suggest that the danger is already considerable and likely to grow in the future. First, the historical record suggests that regional powers have had difficulty resisting the temptation offered by an opponent's vulnerability or the opening of a window of opportunity. In 1967, Egypt's President Nasser closed the Gulf of Aqaba to Israeli shipping, requested the withdrawal of the UN peacekeeping force in the Sinai, and together with Syria, Jordan and Iraq threatened Israel with war on three fronts; a few weeks later Israel preempted the expected Arab attack with devastating consequences for Egypt, Syria and Jordan.

In 1973, Egypt and Syria launched a surprise attack on Israeli forces in the Sinai and the Golan Heights; Israel was dissuaded from preempting at the last minute only by threats that the U.S. would stand aloof if Israel struck first. Israel took advantage of windows of opportunity to attack Egyptian forces in the Sinai in 1956 and Iraq's Osiraq nuclear reactor in 1981. Pakistan's attempted conquest of Kashmir in 1965 was the result of a window of opportunity opening in advance of an expected Indian military build-up; India's intervention in the Pakistan civil war in 1971 and Iraq's attack on Iran in 1980 were at least partly the result of windows opened by turmoil in a neighboring society.

Crossing Dangerous Thresholds

The historical record also reveals that important thresholds have been crossed in recent years. During the 1973 Yom Kippur War, Egypt and Syria launched about two dozen Frog and Scud missiles at Israeli military targets. During the 1980s, Iraq and Iran launched hundreds of missiles at each other's cities; both sides also used chemical weapons against military and civilian targets. During the 1990 Gulf War Iraq launched Scud attacks on Israeli cities as well as military targets in Saudi Arabia. Scud missiles were also used extensively by the Kabul government after the Soviet withdrawal from the Afghan civil war. As these examples suggest, restraints on the use of ballistic missiles and chemical weapons are already fragile and in danger of eroding further.

Second, extrapolation from current trends suggests that first-strike advantages and windows of opportunity will become more widespread in the future. Both the amount and variety of sophisticated weaponry available for purchase has been growing in recent years, in no small part because the end of the Cold War has meant the largest cuts in defense spending since the end of the Second World War. As militaries in the advanced states downsize and restructure, defense industries must find new customers or go out of business. The ability of regional powers to design and produce sophisticated weapons on their own is also getting better as they improve their scientific and technical skills and expand their industrial infrastructures. Both of these developments suggest steady improvements in the missiles and strike aircraft owned by regional powers. In particular, ranges will increase, payloads will become larger and more lethal, and accuracy will become more precise.

But even if offensive capabilities continue to improve, will they improve enough to make surprise attacks something more than a hypothetical possibility? The 1967 Six-Day War offers a benchmark for comparison in this regard. On the morning of June 5, the Israeli Air Force attacked 19 Egyptian air bases, destroying over 300 of Egypt's 340 combat aircraft in less than three hours. The attack on Egypt required virtually the entire Israeli Air Force, but was accomplished using only conventional weapons. A ballistic missile attack on a similar number of targets would likely require only a few dozen nuclear-armed missiles and would be over in minutes rather than hours. Alternatively, missiles armed with chemical warheads could be used to disrupt the victim's air defenses, followed by an air attack, a ground attack, or both.

Yet despite the perils of concentration, geography and limited resources often leave regional powers with no alternative but to locate their forces on a small number of bases within easy reach of a near-by foe. Syria's air force is spread among twenty-two bases; Israel's is concentrated on just eleven.[12]

Attack or Defend?

First-strike advantages and windows of opportunity are likely to appear especially ominous in years to come because regional powers concerned about improvements in a rival's ability to attack face an uninviting choice between matching that ability or attempting to defend against it. The former suggests heightened tensions between states whose forces are better suited to attack than to defend; the latter will be difficult and possibly fruitless because of asymmetries in the relative cost and availability of offensive and defensive weaponry. Ballistic missiles are plentiful and cheap; anti-tactical ballistic missiles are scarce and expensive. Chemical weapons are likewise plentiful and cheap; defensive measures against a chemical attack are laborious and costly. SAMs are cheaper than modern strike aircraft, but the former can be evaded or suppressed. The emerging shape of the offense-defense balance suggests that arms races between regional powers will likely take the form of a competition to improve their ability.

Will such arms races be a prelude to war or a substitute for it?[13] The easier it is for one side to take a commanding but temporary lead over a rival, the greater the danger that one or both sides will conclude that war now is preferable to war later, when conditions may be worse. The ability to strike first depends on the number, speed, accuracy, and destructiveness of available weaponry; the ability to retaliate and thus deter depends on survivability, mobility, and command-and-control. The former attributes are embodied in ballistic missiles armed with unconventional warheads, the spread of which continues unabated; the latter are costly and time-consuming to build into an existing force. The emerging shape of the offense-defense balance suggests that in the post-Cold War world arms races will more likely be the prelude to war than a substitute for it.

Lessons from Recent Conflicts

Third and finally, consider the lessons likely to be drawn from recent wars involving regional powers. Iraq's attempted seizure of the Shatt al Arab led to a prolonged and bloody stalemate with Iran; Argentina's seizure of the Falkland Islands resulted in defeat at the hands of the British; Israel's invasion of Lebanon in 1982 did not achieve the objectives set by the Begin government; and Iraq's seizure of Kuwait was overturned by an overwhelmingly powerful international coalition. On the other hand, "India won both the 1965 and 1971 wars [with Pakistan] with bold offensive operations"[14]; Israel destroyed Iraq's Osirak reactor in 1981 and much of the Syrian air force in a one-day battle in 1982; the United States has used air and naval forces to attack Libya in 1986 and to destroy selected Iraqi targets since the end of the Gulf War in 1991.

The lesson that could easily be drawn is that naked aggression doesn't pay, but carefully planned strikes for limited objectives can cripple a neighbor and yield tangible—albeit temporary—security gains. The keys to success are surprise and speed, destroying without seizing, and keeping a substantial capability to retaliate in reserve. States concerned about a rival's ability to strike first may see much to be gained by a first strike on their rival's most threatening military assets.

Ballistic missiles armed with nuclear warheads are likely to encourage this kind of thinking. Only a few need be fired to destroy a rival's key military bases and command-and-control assets, leaving some in reserve to deter retaliation by the victim. Old-fashioned invasions may not occur very often in the post-Cold War world, but selective attacks on sensitive targets—like air bases, missile storage sites, nuclear reactors or reprocessing plants—may well become more frequent.

The Role of the U.S.

If the spread of sophisticated weaponry is indeed heightening the danger of war between regional powers, what should the United States be doing about it? Two judgments underpin the points that follow: first, that the problem is military as well as diplomatic in nature and thus requires appropriate military policies as well as effective diplomacy;

second, that the federal budget deficit will not disappear for a long time and thus the task for military analysts is to identify solutions that can be implemented despite austere budgets for the foreseeable future.

Concerning the first of these, both the Bush and Clinton Administrations have suggested that the disintegration of the Soviet Union means a larger role for the United States in managing the post-Cold War world, but both have allowed the armed forces to shrink for the sake of deficit reduction and the elusive peace dividend. This sort of thinking is at once shortsighted and practically unavoidable. On one hand, the greater the availability of first-strike weaponry, the greater the likelihood that regional powers whose forces are better suited to attack than to defend will choose war over a tense and uneasy status quo. On the other hand, wars between regional powers are a difficult foreign policy problem for the United States because the dangers often seem remote and even speculative (e.g., nuclear war between India and Pakistan) whereas the budgetary costs of additional power projection forces are immediate and substantial.

There is, however, nothing speculative about the historical record of thresholds crossed and restraints eroded in recent years, which suggests that future wars between regional powers will not be limited to conventional weapons aimed at strictly military targets. Nor can the United States take refuge in its sheltered location in the Western hemisphere. A nuclear war between Israel and Iran or India and Pakistan would not directly menace the United States, but it would be an enormous catastrophe in its own right. It would shatter the nuclear taboo, hasten nuclear proliferation as potential target states scrambled to assemble nuclear retaliatory forces of their own, and scatter fallout that could poison large areas beyond the boundaries of the combatants.

Non-nuclear wars between regional powers pose less of a danger to American interests, but heavily armed regional powers can catalyze enormously destructive wars that threaten important Western interests, like the free flow of oil from the Persian Gulf, and which could also spill over the borders of neighboring states (especially if chemical or biological weapons are used).

Military Solutions

If, however, military policy is constrained by stagnant or declining defense budgets for many years to come, what exactly can be done by way of military solutions? First and foremost is recognition that the value of peacetime armed forces is better measured in terms of what does *not* happen rather than what does. It is better to prevent wars, even far off conflicts, than deal with the consequences after they have begun. Preventing wars between regional powers requires an ability to restrain, reassure, or maybe both; but neither restraint nor reassurance is possible without armed forces that are large and mobile, and thus capable of maintaining a watchful presence near trouble spots or able to get there quickly in force. The better prepared the U.S. is to deter or reassure, the better the chances of preventing or at least containing wars between regional powers before important U.S. interests are threatened and U.S. citizens endangered. Conversely, the deeper the cuts made in current and future defense budgets, the greater the danger that effective action will not be possible when it is urgently needed.

Armed forces that can maintain a presence near trouble spots and project power abroad won't be cheap, but they need not be unduly expensive either. Reconciling needs with resources is more than a ritual for policy wonks, it is an opportunity to reshape the armed forces to better match the post-Cold War world. A post-Cold War military establishment that is merely a small-scale replica of that which existed during the 1980s will not be a good match for the challenges likely to arise during the rest of the 1990s and beyond, for two reasons. First, merely shrinking the armed forces while attempting to preserve all of the services' component parts suggests a loss of effectiveness greater than the loss of personnel or budget authority because the parts that remain no longer fit together very well.

Second, some kinds of armed forces are better suited to the post-Cold War world than others. The ability of the armed forces to contribute to the goals of crisis prevention and crisis management is a function principally of the number and quality of readily available army divisions, naval task forces, and tactical fighter squadrons, and the speed with which they can reach the scene of trouble. The greater the number and visibility of such rapidly deployable units, the greater the services' ability to prevent bad things from happening by restraining or reassuring states contemplating war as a result of ambition or desperation. During the Cold War, strategic nuclear forces were central to the U.S.-Soviet competition. In the post-Cold War world, B-2 Stealth bombers and Ohio-class submarines are likely to be an expensive luxury, unsuited for Third World contingencies and so expensive that building any more of them will drain scarce defense dollars from forces that are better suited for the wars between regional powers that pose the greatest danger to a more peaceful world order. The B-2 has the added drawback of being so expensive (more than $40 billion to build the first batch of 20) that military commanders are unlikely to risk losing one by sending it against a hostile target. Think of it as the most expensive training vehicle in the history of warfare.

Setting Priorities

A similar line of argument can be used to set priorities for dividing available defense funds among the various kinds of general purpose forces. Reserve units are often touted as a way to maintain strength at low cost, but the delays that inevitably arise in making them combat-ready diminish their value relative to active-duty forces. Carrier battle groups and Marine Expeditionary Forces offer a better fit to the demands of the post-Cold War world than Army divisions and Air Force tactical fighter squadrons, because the former are largely self-contained, do not require extensive land bases, and are less dependent on scarce and costly airlift than the latter.

Within each of the services, judgments about the worth of specific programs will depend on the contribution that each can make to preventing or containing wars between regional powers. Within the Navy, for example, nuclear attack submarines are less useful than surface combatants that can maintain a visible presence (for deterrence or power projection) near crisis spots. The very-costly Seawolf submarine is doubly superfluous because the Navy's Los-Angeles-class submarines are already better than any foreign competitor and hardly overworked in view of the collapse of the Soviet Navy. The Seawolf, like the B-2, is a program without a mission, aside from keeping a shipyard busy until it can find something better to do.

Wasteful programs like the B-2 and the Seawolf are especially troublesome because American armed forces are already the most sophisticated in the world—what is needed are more of them to cover potential trouble spots, not further generational leaps in aircraft and submarines.

Future Demands on the Navy

Some new capabilities will of course be needed to cope with the particular mix of dangers presented by the post-Cold War world. A growing danger of war between regional powers in the Middle East, south Asia and east Asia suggests that future demands on the Navy—the service most often called upon to project power to distant regions for purposes of crisis prevention and crisis management—will increase rather than decline. Current policy, however, calls for a 330-ship Navy, or 40% fewer than the 540 ships available in 1990, at the time of the Gulf War with Iraq. While the Navy will retain 12 large-deck, multi-purpose carriers—the ships that are most important to the presence and power projection missions—the carriers themselves are aging and retirements will likely outpace replacements for the foreseeable future.[15] Because of the high costs and long lead-times involved in building new Nimitz-class carriers, perhaps the most promising short-term solution would be to supplement the remaining large-deck carriers with a new class of smaller, less expensive, but still very capable carriers equipped with vertical and short take-off aircraft (VSTOL) like the AV-8B Harrier and the V-22 Osprey.

The Navy's current carrier battle groups are a particularly valuable asset in a milieu in which the danger of war between regional powers is increasing because they offer the ability to perform many tasks within a compact, self-contained formation: project power ashore, defend friendly shipping from air and sea attacks, and conduct sea surveillance and anti-submarine warfare. It would be unrealistic to expect a mid-size carrier operating VSTOL and tilt-rotor aircraft to perform all of these missions as well as a Nimitz-class carrier, but mid-size carriers could perform very capably if relieved of the requirement to project power ashore. The Navy currently has many ways to project power ashore in addition to the attack aircraft carried by the current fleet of large-deck carriers—for example, ship-launched cruise missiles, Marine amphibious units, and naval gunfire. The prerequisite to employing these alternative means is that the ships that carry them be protected from attacks by hostile aircraft, surface vessels, and submarines. This suggests that the proposed new class of midsize carriers be designed to perform three tasks well: air defense of friendly ships and troops ashore, anti-ship operations, and anti-submarine warfare. All three are within the capability of currently available VSTOL and tilt-rotor aircraft. Suitably equipped, a fleet of VSTOL carriers would allow the Navy to use its remaining frigates, destroyers, cruisers and Marine amphibious units to form additional, independently deployable task forces, thereby improving its ability to maintain a presence near trouble spots for purposes of deterrence or reassurance.

Improving the Navy's ability to perform the presence and power projection missions by means of a new class of ships will incur some new budgetary costs, but in a world of heavily armed regional powers the demand for naval task forces is more likely to increase than decline. It will be cheaper and more effective in the long run to assemble the needed capabilities now than to scramble to come up with a response to an unpleasant surprise like a nuclear war in the Middle East or South Asia.

NOTES

1. Scott Sagan, "1914 Revisited," *International Security,* Vol. 11, Fall 1986, pp. 151-155; Salah al-Ameel, *Why Do States Go to War? Prevention, Pre-Emption and the Prospect of Gain* (Ph.D. Thesis: Catholic University, 1994), p. 11.
2. Gerald Steinberg, "Indigenous Arms Industries and Dependence: The Case of Israel," *Defense Analysis,* December 1986, p. 296.
3. The affinity felt by professional military officers for preventive war is discussed by Scott Sagan, "The Perils of Proliferation," *International Security,* 18, Spring 1994, pp. 75-85. See also Jack Levy, "Declining Power and the Preventive Motivation for War," *World Politics,* October 1987, pp. 82-107.
4. Quoted in Paul Doty and Stephen Flank, "Arms Control for New Nuclear Nations," in Robert Blackwill and Albert Carnesale (eds.), *New Nuclear Nations* (New York: Council on Foreign Relations, 1993), p. 69.
5. "Unsweet Missiles of Spring," *The Economist,* March 26, 1988, p. 36.
6. Ibid. See also Janne Nolan, *Trappings of Power* (Washington: Brookings, 1991), pp. 77-81.
7. John Lewis Gaddis, "The Long Peace," *International Security,* Spring 1986, p. 124.
8. Yossi Melman and Dan Raviv, "Why Nobody Will Win the Next War in the Middle East," *Washington Post,* November 6, 1988, p. C2.
9. Bruce Blair, *Strategic Command and Control* (Washington: Brookings, 1985), p. 116; Thomas Schelling and Morton Halperin, *Strategy and Arms Control* (New York: Twentieth Century Fund, 1961), pp. 9-17.
10. See, for example, Scott Sagan, *The Limits of Safety* (Princeton, NJ: Princeton University Press, 1993).
11. Quoted in Lally Weymouth, "Would Israel Strike First?" *Washington Post,* November 11, 1990, p. B2.
12. Al-Ameel, *Why Do States Go to War?,* pp. 119-123; Janne Nolan, *Trappings of Power* (Washington: Brookings, 1991), chapter 4; Melman and Raviv, "Why Nobody Will Win the Next War in the Middle East."
13. Samuel Huntington, "Arms Races: Prerequisites and Results," *Public Policy,* 8, 1948, pp. 41-86.
14. Devin Hagerty, "Nuclear Deterrence in South Asia," *International Security,* 20, Winter 1995/1996, p. 111.
15. Mark Randol and Wallace Thies, "The Opportunity Costs of Large-Deck Carriers," *Naval War College Review,* Summer 1990, pp. 9-31.

☆ ☆ ☆ ☆

PARING DOWN THE ARSENAL

By Frank von Hippel

THE HELSINKI SUMMIT IN MARCH gave a much needed impulse—albeit a modest one—to the long-dormant nuclear arms reduction process. There had been no negotiations since the second Strategic Arms Reduction Treaty (START II) had been signed four years earlier. Although the treaty had been ratified by the U.S. Senate, it had not been ratified by the Russian Duma, where opposition was intense.

By the time the summit convened, it looked as if the treaty might simply unravel, the victim of lingering Cold War-era distrust. But President Boris Yeltsin said at the conclusion of the summit that enough progress had been made to "prepare grounds so that the Duma could positively look at ratifying START II."

That progress included a commitment by President Bill Clinton to begin negotiating a START III agreement after the Duma ratifies START II. The aim of START III, according to Clinton and Yeltsin, would be to reduce the ceiling on the number of deployed strategic warheads on each side to 2,000–2,500 by the end of the year 2007. In contrast, START II called for a limit of 3,500 deployed strategic warheads by 2003.

Frank von Hippel is a professor of public and international affairs at Princeton University. In 1993–94, he served as assistant director for national security in the White House Office of Science and Technology Policy.

It's time to pull missiles off hair-trigger alert and get on with deep cuts in nuclear stockpiles.

The presidents also agreed to "explore possible measures relating to long-range nuclear sea-launched cruise missiles [SLCMs] and tactical nuclear systems." The U.S. military is concerned that Russia retains over 10,000 nuclear warheads while Russia's military is concerned about the remaining hundreds of U.S. bombs deployed in Europe and the lingering SLCM launch capabilities of U.S. attack submarines.

Clinton and Yeltsin also agreed to integrate into the START III process exchanges of information about *total* U.S. and Russian stockpiles of strategic warheads (deployed and nondeployed) and about the elimination of excess warheads. Confidence-building "transparency" arrangements, such as on-site inspections, also would be negotiated.

Finally, Clinton succeeded, after three and a half years of effort, in getting Yeltsin to agree to a dramatic loosening of the terms of the 1972 Anti-Ballistic Missile (ABM) Treaty. That frees the United States to continue to develop and produce mobile long-range land-, sea-, and air-based anti-missile systems for "theater defense." These systems can have virtually unlimited capabilities as long as they are not *tested* against strategic ballistic missiles and are not deployed against Russia's strategic missiles.

While Yeltsin and Clinton reaffirmed the "fundamental significance" of the ABM Treaty to strategic stability and the possibility of further reductions in strategic offensive arms, Yeltsin's decision to go along with U.S. theater missile defense plans may eventually impede future arms-reduction efforts. Analysts in Moscow will continue to point out that mobile U.S. theater defenses could be quickly redeployed as national defenses. Indeed, U.S. missile-defense enthusiasts have already proposed using the navy's upper-tier missile defense system for that purpose.

But if the ballistic-missile-defense problem can be contained, then deeper cuts and other steps to reduce the nuclear danger would be possible. Given the political will, it would be possible, over the course of the next 20 or 25 years, to get the U.S. and Russian nuclear arsenals down from about 10,000 warheads apiece to, say, 200 warheads apiece—and still preserve the principle of nuclear deterrence.

The ultimate objective should be the elimination of all nuclear weapons. But that is still beyond the horizon. Meanwhile, debate over the requirements of elimination should not be allowed to delay the deep reductions that must come first.

Russia's nightmares

At the Joint Summit press conference, Yeltsin, when asked whether the Duma would now ratify START II, responded: "I expect that the State Duma will make a decision based on my advice." This may be the case, but it is not certain.

To understand how the balance might be swayed in the Duma by the Helsinki agreements, it is useful to examine the way in which those agreements dealt with the four main concerns that lay behind the Duma's opposition:

■ **Start II limits were too high to allow Russia to maintain parity with the United States.** START II requires Russia to eliminate most of its land-based multiple-warhead missiles at a time when many of its ballistic missile submarines and bombers are reaching their design lifetimes. As a result, when the START II limits on deployed warheads would come into force at the end of 2003, Russia would probably be able to deploy fewer than 3,000 strategic warheads on its permitted strategic weapon systems. By the year 2010, it would probably be able to deploy fewer than 2,000.

The U.S. START III proposal deals with much of this problem—although the whole issue could have been avoided if President Bush had agreed to the 2,000 warheads proposed by President Yeltsin five years ago.

■ **The United States has a breakout advantage.** The U.S. Defense Department has deliberately structured its proposed START II reductions (in the words of its public report on the "Nuclear Posture Review") to preserve an "upload-hedge" option. That means the United States would be able to deploy twice as many warheads as permitted by START II "should political relations with Russia change for the worse [and/or] START I and START II not be fully implemented."

Both the United States and Russia have about 7,000 strategic warheads deployed today. But because of the very different impact of START II on the two forces, a rapid upload option would not be available to Russia.

The treaty requires Russia to eliminate about 280 land-based ballistic missiles carrying about 2,600 warheads. Because of obsolescence and lack of funds, Russia is also expected to retire 12 submarines and 68 bombers carrying about 1,600 warheads for a total reduction of about 4,200.

In contrast, START II requires the United States to eliminate only 50 MX missiles carrying 500 warheads. The United States also expects to retire four submarines carrying 768 warheads for a total of about 1,200. Most of the remaining U.S. reductions are to be accomplished by "downloading" 500 Minuteman III land-based missiles from three to one warhead each; downloading 336 Navy Trident II missiles from eight to five warheads each; and converting 95 B-1 bombers, which can carry 16 warheads each, to non-nuclear roles.

If the United States ever chose to abrogate START II and upload, it could redeploy stored warheads onto the previously downloaded Trident II and Minuteman III missiles as well as the B-1 bombers. As a result, in the year 2010, for instance, the number of U.S. deployed strategic warheads could still be built back up to about 7,000, while Russia would be able to field only about 1,600.

The impact of the Helsinki summit agreement on this concern will not be clear until the shape of the START III forces are negotiated. However, the proposal to exchange information on stored strategic warheads provides a possible handle on the upload problem.

■ **The United States might deploy a national ballistic-missile defense system.** The Republican congressional leadership continues to press for a commitment to deploy nationwide defenses against ballistic missiles by 2003. This would be done—if necessary—by using the "supreme national interests" escape clause in the ABM Treaty.

Although ballistic missile defense enthusiasts describe their idea as providing a "thin" defense against an accidental or unauthorized launch or against an attack from a rogue nation, many Russian analysts see it differently.

From a Russian perspective, it looks as if the United States could quickly upgrade a thin defense into a system that could serve as a shield from behind which the United States might launch a first strike in a crisis confrontation. Russian analysts also believe that the elimination of Russia's land-based multiple-warhead missiles under START II would make the U.S. missile defense task much easier. For now, the Clinton administration does not believe that there is adequate justification for deployment of a national missile defense. But the administration has agreed to develop hardware that could be deployed by 2003, if a go-decision were made by the year 2000.

On a parallel track, the administration is developing mobile long-range interceptor missiles and space-based sensors for "theater" missile defense. Domestic and Russian analysts alike note that such hardware could become part of a national defense.

As already noted, the Helsinki summit agreement sent a mixed message in response to concerns about the future of the ABM Treaty. Clinton pledged U.S. adherence to the treaty and Yeltsin dropped Russian objections to U.S. theater missile defense programs, which could provide the future wherewithal for a rapid breakout from the treaty.

• **NATO is expanding toward Russia.** Largely at the urging of the United States, NATO is expected to announce in July that it will admit Poland, Hungary and the Czech Republic. NATO's military expansion into the buffer area created by the voluntary Soviet withdrawal has created outrage in Russia across the political spectrum.

The North Atlantic Council announced in December 1996 that NATO members have "no intention, no plans, and no reason" to move its nuclear systems east. At the Helsinki summit, Clinton added, "nor do they foresee any future need to do so." He also agreed to include this language in a new agreement that would be signed by the leaders of all the NATO countries, as well as by Russia. And Clinton assured Yeltsin that NATO does not intend to build up forces permanently stationed in Eastern Europe. Indeed, NATO offered to renegotiate the Conventional Forces in Europe Treaty to formalize this commitment.

For now, these commitments will

help assuage Russian concerns about NATO's short-term expansion plans. In the future, these concerns are likely to focus principally on whether NATO will move to expand all the way up to Russia's border by admitting the Baltic States and perhaps even Ukraine.

Nuclear dangers

Many Western leaders, political and military, are still quietly exultant over having "won" the Cold War and are dismissive of Russia's security concerns. That's a mistake. If nuclear dangers are to be further reduced, Russia's concerns must be dealt with. The Helsinki summit was a good start. But it was not enough, by itself, to calm the waters in Moscow.

There is the danger that Russia—if not reassured by further actions and commitments that the West's intentions are benign, will attempt to deal with its concerns about the continuing high state of readiness of U.S. forces, conventional and nuclear, by attempting to maintain a large portion of its own deteriorating strategic forces on high alert. And Russia may attempt to deal with the abysmal state of its conventional military forces by retaining thousands of tactical nuclear weapons.

Such Russian responses would magnify two of the greatest dangers posed by Russia's deteriorating nuclear forces: the possibility of mistaken or unauthorized launch of strategic missiles, and of leakage of tactical nuclear weapons into the international black market.

A third threat, which will develop if the United States and Russia do not go much further in reducing their nuclear confrontation, will be to the nonproliferation regime. In 1995, in exchange for an agreement by the non-weapon states to an indefinite extension of the Nuclear Non-Proliferation Treaty (NPT), the United States and Russia (and the other weapon states) committed themselves to "systematic and progressive efforts to reduce nuclear weapons globally, with the ultimate goal of eliminating those weapons."

The NPT is the legitimating authority for international actions to stop clandestine nuclear programs such as those mounted by Iraq and North Korea. But if the nuclear powers—particularly the United States and Russia—ignore their NPT obligation to work toward nuclear disarmament, the treaty may become a dead letter.

The United States, which emerged from the Cold War as the only true superpower, must take the lead in launching new initiatives to reduce these dangers by achieving an agreement with Russia to quickly take most nuclear weapons off alert [see "De-alerting"] and by negotiating additional deep cuts beyond START III.

Finally, the United States should join China in adopting a no-first-use nuclear policy, and it should press Russia, Britain, and France to join in. That would go a long way toward strengthening the nuclear nonproliferation regime. After all, how can the role of nuclear weapons be de-emphasized elsewhere if the world's most powerful nation insists that *its* security requires it to reserve the option of using nuclear weapons first?

During the Cold War, the U.S. first-use policy was directed primarily at the Soviet Union, the assumption being that nuclear weapons might be needed to counter a massive Soviet conventional attack on Western Europe.

Today, the Soviet threat is gone. But U.S. think-tank warriors are endlessly creative. Now the possibility that a "rogue state" might use chemical or biological weapons is often cited as the principal justification for preserving a first-use option.

It would be much more supportive of the nonproliferation regime for the United States to push for universal adherence to the Chemical Weapons Convention, which it has signed but—as of early April—not ratified. Similarly, the United States ought to deal with the objections of its biotech industry to greatly strengthening verification provisions for the biological weapons ban.

Warhead control

If the United States and Russia are to move seriously toward deep reductions, they will also have to move toward greater openness regarding the numbers of *non-deployed* warheads; they will have to come to grips with tactical nuclear weapons; and they will have to hammer out some difficult verification issues.

Reserve warheads. No nuclear arms limitation agreement has ever limited nuclear warheads *per se*. The Strategic Arms Limitation Treaties (SALT I and II) and the Intermediate-Range Nuclear Forces Treaty limited launchers and delivery vehicles. START I and II, in addition, limited the numbers of *deployed* warheads and bombs.

As deployed forces become smaller, however, stored warheads become a greater concern. As previously noted, reserve warheads in the United States already worry Russia because of the large upload capacity of the planned U.S. START II forces. Similarly, the U.S. military frets over the very large stockpiles of tactical nuclear warheads that Russia still retains.

One reason for keeping a small number of warheads and bombs in reserve is to provide a source of spares (in case a problem develops with an individual warhead) and to provide samples for destructive examination for the effects of aging.

But a common argument for preserving a large number of bombs and warheads, as the United States plans to do, is to provide backups in case all the weapons of a given *type* develop a disabling defect. In a de-alerted posture, it would be unreasonably provocative, however, to maintain a large stockpile of reserve warheads in addition to the stockpile of de-alerted warheads that had been removed from their launchers.

If the de-alerted warheads included warheads of a different type that could be placed on the same launchers as the deployed warheads, they could serve as spares as well as a reserve for re-enlarging the deployed force, if needed.

The de-alerted warheads could be widely dispersed, so that they would not be tempting targets for a possible first strike. If the START Treaty could be amended to allow it, they might, for instance, be stored in former ICBM silos that had been partially filled with concrete so they were no longer deep enough to hold missiles.

With such arrangements, the United States and Russia could agree to dismantle all stored strategic warheads in

U.S. POST–COLD WAR MILITARY STRATEGY: Arms Control

> ### The Deep Cuts Study Group
>
> Frank von Hippel's essay draws heavily—although it may differ in detail—from the preliminary findings of a study carried out by the Deep Cuts Study Group.
> The members of the group: Von Hippel and Harold Feiveson, Princeton University; Bruce Blair and Janne Nolan, the Brookings Institution; Jonathan Dean, the Union of Concerned Scientists; Steve Fetter, the University of Maryland; James Goodby, Stanford University; George Lewis and Theodore Postol, the Massachusetts Institute of Technology.

excess of treaty limits (2,000–2,500 for START III, for example) and place the recovered fissile material under international safeguards.

Tactical warheads. The United States is reducing its tactical nuclear arsenal to about 1,000 warheads. According to Robert S. Norris and William M. Arkin of the Natural Resources Defense Council, the tactical nuclear stockpile will consist of about 600 B61 bombs and about 350 sea-launched cruise missiles. (See the *Bulletin*'s "NRDC Nuclear Notebook, July/August 1996.)

Russia's approximately 18,000 remaining pre-1991 tactical nuclear warheads will have reached the end of their design lives by about 2003. Thereafter, the size of Russia's tactical nuclear stockpile will be determined by the amount of its post-1991 production.

There seems to be very little new Russian warhead production thus far, because the warhead assembly facilities have been busy dismantling the Cold War stockpile. That suggests that there is an opening for a U.S.-Russian agreement to limit their stockpiles of tactical nuclear weapons to lower levels—to 500 each, for example.

Better yet, why not eliminate them entirely? Reducing the number of U.S. tactical nuclear bombs now deployed in NATO countries to zero is said to be politically difficult because their presence symbolizes the U.S. commitment to defend its NATO allies from nuclear attack. In turn, that commitment is said to make it unnecessary for countries such as Germany to acquire their own nuclear deterrents.

And yet, the United States provides a nuclear guarantee to Japan without basing nuclear weapons there, and it continues to provide such a guarantee to South Korea, although it has withdrawn all nuclear weapons from that country.

A possible compromise would be to leave it up to the individual nuclear powers to decide on the mix between tactical and strategic warheads within a fixed limit. Under that arrangement, the price of keeping a tactical nuclear warhead would become the loss of a strategic warhead.

Verification. Presidents Clinton and Yeltsin have repeatedly agreed in joint summit statements on a desire to make their warhead stockpiles and reductions more "transparent." Their most detailed statement, issued after their May 1995 Moscow summit, affirmed "the desire . . . to exchange detailed information on aggregate stockpiles of nuclear warheads [and] stocks of fissile materials . . . on a regular basis" and "to negotiate . . . a cooperative arrangement for reciprocal monitoring of storage facilities of fissile materials removed from nuclear warheads and declared to be excess to national security requirements."

U.S. and Russian technical experts have conducted joint demonstrations of external radiation measurements that could be used to confirm that sealed containers hold stored plutonium objects of the approximate mass and size expected of "pits" extracted from dismantled nuclear warheads.

However, the implementation of this and other proposed transparency agreements awaits the conclusion of an "Agreement of Cooperation" on the bilateral protection of the classified data that would be revealed through such measurements.

Unfortunately, as Russia became increasingly disillusioned about its security partnership with the United States—and indeed public cooperation with the United States became a political liability for Russian officials—Moscow became unresponsive to U.S. proposals to complete the agreement. It is to be hoped—but not at all assured—that these negotiations will be revived after the Helsinki summit.

In their May 1995 "Joint Summit Statement," Clinton and Yeltsin also agreed on the principles of irreversibility of stockpile reductions: no new civilian nuclear material will be used for weapons and, once fissile material removed from nuclear warheads is declared excess, it will not again be used in weapons.

At the April 1996 summit of the Group of Seven Industrialized Nations in Moscow, the United States, Russia, Britain, and France joined in a pledge that such irreversibility would be made verifiable by "the placing of fissile material designated as not intended for defense purposes under IAEA [International Atomic Energy Agency] safeguards . . . as soon as it is practicable to do so."

The United States has already placed about 10 metric tons of highly enriched uranium and two tons of plutonium under IAEA safeguards at three Energy Department sites at Oak Ridge, Hanford, and Rocky Flats. However, the United States expects to maintain a very large stockpile of weapon-grade uranium for future use as fuel in U.S. and British naval-propulsion reactors.

If this naval-fuel stockpile were placed under IAEA safeguards, materials would have to be withdrawn from safeguards in the future—a bad precedent. This problem could be mitigated by a multilateral agreement that all new naval nuclear reactors would be fueled with non-weapons-usable uranium enriched to less than 20 percent uranium 235. (The U.S. Navy, however, is not enamored of that idea, because the reactors would need larger cores to achieve the same interval between refuelings.)

Another factor complicating the placing of fissile materials from excess weapons under IAEA safeguards is that these materials are mostly in the form of weapons components. The designs of these key components are considered secret by both the United States and Russia.

There has been some discussion among the United States, Russia, and the IAEA regarding the possibility of applying non-intrusive safeguards to these components, which would protect the secret information. However, such procedures would still reveal the average amounts of plutonium and highly enriched uranium in warheads—information that some U.S. weapons designers insist should be kept secret for nonproliferation reasons.

And in Russia, the Ministry of Atomic Energy reportedly considers the isotopic composition of its weapon-grade plutonium to be classified, although the United States does not classify such information.

If such obstacles cannot be overcome, excess fissile materials should be converted to standard ingots, cans of oxide, or other non-classified forms that could be placed under international safeguards. This should be done as soon as it can be assured that the processing will be done without any of the material being stolen.

Getting on with reductions

It now appears that START III negotiations will take place, and they will lead to an agreement that limits deployed strategic warheads to 2,000–2,500 each for the United States and Russia. While START III reductions are under way, the Deep Cuts Study Group, of which I am a member, believes the United States and Russia should reach a START IV agreement that would make deeper reductions to about 1,000 strategic and—at most—100 tactical warheads each, *with stored warheads and warhead components counted in the total.*

That would be a dramatic reduction indeed, considering that both sides seem to be planning to keep 10,000 or so *total* warheads, even though START II limits each of them to fewer than 3,500 *deployed* strategic warheads.

Before reductions to the 1,000-warhead level could be implemented, however, the remaining declared weapon states—Britain, France, and China—would have to be recruited into the disarmament process—at least to the extent of committing not to build up their nuclear arsenals and to exchanging declarations regarding the sizes of their warhead and fissile-material stockpiles.

A global ban on the production of fissile material for weapons and a global agreement to strictly limit stockpiles of weapons-usable fissile materials also would have to be achieved by this stage.

A fissile cutoff. A global ban on the production of fissile material for warheads would cap the size of the potential nuclear-warhead stockpiles of the declared and threshold weapon states, thereby preventing others from building up while the United States and Russia are reducing. All five declared nuclear weapon states have indicated their willingness to join in a fissile cutoff and have also indicated they are not currently producing fissile materials for weapons.

However, Israel and India are believed to still be building up their stockpiles of weapons plutonium, and India—supported by many of the non-weapon states—insists on linking the fissile cutoff to negotiations on "time-bound" nuclear disarmament. Pakistan (the third "threshold" state) wants a linkage to reductions to equal stockpiles. As a result, more than three years after the unanimous vote at the United Nations to pursue a fissile-materials-cutoff treaty, negotiations have not begun.

A possible compromise first step that would achieve the sought-for linkage between the production cutoff and disarmament would be for the threshold states to join the production moratorium on the condition that the weapons states continue their stockpile reductions.

It would probably be necessary to strengthen the credibility of the production-halt declarations with bilateral and multilateral transparency measures and the shutdown of facilities considered too sensitive for intrusive inspections.

Limitations on weapons-usable fissile materials. As nuclear-warhead arsenals become smaller, other stockpiles of weapons-usable materials will become matters of concern, even if they are under international safeguards. China is already worried that Japan could quickly convert its stockpile of IAEA-safeguarded civil plutonium into a large nuclear arsenal.

Much larger stockpiles of separated civil plutonium have accumulated elsewhere. France and Britain each have stockpiles at their commercial reprocessing plants of about 50 metric tons—the equivalent of about 10,000 nuclear warheads. Russia has accumulated about 30 tons at its commercial reprocessing plant. And India has a small but growing stockpile of separated civil plutonium.

Civilian use of plutonium increases the threat of nuclear theft as well as nuclear proliferation. Further plutonium separation should therefore be halted and excess civilian and weapons stocks disposed of.

That will be difficult to achieve, however, given the financial, career, and intellectual investments that have been made in the separation of plutonium and its recycle as nuclear fuel.

There is also another (but still not widely understood) factor that is even more important in sustaining the uneconomic activity of plutonium separation. Commercial spent fuel reprocessing continues largely because the nuclear utilities of some countries, notably Germany and Japan, use it to "export" their radioactive waste disposal problems. (In fact, they only delay the problem rather than solving it, because reprocessing contracts specify that the separated fission-product waste must eventually be returned to the country of origin.)

If the United States were to take the lead in establishing a set of international spent-fuel storage facilities, storage would be seen by many nuclear utilities as an attractive alternative to reprocessing.

Such an effort, however, would somehow have to overcome the inevitable environmental and safety objections that so far have blocked almost all efforts to site national spent-fuel storage facilities.

Deep cuts

In the third stage, reductions would have to become fully multilateral, with Britain, France, and China joining in the negotiations and verification of all warhead and fissile-material stockpiles.

If this were done, reductions to 200 warheads each for the United States, Russia, China, and Western Europe could be achieved by the year 2020. (This assumes that Britain and France would be willing to have their nuclear forces treated as a single West European force.)

A 200-weapon stockpile does not necessarily mean 200 *deployed* weapons, however. The Deep Cuts Study Group believes that each region would need only 10 to 20 deployed weapons; the remainder would be in storage. Ten survivable warheads would still be a terrifying deterrent. A single 450-kiloton Trident II warhead, for example, could destroy an urban area of 200 square kilometers—roughly the size of Washington or St. Louis.

We do not, however, endorse the idea of targeting urban populations—even though such a policy would be no more immoral than today's policy of targeting *thousands* of military targets with the full knowledge that tens of millions of civilians would die as a "collateral" effect.

There would be no need to target cities to have a strong deterrent. Any kind of nuclear retaliation would be devastating. For example, major military bases or key economic facilities such as refineries could be attacked in retaliation for a nuclear strike.

We also assume that, if the nuclear powers could agree on a plan involving reductions to such small numbers of strategic warheads, they could also agree to eliminate tactical nuclear weapons. Alternatively, tactical nuclear weapons could be included in the permitted 200-warhead forces.

Difficulties

The "threshold" nuclear states—Israel, India, and Pakistan—will have to be engaged at some point in the deep-reductions process. Otherwise, it will come to a halt.

As a start, the threshold states should join in a moratorium on fissile-material production and then a formal cutoff treaty. They should also put any nuclear-weapons-usable fissile material that they have produced for civilian purposes under IAEA safeguards. These measures would cap the potential sizes of their arsenals.

At a later stage, they could join in the reductions process by placing agreed amounts of their remaining stocks of unsafeguarded fissile material under international safeguards. Or, consistent with their current policies of keeping their nuclear deterrents undeployed—that is, "in the closet"—one or more of the threshold states might be willing to put all its nuclear materials in a national storage facility that was subject to international perimeter-portal monitoring to verify that the material was not removed.

The form of the material (which might even be weapons components) would not be subject to international inspection, and it would have to be understood that, in a crisis, the owning country would have both the power and the right to order the international monitors to depart.

As for the five declared nuclear powers, there are many uncertainties that could make an agreement on low numbers of weapons difficult. Consider, for instance, the huge quantities of fissile materials that were produced over the decades by the United States and the Soviet Union.

There have been considerable losses at various stages of the production process. As a result, the weapons states cannot even prove to *themselves* that ton-quantities of fissile material have not been hidden away. In February 1996, for example, the United States made public a complete accounting of its plutonium production and use and found that the cumulative "inventory difference . . . between the quantity of nuclear material held according to the accounting books and the quantity measured by a physical inventory . . . for the 50-year period from 1944 to 1994 is 2.8 tonnes."

These inventory differences were attributed to inaccurate predictive codes for production reactors; materials trapped in production facilities (in pipes, for instance); measurement uncertainties—especially for plutonium in difficult-to-assay waste—unmeasured losses in accidental spills; "recording, reporting, and rounding errors"; and so on. The Energy Department believes that there have been no thefts and that there are no hidden stockpiles. But it would be difficult to prove that to the satisfaction of another government suspicious about possible cheating.

Such concerns could be reduced if the United States and Russia—and later, all nuclear weapon and threshold states—launched (as first suggested four years ago by Steve Fetter of the University of Maryland) a joint "nuclear archeology" project to reconstruct the production and disposition history of their nuclear materials, using all available records, interviews with key active and retired personnel, and physical measurements at production facilities.

In the end, however, reductions of the magnitudes proposed here may only be possible when political leaders realize that survivable weapons systems capable of launching just a few warheads are an adequate deterrent even against threats from states armed with much larger nuclear forces.

At the height of the Cold War, when the Soviet Union was threatening to cut off Berlin, a very small and not very survivable Russian force was more than adequate to deter U.S. nuclear planners from proposing a first strike to a desperate U.S. leadership.

For his 1983 book, the *Wizards of Armageddon*, Fred Kaplan interviewed participants in the U.S. nuclear planning process during the 1961 Berlin crisis. He learned that intelligence analyses indicated that the Soviet strategic forces were in "awful shape" in 1961—warheads had not been loaded onto missiles, bombers were not on alert, and almost all of the nuclear submarines were in port. The Soviet early-warning network was riddled with gaps, which would have made it difficult for the Soviets to detect a "less-than-massive U.S. bomber attack," especially if the bombers flew low.

That year, war over Berlin seemed possible, even likely, and White House and Pentagon officials searched for a way to stand firm while—in President Kennedy's words—avoiding "humiliation or holocaust." After all, writes Kaplan, if the Soviets went all out in capturing and defending Berlin with conventional forces, they would win. Berlin was an isolated enclave behind the "Iron Curtain" that divided Europe. If it came to war, the United States would have to use nuclear weapons.

The Pentagon prepared a detailed strike plan with information on the precise location of Soviet nuclear targets. The data were fed into a mathematical model, which indicated that a counterforce attack was feasible and could be carried out with high confidence.

Nevertheless, the study also indicated that a few Soviet bombs and missiles would survive. If the Soviets retaliated with nuclear weapons, two to three million Americans would die, under best-case assumptions. In the worst case, as many as 10 to 15 million would perish, along with many millions of Europeans. Writes Kaplan:

"If ever in the history of the nuclear arms race, before or since, one side had unquestionable superiority over the other, one side truly had the ability to devastate the other side's strategic forces, one side could execute the Rand counterforce/no-cities option with fairly high confidence, the autumn of 1961 was that time. Yet approaching the height of the gravest crisis that had faced the West since the onset of the Cold War, everyone said 'No.'"

What is needed

Technically, there is no absolute obstacle to the staged reductions proposed here. However, as demonstrated by the analysis of the history of the Pentagon's Nuclear Posture Review by Janne Nolan of the Brookings Institution, there will not be a deep-cuts policy as long as the development of the policy is left to the nuclear targeteers.

The failure of the Nuclear Posture Review should be contrasted with the high-level process in which President Bush, his national security adviser, the secretary of defense, and the chairman of the Joint Chiefs of Staff were personally involved in August and September 1991. That process quickly resulted in a decision to initiate a parallel U.S.-Soviet process to eliminate army nuclear weapons and to store or destroy all the nuclear weapons then on surface naval ships.

If the Clinton administration wants to remove U.S. and Russian missiles from their launch-on-warning postures and to initiate a deep cuts process, its national security team will have to engage these issues with similar intensity. Bill Clinton is said to hunger for a prominent place in the history books. No other issue presents a finer opportunity, either for him or for the world.

Article 31

> "Because of the global upsurge in ethnic and sectarian conflict, policymakers have become more attuned to the role played by [light] arms in sparking and sustaining low-level warfare and have begun to consider new constraints on trade in these munitions... Although heavy weapons sometimes play a role, most of the day-to-day fighting is performed by irregular forces armed only with rifles, grenades, machine guns, light mortars, and other 'man-portable' munitions."

The New Arms Race: Light Weapons and International Security

MICHAEL T. KLARE

For most of the past 50 years, analysts and policymakers have largely ignored the role of small arms and other light weapons in international security affairs, considering them too insignificant to have an impact on the global balance of power or the outcome of major conflicts. Nuclear weapons, ballistic missiles, and major conventional weapons (tanks, heavy artillery, jet planes) are assumed to be all that matter when calculating the strength of potential belligerents. As a result, international efforts to reduce global weapons stockpiles and to curb the trade in arms have been focused almost exclusively on major weapons systems. At no point since World War II have international policymakers met to consider curbs on trade in light weapons, or to restrict their production.

Recently, world leaders have begun to take a fresh interest in small arms and light weapons. Because of the global upsurge in ethnic and sectarian conflict, policymakers have become more attuned to the role played by such arms in sparking and sustaining low-level warfare, and have begun to consider new constraints on trade in these munitions. "I wish to concentrate on what might be called 'micro-disarmament,'" United Nations Secretary General Boutros Boutros-Ghali declared in January 1995. By that, he explained, "I mean practical disarmament in the context of the conflicts the United Nations *is actually dealing with*, and of the weapons, most of them light weapons, that are actually killing people in the hundreds of thousands" (emphasis added).

This focus on the conflicts the United Nations is "actually dealing with" represents a major shift in global priorities. During the cold war, most world leaders were understandably preoccupied with the potential threat of nuclear war or an East-West conflict in Europe. Today policymakers are more concerned about the immediate threat of ethnic and sectarian warfare. While such violence does not threaten world security in the same catastrophic manner as nuclear conflict or another major war in Europe, it could, if left unchecked, introduce severe instabilities into the international system.

This inevitably leads, as suggested by Boutros-Ghali, to a concern with small arms, land mines, and other light munitions; these are the weapons, he notes, that "are probably responsible for most of the deaths in current conflicts." This is true, for instance, of the conflicts in Afghanistan, Algeria, Angola, Bosnia, Burma, Burundi, Cambodia, Kashmir, Liberia, Rwanda, Somalia, Sri Lanka, Sudan, Tajikistan, and Zaire. Although heavy weapons sometimes play a role, most of the day-to-day fighting is performed by irregular forces armed only with rifles, grenades, machine guns, light mortars, and other "man-portable" munitions.

SMALL ARMS, GLOBAL PROBLEMS

The centrality of light weapons in contemporary warfare is especially evident in the conflicts in Liberia and Somalia. In Liberia, rival bands of guerrillas—armed, for the most part, with AK-47 assault rifles—have been fighting among themselves for

---

MICHAEL T. KLARE *is a professor of peace and world security studies at Hampshire College and director of the Five College Program in Peace and World Security Studies. He is the author of* Rogue States and Nuclear Outlaws: America's Search for a New Foreign Policy *(New York: Hill and Wang, 1995).*

> ### Light Weapons in Worldwide Circulation
>
> ASSAULT RIFLES:
> - Russian/Soviet AK-47 and its successors
> - U.S. M-16
> - German G3
> - Belgian FAL
> - Chinese Type 56 (a copy of the AK-47)
> - Israeli Galil (also a copy of the AK-47)
>
> MACHINE GUNS:
> - U.S. M-2 and M-60
> - Russian/Soviet RPK and DShK
> - German MG3
> - Belgian MAG
> - Chinese Type 67
>
> LIGHT ANTITANK WEAPONS:
> - U.S. M-20 and M-72 rocket launchers
> - U.S. Dragon and TOW antitank missiles
> - Russian/Soviet RPG-2 and RPG-7 rocket-propelled grenades (and Chinese variants, Types 56 and 69)
> - French-German MILAN antitank missiles
>
> LIGHT MORTARS:
> - Produced by many countries in a variety of calibers, including 60 mm, 81 mm, 107 mm, and 120 mm.
>
> ANTIPERSONNEL LAND MINES:
> - U.S. M-18A1 "Claymore"
> - Russian/Soviet PMN/PMN-2 & POMZ-2
> - Belgian PRB-409
> - Italian VS-50 and VS-69
> - Chinese Types 69 and 72
>
> SHOULDER-FIRED ANTI-AIRCRAFT MISSILES:
> - U.S. Stinger
> - Russian/Soviet SAM-7
> - British Blowpipe
> - Swedish RBS-70

stepped on or driven over) is a common feature of many of these conflicts. These munitions, which can cost as little as $10 apiece, are planted in roads, markets, pastures, and fields to hinder agriculture and otherwise disrupt normal life. An estimated 85 million to 110 million uncleared mines are thought to remain in the soil of some 60 nations, with the largest concentrations in Afghanistan, Angola, Cambodia, and the former Yugoslavia. Each year some 25,000 civilians are killed, wounded, or maimed by land mines, and many more are driven from their homes and fields.

There are many reasons why small arms, mines, and other light weapons figure so prominently in contemporary conflicts. The belligerents involved tend to be insurgents, ethnic separatists, brigands, and local warlords with modest resources and limited access to the international arms market. While usually able to obtain a variety of light weapons from black-market sources or through theft from government arsenals, they can rarely afford or gain access to major weapons systems. Furthermore, such forces are usually composed of ill-trained volunteers who can be equipped with simple infantry weapons but who lack the expertise to operate and maintain heavier and more sophisticated equipment.

Logistical considerations also mitigate against the acquisition of heavy weapons. Lacking access to major ports or airfields and operating largely in secrecy, these forces must rely on clandestine and often unreliable methods of supply that usually entail the use of small boats, pack animals, civilian vehicles, and light planes. These methods are suitable for delivering small arms and ammunition, but not heavy weapons. Tanks, planes, and other major weapons also require large quantities of fuel, which is not easily transported by such rudimentary methods.

The character of ethnic and sectarian warfare further reinforces the predominance of light weapons. The usual objective of armed combat between established states is the defeat and destruction of an adversary's military forces; the goal of ethnic warfare, however, is not so much victory on the battlefield as it is the slaughter or the intimidation of members of another group and their forced abandonment of homes and villages ("ethnic cleansing"). In many cases a key objective is to exact retribution from the other group for past crimes and atrocities, a task best achieved through close-up violence that typically calls for the use of handheld weapons: guns, grenades, and machetes.

While the weapons employed in these clashes are relatively light and unsophisticated, their use can

control of the country, bringing commerce to a standstill and driving an estimated 2.3 million people from their homes and villages. In Somalia, lightly armed militias have been similarly engaged, ravaging the major cities, paralyzing rural agriculture, and at one point pushing millions to the brink of starvation. In both countries, UN-sponsored peacekeeping missions have proved unable to stop the fighting or disarm the major factions.

The widespread use of antipersonnel land mines (small explosive devices that detonate when result in human carnage of horrendous proportions. The 1994 upheaval in Rwanda resulted in the deaths of as many as 1 million people and forced millions more to flee their homeland. Similarly, the fighting in Bosnia is believed to have taken the lives of 200,000 people and has produced millions of refugees.

Although the availability of arms is not in itself a cause of war, the fact that likely belligerents in internal conflicts are able to procure significant supplies of light weapons has certainly contributed to the duration and intensity of these contests. Before the outbreak of violence in Rwanda, for example, the Hutu-dominated government spent millions of dollars on rifles, grenades, machine guns, and machetes that were distributed to the army and militia forces later implicated in the systematic slaughter of Tutsi civilians. In Afghanistan, the fact that the various factions were provided with so many weapons by the two superpowers during the cold war has meant that bloody internecine warfare could continue long after Moscow and Washington discontinued their supply operations. The ready availability of light weapons has also contributed to the persistence of violence in Angola, Kashmir, Liberia, Sri Lanka, and Sudan.

The widespread diffusion of light weapons in conflict areas has also posed a significant hazard to UN peacekeeping forces sent to police cease-fires or deliver humanitarian aid. Even when the leaders of major factions have agreed to the introduction of peacekeepers, local warlords and militia chieftains have continued to fight to control their territory. Fighting persisted in Somalia long after American and Pakistani UN peacekeepers arrived in 1992, leading to periodic clashes with UN forces and, following a particularly harrowing firefight in October 1993, to the withdrawal of American forces. Skirmishes like these were also a conspicuous feature of the combat environment in Bosnia before the signing of the Dayton peace accords, and remain a major worry for the NATO forces stationed there today.

Even when formal hostilities have ceased, the diffusion of light weapons poses a continuing threat to international security. In those war-torn areas where jobs are few and the economy is in ruins, many demobilized soldiers have turned to crime to survive, often using the weapons they acquired during wartime for criminal purposes or selling them to combatants in other countries. During the 1980s, South African authorities provided thousands of guns to antigovernment guerrillas in Angola and Mozambique; these same guns, which are no longer needed for insurgent operations, are now being smuggled back into South Africa by their former owners and sold to criminal gangs. Some of the guns provided by the United States to the Nicaraguan contras have reportedly been sold to drug syndicates in Colombia.

Maiming Progress

It is no longer possible to ignore the role of small arms and light weapons in sustaining international conflict. Although efforts to address this problem are at an early stage, policymakers have begun to consider the imposition of new international constraints on light weapons trafficking. The UN, for example, has established a special commission—the Panel of Governmental Experts on Small Arms—to look into the problem, while representatives of the major industrial powers have met under the auspices of the Wassenaar Arrangement (a group set up in 1996 to devise new international controls on the spread of dangerous military technologies) to consider similar efforts. Despite growing interest, movement toward the adoption of new controls is likely to proceed slowly because of the many obstacles that must be overcome. (Only in one area—the establishment of an international ban on the production and use of antipersonnel land mines—is rapid progress possible.)

One of the greatest obstacles to progress is the lack of detailed information on the international trade in small arms and light weapons. Although various organizations, including the United States Arms Control and Disarmament Agency (ACDA) and the Stockholm International Peace Research Institute (SIPRI) have long compiled data on transfers of major weapons systems, no organization currently provides such information on light weapons. Those who want to study this topic must begin by producing new reservoirs of data on the basis of fragmentary and anecdotal evidence. Fortunately, this process is now well under way, and so it is possible to develop a rough portrait of the light weapons traffic.[1]

---

[1] Three basic sources constitute a provisional database on the topic: Jeffrey Boutwell, Michael T. Klare, and Laura W. Reed, eds., *Lethal Commerce: The Global Trade in Small Arms and Light Weapons* (Cambridge, Mass.: American Academy of Arts and Sciences, 1995); Michael Klare and David Andersen, *A Scourge of Guns: The Diffusion of Small Arms and Light Weapons in Latin America* (Washington, D.C.: Federation of American Scientists, 1996); and Jasjit Singh, ed., *Light Weapons and International Security* (New Delhi: Indian Pugwash Society and British-American Security Information Council, 1995).

SUPPLY AND DEMAND

There is no precise definition of light weapons. In general, they can be characterized as conventional weapons that can be carried by an individual soldier or by a light vehicle operating on backcountry roads. This category includes pistols and revolvers, rifles, hand grenades, machine guns, light mortars, shoulder-fired antitank and anti-aircraft missiles, and antipersonnel land mines. Anything heavier is excluded: tanks, heavy artillery, planes, ships, and large missiles, along with weapons of mass destruction.

Small arms and light weapons of the types shown in the table on page 174 can be acquired in several ways. All the major industrial powers manufacture light weapons of various types, and tend to rely on domestic production for their basic military needs. Another group of countries, including some in the third world, has undertaken the licensed manufacture of weapons originally developed by the major arms-producing states. The Belgian FAL assault rifle has been manufactured in Argentina, Australia, Austria, Brazil, Canada, India, Israel, Mexico, South Africa, and Venezuela, while the Russian/Soviet AK-47 (and its variants) has been manufactured in China, the former East Germany, Egypt, Finland, Hungary, Iraq, North Korea, Poland, Romania, and Yugoslavia. All told, about 40 countries manufacture at least some light weapons in their own factories. All other nations, and those countries that cannot satisfy all of their military requirements through domestic production, must rely on the military aid programs of the major powers or the commercial arms market.

Historically, the military aid programs of the United States and the Soviet Union were an important source of light weapons for developing nations. In addition to the major weapons supplied by the superpowers to their favored allies, both Moscow and Washington also provided vast quantities of small arms, grenades, machine guns, and other light weapons. Today, direct giveaways of light weapons are relatively rare (although the United States still supplies some surplus arms to some allies), so most developing nations must supply their needs through direct purchases on the global arms market.

Unfortunately, there are no published statistics on the annual trade in light weapons. However, the ACDA has estimated that approximately 13 percent of all international arms transfers (when measured in dollars) is comprised of small arms and ammunition. Applying this percentage to ACDA figures on the value of total world arms transfers in 1993 and 1994 would put global small arms exports at approximately $3.6 billion and $2.9 billion, respectively (in current dollars). Adding machine guns, light artillery, and antitank weapons to the small arms category would probably double these figures to some $6 billion per year, which is about one-fourth the total value of global arms transfers.

Further data on the sale of small arms and light weapons through commercial channels are simply not available. Most states do not disclose such information, and the UN Register of Conventional Arms (an annual listing of member states' arms imports and exports) covers major weapons only. However, some indication of the scope of this trade can be obtained from the information in *Jane's Infantry Weapons* on the military inventories of individual states. The FAL assault rifle is found in the inventories of 53 third world states; the Israeli Uzi submachine gun is found in 39 such states; the German G3 rifle in 43 states; and the Belgian MAG machine gun in 54 states.

For established nation-states (except those subject to UN arms embargoes), the commercial arms trade provides an ample and reliable source of small arms and light weapons. For nonstate actors, however, the global arms market is usually closed off. Most countries provide arms only to other governments, or to private agencies that employ or distribute arms with the recipient government's approval. (Such approval is sometimes given to private security firms that seek to import firearms for their own use, or to gun stores that sell imported weapons to individual citizens for hunting or self-defense.) All other groups, including insurgents, brigands, and ethnic militias, must rely on extralegal sources for their arms and ammunition.

THE OTHER ARMS MARKETS

Nonstate entities that want weapons for operations against the military forces of the state or against rival organizations can obtain arms in three ways: through theft from government stockpiles; through purchases on the international black market; and through ties to government agencies or expatriate communities in other countries.

Theft is an important source of arms for insurgents and ethnic militias in most countries, especially in the early stages of conflict. The fledgling armies of Croatia and Slovenia were largely equipped with weapons that had been "liberated" from Yugoslav government arsenals. Weapons seized from dead or captured soldiers also figure prominently in the arms inventories of many insurgent forces. Thus the mujahideen of Afghanistan relied largely on captured Soviet weapons until they began receiving arms in large quantities from outside sources. Many of the guerrilla groups in Latin America have long operated in a similar fashion.

For those insurgent and militia groups with access to hard currency or negotiable commodities (such as diamonds, drugs, and ivory), a large variety of light weapons can be procured on the international black market. This market is composed of private dealers who acquire weapons from corrupt military officials or surplus government stockpiles and ship them through circuitous routes—usually passing through a number of transit points known for their lax customs controls—to obscure ports or airstrips where they can be surreptitiously delivered to the insurgents' representatives. Transactions of this sort have become a prominent feature of the global arms traffic, supplying belligerents around the world. The various factions in Bosnia, for example, reportedly obtained billions of dollars in arms through such channels between 1993 and 1995. Many other groups, including the drug cartels in Colombia and the guerrilla groups in Liberia, have also obtained arms in this fashion.

Finally, insurgents and ethnic militias can turn to sympathetic government officials or expatriate communities in other countries for weapons (or for the funds to procure them from black-market suppliers). During the cold war, both the United States and the Soviet Union—usually operating through intelligence agencies like the CIA and the KGB—supplied weapons to insurgent groups in countries ruled by governments allied with the opposing superpower. At the onset of the 1975 war in Angola, for example, the CIA provided anticommunist insurgents with 20,900 rifles, 41,900 anti-tank rockets, and 622 mortars; later, during the Reagan administration, the United States supplied even larger quantities of arms to the contras in Nicaragua and the mujahideen in Afghanistan. The KGB also supplied insurgent groups with arms of these types, often routing them through friendly countries such as Cuba and Vietnam.

Superpower intervention has largely ceased with the end of the cold war, but other nations are thought to be engaged in similar activities. The Inter-Services Intelligence (ISI) agency of Pakistan is believed to be aiding in the covert delivery of arms to antigovernment insurgents in Kashmir. Likewise, the government of Iran has been accused of supplying arms to Kurdish separatists in Turkey, while Burkina Faso has been charged with aiding some of the guerrilla factions in Liberia. Expatriate groups have also been known to supply arms to associated groups in their country of origin. Americans of Irish descent have smuggled arms to the Irish Republican Army in Northern Ireland, while Tamil expatriates in Canada, Europe, and India are thought to be sending arms (or the funds to procure them) to the Tamil Tigers in Sri Lanka.

A DUAL STRATEGY FOR ARMS CONTROL

What are the implications of all this for the development of new international restraints on light weapons trafficking? We are dealing with two separate, if related, phenomena: the overt, legal transfer of arms to states and state-sanctioned agencies, and the largely covert, illicit transfer of arms to insurgents, ethnic militias, and other nonstate entities. While there is obviously some overlap between the two systems of trade, it is probably not feasible to deal with both through a single set of controls.

Any effort to control the light weapons trade between established states (or their constituent parts) will run into the problem that most government leaders believe the acquisition of such weaponry is essential to the preservation of their sovereignty and therefore sanctioned by the United Nations charter. Many states are also engaged in the sale of light weapons and would resist any new constraints on their commercial activities. It is unlikely, therefore, that the world community will adopt anything resembling an outright ban on light weapons exports or even a significant reduction in such transfers.

This does not mean that progress is impossible. It should be possible to insist on some degree of international transparency in this field. At present, governments are under no obligation to make available information on their imports and exports of light weapons. By contrast, most states have agreed to supply such data on major weapons systems, for release through the UN Register of Conventional Arms. Although compiling data on transfers of small arms and light weapons would undoubtedly prove more difficult than keeping track of heavy

> *For those...with access to hard currency or negotiable commodities (such as diamonds, drugs, and ivory), a large variety of light weapons can be procured on the international black market.*

weapons (because small arms are normally transferred far more frequently, and with less government oversight, than heavy weapons), there is no technical reason why the UN register could not be extended over time to include a wider range of systems. Including light weapons in the register would enable the world community to detect any unusual or provocative activity in this area (for example, significant purchases of arms and ammunition by a government that is supposedly downsizing its military establishment in accordance with a UN-brokered peace agreement) and to respond appropriately.

The major arms suppliers could also be required to abide by certain specified human rights considerations when considering the transfer of small arms and light weapons to governments involved in violent internal conflicts. Such sales could be prohibited in the case of governments that have suspended the democratic process and employed brutal force against unarmed civilians. An obvious candidate for such action is Burma, whose military leadership has usurped national power, jailed pro-democracy activists, and fought an unrelenting military campaign against autonomy-seeking minority groups. Human rights considerations have already figured in a number of UN arms embargoes—such as that imposed on the apartheid regime in South Africa—and so it should be possible to develop comprehensive restrictions of this type.

Finally, the world community could adopt restrictions or a prohibition on the transfer of certain types of weapons that are deemed to be especially cruel or barbaric in their effects. The first target should be the trade in antipersonnel land mines. President Bill Clinton called for a worldwide ban on the production, transfer, and use of such munitions in May 1996. Many other leaders have promised to support such a measure, but more effort is needed to persuade holdout states to agree. In addition to land mines, a ban could be imposed on bullets that tumble in flight or otherwise reproduce the effects of dumdum bullets (a type of soft-nosed projectile that expands on impact and produces severe damage to the human body). Bullets of this type where outlawed by the Hague Convention of 1899, but have reappeared in other forms.

STOPPING BLACK-MARKET TRAFFIC

An entirely different approach will be needed to control the black-market traffic in arms. Since such trafficking violates, by definition, national and international norms regarding arms transfers, there is no point in trying to persuade the suppliers and recipients involved to abide by new international restraints on the munitions trade. Instead, governments should be asked to tighten their own internal controls on arms trafficking and to cooperate with other states in identifying, monitoring, and suppressing illegal gun traffickers.

As a first step, all the nations in a particular region—such as Europe or the Western Hemisphere—should agree to uniform export restrictions and establish electronic connections between their respective customs agencies to permit the instantaneous exchange of data on suspect arms transactions. These measures should prohibit the export of arms to any agency or firm not subject to government oversight in the recipient nation, and the use of transshipment points in third countries that do not adhere to the uniform standards. At the same time, the law enforcement agencies of these countries should cooperate in tracking down and prosecuting dealers found to have engaged in illicit arms transfers. Eventually these measures could be extended on a worldwide basis, making it much more difficult for would-be traffickers to circumvent government controls.

It is unrealistic, of course, to assume that these measures will prevent all unwanted and illicit arms trafficking—there are simply too many channels for determined suppliers to employ. Nor should airtight control be the goal of international action. Rather, the goal should be to so constrict the flow of weapons that potential belligerents (including nonstate actors) are discouraged from achieving their objectives through force of arms and seek instead a negotiated settlement. Such controls should also be designed to reduce the death and displacement of civilians trapped in conflict areas, and to impede the activities of terrorist and criminal organizations.

Obviously, it will not be possible to make progress so long as policymakers view the trade in small arms and light weapons as a relatively insignificant problem. Educating world leaders about the dangerous consequences of this trade in an era of intensifying ethnic and sectarian conflict is a major arms control priority. Once these consequences are widely appreciated, it should be possible for the world community to devise the necessary controls and make substantial progress in curbing this trade.

Historical Retrospectives on American Foreign Policy

American foreign policy tends to be present and future oriented. It is the present that defines the foreign policy challenges that must be met and provides policymakers with opportunities to be seized. It is in the present that policymakers struggle to pass legislation, adjust policies to available resources, and make choices against a backdrop of incomplete information and conflicting interpretations of the national interest. The legitimacy of future-oriented thinking in these circumstances is readily acknowledged. The goal is not just to meet American foreign policy goals today but also tomorrow, next year, and in the next decade. The obvious problem is that the future does not provide a concrete standard against which to evaluate policy. People are free to read what they will into the future, and the future they see will differ from person to person, depending upon such things as their views of human nature, their faith in the ability of science and technology to solve environmental and social problems, and how much importance they give to chance and accident.

It is different with the past. The past both attracts and repels us, and for that reason its place in policy deliberations is less secure. We are drawn to the past by the desire to avoid repeating its failures and the hope of duplicating its successes. We want no more Vietnams, Bosnias, or Somalias, but we do wish for another Marshall Plan. We often turn our backs to the past out of the conviction that the present and future bear little resemblance to it that history has little to teach us. Thus we run the risk of learning the wrong lessons.

The relationship of the past to the present and future affects much of the controversy over the nature of the post–cold war international system. Just how different is this system from that of the cold war or earlier ones? Can a leader such as Saddam Hussein be equated with Adolf Hitler, or is that analogy misleading and dangerous? What insights can we gain from the way the cold war competition between the United States and Soviet Union was played out? How different is the mass exodus from Cuba in 1994 from those that occurred during the cold war? Can we respond to it the same way? Should we adopt a different policy? Answering such questions is difficult, because in spite of its more concrete nature, the past can be an elusive database to work from.

One reason for this is that our understanding of the past is never complete or final. New information is constantly coming forward that requires us to rethink established truths and entertain new explanations for why an event occurred. This is especially true in the case of American foreign policy. Not only are many of the most crucial decisions made in small group settings and surrounded in secrecy, with only fragmentary information being made available through the press, but virtually the entire history of the cold war has been written from an American perspective and with American sources. As Russian archives open up, we can expect to see a new wave of cold war studies. Second, the past does not lend itself to a single interpretation. Just as with the future, different philosophical, conceptual, or strategic starting points yield different insights and lessons. Third, it is not always clear where to look for lessons. The debate over whether the United States should send troops to Bosnia produced an abundance of historical parallels. Vietnam, Beirut, Somalia, and Grenada were all cited by political commentators as the proper starting point for thinking about this policy problem.

The three readings in this unit are concerned with achieving a better understanding of the past so that American foreign policy might enjoy successes in the present and the future. The first two essays address recent foreign policy initiatives by the United States. In "Closing the Gate: The Persian Gulf War Revisited," Michael Sterner looks at the question of whether there was anything that might have been done militarily to alter the political outcome of the war.

Susan Woodward, in "Bosnia after Dayton: Year Two," examines the current situation in Bosnia in light of the goals of the Dayton Accords. She concludes that the most likely outcome is an extremely weak, fragile, and relatively unstable country.

The final reading is "Midnight Never Came," in which Mike Moore traces the back-and-forth movement of *The Bulletin of the Atomic Scientists'* "Doomsday Clock" toward midnight and the onset of a global nuclear war. His ac-

UNIT 8

count provides insight into the nature of U.S.–Soviet cold war competition and the difficulties of negotiating an end to the nuclear arms race. It also provides us with a baseline from which to judge contemporary efforts to put the nuclear genie back in the bottle.

Looking Ahead: Challenge Questions

Which events are more important to learn from, successes or failures? In studying the past, what should policymakers look for? List the three most important events in the cold war that policymakers should learn from.

How can we improve the ability of the government to learn from the past?

Looking back over the Clinton administration, how would you rate its ability to learn from the past?

Which post-cold war American foreign policy initiative will be most studied in the future?

Where would you place the minute hand on the Doomsday Clock today? What events would cause you to move it forward or backward?

What are the lessons of Bosnia for future American diplomatic peace initiatives?

What are the lessons of the Persian Gulf War for the future use of American military power?

Identify a major foreign policy event from each decade of the cold war that holds important lessons for the future. Justify your choices.

Article 32

> As the Persian Gulf War fades into memory, a revisionist reading of the war's aims and strategy has gained critical favor among those who see it as having been the last best hope for relieving the Middle East of Saddam Hussein. In response to this reinterpretation, Michael Sterner examines whether "there is anything the coalition did not do militarily that could have changed the political outcome of the war. To answer that we need to look not only at what coalition forces might have done, but at what the impact of those actions would likely have been in Iraq."

Closing the Gate: The Persian Gulf War Revisited

MICHAEL STERNER

As soon as it became apparent that the Persian Gulf War had not resulted in the ouster of Saddam Hussein, a host of articles, books, and other commentary began to appear second-guessing American war aims and Washington's decision to bring the war to an end. At the very least—so the argument went—the Bush administration had ended the war prematurely, allowing significant Iraqi forces to escape, which Saddam was then able to use to suppress the Shiite and Kurdish uprisings. Some critics faulted Washington's war goals from the outset, saying it should have pressed the war to the point of unconditional Iraqi surrender, or at least have occupied Iraqi territory to impose much tougher terms on Baghdad.

All this commentary has been generated by the disparity between one of the most complete battlefield victories in military history and the problematic political results that have been the war's legacy. Six years after the war's end, Saddam's repressive regime is still in power; the contest of wills between the Iraqi leader and the coalition victors has not ended but has merely been transferred to the UN Security Council; regional security has been only half achieved, requiring the United States to maintain large forces for rapid deployment to the Gulf; and Washington is faced with the dilemma that economic sanctions are hurting the Iraqi people more than Saddam's regime. It is not surprising that so many have rushed in to explain this discordant result.

Much of the commentary is more a cri de coeur than a systematic analysis. *New York Times* columnist William Safire declared on January 13, 1992, that George Bush had "snatched defeat from the jaws of victory." In a January 9, 1996, interview on the PBS program *Frontline,* former British Prime Minister Margaret Thatcher came up with the epigrammatic but hardly profound comment that "There is the aggressor, Saddam Hussein, still in power. There is the president of the United States, no longer in power. I wonder who won?" Even as good an analyst as Jeffrey Record clearly goes over the top when he says in his 1993 book, *Hollow Victory,* that the Gulf War "was a magnificent military victory barren of any significant diplomatic gains."

The initial postwar debate has been revived

MICHAEL STERNER *is a retired diplomat who served as ambassador to the United Arab Emirates and as deputy assistant secretary of state for Near East and South Asian affairs.*

recently by the publication in 1995 of *The General's War*, by Michael Gordon and Bernard Trainor, and by the 1995 memoirs of former Chairman of the Joint Chiefs of Staff General Colin Powell and Arab Forces commander General Khaled bin Sultan. Gordon, a *New York Times* correspondent, and Trainor, a retired Marine general now at Harvard, offer one of the best accounts of the war. They do not waste time on the we-should-have-marched-to-Baghdad argument—recognizing that this option was never in the cards—but make two judgments that deserve serious consideration: that the United States ended the war too soon, allowing much of the Iraqi Republican Guard to escape with its heavy equipment; and that, as they noted in a February 1, 1995, *Charlie Rose Show* interview on PBS, American willingness to withdraw unconditionally from Iraqi territory deprived the United States of "the opportunity to create the conditions to overthrow Saddam Hussein."

Yet Gordon and Trainor, along with most other critics of the way the war ended, rather breezily leave it at that, failing to explain how, in bringing the war to an "optimal" military close, conditions would have been created that would have led to the overthrow of Saddam. The crucial question is whether there is anything the coalition did not do militarily that could have changed the political outcome of the war. To answer that we need to look not only at what coalition forces might have done, but at what the impact of those actions would likely have been in Iraq.

SETTING WAR AIMS

Iraq's invasion of Kuwait on the morning of August 2, 1990, took Arab and Western governments by surprise. The first concern in Western capitals was to erect a defense of Saudi Arabia against a possible continuation of Iraq's move southward. But on the day of the invasion, the UN Security Council condemned Iraq's action and demanded its unconditional withdrawal; this immediately raised the question of what the United States, as Western leader, would do to put teeth into this resolution. Pondering this, President Bush proceeded to Aspen, Colorado, for a previously scheduled conference, where he met with British Prime Minister Thatcher. Thatcher urged a tough response, but as she herself records, found Bush already disposed to be very firm.

In this respect the president appears to have been well out ahead of some of his senior advisers. Colin Powell records in *My American Journey* surprise and admiration at how quickly Bush made up his mind that Iraq would have to be ejected from Kuwait, whatever it took.[1] On August 5, Bush told reporters that "this will not stand, this aggression . . ." Three days later, in an address to the nation, the president set forth American objectives: 1) the immediate, complete, and unconditional withdrawal of Iraqi forces from Kuwait; 2) the restoration of Kuwait's legitimate government; 3) the security and stability of Saudi Arabia and the Persian Gulf; and 4) the safety and protection of Americans abroad.

Achieving the third objective could reasonably be supposed to require the destruction of Iraq's war-making capability over and above Iraq's eviction from Kuwait; nevertheless, it is notable that the statement did not contain a call for Saddam Hussein's replacement, or any other intervention in Iraqi internal affairs. This program of clearly defined and limited goals remained remarkably constant throughout the following months. Richard Haass, the administration's Middle East adviser on the National Security Council, said in a June 10, 1996, interview with this author that while it became tactically necessary for coalition forces to invade Iraqi territory to carry out a war plan that ensured Iraq's overwhelming military defeat, this did not change the political strategy. "The elimination of Saddam was a war hope but never a war aim." In his memoir, Colin Powell says that "In none of the meetings I attended was dismembering Iraq, conquering Baghdad, or changing the form of government ever seriously considered. We hoped that Saddam would not survive the coming fury. But his elimination was not a stated objective. What we hoped for, frankly, in a post-war Gulf region, was an Iraq still standing, with Saddam overthrown."

In public comments before, during, and after the war, Bush expressed the hope that the Iraqi people would overthrow Saddam Hussein, but this never became a United States policy objective. Powell, among others, regretted the tendency on the part of the president to personalize American war aims, and worried—correctly as it turned out—that it would raise expectations that might prove impossible to fulfill.

---

[1]Powell was initially very cautious about setting forth objectives that might require the use of United States military force when it was unclear whether there would be public support for it. He is quoted by Gordon and Trainor in *The General's War* as saying, at a meeting with Defense Secretary Dick Cheney on August 2, "I don't see the senior leadership taking us into armed conflict for the events of the last twenty-four hours. The American people don't want their young dying for $1.50 gallon [sic] oil . . ."

Several factors combined to solidify the decision to keep United States war aims carefully limited. Extending the war to include political objectives in Iraq would have been vigorously opposed by all of the Arab coalition members and most of the European members as well.[2] American policymakers were also aware that intervention in Iraq would have radically altered Arab public opinion about the conflict. Expelling Iraq from Kuwait had the support of a significant segment of the Arab public that would have turned against the United States had there been an attempt to invade Iraq with the purpose of installing a new government. Moreover, American sponsorship would have been a long-term political liability for a new Iraqi government.

Certainly the most compelling reason to avoid intervention in Iraqi internal affairs would have been the profoundly altered nature of the mission undertaken by the United States. Instead of a mission that could have had a clear ending (the expulsion of the Iraqis from Kuwait), the United States would have undertaken one that would have required the invasion and occupation of Iraq. This held excellent prospects of bogging down American forces for an indefinite period, without any assurance that the end result would not be a splintering of Iraq along ethnic and religious lines—which was not perceived as being in the United States interest. There would also have been the problem of seeking congressional support for a wider war; it must be remembered that the Senate approved military action for even the administration's limited war objectives by a margin of only a few votes. From the numerous memoirs and interviews since the war, it is apparent that senior United States policymakers from the president on down were aware of these considerations, and that they found them compelling.

THE 100-HOUR WAR'S END

The ground war strategy that General Norman Schwarzkopf and his planners devised called for a thrust directly north from Saudi Arabia by United States marines and Arab forces that would "fix" the Iraqi forces in Kuwait in battle, while two United States army corps, including British and French divisions, swung far to the west and north through Iraqi territory to cut off the Iraqi lines of retreat and engage Iraq's Republican Guard divisions, which were positioned just north of the Iraq-Kuwait border. The only flaw in this outstandingly successful plan was that progress in the eastern sector was so rapid that it exposed the flank of the advancing forces, causing Schwarzkopf to push forward the launching of the two western corps by nearly 24 hours. Then, as the conflict turned into an Iraqi rout, it was feared the "left hook" would not arrive in time to engage the Republican Guard divisions before most of them had been withdrawn northward across the Euphrates River.

> *"The elimination of Saddam was a war hope but never a war aim."*

Even so, after the four days of fighting between February 24 and 27, 1991, the results were overwhelmingly impressive: Kuwait City had been liberated; most of the Iraqi divisions in Kuwait had been overrun with minimal resistance; some 82,000 Iraqi soldiers had been captured; in tank battles on February 26 and 27, several of the Iraqi Republican Guard heavy divisions had been badly mauled; and United States forces were astride the main road between Basra and Baghdad, and within 25 miles of Basra itself. All this had been accomplished with an almost miraculously low allied casualty rate (260 killed, of whom 146 were American).

Although postwar interviews and memoirs have tossed the ball back and forth as to who was most anxious to end the fighting, there is no basic disagreement among the participants about how the decision was reached. According to Schwarzkopf's account, he received a call mid-afternoon February 27 from Powell, who said it was time to give thought to a cease-fire, adding that people at home were beginning to be upset by reports of unnecessary slaughter of fleeing Iraqi troops along Kuwait's "Highway of Death." (That day's *Washington Post*, for example, had carried a story with the headline, "'Like Shooting Fish in a Barrel,' US Pilots Say.") Schwarzkopf says he told Powell he would like to have another day to finish the job. "The five-day war. How's that sound?"

---

[2] In his memoir, *Desert Warrior*, General Khaled bin Sultan says, "The Syrians told me very clearly, and the Egyptians somewhat more tactfully, that they could not consider entering Iraq, nor indeed could any Arab troops including our own."

32. Closing the Gate

At 9 P.M. in Riyadh (1 P.M. EST), Schwarzkopf gave a briefing to reporters at which he said the coalition's objectives had basically been achieved. He claimed 29 Iraqi divisions had been rendered completely ineffective and, pointing to a map where the remaining Iraqi forces south of the Euphrates were located, said, "The gates are closed. There is no way out of here." Pressed on this by a reporter, Schwarzkopf said he did not mean that no one was escaping, but that the gate was closed on Iraq's "military machine."

In Washington, shortly after Schwarzkopf's briefing, a meeting of Bush and his senior advisers on the war was convened. Powell told the group about the battlefield results. There was general agreement that the war's objectives had largely been achieved, and concern was expressed that the war not be pursued to the point of needless slaughter. Powell expressed the view that the time was coming to end the war. According to Powell's account, he suggested "tomorrow" and the president said, "Why not today?" A call was placed to Schwarzkopf in Riyadh. Powell told him the president was thinking of going on the air at 9 P.M. EST (5 A.M. Riyadh time) to announce a suspension of hostilities, and asked if he had any problem with that. Schwarzkopf, after some thought, said he had none, but wanted to check with his commanders. He did so, and reports in his memoir that "nobody seemed surprised."[3]

In Washington the war council met again at 5:30 P.M. and reached a final decision: the United States would announce a "suspension of offensive combat operations" for midnight EST, or 8:00 A.M. February 28 on the battlefield. The change from the earlier time of 5:00 A.M. was evidently made entirely for PR reasons; the extra three hours allowed the administration to refer to a "100-hour war" (Schwarzkopf comments sardonically, "I had to hand it to them: they really knew how to package an historic event," but acknowledges the change made little difference on the battlefield).

The White House wanted to add the stipulation that those Iraqi forces left in the "Basra pocket" would have to abandon their equipment and walk home. When this was conveyed to Schwarzkopf, a member of his staff pointed out that it would be impossible to enforce this without keeping up allied attacks. Schwarzkopf says, "He was right, of course. There was a considerable amount of armored equipment—perhaps two divisions worth—pushed up against the pontoon bridges at Basra..." Schwarzkopf told this to Powell, still at the White House meeting, who says, "We were all taken slightly aback," but no one felt it changed the basic equation. As Powell puts it, the Iraqi army's back was broken; there was no need to fight a war of annihilation. All participants agree that no dissenting views were expressed at the meeting.[4]

National security adviser Brent Scowcroft later said in an interview that he had misgivings about ending the war prematurely, but admits he did not voice them at the time. Schwarzkopf told David Frost in an interview after the war that "frankly, my recommendation had been, you know, continue the march..." but quickly backed down when an angry Colin Powell reminded him that he had every opportunity to press this view during the February 27 discussions, but did not. (In his memoirs, Schwarzkopf says he basically agreed with the White House decision and does not mention the Frost interview.)

The CIA estimates that at the time of the suspension of hostilities Iraq had lost, to all causes, 75 percent of the tanks it had in the Kuwait Theater of Operations (KTO), more than 50 percent of its armored personnel carriers (APCs), and nearly 90 percent of its artillery. Since about half of Iraq's prewar armed forces had been in the KTO, the magnitude of this disaster can easily be judged.

Even so, the CIA estimate also notes that almost 50 percent of the Republican Guard's major combat equipment in the KTO escaped destruction and remained under Iraqi control. As the Iraqis prepared for another day of battle on February 28, the remnants of four Guard armored and infantry divisions were drawn up in defensive positions west and south of Basra in the hope of delaying the allied advance so that more Iraqi units could escape northward. There is little question that much of their equipment could have been destroyed or captured

---

[3] This does not square entirely with an interview given to Gordon and Trainor by Lieutenant General Calvin Waller, the deputy commander of allied forces in the Gulf, who said he forcefully told Schwarzkopf at the time that ending the war so soon was a mistake. It does, however, accurately reflect the view of Lieutenant General John Yeosock, the commander of the Third Army. While Yeosock had earlier told Schwarzkopf he would have preferred another day to "finish the job," when informed of the White House's decision he thought it was "a reasonable call." "If I had felt strongly otherwise, I would have fought Norm about it." Lieutenant General John Yeosock, telephone interview with author, July 1, 1996.

[4] This summary of events draws from Gordon and Trainor, the memoirs of Powell and Schwarzkopf, and Richard M. Swain, *"Lucky War": The Third Army in Desert Storm* (Ft. Leavenworth, Kans.: U.S. Army Command and General Staff College Press, 1994).

in another day of fighting. The troops and plans were in place that could have done so, and allied air power would have pounded Iraqi units trying to get across the bridges over the Shatt al Arab waterway.

But it is important to emphasize that the *total* destruction of the Guard units was never an attainable option. At least some of the Guard (probably mainly infantry units) had already been withdrawn across the Euphrates by the time hostilities had ceased. Moreover, equipment isn't everything, and was perhaps not even the most important thing for the Guard's next job, suppressing internal unrest. Gordon and Trainor point out that the Guard had saved its command headquarters units, which enabled it to quickly organize the remnants of the Guard field force into cohesive units. Even after the devastation of another day of fighting, this leadership cadre could well have been among the survivors.

Furthermore, had the Guard units defending Basra withdrawn into the built-up areas of Basra and Zubair, they would have posed a dilemma for the allies. The coalition had no intention of engaging in street-to-street fighting in Iraqi cities, a proposition that would certainly have entailed a higher rate of allied casualties, not to mention many Iraqi civilian casualties. While the allies might have been able to bottle up some Republican Guard units in Basra by cutting off all escape routes north, there would have been no way to compel them to surrender or abandon their equipment without a prolonged blockade.

The Talks at Safwan

American handling of the cease-fire talks that took place under a tent at Safwan on March 3, 1991, has added further fuel to the revisionist charge that the allies "gave away" the peace. In his memoir, Schwarzkopf, who conducted the talks for the coalition, says he regrets his decision to allow the Iraqis to fly armed helicopters when the Iraqis said they needed these flights because of the damage done to their transportation system. To be fair to Schwarzkopf, most of this criticism was made later when the role that Iraqi helicopter gunships played in the suppression of the uprisings in the south became known. Once the decision had been reached to end the fighting, Schwarzkopf believed his job was to get allied prisoners of war back, establish clear cease-fire lines to avoid further clashes with the Iraqis, and begin as soon as possible to evacuate American soldiers for their triumphant welcome back home. Understandably, he would have felt that if anything beyond this had been required,

it was up to Washington to give him instructions. But beyond receiving approval for his own suggested military agenda, Schwarzkopf received no instructions from Washington to use the United States position on the battlefield as leverage to support political objectives in the postwar situation.

It is thus unrealistic to blame Schwarzkopf for having assured the Iraqis prematurely of American willingness to evacuate Iraqi territory. This was an important point for the Iraqis, and had it not been granted the implementation of other conditions of the cease-fire that were important to the allies would have been complicated. What, exactly, could the allies have achieved by continuing to occupy Iraqi territory? United States willingness to withdraw could not have been used as leverage to prevent Baghdad from suppressing the southern Shiite and northern Kurdish uprisings; Saddam would have waited the United States out, especially when he sensed that above all Washington wanted to bring American troops home as soon as possible.

The uprisings had no chance when they failed to spread to Baghdad and the central Sunni towns, the political nerve center of the country.

The Kurdish and Shiite Uprisings

The first incidents of rebellion in Iraq took place in the southern Sunni towns of Abu'l Khasib and Zubair immediately after the suspension of hostilities. They were touched off by disaffected and angry Iraqi troops straggling northward from the battlefield. Gunshots, and in some cases tank rounds, were fired at posters of Saddam; these incidents quickly generated more widespread demonstrations on the part of the civilian population. The uprising spread rapidly to other cities and towns in the south: Basra on March 1; Suk al-Shuyukh on March 2; Nassiriya, Najaf, and Kufa on March 4; Kerbala on March 7.

The best analysis of the uprisings is an article in the May–June 1992 issue of *Middle East Report* by Falah Abd al-Jabar, a London-based Iraqi journalist with good connections to the Iraqi opposition, who had also talked with participants in the uprisings. Abd al-Jabar writes that "a detailed account of what happened in each city is impossible, but reports in various outlawed Iraqi publications speak of a series of events remarkably similar in every case. Masses would gather in the streets to denounce Saddam Hussein and Ba'thi rule, then march to seize the mayor's office, the Ba'th Party headquarters, the secret police (mukhabarat) building, the prison and the city's garrison (if there was one). People shot as they went at every poster or wall relief of the dictator. As the cities came under rebel control, the insurgents cleaned out Ba'thists and mukhabarat."[5]

But, beyond these outbursts of rage at the apparatus of state control, the uprisings seemed to go nowhere. Although rebels were in control of these towns for several days, their leadership was fragmented and ineffective. Refugees fleeing south continued to report "chaotic conditions" in the towns under rebel control. No effort appears to have been made to restore order and organize a defense against the suppression that was inevitably to come. There was no evident communication between the rebel leadership in the various towns (ironically the air war's devastation of the Iraqi communications system made this even more difficult) and no apparent effort to convey what was happening in the south to the segments of the Baghdad population that might also have been ready to revolt.

As Abd al-Jabar points out, the revolt in the south was at a critical disadvantage. "First, it was close to the front lines where Republican Guard units were still stationed. Second, while the conscripted military was ripe for rebellion, it was politically immature. And thirdly, the Islamists, in the euphoria of apparent early success, joined in and raised a disastrous slogan: Ja'fari [Shiite] rule." Abd al-Jabar also notes that the Iraqi political opposition was surprised by the uprisings and totally unprepared to offer leadership.

The sectarian aspect was probably the most critical factor. Iraqi Shia who had fled to Iran during the Iraq-Iran War began to come back across the border, some displaying pictures of the Ayatollah Ruhollah Khomeini and Iraqi opposition figure Muhammad Bakr al-Hakim, who had organized the "Supreme Assembly of the Islamic Revolution in Iraq" in 1982 and was now based in Iran. Iran's behavior during the crisis was in fact quite cautious, and the role of the Iraqi exiles was limited—they did not start the uprisings, nor were they the majority element—but their attempt to co-opt the revolt in the name of Islam was enough to give the rebellion a sectarian character. This undermined the appeal of the uprising in the politically important central Sunni-dominated part of the country and, as Abd al-Jabar says, "provided an opportunity for Saddam to garner domestic support and regain implicit if undeclared international support." The sectarian aspect was underscored when uprisings began in the Kurdish region a few days later.

Meanwhile, the Iraqi military command reorganized the surviving elements of the Republican Guard and used them to restore control in the south. By all accounts they went at this with a vengeance. A Jordanian photographer reported seeing Guard tanks in the streets of Basra on March 4 "destroying everything in front of them." Reprisals were swift and brutal. Refugees reported fierce fighting for several days, but the tide turned rapidly. By March 7 loyalist troops were reported to be in control of Basra; after heavy shelling by government forces the rebellion was quelled in Kerbala on March 12 and in Najaf the next day. A further break for Saddam was that the rebellion in the Kurdish areas did not begin until after suppression of the southern revolt was well under way (the first reports of unrest in the north appeared in the international press March 7). While reinforcements in the form of two Guard brigades (a force of about 7,500 men) were sent from the northern part of the country and apparently participated in the sieges of Kerbala and Najaf, the basic job of suppression was performed by Republican Guard troops that had been in the Kuwait theater during the Gulf War. According to one analyst, the Iraqi command succeeded in putting together, out of the remnants of the Gulf War forces, about five effective divisions with some 50,000 to 60,000 troops.[6]

The uprisings had no chance when they failed to

---

[5] The phrase "cleaned out" should not be misunderstood; hundreds of government security and Baath Party personnel were killed in the fighting or executed by the rebels after summary trials in the cities they took over.

[6] Roland Danreuther, *The Gulf Conflict: A Political and Strategic Analysis*, Adelphi Paper no. 264 (London: Institute for International and Strategic Studies, 1991–1992).

spread to Baghdad and the central Sunni towns, the political nerve center of the country. Although Teheran radio broadcast reports of massive demonstrations in Baghdad, there has never been independent confirmation that any disturbances took place there.

The uprising in the south posed an uncomfortable dilemma for the United States. Washington did not want to appear to be standing by with folded arms as Saddam put down the rebellion with ruthless efficiency; at the same time, the administration was determined not to be sucked back into military involvement in Iraq. As Lawrence Freedman and Efraim Karsh have pointed out in their 1992 study, *The Gulf Conflict,* Saddam was astute in the days right after the war in accepting without dispute the immediate postwar Security Council resolutions and in scrupulously observing the terms of the cease-fire, thus reinforcing the coalition powers' disposition to call it a mission accomplished and go home.

Also reinforcing the tendency toward nonintervention was the sketchiness of the intelligence available to Washington. No one really knew who the leaders of the uprisings were, how much support they had, or what the Iranian role was. Richard Haass says policymakers were concerned about the reports of Iranian involvement and the "dismemberment of Iraq; we didn't want to see an Islamic Republic established in the south." Colin Powell goes further in saying, "Nor, frankly, was their [the rebels] success a goal of our policy," and he indicates his agreement with a telegram by Charles Freeman, the American ambassador in Saudi Arabia at the time, which said, "It is not in our interest to destroy Iraq or weaken it to the point that Iran and/or Syria are not constrained by it." Much of the retrospective commentary has been clothed in these geopolitical terms, but the most powerful considerations at the time were a strong bias against becoming re-engaged with Iraq, no matter what the perceived benefits, and a very unclear picture as to what any form of intervention could accomplish. The result was an embarrassing two weeks of belligerent warnings to the Iraqis accompanied by determined inactivity.

Was there anything the United States could have done to help the rebels? It certainly could have used its airpower to suppress the helicopter gunships. But, undeniably effective as the helicopters were in helping to quell the rebellion, their absence would probably not have made the difference between failure and success for the uprisings. The problem for the United States and its allies was that, having decided that they were not prepared to commit ground forces to establish, if necessary, a protectorate for the south, any half-measures raised the question, "How far do we go if the last half-measure fails? And what does a failed intervention do to allied interests in the region?" The Bay of Pigs experience certainly comes to mind as a cautionary precedent.

TWENTY-FOUR HOURS IN THE BALANCE

Compared with the meticulous planning that characterized preparations for the Persian Gulf War—especially the decision to concentrate overwhelming force to make sure the allied victory was a complete one—United States decision making to end the war had a decidedly ad hoc quality to it. Some allowance must be made for the "fog of war"—in particular the difficulty of getting timely and accurate battlefield damage assessments—and the surprising rapidity of the Iraqi collapse. Even so, once the main objective of liberating Kuwait had been achieved, Washington decision makers seemed to lose interest in the information that was available about the condition of the Iraqi army. Instead, they were preoccupied with the adverse publicity of the "Highway of Death" media reports, and with an overwhelming sense of relief that such a brilliant military victory had been achieved at so little cost.[7] Why press one's luck with another day of fighting? The mood at the political level was reinforced by the military high command's determination to make this war turn out differently from the Vietnam experience, with its ill-defined objectives, incremental reinforcements, and waning public support. In this atmosphere, even the news that the gate wasn't really closed on the Republican Guard was brushed aside.

One must respect the enormous responsibility that any president bears in making a decision that would add even a few names to those that were already on the allied casualty list, and it is certainly to the credit of George Bush and Colin Powell that they were thinking humanely about Iraqi casualties as well. It is also true that the stated objectives of the war were achieved by the morning of February 28. We can accept that the ouster of Saddam

---

[7]President Bush has stressed the adverse publicity aspect in postwar statements, most recently, for example, in an article written for the German newspaper *Welt am Sonntag* (Hamburg) on September 22, 1996: "If we had continued the war one more day, just to destroy more tanks and to kill more pitiful soldiers retreating on the highway toward Basra with hands raised, public opinion would have immediately turned against the coalition."

Hussein was indeed only a "war hope" and not a war aim.

But Bush had voiced hope of Saddam's ouster often enough, and any thought given to the postwar situation would have concluded that the survival of the Saddam regime would make the American objective of regional stability far more difficult to achieve. Policymakers at the time could not have known that a rebellion in the southern cities was about to break out. But from their own postwar testimony they were hoping for a coup of some sort, probably from within the armed forces. Recognizing the role the Republican Guard played in supporting the regime, it would have been logical to make sure maximum damage had been inflicted on the Guard. This, indeed, had been Powell's and Schwarzkopf's objective in planning the war from the beginning. From what policymakers knew at the time, continuing the war for another 24 hours to achieve that objective would have made sense. It was in part the universal conviction in Washington that no political leader could survive the catastrophe that had been inflicted on Saddam that made them casual about relating military results to Iraq's internal political situation.

But, from what we now know about the uprising that did take place, and about the internal situation in Iraq, it is hard to make the case that another day of fighting would have made the difference between Saddam's survival and ouster. No doubt the task of suppression would have taken somewhat longer if the regime had been deprived of the use of heavy armor and helicopters; but the ultimate outcome of a battle between battered but still disciplined troops and a rebellion that was disorganized and lacking in overall leadership or any plan of action beyond taking revenge on local officials was never in doubt. As Defense Intelligence Agency historian Brian Shellum put it in an interview, well-led soldiers with rifles in trucks—and Saddam had plenty of those—would have been enough in the end to do the job. And as another analyst has written—and this is at the heart of the matter—what Saddam had to do in the ashes of defeat was to maintain the nerve of the inner ruling group,[8] and he managed to do it.

[8] Danreuther, op. cit., p. 63.

> "The most likely compromise between the current reality in Bosnia and the goal of Dayton is an extremely weak, fragile, and relatively unstable country—a country in name and international recognition only without a central capacity to manage trade and finance, one that might continue to demand external assistance and protection for a long time."

Bosnia after Dayton: Year Two

Susan L. Woodward

The Dayton accord of November 21, 1995, to end the nearly four years of war in Bosnia and Herzegovina was a turning point: in the most violent and disruptive war in Europe in 50 years; in a Balkan crisis that could still destabilize the most geostrategically sensitive area of the continent; and in American leadership in the post–cold war era. Dayton established a "general framework agreement for peace" intended to consolidate the cease-fire signed October 10, 1995; it is also designed to set the conditions for a sustainable peace with international assistance and ensure a united, sovereign, and viable Bosnia and Herzegovina.

When the NATO-led force to implement the accord (IFOR) took over command from the UN Protection Force (UNPROFOR) on December 20, 1995, scholars of peace settlements emphasized that the Dayton accord's success would depend on international commitment to its implementation. The record of the first year adds two more lessons: that the terms of the accord also matter to the outcome, and that the outside powers in charge of implementation (American and European organizations primarily) can create difficulties of their own if they are not prepared.

Much has been accomplished. The spectacular success of IFOR in separating the warring parties, demobilizing armies, and removing police checkpoints has stopped the fighting. Prisoners of war have been exchanged, and confidence-building measures among the armies of the three warring parties operate well. Elections at the national, entity, and cantonal levels took place on schedule on September 14, 1996, with minimal violence. Bosnia had joined the IMF and the World Bank before the elections, and aid for economic reconstruction had begun to flow by June. No one visiting Bosnia and Herzegovina in the summer of 1996 could fail to sense the change in mood since IFOR's arrival: the tentative hopefulness, the slow improvement in physical conditions, the willingness to admit a longing to see close relatives and friends on the other side of military confrontation lines, and the nearly universal desire for a job and normal life.

Nonetheless, the results of the September elections were disheartening to many. Far from providing a smooth transition and easy exit for IFOR, the elections predictably gave a democratic stamp of approval to the three nationalist parties that had waged the war. Irregularities in voter lists, accusations that conditions for a free and fair election did not exist, and fears of violence led the Organization for Security and Cooperation in Europe (OSCE) mission to postpone municipal elections indefinitely. The three ruling parties have continued their prewar and wartime policies of seeking total party control

---

SUSAN L. WOODWARD *is a senior fellow in the Foreign Policy Studies program at the Brookings Institution. She is the author of* Balkan Tragedy: Chaos and Dissolution after the Cold War *(Washington, D.C.: Brookings Institution Press, 1995) and* Socialist Unemployment: The Political Economy of Yugoslavia, 1945-1990 *(Princeton, N.J.: Princeton University Press, 1995). In 1994 she served as head of the analysis and assessment unit in the office of the special representative to the* UN *secretary general for the former Yugoslavia in Zagreb.*

within their own community, pursuing their definition of national political and economic interests in all encounters, and collaborating with each other on a division-of-spoils principle by competing for party control of specific ministries and jurisdictions while locking competitors out.

The tight and inflexible deadlines set to allow American soldiers to leave in 12 months, and the lack of organization and funding for the civilian operation until late spring, did little to counteract the human and physical forces working for separation. The resources of the international intervention—territorial demarcations, humanitarian aid, economic assistance, electoral laws, government ministries, and population resettlements—increased the ruling parties' advantages over opposition parties. Whether one looks at communication, the settlement of refugees and displaced persons, or political power, the goal of a multiethnic, unified Bosnia was further from realization than at the time of the Dayton signing.

Despite a painfully long wait for American commitment, consensus that the departure of NATO forces without a follow-on force would see an almost immediate resumption of the war was taken to heart. On December 20, 1996, the 55,000-person IFOR handed over command to a Stabilization Force (SFOR) of 31,000 to be deployed for another 18 months under United States army General William Crouch. It plans to downsize after 12 months to a much smaller Deterrence Force (DFOR).[1] The major powers have recognized that their own lack of coordination and preparation for civilian tasks has contributed substantially to slowing the pace of the civilian aspects of the accord and allowed the parties to play one international organization or foreign power off against another. The second annual conference on civilian implementation, held in London on December 4 and 5, 1996, aimed to improve coordination under the authority of the Office of the High Representative, but not to hand it any power, and to improve enforcement through assertive, coordinated use of economic conditionality against local parties that do not comply.

Will a commitment to maintain a military presence for 18 more months, improved coordination on the civilian side, and greater willingness to enforce the accord lead to success? Already United States officials have quietly shifted to more modest goals of preventing a resumption of war but leaving the political outcome to the parties themselves. Their European allies have long given priority to regional stability, although for some countries, such as Italy or Germany, this requires a certain political outcome in Bosnia. Officials on both sides of the Atlantic, however, remain convinced (or is it hopeful?) that the *process* of implementing the Dayton accord will work.

SILENT OCCUPATION

The peace process in Bosnia and Herzegovina is a silent occupation. Both military and civilian officials repeat almost daily that peace will not come to Bosnia unless the parties want it, and that the international community is there only to assist the parties in implementing their agreement. Nonetheless, the process is strictly governed by the document negotiated at Dayton, Ohio, and by the instructions and vigilant oversight of its international implementers.

For the three warring parties, the [Dayton] accord is only a truce...

The Dayton accord is a shopping list of compromises drawn up by the negotiators, then bargained and revised by one representative of the three warring parties (President Alija Izetbegovic) and the presidents of neighboring Croatia and Serbia, representing the other two Bosnian parties. A set of 11 annexes commits the outside powers and local parties to specific tasks for its realization. Its virtue is to legitimize an international military intervention force and civilian administration—and above all American troops—with consent, leaving intact international norms of sovereignty.

But that pledge of consent and cooperation was given by only one of the three warring parties' leaders—President Izetbegovic, leader of the Bosnian Muslims (now preferring the label Bosniac), whom the negotiators took to represent the whole of a sovereign Bosnia. The Bosnian Croat and Bosnian Serb delegations refused to sign the accord. American negotiators looked instead to Croatian President Franjo Tudjman and Serbian President Slobodan Milosevic, as imputed patrons and suppliers of political protection and military support to their Bosnian conationals, to ensure the cooperation of their Bosnian counterparts, and thus to signal that sovereignty cannot be divided or shared. For the three warring parties, the accord is only a truce while they continue to pursue their wartime goals by other means.

---

[1] SFOR includes 8,500 American soldiers on the ground; the 13,500 soldiers who will be part of DFOR will include 5,500 Americans.

Behind the commitment to a united and sovereign Bosnia, however, lies a complex agreement that is structured around two separate cease-fires, prescribing four competing and only partial strategies for peace, and containing no overall conception of a final political outcome. The kernel of the Dayton accord is the Washington Agreement of March 1994 between the Bosniacs of the Party of Democratic Action (SDA) and the Bosnian Croats' Party of Croatian Democratic Union (HDZ) to cease hostilities and form a federation. Dayton extends this agreement to the remaining territory of Bosnia, recognizing Serb areas as a separate entity, Republika Srpska. The state of Bosnia and Herzegovina is comprised of these two constitutional entities—the Bosniac-Bosnian Croat federation and the Serb Republic. These two bilateral agreements are, in fact, on separate tracks, the first having begun in March 1994 and the second after the formal signing of the Dayton accord in Paris on December 14, 1995, with different dynamics and separate international tutelage.

No Coherent Strategy for Peace

The lists of tasks in the Dayton accord do not form a coherent strategy for peace but four implicit and partial strategies that are in conflict. First, implementation of the two cease-fires follows the logic of classic peacekeeping. Vast global experience with ending civil wars demonstrates that no matter how much parties to armed conflict desire peace and behave in a conciliatory fashion toward their former enemies, there is a vulnerable transition period between war and peace when neither side can trust the other. The belligerents need outside parties who are willing to provide a psychological bridge until individuals begin to believe that the war is over and reorient their behavior toward peace and reconciliation.

The first stage of such assistance is from foreign military personnel who oversee the separation of military forces, their demobilization, the restoration of freedom of movement for civilians, and the transfer of security functions to civilian police. The next step is economic aid and reconstruction to provide demobilized soldiers opportunities to work while international monitoring of human rights and civilian police forces continues to provide psychological security as the trust necessary to a political settlement is rebuilt.

The specific tasks of IFOR were limited to the second of the two cease-fire agreements and this first stage of peace: to separate the warring parties along a zone of separation between the Bosniac-Croat Federation and the Serb Republic called the inter-entity boundary line (IEBL); oversee the transfer of political authority between the two Bosnian entities where the front line of October 1995 and the IEBL drawn at Dayton did not coincide; help the parties negotiate hundreds of minor adjustments in that IEBL; and monitor compliance and subsequent confidence-building measures among the three armies.

The political character of these two cease-fires is different, however. The purpose of the federation for its patrons, Washington and Bonn, was to end the fighting between Bosnian Croats and Bosnian Muslims (which, at the time of the Washington Agreement, was especially vicious in central Bosnia) by reviving their anti-Serb alliance of October 1991–October 1992 and redirecting their military forces in common action against the Bosnian Serbs. The Dayton agreement preserves this attitude. Diplomatic attention, economic aid, and technical assistance have been largely directed to the federation to transform it from a tactical wartime alliance into a real federation. Economic sanctions remained on the Bosnian Serbs until they had demonstrated their cooperation with the cease-fire through its full 120 days of implementation in March 1996. World Bank aid focused solely on the federation until summer; by year's end, 98.7 percent of all public assistance had gone to the federation, with only 1.3 percent to the Serb Republic. No IFOR military assets were deployed along the Croat-Muslim confrontation line, which is not even recognized by the Dayton accord. American principals still perceive the greatest danger to the Bosnian state to be the Bosnian Serb's military capacity, and an overriding purpose of the federation and the Dayton accord was to create a military balance to deter renewed military expansion by Bosnian Serbs.

This attitude toward the Bosnian Serbs, American theories of war termination, and the view of the Clinton administration that the war was external aggression made possible by a military asymmetry (especially of heavy weaponry) yield a second strategy that is not fully compatible with the peace-keeping mission of IFOR/SFOR troops. This strategy says that the Dayton cease-fire will not become a sustainable peace until there is a military balance between the two entities and the Bosnian government has the capacity for self-defense. Annex 1-B on "military stabilization" contains elements of arms control demanded by Europeans at Dayton, but it is premised on the prior, bilateral military balance.[2]

Stabilization—a primary goal of the SFOR mission in 1997—began with the staged lifting of the arms embargo on the Bosnian government (light weapons after three months, and heavy weapons and aircraft after six) and a commitment by American negotiators at Dayton to "train and equip" a Bosnian army (a united army of the federation, not a pan-Bosnian army) able to defend against Bosnian Serbs. The signatures of Presidents Milosevic and Tudjman are meant to guarantee that they have abandoned plans to partition Bosnia between them and to guarantee Bosnian sovereignty within its prewar republican borders. In October 1996 a separate agreement was signed, under French auspices, on mutual recognition between Izetbegovic and Milosevic.

More significant is the informal guarantee implied in the American military and diplomatic presence. Europeans focus instead on a regional arms control regime, negotiated at Vienna on the treaty on Conventional Forces in Europe principles of transparency, cooperation, and stable force levels for Bosnia, Croatia, and Yugoslavia, and between the parties within Bosnia and Herzegovina, and on a ratio of forces agreed at Dayton based on population (5:2:2 for Yugoslavia, Croatia, and Bosnia, and 2:1 for the federation and the Serb Republic). An important monitoring task for SFOR in 1997, this regime requires some armies (particularly in Yugoslavia and the Serb Republic) to cut their holdings of heavy weapons (tanks, artillery, combat aircraft and vehicles, attack helicopters) while permitting others to build up.[3]

Although Dayton is explicitly a negotiated agreement and not a victors' justice, some of the accord's tasks also reflect a moral indictment and political judgment on war guilt. This aspect, a demand for justice, represents in part the broader foreign policy goals and position of the Clinton administration to deter rogue states (as it labels Serbia) and serious violations of international humanitarian law in the future, and in part a set of conditions for signing the accord made by President Izetbegovic. For Izetbegovic, the Dayton accord is not a just peace, and without justice, there will be no peace. In the words of the negotiators, the accord "takes sides" politically with Izetbegovic's party, the SDA, on the argument that his constituency, the Bosnian Muslims, was the primary victim of aggression and genocide and that he represents the political value of multiethnic cooperation.

This third strategy has two separate elements. One assumes that without a sense of justice, there will be no end to the cycles of retribution and revenge. Bosnian citizens must be persuaded that there is a universal standard the international community is willing to enforce, however belatedly; Muslims must feel vindicated; and Serbs must have the indictment of collective guilt removed by holding individual political and military leaders responsible for the war. "Ethnic cleansing" must therefore be reversed, giving all persons the right to return to their prewar homes or receive compensation.

> *For Izetbegovic, the Dayton accord is not a just peace, and without justice, there will be no peace.*

The International Criminal Tribunal for the former Yugoslavia, set up at The Hague in 1994, will judge serious violations of international humanitarian law in addition to improving the institutional capacity and obligation of the international community to intervene in the future. Those indicted by the tribunal are prohibited from running for or holding public office, and a conditionality clause bars any community not cooperating with the tribunal from receiving economic aid. All members of the international force are prohibited from contact with those who have been indicted and are obliged to arrest and hand over to the tribunal any they encounter. Congressional legislation prohibits American economic assistance to any community that does not cooperate with the tribunal (which is interpreted to mean the entire Serb Republic as long as Bosnian Serb leaders Radovan Karadzic and General Ratko Mladic are not at The Hague) and to projects that do not promote multiethnic cooperation.

The other element of the just peace strategy is a political process aimed at removing radical

---

[2] American diplomats attribute the October 1995 cease-fire and the Dayton agreement to the success of this approach: creating a military balance between the Serbs and the federation by encouraging joint operations between the Bosnian government army and the Croat Defense Council and looking the other way at arms deliveries to the federation; nurturing military cooperation between Bosnia and a Croatia that had received outside assistance in equipping and training its army; and using NATO to bomb Bosnian Serb military targets.

[3] By basing the ratios on population, and not on economic capacity, the burden of defense expenditures may become a serious limit on growth; reductions in military manpower are not mentioned, which suggests an additional reason for concern about economic burden; and the wisdom of adding offensive combat equipment that none of the three parties currently holds is questionable.

nationalists and freeing the vast majority of innocent civilians to reconnect and reconcile. In the American version of this strategy, the removal from any influence and power of Karadzic and Mladic through their arrest would enable more moderate leaders to win in elections and lead the Bosnian Serbs on a path toward reintegration. The September elections were thus to be an essential step in completing the defeat of Karadzic's party, a defeat that had begun with the Croatian military offensives and NATO bombing campaign of the summer of 1995, and Milosevic's concessions on territory made at Dayton.

The Bosnian government version, presented at Dayton by then-Foreign Minister Mohamed Sacirbey, is to counteract the concessions it made to obtain American military support for Bosnian sovereignty—accepting the right of Bosnian Serbs to self-governance within their 49 percent of Bosnian territory (the Serb Republic) and relinquishing military plans for further territorial acquisitions—with a political strategy to regain control over the entire territory of Bosnia and Herzegovina. This would begin with the immediate "liberation" of Sarajevo and continue with the right of all Bosnian citizens to return to their prewar homes and vote in their localities of residence in 1991.[4] Thus, while international actors remove radical Serb nationalists from above, the right of all displaced persons and refugees to vote in their home locality of 1991 and the international commitment to monitor human rights and supervise elections would initiate a process from below that ensnares Serb politicians in a maze of human rights obligations and changes the social composition in favor of voters who will be loyal to Sarajevo. In the long run, majoritarian principles would win out in both the federation and the Serb Republic.

ECONOMIC REVIVAL

National elections had an additional purpose for the international force: to enable IFOR to exit Bosnia. Elections would create a government (the "common institutions" of the two entities) able to provide civilian security and restore normal life before the staged withdrawal began, and the military balance created by a trained and equipped federation army would deter a new war. Essential to this process of normalization, however, is a fourth element of peacebuilding: the strategy Americans liken to the Marshall Plan.

There is a widespread recognition in the United States government and among Europeans that a devastated economy, destroyed infrastructure, and demobilized soldiers without a chance of employment provide miserable prospects for peace. Economic revival following close on the heels of a cease-fire can reincorporate demobilized soldiers into society, wean leaders from war by enriching them through commercial rather than war profits, and bring people from all sides of the war back into contact through markets and trade. The cease-fire becomes anchored in society and political solutions can emerge. In the language of peacekeeping strategy, which it complements, the revival of economic activity is a confidence-building measure and the essential follow-on to end a war definitively.

DAYTON'S ACHILLES' HEEL

The Dayton agreement stopped the war before any of the three warring parties had achieved their political goals. It recognized the nationalist goals of all three governing parties, legitimized the ethnic principle of rule, and completed the aim of the war—to change the geographical distribution of the population to make national control over territory irreversible—with the transfer of the one remaining exception, the Serb-held suburbs of Sarajevo, to federation control in February 1996. By expecting these political party leaders with nationalist goals to act with the accountability of governments in implementing their agreement, the international community appears to support their ambitions to create separate party-states in which each dominates and none becomes a minority. But the accord does not affirm the irreducible element for each of the three parties—external recognition of their national right to self-governance—nor does it choose among their conflicting political views of a Bosnian state. The Dayton accord is not a political settlement.

For some, Dayton is "the last will and testament of Bosnia," providing a cover for its effective partition, while for others it initiates a workable process to reintegrate Bosnia. American officials honestly represented their diplomatic objectives as a compromise between the realistic and moralistic goals of the Clinton administration. To stop the war they would accept that Bosnia had been effectively partitioned and make no guarantees of a political turnaround, but they would do as much as possible

---

[4] Bosnian Prime Minister Hasan Muratovic first referred to the Serb exodus as "liberation." The term "liberation" has come to be applied by Bosniac politicians, including President Izetbegovic and former Prime Minister Haris Silajdzic, to the entire territory of the former republic; for example, it was the theme of Izetbegovic's first public appearance since Dayton, at an election rally in Gorazde on May 4, 1996.

during one year to assist the Bosnian government leadership of Alija Izetbegovic and the multiethnic goal. What the Bosnian government made of this assistance would be up to it.

The political dilemma of integration or partition tends to focus attention on recalcitrant Serbs, but it is relations within the Bosniac-Croat federation that pose the greatest threat to the Dayton accord and the peace operation. The political positions of the federation's two parties have grown further apart now that the strategic shifts favoring Croats and the cessation of hostilities with Serbs shift the two parties' objectives from territorial to economic and political goals. The Bosnian Croat HDZ, which faces no political opposition in the territory it controls, has no intention of abandoning what it considers to be its national rights to territorial sovereignty and economic assets within or moving through that territory. It views unification with Bosnian Muslims to be a threat to those rights, the federation commitment to unity a facade that can drop with the end of hostilities, and the political independence of the ministate the Croats have created called the Croat Republic of Herzeg-Bosna within the Bosnian union to be legitimated by the recognition of a Serb Republic of Bosnia-Herzegovina.

But the Bosniac SDA also claims national rights to sovereignty and territory—for the Muslim nation—and has no intention of abandoning its internationally recognized position as the legitimate government over the entire territory in Bosnia's recognized borders. It has worked hard to overcome its strategic and economic dependence on the Croats by monopolizing as much international military and economic aid as possible; it has also insisted on the right of Muslims to return home to escape its current confinement to less than 25 percent of Bosnian territory. Croat demands for national parity in federal offices and for divided ("separate but equal") municipalities have been countered by an insistence on majoritarian rule. Unfortunately, each party can find justification for its own position in the constitution that was a part of the Dayton accord.

In essence, the three Bosnian parties do not feel the political compromise engineered at Dayton to be their agreement. They will cooperate with representatives of the international community insofar as it suits their party and national interests, but they are not committed to making it work beyond that. Their method is to fasten onto particular rights granted in the accord that suit their long-term political goals and challenge outsiders to make a clearer commitment and recognition of those particular rights and against another party or interpretation.

The ambiguity of the agreement is increased by the contradictions among its peace strategies: between the essential impartiality of the military forces and the political support for the Izetbegovic government; between the federation and the Serb Republic; between the trade and cooperation essential to the survival of all three communities and the programs for military balance that encourage parties to maintain troop deployments and raise police checkpoints around points of dispute or vulnerability on internal frontiers; between the slow timeline of peacekeeping and the security necessary for refugee return and reconciliation, and the quick timeline of deadlines and the political process designed to allow an early troop exit. The burden of these contradictions fell on IFOR commanders during 1996, and they reacted by raising the specter of "mission creep" to resist pressures to perform any task that could be seen to compromise their impartiality.

The Dayton answer to the political dilemma about whether the accord partitions or unifies Bosnia is contained in a constitutional balancing act that combines a single country with substantial devolution of power and jurisdictions. The Dayton constitution's construction of a Bosnian state actually resembles the European Union, with a common market (based on a customs union with exchangeable but separate currencies); a parliament representing the three nations (in two entities); a shared, large-scale infrastructure; and a bureaucracy to staff these foreign and economic functions that is financed by equal (not proportional) contributions from the three communities.

The primary jurisdiction of the common (state) government is foreign policy, not relations that tie politicians to domestic issues and constituents. It thus risks having the same "democracy deficit" as the European Union and similar obstacles to political integration from jealously guarded national sovereignties. No powers or functions of this common government exist to inspire loyalty or identity among all Bosnian citizens (with the possible exception of the Commission on Human Rights). The accord creates few rewards for power, status, or wealth in the center and in common institutions that would nurture centripetal over centrifugal forces or instill a sense of protection for people who wish to choose nonethnic identities (against pressures from their own group to conform). Even the responsibility for defense has been handed to the two entities.

It is clear that radical decentralization does not resolve the dilemma. All aspects of the implementation process in the first year (as they will be in 1997 as well) were dominated by the electoral motives of the three political parties and their view of elections as the current alternative to war, securing further or expanding their control of territory. Negotiations over foreign aid and technical assistance have dragged on while the parties fight over who has authority to sign public contracts, who gains which government portfolios (and the jurisdiction, the patronage, and the funds they bring), and whether they will form a central bank and common customs regime.

The bureaucratic rules of the EU, the IMF, and the World Bank—the leaders in economic reconstruction—require them to work with counterparts who can guarantee that they will eventually repay the loans. There cannot be aid without a country program, and there cannot be a country program without a country. If each of the three parties to the Dayton agreement has authority only over a part of Bosnian territory, who is that counterpart? Even more complex are the obstacles to resettlement and to economic revival that have arisen where ownership rights to housing or firms have been divided by new borders between municipalities or entities.

The case of Mostar is particularly instructive of the difficulties facing the Dayton implementation. Beginning in July 1994, the European Union Administration in Mostar (EUAM) fielded a civilian administration in the city that would replace the United Nations peacekeepers with a massive infusion of financial and administrative assistance and a multinational police force. The strategy of the EUAM was to use economic incentives and reconstruction to bring Croats and Muslims together again. Much has been accomplished: water, electricity, public transport, and fire brigades have been restored, all schools repaired and opened, the medical system revived, new apartments built to entice refugees to return, and some bridges rebuilt. But the city remains as divided as ever, violence erupts frequently, expulsions continue, and the EUAM was unable to push the parties to cooperate or fulfill their commitments.

BOSNIA'S ITALIAN FUTURE?

As SFOR begins its 18-month deployment, the World Bank reorients its program toward sustainability through macroeconomic structural reform, and the Office of the High Representative tries to use its enhanced authority for greater compliance to the Dayton accord through assertive conditionality, the prospects for Bosnia are murky. The reality of the country's separation into three ethnically homogeneous parastates is countered by the enthusiasm of the international operators that the Dayton accord "will work." It is too soon to predict a favorable outcome along the lines of the accord or whether there will be a progressive reconstitution of a Bosnian state in a civic direction, beginning with greater success for non-nationalist parties in the 1998 elections.

The primary tasks in 1997 are to get the common institutions working, hold the postponed municipal elections, and repatriate refugees being expelled from northern Europe. But the process of elections and the right of return will, as in 1996, continue to exacerbate the political contest of wills between the three parties, each obstructing the return of displaced persons and refugees of other groups who would dilute their electoral base and are perceived as threats to territorial sovereignty and national control.

If the economic situation remains bleak and stagnation sets in, refugees will not return and the remaining moderates, professionals, and members of the skilled younger generation will leave. High unemployment will reinforce ethnic partition, prevent return, and delay resettlement through real or imagined job discrimination. If the masses of unemployed, aimless young men now roaming city streets—many still armed—do not find employment, conditions will grow for violent incidents that could spark escalation, criminal gangs and mafia-like rackets, drug and arms smugglers, and extremist organizations and militia. Western concerns about Iranian ambitions, or a West Bank/Gaza hothouse, could be self-fulfilling in the social conditions of cities overwhelmed by displaced peasants and an urban underclass.

The most likely compromise between the current reality in Bosnia and the goal of Dayton is an extremely weak, fragile, and relatively unstable country—a country in name and international recognition only without a central capacity to manage trade and finance, one that might continue to demand external assistance and protection for a long time. There is a more worrisome scenario. There could be a repetition of the Italian experience with post-World War II reconstruction that transformed local crime families into an international criminal network based on control of construction activities and transport-related operations, foreign assistance channeled through public corporations and a dominant political party, state corruption, rapid "privatization" for those with ready cash, and continuing insecurity that favors protection rackets. This is not the usual view of the Marshall Plan, but it cannot be ignored.

MIDNIGHT Never Came

MIKE MOORE

FOR NEARLY FIVE DECADES, the *Bulletin's* Doomsday Clock has told the world what time it is.

The best known symbol of the Nuclear Age—the *Bulletin*'s "Doomsday Clock"—had a hard-to-ignore debut. Early *Bulletins* were newsletters, lacking magazine-style covers. But when the June 1947 *Bulletin* arrived, it had a first-ever cover—a pay-attention-to-me jack-o'-lantern orange cover. Imprinted over the orange: a boldly simple seven-inch by seven-inch clock face. The hour hand was at 12; the minute hand at about seven minutes to. Humankind, the clock said, was in dire straits.

The clock dominated most *Bulletin* covers until 1964, although, thankfully, less garish hues were generally used for the background. The clock, said an editorial in the July 1947 issue, "represents the state of mind of those whose closeness to the development of atomic energy does not permit them to forget that their lives and those of their children, the security of their country and the survival of civilization, all hang in the balance as long as the specter of atomic war has not been exorcized."

And so the *Bulletin* Clock (first called "The Clock of Doom" and then "The Doomsday Clock") entered folklore as a symbol of nuclear peril and a constant warning that the leaders of the United States and the Soviet Union had better sit up and fly right.

Editorial cartoonists in the Western hemisphere and Europe pirated the clock shamelessly, using it as an off-the-rack metaphor for the general madness of the Nuclear Age. In most cartoon incarnations, the clock was either a windup alarm clock or a globe with hour and minute hands. Either way, it was rigged to an explosive—sometimes dynamite, but usually a hulking nuclear bomb.

The clock also became a deadline-friendly factoid for journalists. Whenever U.S.-Soviet relations hit a bad patch, dozens of reporters and editors would call from as far away as Germany and New Zealand. "Are you going to change the clock?" In the post–Cold War era, reporters call and ask the same question whenever someone, say France, does something dumb, like resuming nuclear tests.

The clock has insinuated itself into the brick and limestone halls of academe. How many professors over the years have referred to the clock—approvingly or disparagingly—in history and international relations classes? No one knows, of course. But at least one academic, Joel Slemrod, a professor of business and economics at the University of Michigan, has used the clock in a research study. After postulating that ordinary people are likely to spend more when the international situation looks uncertain and gloomy and save more when it looks as if there will be a morrow, he found a positive correlation between clock

---

Mike Moore is editor of the Bulletin.

moves and savings rates. (Not that the clock caused variations; it merely served as a dandy barometer of East-West tensions.)

Politicians have also used the clock, no matter where they stood on the peace-and-security continuum. For hawks, the clock was a handy reminder of how dangerous the world was, thus justifying yet another multi-billion-dollar arms buildup. For doves, the clock also said the world was dangerous, but that called for conciliatory gestures and arms control treaties. Sen. Tom Harkin, an Iowa Democrat and a member in good standing of the olive branch school of international relations, titled his 1990 book on the perils of Cold War thinking, *Five Minutes to Midnight*.

It moves!

The clock was the creation of a Chicago artist known as Martyl, the wife of physicist Alexander Langsdorf, a *Bulletin* founder. Years later, Martyl said she hit upon the idea "to symbolize urgency." She got that message across by using just the final quadrant of a clock face, which clearly suggested that the end of time was nigh. As for putting the minute hand at seven—that was, she said, merely a matter of "good design."

The minute hand stayed at seven minutes to the hour until the fall of 1949, when President Harry S. Truman announced that the United States had evidence that there had been an atomic explosion in the Soviet Union.

The Soviets promptly disputed Truman. In a statement issued by Tass (and reprinted in the October issue of the *Bulletin*) the Soviet government claimed that U.S. experts had confused a large conventional explosion with an atomic explosion. That was understandable, explained Tass; the Soviet Union was blasting a lot as it built hydroelectric stations, canals, and the like. And, too, did not Western reporters recall that the Soviet Union had announced in November 1947 that it already had the weapon "at its disposal"?

The editors of the *Bulletin*, always mindful that Soviet leaders often lied, didn't buy the Tass explanation. Truman was right; the Soviet Union had set off an atomic detonation, and that was proof that the East-West nuclear arms race, long predicted by the *Bulletin*, was well under way.

"We do not advise Americans that doomsday is near and that they can expect atomic bombs to start falling on their heads a month or a year from now," wrote Editor Eugene Rabinowitch in an October 1949 essay. "But we think they have reason to be deeply alarmed and to be prepared for grave decisions."

In the October 1949 issue, the *Bulletin* moved the clock's minute hand for the first time, to three minutes to midnight.

Birth of the "evil thing"

The Soviet atomic explosion caught the Truman administration flat-footed. Gen. Leslie R. Groves, the director of the wartime Manhattan Project, had repeatedly predicted that it would take the Soviet Union a generation or more to make a bomb. Truman was even more confident; he believed that the Soviet Union lacked the scientific and industrial competence to *ever* mount a successful atomic bomb program.

The *Bulletin* was founded in December 1945 on the contrary notion. Back then, most of the scientists connected with the *Bulletin* believed that Soviet scientists and Russian industry were fully capable of building an atomic bomb in just a few years. (In November 1945, Harold C. Urey, a *Bulletin* founder, told the Senate Special Committee on Atomic Energy that "we should not think of a longer time than about five years.") The way to avoid a destructive nuclear arms race, the *Bulletin* said, was to put the control of nuclear energy, including weapons, into the hands of an international agency.

That didn't happen, of course. And now the Soviet fission explosion had given new urgency to a secret, high-level U.S. debate that had been simmering since the early days of the Manhattan Project: should the United States build a "Super," a "hydrogen bomb" far more powerful than the largest fission weapon?

A host of scientists advising the government opposed the Super. Morally, it would be so large as to be potentially genocidal. From a utilitarian point of view, it would serve no clear military purpose; fission bombs would be all anyone really needed. Physicists I.I. Rabi and Enrico Fermi, both key scientists during the Manhattan Project, described a hydrogen bomb as an "evil thing." James Conant, an adviser to Roosevelt and Truman on nuclear matters, said the "world is loused up enough"—it didn't need a hydrogen bomb.

In the end, anti-Super reservations were washed away in a tide of *Realpolitik*. Truman's key political advisers, including Secretary of State Dean Acheson, were convinced that the Soviets could—and would—build an H-bomb. Given that, it would be intolerable for the United States not to. (Today we know that the Soviets did indeed push ahead from fission to fusion, with scarcely a pause.)

On October 31, 1952, the United States tested its first true thermonuclear device, a thuggish thing called "Mike" that had a yield nearly a thousand times greater than the Hiroshima bomb. The islet of Elugelab in the Pacific, upon which it was detonated, disappeared, leaving a crater 160 feet deep and more than a mile wide. Nine months later, in August 1953, the Russians exploded a less powerful but still awesome thermonuclear device.

The September 1953 *Bulletin* cover was remade at the last minute, as soon as word of the Soviet test got out, and the minute hand moved to two minutes to midnight. In the following issue—October 1953—Editor Rabinowitch said:

"The hands of the Clock of Doom have moved again. Only a few more swings of the pendulum, and, from Moscow to Chicago, atomic explosions will strike midnight for Western civilization."

Massive retaliation and a "cohesive force"

In the 1950s, the U.S. consumer society boomed as a prosperous suburban lifestyle spawned highways, barbecue grills, TV sitcoms, and children. But abroad, the news was mostly bad. The Soviets were building nuclear weapons at a rapid pace, and they had even produced a few intercontinental ballistic missiles. (Emphasis on "few." Ardent Cold Warriors, including Democratic presidential candidate John F. Kennedy, charged that a complacent President Eisenhower had let the Russians pull ahead in ballistic weapons, thus producing a "missile gap." But it was a phantom gap, the product of misinterpreted intelligence, over-reliance on worst-case scenarios, anti-Soviet hysteria, and cynical domestic political calculation.)

In Europe, homegrown attempts to introduce democratic reforms in Hungary, encouraged by "liberation" rhetoric from Washington, had been aborted by Russian tanks. And in divided Germany, U.S.-Soviet relations were in perpetual crisis over the future of West Berlin, a let-it-all-hang-out oasis of capitalism in the heart of drab East Germany.

1960

On the other side of the world, the Korean Peninsula, where the United States (with help from U.N. and South Korean allies) had fought North Korean and Chinese soldiers, was still a potential flashpoint. The Korean war had not quite ended; it was merely on hold.

Farther south, Communist China and the old Chinese warlord, Chiang Kai-shek, were at one another's throats. At the end of a bloody civil war, Chiang and his remaining troops had taken refuge on the island of Formosa, just off the Chinese mainland, and war in the Formosa Straits seemed perennially possible. As Chiang's protector, the United States would surely be involved.

In the Korean War, Eisenhower hinted broadly that he might use nuclear weapons to bring the war to an end. As for the war of nerves in the Formosa Straits, the president got the message across that the United States would not shrink from using nuclear weapons to protect Chiang.

In Southeast Asia, the colonial French government had suffered a humiliating defeat in Indochina, and there was anti-colonial, nationalist, and separatist turmoil from the South China Sea to the Bay of Bengal. In fact, the colonial world was everywhere in revolt, and the Soviet Union and the United States were in sharp competition to win the affection—or at least to buy the allegiance—of the newly independent nations.

Some Third World leaders had already become adept at playing Americans and Russians off one another. But when Col. Gamal Abdel Nasser announced Egypt's neutrality, Eisenhower grew tired of the game, and a U.S. offer to help finance a high dam on the upper Nile was withdrawn. In retaliation, Nasser nationalized the British- and French-owned Suez Canal; toll revenues from the canal would build the dam.

In late 1956, the Israelis invaded Egypt and were soon joined by the British and the French. Their unspoken agenda: to regain the canal and topple Nasser.

Eisenhower was in a bind. If the United States supported its friends—the British, French, and Israelis—Nasser might turn to the Soviet Union for help. After that, anything could happen. Eisenhower took the cautious route: his administration condemned the invasion at the United Nations. The invading troops withdrew, the Soviets stayed out of the fracas, Nasser paid $81 million for taking the canal, and the Russians eventually financed the Aswan High Dam.

Despite the tumult and bloodshed, Rabinowitch found reasons in January 1960 to be moderately encouraged by the way the decade had unfolded, at least on the nuclear front. He noted, for instance, that the "Suez expedition was called off after the fighting was well under way—in fact, when it was almost over—although vital interests of two great powers had to be sacrificed."

The Suez outcome suggested that the "world map has been frozen by universal fear of a great war," he explained. In the pre-nuclear era, turmoil in many parts of the world would have led to a major war. But now, "war threats and counterthreats have become bluffs and counterbluffs."

Rabinowitch was right. Talk was often bellicose—"massive retaliation" and "we will bury you" are only two of the truly memorable phrases from the decade. But the Soviets and the Americans had clearly become cautious vis-á-vis one another's vital interests. Direct confrontation between the superpowers was generally to be avoided; confrontation by proxy was just rearing its head.

Meanwhile, there were at least a few positive signs of multinational cooperation—among them, the International Geophysical Year, the efforts of U.N. organizations such as UNESCO and UNICEF, and the Pugwash meetings involving Soviet and Western scientists. Rabinowitch believed that "a new cohesive force has entered the interplay of forces shaping the face of mankind, and it is making the future of man a little less foreboding."

The minute hand was again put at seven minutes to midnight, its original setting.

> *By 1960, fear of a great war froze the world map, and threats became bluffs.*

Fear keeps the peace

People sometimes assume that the minute hand of the clock is moved frequently. In fact, the clock has been reset just 14 times in its 48 years. Clock moves reflect major trends, not transient events. For instance, the Cuban missile crisis in October 1962 failed to produce so much as a blip in the clock. The crisis—a frightening exception to the still developing "rule" that the United States and Soviet Union should not directly confront one another—came and went too fast for the *Bulletin* to act on it.

A year after the missile crisis, in October 1963, the *Bulletin* moved the minute hand back in recognition of the signing of the Partial Test Ban Treaty, an agreement banning atmospheric nuclear testing. Rabinowitch explained in his editorial that the treaty was not a "significant step toward disarmament"—after all, underground tests would continue. Nor would the treaty prevent additional nations from acquiring nuclear weapons, Rabinowitch added. Indeed, he believed that China would shortly join the nuclear club. (China's first test of a fission device came in October 1964.)

Nevertheless, the treaty, said Rabinowitch, was tangible evidence that the "cohesive force" was still alive and well. Both sides of the East-West confrontation continued to experience "naked fear for survival," and that fear helped keep the peace. The treaty also suggested that "the forces of realism" were winning; on both sides of the East-West divide, "obstinate dogmatism" was in retreat.

The minute hand was moved back to 12 minutes to midnight.

Failure of imagination

By 1968, it was clear to Rabinowitch that the "dogmatists" had not been routed, after all. Cooperation between and among nations, never a strong trend, had waned. Nationalism and "international anarchy" were in flower.

"De Gaulle's France and Mao's China led the way," said Rabinowitch in the January 1968 issue. "Both devoted enormous efforts to the development of nuclear weapons as a visible sign of their sovereignty, and a guarantee of freedom of action.

"Stirrings of military nationalism appeared all over the globe. India and Pakistan went to war in 1965; Israel and the Arab countries did the same in 1967. And the United States was already embarked on a growing military intervention in Southeast Asia, without the U.N. label that had so irritated American nationalists in the Korean conflict."

Rabinowitch seldom expected much from Soviet leaders, whom he generally thought to be benighted and paranoid, but he expected a lot of American leaders. The United States, despite its many flaws, was still the last best hope of mankind. More than any other nation, it could demonstrate—by example—that military spending was wasteful, and that it was far better to help Third World nations develop their own peace-time economies then to supply them with arms.

But American leadership—particularly the administration of Lyndon B. Johnson—had not been up to the task. The great U.S. failure of the 1960s, said Rabinowitch, was not so much a "sin of commission"—the Vietnam War—as a "sin of omission," a failure to use American power and wealth in imaginative ways to lead a worldwide mobilization of technical, economic, and intellectual resources for the building of a viable world community. "The day of reckoning may be approaching, not in the form of American withdrawal and communist takeover in the Far East, but in a wave of world hunger, and the accompanying surge of world anarchy."

The minute hand was moved up to its original slot, seven minutes to midnight.

34. Midnight Never Came

A "first step"

The previous year's clock editorial, called "The Dismal Record," reflected disappointment over missed opportunities. But in Geneva, a process had been going on since the mid-1960s that looked promising. On the theory that it only takes one spark to start a forest fire, nations—nuclear as well as non-nuclear—were attempting to limit the "horizontal" spread of nuclear weapons.

Many of the non-nuclear weapon states were also fearful of "vertical" proliferation in the United States and the Soviet Union, while they remained enamored of nuclear power, which was seen as the cure for virtually all ills. In 1968, a deal was finally struck: Under the terms of the Nuclear Non-Proliferation Treaty (NPT), the nuclear weapon states would help non-nuclear weapon states develop nuclear power. In turn, the "have-not" states would agree not to develop or obtain nuclear weapons.

Finally, the five nuclear weapon states promised to work toward a cessation of the nuclear arms race and eventual disarmament. More than 100 nations signed the NPT, although some of the holdouts were worrisome—especially Israel, India, Pakistan, South Africa, Argentina, and Brazil.

But even with holdouts, Rabinowitch was heartened by the deal, if not overwhelmed. In the April 1969 issue, he wrote: "This treaty reasserts the common interests of all signatories in avoiding new instabilities, bound to be introduced into the precarious balance of nuclear terror with the emergence of new nuclear nations...."

"The great powers have made a first step. They must proceed without delay to the next one—the dismantling, gradually, of their own oversize military establishments. Otherwise the hope raised by the treaty will prove futile."

The minute hand was moved back to ten minutes to midnight.

Parity cometh

In 1964, Stanley Kubrick released *Dr. Strangelove*, a wickedly funny satire of deterrence theory, and Sidney Lumet gave audiences *Fail Safe*, an earnest and plodding essay on the same topic. Both films explored scenarios in which U.S. bombers erroneously attack the Soviet Union with nuclear weapons. In *Fail Safe*, Moscow and New York are destroyed; in *Strangelove*, the planet is fatally irradiated by a secret Soviet "Doomsday Machine."

In a sense, Kubrick and Lumet were cockeyed optimists. Sure, things didn't turn out so well for a few million people (*Fail Safe*) or a few billion (*Strangelove*), but in each case, a fictional president had hours to correct the original attack-the-Soviets mistake. But in the real world, the time scale was about to be reduced to minutes. There would no time for reflective assessment, no time for call-backs.

By the mid-1960s, the United States and the Soviet Union were working on antiballistic missile systems (ABMs), with the Russians showing far more enthusiasm for the concept than the Americans. To Soviet leaders, a defense system seemed reasonable, even morally compelling. But in the United States, a host of influential policy-makers, including Defense Secretary Robert S. McNamara, argued that an effective ABM system would be dangerous.

Mutual terror, went the argument, was still the great peacekeeper. As long as both sides knew that each could destroy the other, no matter who struck first, an uneasy peace would prevail. But ABMs had the potential for disrupting that rickety balance of terror. They would encourage a rapid acceleration of the nuclear arms race, because increases in offensive weapons were the surest and cheapest way of offsetting advances in defensive systems.

And in moments of high East-West tension, the side that believed that it had the most effective ABM system might be tempted to launch a first strike, confident that it could ride out the weakened retaliatory attacks with minimal damage.

But in an obscene game of chicken, the side that feared a preemptive first strike might well launch its own preemptive attack. Meanwhile, the other side, assuming that the enemy would reason thusly, would have even more reason to strike first....

Fear of Russian progress on ABMs inspired the United States to enhance its offensive forces by developing missiles that carried "multiple independently targetable reentry vehicles"—MIRVs. The last stage of an ICBM was merely a "bus" carrying several warheads, each of which could be released at a different time in a preplanned sequence. Thanks to in-flight course corrections by the bus, the warheads would have different ballistic trajectories and different targets.

In this new post-*Strangelove* world, an enemy who struck first would have a clear advantage, said nuclear strategists. Because one MIRVed ICBM could theoretically knock out several enemy missiles in their silos, the side that struck first could retain many of its missiles for a possible second strike.

The only way to level the "bolt-from-the-blue" playing field was for the target nation to launch its missiles *before* they could be destroyed in their silos. In a MIRVed use-'em-or-lose-'em world, the U.S. and Russian command authorities might have just minutes to make a launch–no launch decision, even if the information they had was muddled and ambiguous.

By the late 1960s, U.S. and Soviet leaders had come to suspect that the two nations were lurching toward an abyss. In an attempt to pull back from the edge, the Strategic Arms Limitation Talks (SALT) began in Helsinki in November 1969.

The central idea of SALT was that the United States and the Soviet Union would give up their respective dreams of achieving clearcut nuclear superiority. Instead, they would begin a process designed to produce a rough sort of "parity." In turn, that might bring a measure of predictability and stability to East-West relations.

In 1972, two agreements were signed. One, the Anti-Ballistic Missile Treaty, effectively put an end to most ABM work, thus making an out-of-control nuclear arms race less likely. In effect, the treaty said that each nation must remain vulnerable to the other side's missiles; continued willingness to abide by a mutual suicide pact had become the Golden Rule of deterrence theory.

Meanwhile, the five-year SALT Interim Agreement froze the number of ballistic missile launchers—that is, the number of land-based missile silos and submarine-based missile launch tubes—at 1972 levels. It was an exceedingly modest start toward nuclear arms control; it did not actually limit the number of missiles each side could have or the number of warheads that a given missile might carry.

Bernard T. Feld, a member of the *Bulletin*'s Board of Directors, was generally pleased with the ABM Treaty, but wary of the Interim Agreement. Feld, whose sarcasm was not always hidden, wrote the clock editorial for the June 1972 issue:

"Now we have been presented with the greatest step towards world peace since the Sermon on the Mount, and we are torn between the impulse to cry 'bravo' and the desire to shout 'fraud.'"

MIRVed missiles were meant to counter the ABM "threat," he said. But now the ABM threat had faded—yet MIRVs remained. That was "because we are too far along with deployment and the Russians too far behind—an asymmetry that we do not want to give up and they do not want to freeze. So we have accepted that we will both go to MIRV, after which it will be too late to avoid MIRV without unacceptably intrusive inspection."

The ABM Treaty was fine, but the Interim Agreement was thin gruel. Nonetheless, the United States and the Soviet Union *had* ac-

By 1972, agreements controlling nuclear arms proliferation were signed, and a limitation on the number of missiles was established.

cepted the principle of parity, and that was a foundation to build upon. The minute hand was moved back to 12 minutes to midnight.

Premature optimism

The cover of the September 1974 *Bulletin* was an editorial cartoon come to life. It featured a photo of an alarm clock with its minute hand approaching midnight. The clock, a battery, and a globe were wired together into a primitive time bomb.

1974

It was not a wholly unreasonable image, given the facts: instead of reducing their numbers, the United States and the Soviet Union were MIRVing and modernizing their nuclear arsenals at an alarming rate; India had exploded a nuclear device; and SALT II was at an impasse.

Founding Editor Rabinowitch had died in 1973. Feld was now editor-in-chief, but his deputy, Editor Samuel H. Day, wrote the September 1974 clock editorial:

"Despite the promise of the 1972 accords, it is now apparent that the two nuclear superpowers are nowhere near significant agreement on strategic arms limitations. The failure was manifest at the recently concluded summit conference in Moscow. This in itself is cause for concern in view of the arms buildup which has continued during the course of the negotiations, and particularly since 1972.

"In anticipation of [arms] limitations agreements that have never come to pass or were of little consequence, more and more weapons have been built and tested, and more and more weapons systems have been developed and deployed. Far from restraining the forces which it was intended to curb, SALT has sustained and nourished them, providing acceptable channels for conducting business as usual."

The *Bulletin*'s optimism in resetting the clock to 12 minutes to midnight in 1972 had been "premature," said Day. The "danger of nuclear doomsday is measurably greater today than it was in 1972."

The minute hand was moved up to nine minutes to midnight.

Nucleoholics, greed, and irrationality

As the *Bulletin* entered its thirty-fifth year, Editor-in-Chief Feld offered a general assessment of the world situation in the January 1980 issue. It was not a happy prospect. SALT II negotiations had concluded in 1979, and it took a heroic act of optimism to conclude that much had been accomplished. Weapon ceilings were set so high, and MIRVed weapons had become so commonplace, that a nuclear Armageddon seemed as likely now as when the talks began. Feld wrote:

"More than ten years after the start of the SALT negotiations, we are still struggling with the acceptance of an agreement which, far from embodying significant nuclear disarmament, retains—if it does not encourage—the accumulation of astronomical numbers of deliverable nuclear weapons by both the so-called 'superpowers'; which is not yet able to address the dangers of an irrational and growing nuclear confrontation in Europe; and which has not even begun to take the minimum steps of restraint needed to shore up a rapidly deteriorating nonproliferation regime."

The United States and the Soviet Union, said Feld, were equally to blame. The former had a "self-defeating propensity for the premature introduction of destabilizing new technologies." The latter was stubbornly wedded to the sanctity of large numbers of huge missiles to counterbalance a lack of technical sophistication. Both had "been behaving like what may best be described as 'nucleoholics'—drunks who continue to insist that the drink being consumed is positively 'the last one,' but who can always find a good excuse for 'just one more round.'"

But the accelerating arms race was just one source of instability, albeit the darkest. Feld said that increased competition among nations for ever more scarce resources, often a cause of conflict and war, would get worse in the coming decades, not better. The developed world used a disproportionate share of the world's resources and would continue to do so. Conservation did not come naturally to the affluent. Meanwhile, the developed world made only token efforts to help improve living conditions in the poorest nations of the Third World.

Also serious was a "spreading trend toward irrationality in the national and international conduct of many states, of peoples aspiring to nationhood, and dissident minorities (down to minorities comprising only a few individuals) within nations. Each one of us can easily find many examples of this trend toward a return to the the social and political behavior of the Middle Ages: the provisional branch of the Irish Republican Army or the Italian Red Brigade; the religious fanaticism now in control in Iran and other parts of the Islamic world; the systematic dismemberment of Lebanon, the outstanding modern example of a secular democratic state; the genocidal orgy in Cambodia, demonstrating the contemporary possibility that innocent people may, without choice, end up both red and dead while the rest of the world impotently stands by."

Despite his gloomy analysis, Feld reminded readers that the *Bulletin* was "essentially optimistic," and he exhorted the *Bulletin* community not to give up on SALT or the SALT process. But for now, the minute hand of the clock was moved up to seven minutes to midnight, where it had started in 1947.

"War-fighting," anyone?

Just 12 months later, the outlook for the world seemed even dimmer. The Soviet Union had dispatched tanks, troops, and dive bombers to Afghanistan in December 1979 to prop up a puppet government, further poisoning a none-too-cordial relationship between Moscow and Washington. President Jimmy Carter, who had sent SALT II to the Senate for ratification, condemned the Soviets for "invading" their neighbor, cancelled U.S. participation in the upcoming Olympic Games in Moscow, and asked the Senate to postpone action on SALT II.

More chillingly, the Carter administration, in an attempt to bring order to decades of jury-rigged nuclear-response plans and to enhance the "credibility" of deterrence, had devised a wider range of nuclear options, including the implementation of command-and-control measures that would—in theory—insure that the United States could fight a "protracted nuclear conflict."

Then in November 1980, former governor and movie star Ronald Reagan, a defense hawk who had campaigned on the premise that the United States had become dangerously weak vis-á-vis the Soviet Union, was elected president. SALT II was "fatally flawed," said Reagan, and the Soviets routinely flouted SALT provisions. In contrast, the United States, which played by the rules, had laced itself into a straitjacket. The way to end the Cold War, Reagan said, was to *win* it. Feld wrote in the January 1981 issue:

"Nuclear weapons—more and more unambiguously aimed at war-fighting rather than war-deterrence—are now being rapidly deployed by the East and West in Europe. The Russian SS-20 and the U.S. MX blatantly announce a new race in improved missile accuracy and mobility, heralding the acceptance of counterforce first-strike by both sides.

"These ominous signs of deterioration are cast into starker relief by the flat unwillingness of either the United States or the Soviet Union to reject publicly, and in all circumstances, the threat of striking the other first. Both sides willfully delude themselves that a nuclear war can remain limited or even be won. In 1980, both sides officially declared nuclear war 'thinkable.'"

The minute hand was moved up to four minutes to midnight.

Ideologues take control

The early Reagan years alarmed the *Bulletin*'s editors, along with millions of other people in the United States and Western Europe. Reagan, who may have believed more ardently than any previous president in the ultimate abolition of nuclear weapons, nevertheless expanded and accelerated a weapons buildup that Jimmy Carter had begun. Reagan also seemed to enjoy tossing incendiary rhetoric into the dry-as-straw East-West barn. In his first presidential news conference, he asserted that Soviet leaders "reserve unto themselves the right to commit any crime, to lie, to cheat."

1984

While the comment would not have raised an eyebrow if a historian had uttered it, it seemed recklessly provocative coming from the commander-in-chief of the most powerful nation on earth. Two years later, Reagan trumped his any-crime-any-time comment by calling the Soviet Union the "Evil Empire" in a speech redolent of Old Testament rhetoric about the final showdown between the forces of Good and Evil.

To manage domestic affairs, Reagan surrounded himself with moderates and pragmatists. But in foreign affairs, many of his key advisers were anti-Soviet ideologues—hardliners who believed that the United States should throw out the idea of nuclear parity. Eugene Rostow, for instance, became director of the Arms Control and Disarmament Agency. Previously, he had been co-chair (with Paul Nitze) of the Committee on the Present Danger, a Carter-era organization dedicated to persuading the nation that the Soviet Union was dangerously ahead of the United States in nuclear weaponry.

In 1983, Reagan announced the Strategic Defense Initiative (SDI), resurrecting the long-dead fantasy of unfurling an anti-ballistic missile umbrella over the United States. The president's March 23 speech came as a surprise to almost everyone, including some of Reagan's closest advisers. The space-based SDI plan was quickly dubbed "Star Wars," after the movie trilogy of that name.

Reagan's Star Wars plan, if developed and deployed, would surely violate the ABM Treaty, critics said. It would lead to a resumption of an all-out nuclear arms race. And—as a final irony—it almost surely would not work in the event of an all-out attack. The *Bulletin*'s first unsigned clock editorial appeared in the January 1984 issue:

"As the arms race—a sort of dialogue between weapons—has intensified, other forms of discourse between the superpowers have all but ceased. There has been a virtual suspension of meaningful contacts and serious discussions. Every channel of communications has been constricted or shut down; every form of contact has been attenuated or cut off. And arms control negotiations have been reduced to a species of propaganda."

The minute hand was moved up to three minutes to midnight.

Breakthrough

Western Europe had been seen as a potential nuclear battleground virtually since the beginning of Nuclear Time. In the 1950s, U.S. bombers with nuclear weapons had been stationed in England and tactical nuclear weapons had been deployed with NATO troops, all to discourage the Soviet Union from gobbling up Bonn and Paris and London and Rome without a burp. In the 1950s, the West European nations were generally comfortable basking in the shade of the U.S. nuclear umbrella. The threat of nuclear retaliation, went the conventional wisdom, kept the Russian bear in hibernation and away from the Fulda Gap.

When the Soviets caught up, in a rough sort of way in the 1960s, nuclear intimidation was no longer a game of solitaire. If the NATO nations, led by the United States, used nuclear weapons to fend off a Soviet invasion, the Soviets could now strike the United States. Given that, would the United States actually come to the aid of Europe if it meant possible national suicide?

1988

This "coupling" debate, always surreal, had waxed and waned through the 1960s and 1970s. Britain developed nuclear weapons in part to maintain its "special relationship" with the United States. In contrast, Charles DeGaulle had so little confidence in U.S. nuclear commitments that he insisted that France have its own independent nuclear retaliatory force.

In the late 1970s, in an attempt to enhance

deterrence and tighten the coupling between Europe and the United States, the West European members of NATO obtained a U.S. promise to deploy 464 ground-launched nuclear-tipped cruise missiles on NATO soil, as well as 108 nuclear-armed Pershing II intermediate-range ballistic missiles.

In theory, the missiles would counterbalance a nasty-looking Soviet force of 243 triple-warhead SS-20 missiles aimed at NATO targets. They would also be bargaining chips. Deployment—even the threat of deployment—would give the West additional leverage in pushing for a treaty that would sharply constrain such weapons worldwide.

In the early 1980s, as deployment of the new missiles loomed and NATO and Soviet rhetoric became more alarming, popular opposition in Western Europe became a force to be reckoned with. In the fall of 1981, more than 250,000 people turned out for a protest in Bonn; the following month, some 400,000 protested in Amsterdam.

Deploying Pershing missiles that could hit Soviet targets in five to 10 minutes was utterly mad, said the protesters in Europe and in the United States. It would make the Soviets even more edgy, ultimately leading to an unintentional but devastating nuclear war. ABC-TV's two-part movie, *The Day After*, linked Pershing deployment to a civilization-ending war. It played to huge audiences on two continents.

The fact that the United States and the Soviet Union eventually signed an Intermediate-range Nuclear Forces (INF) Treaty in December 1987—which eliminated all such weapons (including Pershing IIs and SS-20s) rather than merely cutting their numbers—struck many people, including the editors of the *Bulletin*, as near-miraculous. But it wasn't quite that. Public opinion in Western Europe and the United States had made it plain to the Reagan administration that people were fed up with having to live at Ground Zero. Public pressure to do something about the nuclear arms race had become a potent political movement.

As surprising as Reagan's agreement to the INF Treaty may have been, it was even more startling to learn that the Soviet Union, long victimized by constipated and unimaginative leadership, finally had a top man—Mikhail Gorbachev—with the wit and the imagination and the courage to finally end the Cold War. The editorial in the January-February 1988 *Bulletin* said:

"For the first time the United States and the Soviet Union have agreed to dismantle and ban a whole category of nuclear weapons. They have crafted provisions that enable each to be confident that the other will comply with the treaty's terms. The agreement they have fashioned can serve as a model for future accords. That agreement would not have been possible without the leadership displayed by General Secretary Mikhail Gorbachev and President Ronald Reagan. We applaud them."

The minute hand was moved back to six minutes to midnight.

The great melt

The Berlin Wall came down at the end of 1989, symbolizing the end of the Cold War. Gorbachev had long realized that the Soviet Empire, which had rested on a foundation of fear and intimidation for more than four decades, could not be sustained. His goals were to shore up Soviet society, to repair the collapsing Soviet economic machine, to introduce democratic reforms, to end Soviet isolation from the Western world, and to bring new life—"new thinking"—to the desperately outdated Communist Party.

Meanwhile, new thinking was far advanced in Poland, Czechoslovakia, Hungary, East Germany, Romania. Men and women who had danced tepidly to Moscow's balalaika since the end of World War II would do it no longer. Revolution was in the air from the North Sea to the Black Sea. And Gorbachev was not about to send tanks into Eastern Europe, as his predecessors had, to keep the East Bloc nations in line. The editorial in the April 1990 *Bulletin* remarked:

"Now, 44 years after Winston Churchill's 'Iron Curtain' speech, the myth of monolithic communism had been shattered for all to see, the ideological conflict known as the Cold War is over, and the risk of global nuclear war being ignited in Europe is significantly diminished...."

The minute hand was moved back to 10 minutes to midnight.

The coup that failed

The old era ended abruptly. Few had anticipated it; even fewer seemed to have a clear notion of what would—or should—come next. From a Washington perspective, change was good as long as it didn't get out of hand. The Reagan and Bush administrations had come to see Gorbachev as an ally, as a friend, as a bulwark against chaos in a troubled Soviet Union.

Back home in Russia, Gorbachev didn't have a prayer. He was said to be chiefly responsible for every problem and disgrace tormenting the Soviet Union—ranging from the nation's decline as a world power to its free-falling economy to an increase in public drunkenness to the imminent dissolution of the Union itself.

By the the beginning of 1991, the general secretary was foundering, although official Washington seemed not to know it. The end came in late August, when reactionaries mounted a near-bloodless coup. The coup failed to install a government of revanchist communists, but Gorbachev was finished, although he remained in office through the remainder of the year.

Discredited and virtually deposed, yes. But Gorbachev had not been a failure. Beginning in 1985, when he took over as general secretary, Gorbachev had forced democratic reforms onto the moribund Soviet system. Although the reforms helped foment the turmoil that led to his downfall, they had become so ingrained by August 1991 that a successful right-wing coup was not possible. As unpopular as Gorbachev had become, the rightist alternatives looked worse to most Russians.

Shortly before the coup attempt, Gorbachev had signed the Strategic Arms Reduction Treaty, the Reagan-era successor to SALT and the first nuclear arms agreement that mandated steep rollbacks in so-called "strategic" weapons. And in September and October, as the Soviet Union sputtered to an end, Presidents Bush and Gorbachev announced a series of unilateral but parallel initiatives taking most intercontinental missiles and bombers off hair-trigger alert, and withdrawing thousands of tactical nuclear weapons from forward bases. The *Bulletin* editorial in the December 1991 issue said:

"The 40-year-long East-West nuclear arms race has ended. The world has clearly entered a new post–Cold War era. The illusion that tens of thousands of nuclear weapons are a guarantor of national security has been stripped away. In the context of a disintegrating Soviet Union, large nuclear arsenals are even more clearly seen as a liability, a yardstick of insecurity...

"We believe that Presidents Bush and Gorbachev have guided their respective nations to a historic intersection of mutual interests. Continuing boldness and imagination are called for. Men and women throughout the world must vigorously challenge the bankrupt paradigms of militarism if we are to achieve a new world order. The setting of the *Bulletin* Clock reflects our optimism that we are entering a new era."

The minute hand of the clock was pushed back to 17 minutes to midnight.

Off the scale

The new man in Moscow was Boris Yeltsin, a self-styled radical democrat. As president of the Russian Federation, he presided over the formal demise of the Soviet Union. Russia, he said, would adhere to the letter and the spirit of arms control agreements negotiated by the old Soviet Union.

To symbolize the dramatic nature of the changes marked by the the 1991 clock move, the *Bulletin*'s Board of Directors had moved the minute hand "off the scale," to 17 minutes to midnight. By *Bulletin* standards, that represented an unprecedented burst of enthusiasm and optimism.

In May 1946, Albert Einstein, one of the *Bulletin*'s more notable godfathers, looked toward the future and said: "The unleashed power of the atom has changed everything save our modes of thinking, and thus we drift toward unparalleled catastrophe."

The goal of the *Bulletin*—founded 50 years ago in December—has been to render that wonderfully apt Einstein quote obsolete. The *Bulletin* has been—and still is—committed to changing the way people think about war-and-peace issues. Its "Clock of Doom," as Eugene Rabinowitch used to call it, has been a major part of that effort.

The clock quickly became the symbol of the *Bulletin*. But it also came to symbolize something far larger than a magazine published in Chicago, just blocks from where the first controlled, self-sustaining nuclear reaction took place. The clock became an icon of the Nuclear Age, a centerpiece of pop culture, an image so clearly on target that if the *Bulletin* had not invented it, a Nehru or a Cousins or a Kennedy would have come up with it eventually.

The *Bulletin* Clock is not just the property of a magazine. It belongs to everyone who cares about the future of humankind.

Index

Acheson, Dean, 63, 100, 101, 216
Adams, John Quincy, 94, 96-97
Afghanistan, 27, 39, 69, 81, 89, 134, 166, 167, 176, 180, 192, 193, 194, 196, 221
African National Congress, 67
Aganbegyan, Abel, 135, 136
Agency for International Development (AID), 40
Aideed, Mohamed Farah, 143, 144, 145
Albright, Madeleine, 110, 151; on bipartisan foreign policy, 8-11
Algeria, 63, 65, 68-69, 71, 167, 192
Angola, 89, 108, 192, 193, 194, 196
Anti-Ballistic Missile (ABM) Treaty, 38, 50, 131, 185, 220
apartheid, 66, 109, 197
Argentina, 108, 109, 195, 219
Armenia, 166
arms sales: campaign finance and, 120-123; in post–cold war world, 176-184, 185-191, 192-196; technology and, 124-128
Asia-Pacific Economic Cooperation (APEC), 31, 44, 66, 67
Aspin, Les, 121, 140, 145
Association of Southeast Asian Nations (ASEAN), 46, 66, 67
Atlantic Alliance, 36, 39, 53, 58
Australia, 40, 91, 195
Austria, 195
Azerbaijan, 166

Bahrain, 167
Baker, James, 8, 9, 10, 100, 103, 104, 136
Bangladesh, 29
Belarus, 10, 61
Biafra, 28
biological weapons, 176, 177, 178, 182
Birman, Igor, 135, 136
Bolivia, 70
Bosnia, 9, 12, 13, 24, 28, 37, 45, 81, 83, 84, 85, 95, 108, 109, 110, 111, 112, 113, 131, 143, 166, 167, 172, 174, 192, 194, 196, 208-214
Boutros-Ghali, Boutros, 143, 193
Brazil, 65, 68, 70, 123, 166, 167, 219
Brezhnev, Leonid, 134, 135
Britain, 18, 31, 49, 56, 63, 91, 181, 187, 189, 217
Brunei, 42, 46
Burkina Faso, 196
Burma, 19, 28, 192, 197
Burundi, 108, 113, 192
Bush, George, 8, 10, 11, 20, 27, 54, 81, 83-84, 129, 132, 140, 142, 143, 147, 182, 223, 224. See also Persian Gulf War
Bush, George W., 116-117

Cairo Declaration, 49
Cambodia, 27, 28, 108, 113, 192, 193
campaign finance, foreign contributions to, 120-123
Canada, 18, 67, 195, 196; NAFTA and, 116-119
capitalism, 16, 105
Carter, Jimmy, 24, 132, 145, 176, 221, 222
Casey, William, 129, 130, 131, 132, 133, 134, 135, 137
Caucasus, 169

Central Intelligence Agency (CIA), 15; cold war and, 129, 143, 149, 156
Chechnya, 19, 28, 108, 114
chemical weapons, 10-11, 38, 147-151, 176-184
Chile, 67, 108, 109, 121, 122, 123
China, 13, 20, 21, 28, 39-44, 61, 63, 69, 70, 91, 92, 99, 100, 104, 161, 166, 167, 168, 169, 173, 178, 187, 189, 190, 195, 217, 218; realpolitik and, 45-52
Chirac, Jacques, 35, 62
Christopher, Warren, 35, 122, 142, 144, 145
Churchill, Winston, 141, 223
Clinton, Bill, 8, 12-14, 17, 24, 29, 34, 44, 48, 51, 53, 55, 58, 64, 65, 71, 76, 84, 85, 99, 104, 111, 112, 113, 114, 117, 119, 120, 121, 123, 132, 147, 148, 174, 175, 182, 185, 186, 188, 191, 197, 212; meritocracy in administration of, 140-142; Somalia and, 143-146
CNN effect, 83
cold war, end of, 12, 13, 14, 17, 18, 19, 21, 22, 24, 27, 39, 47, 53, 54, 55, 56, 59, 60, 64, 68, 75, 80, 81, 83, 86, 87, 88, 98, 120, 141, 151, 172-173, 175, 192, 215, 216; CIA and, 129-137; NATO and, 34-38; warfare and, 176-184
Colombia, 19, 196
colonialism, 26
communism, 24, 43, 135, 142
Comprehensive Test Ban Treaty, 151
Conference on Security and Cooperation in Europe (CSCE), 56
containment, 14, 169
Conventional Forces in Europe (CFE) Treaty, 35, 186
Croatia, 108, 111, 195, 208-214
Cuba, 13, 131, 169, 196
Cumings, Bruce, 100, 101
Cyprus, 68
Czech Republic, 60, 61, 186, 223

Dayton Accords, 37, 111, 194, 208-214
De Gaulle, Charles, 218, 222
decapitation, 179-180
deliberate war, in the post–cold war world, 176-184
democracy, 12, 14, 16, 24, 30, 50, 51, 56, 73, 74, 160
Deutch, John, 130, 132, 136, 137, 140, 149
diplomacy, foreign policy and, 8-11
Dodge Plan, 100
Dole, Bob, 116, 119, 149
dominant maneuver, military technology and, 126
Doomsday Clock, 215-224
drug trafficking, 9, 19, 58
dumdum bullets, 197

East Timor, 28, 66
Ecuador, 39, 66
Egypt, 40, 63-64, 69, 70, 73, 143, 167, 173, 180, 195, 217
Eisenhower, Dwight, 63, 131, 132, 217
El Salvador, 63, 70
elections, and foreign contributions, 120-123
environmental issues, 9, 69, 117
Eritrea, 28

Ethiopia, 69, 70, 108, 109
ethnic issues, 27, 39, 61, 108, 111, 143, 192, 193; Bosnia and, 208-214
European Community (EC), 26, 30, 53, 55-56, 58, 68, 168, 213, 214
European Monetary System, 30
Export-Import Bank, 121

Falkland Islands, 181
Feinstein, Dianne, 118, 121
Feld, Bernard T., 220, 221-222
Finland, 195
First Wave, Toffler's theory of, 125
focused logistics, military technology and, 126
fog of war, 125
foreign aid, 160-161
France, 18, 25, 39, 49, 68, 160, 168, 187, 189, 215, 217, 218, 222
Friedberg, Aaron, 100, 104
full-dimension protection, military technology and, 126
fundamentalism, Islamic, 27, 66, 68, 71-77, 85

Gates, Robert, 129, 131, 132, 133, 134, 135, 137
General Agreement on Tariffs and Trade (GATT), 31, 84, 163
genocide, 108, 111, 115
Gergen, David, 140, 145
Germany, 13, 16, 18, 53, 54, 56, 60, 62, 80, 133, 160, 189, 195, 223; foreign aid to, 99-105. See also Nazi Germany
Golan Heights, 85, 178, 180
Goldstone, Richard, 110, 112, 113
Gorbachev, Mikhail, 36, 130, 131, 136, 155, 223-224
Gordon, Michael, 201, 204
Gosende, Robert, 143, 145
Greater East Asian Co-Prosperity Sphere, 101
Greece, 13, 26, 68, 94
Grenada, 172
Group of Seven, 35, 167, 188
Guatemala, 108
guerrilla warfare, 127

Haass, Richard, 201, 206
Haig, Alexander, 132, 133
Haiti, 11, 13, 28, 29, 39, 45, 63, 70, 81, 83, 84, 95, 97, 108, 113-114
Hamas, 71, 73
Hartung, William, 129, 130
Helms, Jesse, 147, 148, 151
Herzegovina, 110, 111, 208-214
Hinduism, 27
Hizballah, 73, 74
Holocaust, 108
Honduras, 108, 109
Hong Kong, 13
human rights, 12, 26, 28, 29, 30, 45, 49, 56, 63, 76, 108, 123, 160, 167, 197, 213
Hungary, 60, 61, 121, 150, 186, 195, 223
Hussein, Saddam, 9, 28, 81, 82, 103, 113, 128, 150, 177, 179, 180. See also Persian Gulf War

225

inadvertent war, in the post–cold war world, 176–184
India, 29, 42, 65, 69, 88, 104, 166, 176, 177, 178, 179, 180, 181, 182, 189, 190, 195, 196, 218, 219
Indonesia, 28, 42, 65, 66–67, 68, 121, 166
Inner Mongolia, 49
Interamerican Development Bank, 161
Intermediate-Range Nuclear Forces (INF) Treaty, 223
International Atomic Energy Agency (IAEA), 131, 188, 189
International Monetary Fund, 68, 208, 214
Iran, 13, 26, 61, 76, 85, 128, 134, 145, 167, 174, 177, 178, 181, 182; sanctions against, 165–169. See also Persian Gulf War
Iraq, 10, 13, 28, 39, 68, 85, 95, 97, 99, 108, 113, 127, 131, 155, 166, 169, 172, 173, 176, 177, 178, 180, 181, 183, 187, 195. See also Persian Gulf War
Ireland, 133, 196, 221
Iron Curtain, 191, 273
Islam, 19, 27, 66, 68, 69, 89, 166. See also fundamentalism, Islamic
isolationism, 25, 47, 81
Israel, 10, 20, 39, 40, 63, 66, 69, 71, 85, 89, 133, 167, 173, 176, 177, 178, 180, 181, 189, 190, 195, 217, 219
Italy, 68, 133, 221
Itzetbegovic, Alija, 209, 211, 213

Jacobinism, 26, 28
Japan, 13, 16, 18, 20, 21, 39–44, 45, 46–48, 50, 54, 63, 67, 70, 82, 84, 160, 167, 173, 174, 189; foreign aid to, 99–105; trade and, 162–164; and war crimes trials, 108–115
Java, 66
John Paul II, Pope, 132–133
Johnson, Lyndon B., 132, 218
Joint Vision 2010, 126, 127, 128
Jordan, 10, 66, 180
judicial intervention, international, war crimes and, 108–115

Kant, Immanuel, 24, 26
Kaplan, Fred, 190–191
Karadzic, Radovan, 110, 211, 212
Kashmir, 69, 180, 192, 194
Kautsky, Karl, 102–103
Kazakhstan, 10
Kennan, George, 80, 101–102; on American principles, 94–98
Kennedy, John F., 11, 87, 131, 132, 145, 190, 217
Khomeini, Ayatollah Ruhollah, 169, 205
Kissinger, Henry, 8, 63
Kohl, Helmut, 36, 62
Kosovo, 112
Kurdish people, 28, 108, 113, 123, 204–205
Kuwait, 20, 39, 63, 66, 99, 108, 113, 128, 155, 167, 172, 181. See also Persian Gulf War

laissez-faire, 26, 29
Lake, Anthony, 17, 24, 29, 103, 129, 132, 143, 145
League of Nations, 30
Lebanon, 20, 39, 84, 85, 89, 95, 167, 172, 181
Lee Teng-hui, 45, 48, 50
Lenin, V. I., 102–103, 105
liberal internationalism, 24–31
Liberia, 28, 39, 108, 114, 192, 194, 196

Libya, 10, 68, 149, 167, 172, 176, 181
light weapons, 192–196
Lott, Trent, 147, 151
Lugar, Richard, 9, 147
Lundberg, Kirsten, 130–131

MacEachin, Douglas, 130, 131
Macedonia, 68
Malaysia, 42, 46
Mali, 69
Mandelbaum, Michael, 35, 85
Manhattan Project, 216
maquiladoras, 118
Marshall, Andrew, 125
Marshall, George, 11
Marshall Plan, 57, 59, 100, 212, 214
Marx, Karl, 18, 27, 31
media, foreign policy and, 82–83, 87–93
meritocracy, Clinton administration as, 140–142
Mexico, 9, 12, 13, 19, 65, 173, 195; NAFTA and, 116–119
military issues: campaign finance and, 120–123; after the cold war, 176–184, 185–191, 192–196; technology and, 124–128; and use of force, 172–175
Mill, John Stuart, 24, 25
Milosevic, Slobodan, 103, 111, 112, 209, 211, 212
mines, antipersonnel, 193
Mladic, Ratko, 111, 211
Montenegro, 112
Morocco, 68
Mozambique, 194
Mubarak, Hosni, 65, 66
Muslim Brotherhood, 73–74, 75

Nasser, Gamal Abdul, 180, 217
National Security Act, 15
nationalism, 69
Navy, U.S., in the post–cold war world, 183–184
Nazi Germany, 61; war crimes and, 108–115
Netherlands, 89
New Deal, 30
Nicaragua, 172, 196
Nixon, Richard, 63, 132
North American Development Bank, 116
North American Free Trade Agreement (NAFTA), 9, 14, 19, 31, 65, 140
North Atlantic Treaty Organization (NATO), 13, 17, 21, 39, 56, 57, 59, 68, 84, 99, 103, 112, 116–119, 135, 186–189, 194, 208, 222, 223; enlargement of, 60–61; Russia and, 34–38
North Korea, 11, 13, 39–44, 45, 85, 99, 103, 104, 127, 131, 149, 173, 176, 187, 195
nuclear weapons, 26, 41–42, 85–86, 131, 135, 185–191, 192; Doomsday Clock and, 215–224; in post–cold war world, 176–184
Nunn, Sam, 53, 143, 147
Nye, Joseph, 42, 103, 140

official development assistance, 160–161
Open Skies agreement, 38
Organization for Security and Cooperation in Europe (OSCE), 112, 208
Organization of Petroleum Exporting Countries, 165
organized crime, 9
Ottoman Empire, 63

Pakistan, 19, 20, 65, 69, 70, 88, 103, 143, 167, 176, 177, 178, 179, 180, 181, 182, 190, 194, 218, 219
Palestine, 10, 39
Panama, 39, 172
Partial Test Ban Treaty, 218
Partnership for Peace, 39
Pax Americana, 99, 104
peacekeeping, United Nations, 28–29, 114, 194; Somalia and, 143–146
Perry, William, 46, 103, 123, 140
Persian Gulf War, 27, 75, 81, 83, 104–105, 113, 128, 172, 175, 178, 181, 183, 200–208
Peru, 39
Philippines, 39, 42, 46, 70
Pipes, Daniel, 71–77
pivotal states, and U.S. foreign policy, 63–70
Poland, 36, 61, 132–133, 174, 186, 195, 223
population growth, global, 9, 69
Powell, Colin, 129, 145, 201, 203
precision engagement, military technology and, 126
preventive vs. preemptive war, 177, 179, 219
Primakov, Yevgeny, 34, 36, 61
Proposition 187, 118

Qaddafi, Muammar, 68, 150

Rabinowitch, Eugene, 216, 217, 218, 220
Reagan, Ronald, 11, 54, 85, 86, 129, 132, 134, 135, 136, 176, 221, 222, 223, 224
realpolitik, 216; China and, 45–52; liberal internationalism and, 26–27
reconnaissance satellites, 178
revolution in military affairs (RMAs), technology and, 124–128
Romania, 60, 61, 121, 195, 223
Roosevelt, Franklin D., 27, 175, 216
Rostow, Eugene, 102, 222
Rousseau, Jean Jacques, 24, 25, 26
Russia, 10, 13, 19, 50, 63, 70, 150, 166, 167, 168, 169, 173, 175, 195; arms race and, 185–191; NATO and, 34–38, 60–61. See also Soviet Union
Rwanda, 28, 39, 63, 83, 95, 108, 110, 112, 114, 115, 192, 194

Sachs, Jeffrey, 161
Sacirbey, Mohamed, 212
Sadat, Anwar, 177
Safire, William, 200
Salinas de Gortari, Carlos, 119
sanctions, against Iran, 165–169
Santayana, George, 137
satellites, reconnaissance, 178
Saudi Arabia, 63, 65, 73, 167, 173, 174, 178, 180
Schumpeter, Joseph, 20
Schwarzkopf, Norman, 10, 202–203, 204
Scowcroft, Brent, 129, 143, 149, 203
Second Wave, Toffler's theory of, 125
self-determinism, 26–27, 30
Serbia, 28, 29, 111, 112, 131, 208–214
Sese Seko, Mobutu, 86
Shalala, Donna, 142
Shalikashvili, John, 126
sharia, 73
Shellum, Brian, 207
Shevardnadze, Eduard, 135, 136
Shiite Muslims, 204–205
Shinn, David, 145
Shklar, Judith, 24
Shultz, George, 130, 133
Singapore, 18, 121

226

Six-Day War, 179, 180
Slemrod, Joel, 215
Slovakia, 61
Slovenia, 60, 195
Smith, Adam, 100
Smith, Leighton, 112
Smith, Tony, 24
Solana, Javier, 35
Somalia, 20, 28, 39, 45, 82, 85, 95, 108, 127, 143–146, 172, 174, 192, 193, 194
South Africa, 65, 69–70, 109, 176, 195, 197, 219
South Korea, 17, 18, 39–44, 63, 84, 99, 104, 173
South Molucca, 89
Soviet Union, 11, 16, 26, 27, 40, 42, 56, 81, 89, 99, 131, 132–137, 148, 176, 178, 180, 182, 183, 196, 215. *See also* Russia
Spain, 18, 68
Spratly Islands, 49, 52
Sri Lanka, 108, 114, 192, 194, 196
stealth technology, military, 126, 183
Steiner, George, 141
Stephanopoulos, George, 141
Sterling, Claire, 132
Stockwell, David, 145
Strategic Arms Limitation Treaties (SALT), 187, 220, 221, 224
Strategic Arms Reduction Treaty (START), 38, 61, 185, 186, 189
Strategic Defense Initiative, 134, 222
Stuetzle, Walther, 61
Sudan, 76, 166, 167, 192, 194
Suharto, Indonesia's president, 66
survivability vs. control, modern warfare and, 179–180
Sweden, 135
Syria, 68, 85, 149, 180, 181, 206

Tadic, Dusan, 112
Taft, Robert, 100
Taiwan, 18, 43, 44, 45, 46, 48–50, 99, 104
Tajikistan, 39, 166, 192

Talbott, Strobe, 35, 140, 141–142
Tarnoff, Peter, 143
technology, military, 124–128
terrorism, 86, 89, 132–134, 150, 167
Tet offensive, 81, 88
Thatcher, Margaret, 200, 201
Third Wave, Toffler's theory of, 125
Thucydides, 25
Tibet, 28, 43, 49
Tighe, Eugene, 133
Toffler, Alvin and Heidi, 125
torture, 114
totalitarianism, 72
trade: Japan and, 162–164; NAFTA and, 116–119
Trainor, Bernard, 201, 204
Truman, Harry, 11, 15, 16–17, 129, 132, 175, 216
Tudjman, Franco, 209, 211
Tunisia, 68
Turkey, 13, 28, 63, 65, 68–69, 70, 94, 121, 123, 143, 167, 196
Turner, Stansfield, 129, 132
Tyson, Laura D'Andrea, 142

Uganda, 166
Ukraine, 37, 173
United Arab Emirates, 167
United Nations, 27, 28–29, 40, 43, 50, 131, 167, 168, 173, 180, 189, 192, 194, 196, 197, 201, 208, 209, 218; Somalia and, 143–146; war crimes, and, 108–115
Urey, Harold C., 216
Uzbekistan, 167

Vandenberg, Hoyt Sanford, 11, 100, 132
Venezuela, 195
verifiability, for chemical weapons, 149
Versailles Treaty, 60
Vietnam, 17, 26, 42, 46, 63, 81, 82, 83, 88, 100, 127, 133, 134, 143, 145, 169, 176, 196, 206
Vinson, Carl, 15

von Ribbentrop, Joachim, 110
Walzer, Michael, 28
war, after the cold war, 176–184, 192–196. *See also* military issues
war crimes, 108–115
Warner, Andrew, 161
Warner, John, 143
War of 1812, 89
Warsaw Pact, 34, 129, 134–135, 136
Washington, George, 96
Wassenaar Arrangement, 194
Webster, William, 132, 133
Weinberger, Caspar, 149
Welch, Jack, 91
White House Situation Room, 152–157
Williams, John, 72
Wilson, Pete, 118
Wilson, Woodrow, 21, 24, 27, 29
Wolfowitz, Paul, 132
Woolsey, James, 130, 132, 149
World Bank, 40, 161, 208, 214
World Trade Organization, 14, 19, 162–163
World War I, 11, 60
World War II, 16, 54, 59, 82, 97, 104, 141, 142, 176, 178, 180; war crimes trials of, 108–115

Xinjiang, 49

Yamashita, Tomoyuki, 108
Yeltsin, Boris, 34, 35, 36, 61, 185, 186, 188, 224
Yom Kippur War, 179, 180
Yugoslavia, 18, 27, 39, 111, 112, 113, 114, 131, 193, 195

Zaire, 39, 65, 86, 192
Zhirinovsky, Vladimir, 34
Zumwalt, Elmo, 151
Zyuganov, Gennady, 34

Credits/Acknowledgments

Cover design by Charles Vitelli

1. **The United States and the World: Strategic Choices**
Facing overview—Illustration by Mike Eagle.

2. **The United States and the World: Regional and Bilateral Relations**
Facing overview—United Nations photo. 41—Embassy of South Korea photo.

3. **The Domestic Side of American Foreign Policy**
Facing overview—AP/Wide World photo.

4. **The Institutional Context of American Foreign Policy**
Facing overview—Library of Congress photo.

5. **The Foreign Policy-making Process**
Facing overview—The White House photo.

6. **U.S. International Economic Strategy**
Facing overview—United States Lines photo.

7. **U.S. Post–Cold War Military Strategy**
Facing overview—AP/Wide World photo by Karsten Thielker.

8. **Historical Perspectives on American Foreign Policy**
Facing overview—AP/Wide World photo by Enric R. Marti.

PHOTOCOPY THIS PAGE!!!

ANNUAL EDITIONS ARTICLE REVIEW FORM

■ NAME: _____ DATE: _____

■ TITLE AND NUMBER OF ARTICLE: _____

■ BRIEFLY STATE THE MAIN IDEA OF THIS ARTICLE: _____
_____

■ LIST THREE IMPORTANT FACTS THAT THE AUTHOR USES TO SUPPORT THE MAIN IDEA:
_____
_____
_____
_____

■ WHAT INFORMATION OR IDEAS DISCUSSED IN THIS ARTICLE ARE ALSO DISCUSSED IN YOUR TEXTBOOK OR OTHER READINGS THAT YOU HAVE DONE? LIST THE TEXTBOOK CHAPTERS AND PAGE NUMBERS:
_____
_____
_____
_____

■ LIST ANY EXAMPLES OF BIAS OR FAULTY REASONING THAT YOU FOUND IN THE ARTICLE:
_____
_____
_____
_____

■ LIST ANY NEW TERMS/CONCEPTS THAT WERE DISCUSSED IN THE ARTICLE, AND WRITE A SHORT DEFINITION:
_____
_____
_____
_____

*Your instructor may require you to use this ANNUAL EDITIONS Article Review Form in any number of ways: for articles that are assigned, for extra credit, as a tool to assist in developing assigned papers, or simply for your own reference. Even if it is not required, we encourage you to photocopy and use this page; you will find that reflecting on the articles will greatly enhance the information from your text.

We Want Your Advice

ANNUAL EDITIONS revisions depend on two major opinion sources: one is our Advisory Board, listed in the front of this volume, which works with us in scanning the thousands of articles published in the public press each year; the other is you—the person actually using the book. Please help us and the users of the next edition by completing the prepaid article rating form on this page and returning it to us. Thank you for your help!

ANNUAL EDITIONS: American Foreign Policy 98/99
Article Rating Form

Here is an opportunity for you to have direct input into the next revision of this volume. We would like you to rate each of the 34 articles listed below, using the following scale:

1. **Excellent: should definitely be retained**
2. **Above average: should probably be retained**
3. **Below average: should probably be deleted**
4. **Poor: should definitely be deleted**

Your ratings will play a vital part in the next revision. So please mail this prepaid form to us just as soon as you complete it.
Thanks for your help!

Rating	Article	Rating	Article
	1. Building a Bipartisan Foreign Policy: Diplomacy and Economics		18. When Money Talks, Congress Listens
	2. Starting Over: Foreign Policy Challenges for the Second Clinton Administration		19. Racing toward the Future: The Revolution in Military Affairs
	3. A New Realism		20. Ending the CIA's Cold War Legacy
	4. The Crisis of Liberal Internationalism		21. The Curse of the Merit Class
	5. Don't Isolate Us: A Russian View of NATO Expansion		22. How the Warlord Outwitted Clinton's Spooks
	6. Reluctant Guardian: The United States in East Asia		23. Playing Politics with the Chemical Weapons Convention
	7. Chinese Realpolitik		24. Inside the White House Situation Room
	8. America and Europe: Is the Break Inevitable?		25. Foreign Aid
	9. The Folly of NATO Enlargement		26. A U.S.–Japan Trade Agenda
	10. Pivotal States and U.S. Strategy		27. Adjusting to Sanctions
	11. The U.S. and Islamic Fundamentalists: The Need for Dialogue		28. Soldiering On: U.S. Public Opinion on the Use of Force
	12. The Common Sense		29. Deliberate and Inadvertent War in the Post–Cold War World
	13. The Shrinking of Foreign News: From Broadcast to Narrowcast		30. Paring Down the Arsenal
	14. On American Principles		31. The New Arms Race: Light Weapons and International Security
	15. Why America Thinks It Has to Run the World		32. Closing the Gate: The Persian Gulf War Revisited
	16. International Judicial Intervention		33. Bosnia after Dayton: Year Two
	17. The Politics of NAFTA: Why Is Texas So Much Hotter for NAFTA than California?		34. Midnight Never Came

(Continued on next page)

ABOUT YOU

Name _____ Date _____

Are you a teacher? ❏ Or a student? ❏

Your school name _____

Department _____

Address _____

City _____ State _____ Zip _____

School telephone # _____

YOUR COMMENTS ARE IMPORTANT TO US !

Please fill in the following information:

For which course did you use this book? _____

Did you use a text with this ANNUAL EDITION? ❏ yes ❏ no

What was the title of the text? _____

What are your general reactions to the Annual Editions concept?

Have you read any particular articles recently that you think should be included in the next edition?

Are there any articles you feel should be replaced in the next edition? Why?

Are there any World Wide Web sites you feel should be included in the next edition? Please annotate.

May we contact you for editorial input?

May we quote your comments?

ANNUAL EDITIONS: AMERICAN FOREIGN POLICY 98/99

BUSINESS REPLY MAIL

First Class   Permit No. 84   Guilford, CT

Postage will be paid by addressee

Dushkin/McGraw·Hill
Sluice Dock
Guilford, CT 06437

No Postage
Necessary
if Mailed
in the
United States